Through the Darkness

Through the Darkness

A Story of Love from the Other Side

Charlie Bynar

GFB

Some names, identities, and circumstances have been changed in order to protect the privacy of individuals.

Copyright © 2025 by Charlie Bynar

All rights reserved.

No part of this book may be reproduced, or stored in a retrieval system, or transmitted in any form or by any means, electronic, mechanical, photocopying, recording, or otherwise, without express written permission of the publisher.

GFB

Published by Girl Friday Books™, Seattle
www.girlfridayproductions.com

Produced by Girl Friday Productions

Cover design and all images courtesy of the author.
ISBN (paperback): 978-1-964721-22-4
ISBN (ebook): 978-1-964721-23-1

Library of Congress Control Number: 2024921430

First edition

FOR ISAAC AND CHRIS

CONTENTS

Acknowledgments ix
Author's Note xi
Preface xiii

1. Angel Biscuits 1
2. The Girl of His Dreams 10
3. Entangled Particles 16
4. I Miss You 26
5. The Top of the Mountain 37
6. Platitudes 46
7. Time: The Greatest Force 54
8. The Deep End 62
9. Thin Ice 69
10. The Silver Lining 79
11. Not Crazy After All 86
12. Sumerian Tablets 93
13. Queen Ant Melba 101
14. Guilt and Shame 111
15. Nonlinear Time 123
16. The Quiet of the Storm 130
17. Borrowed Time 136
18. Under Wraps 143
19. Forgiveness 149
20. New Friends 157

21. Expert's Opinion	167
22. Life Lessons	176
23. Long Live the Queen	184
24. King Solomon and Sir Isaac Newton	194
25. Isaac's Ashes	202
26. Houston	211
27. Two Reasons	221
28. Sister Teresa	230
29. An Old Soul	238
30. Forever Isaac	251
31. Lunch on the Pier	263
32. Isaac Was Here	274
33. Good Job, Mom	283
34. Two or Three Days	293
35. Trust	301
36. Homeward Bound	309
37. The Celebration	322
Epilogue	329
Bibliography	333
About the Author	349

ACKNOWLEDGMENTS

I would like to express my sincere thanks to the following people: my sister Teresa Mackie for her undying support and always coming to my rescue ever since we were little waifs growing up in Idaho; my aunt Mable Kite for the beautiful details about the Williams family; Dr. Katherine Kula, expert medical witness, for reviewing Isaac's birth records and supporting my conclusions; Allison DuBois for her life-changing reading; Tarra of Sedona for invaluable life lessons; Tom McMullan for his thoughtful insights; Lloyd Jassin for his legal counsel; Jeffrey Bub for his physics expertise; Dan Brown for his MasterClass; Mark Ireland for his insight; Jessica Sindler, Shari Strong, Erin Cusick, and Melody Moss for their editing; Donald Stefanski, Potoula Pappas, Carol Jean Gray, and Omar Shehryar for their help and support; and Florian Johnson for translating Diné Bizaad to English.

AUTHOR'S NOTE

This is a true story.

PREFACE

IN THE WAKE OF THE STORM, I sat at my kitchen table, drinking coffee, trying to make sense of everything that had happened. One minute, I was remembering my cat, Schmiggs, sitting on the kitchen table. Black saucers filled his green eyes as he craned his neck, clearly looking at something—someone—down the hall that I couldn't see. The next minute, I remembered the four messages I had received from my dead son while I was sleeping. The dream visits really got my attention, since I'd never experienced anything like that before. I began to replay random events from the last three and a half years in my mind, jumping from one thought to another in no particular order. There were the little yellow ants with their dark eyes; the grand idea that death was an illusion; scientific theories and explanations about entangled particles; the remarkable thing that happened with the laundry light; the extraordinary event with my aunt Mable—nothing less than a miracle; the hawk coming out of nowhere; the fucking medical records; contemplating suicide from a place of pure darkness; the crazy thing with the moon; the reading from the world-renowned psychic medium; the endless and somewhat tiring menu of life lessons and their "gifts" of new perspectives (obviously, I'm still working on some of those); my mom's ancestors from the Deep South; Houston, which I now despise—sorry, Houstonians, nothing personal; cosmology; and of course, debates about science, religion, and the Sumerian tablets.

I wanted—I *needed*—to make sense of what had happened and put my thoughts in order, so I decided to write a book. Since my story involves my dead son, the following narrative revolves around two worlds: The first is my present-day life, which includes my husband and me, and the second is the other side—a place where everyone goes after they die and is restored to perfect health. This approach allowed me to truthfully record the events in my present-day life as they unfolded, and it also provided a space to speculate about how my son might have influenced those events from the other side and how those two worlds might have intersected.

Honestly, it has been an extraordinary journey . . . so extraordinary that some people questioned whether the things I told them were the truth. Then again, people often question things they haven't experienced, because they have no reference point. I understand. Before it happened to me, I wouldn't have believed it, or at least I would have been very skeptical. So let me assure you, although I've taken the liberty to imagine the other side and how my son might have influenced my life from there, everything else depicted in these pages truly happened!

1

ANGEL BISCUITS
April 21, 2017

CHARLIE WOKE IN A PANIC, only to realize she was still trapped in the same nightmare: one she had fallen into three days earlier after her ex-husband found Isaac, her only child, dead on his bedroom floor. Her heart pounded as she stared blankly into the darkness, hearing only the sound of her own heavy breathing.

Her forehead and chest felt sweaty. She threw back the covers and sat on the edge of the bed. *I can't fucking believe the worst thing that could ever happen—has happened.* She wiped her brow and, not wanting to wake her husband, Chris, quietly got out of bed and put on her worn slippers and Isaac's gray-and-maroon hoodie, which she had started wearing after his death to feel closer to him. She walked to the living room, lit a small candle, and placed it on a small table among the collection of little treasures that she and Isaac had gathered from around the world, including a conch shell, some little boxes, and several fossils. Gradually, her heartbeat slowed to its normal rate and rhythm, but she remained in a state of shock. Disbelief.

At five feet tall, with brown eyes, short brown hair, and a medium build, Charlie was unremarkable in her physical appearance. She generally had a quality of fierce independence and single-minded determination that set her apart from others, but now, she was crushed by Isaac's death.

Charlie walked into the dark kitchen and turned on the stove light. She filled the espresso machine's basket with freshly ground coffee beans, placed a Starbucks mug under it, and watched the creamy espresso pour into the steaming hot water. As she sipped the coffee, the hot elixir warmed her hands and small frame, but nothing could warm her broken heart.

Hearing the noise from the kitchen, their two rescue dogs ran in to see what was for breakfast. Dexter Do-Little, a well-mannered Pomeranian, spent most of his time curled up on Charlie and Chris's bed, while Cobalt Curly-Tail, an overweight heeler-collie mix, spent his time obsessing over food and chasing the gray squirrels living in the backyard underneath the patio deck.

As Charlie prepared their food, they wagged their tails excitedly. Not wanting to miss any opportunity for a treat, Schmiggs, their rescued black-and-white Norwegian forest cat, jumped onto the counter and meowed, his voice harsh and raspy. Charlie gave the dogs their breakfast, took the tuna fish from the refrigerator, and gave her cat a scoop in his dish on the counter. After Schmiggs finished eating, he sat licking his paws and cleaning his long white whiskers, his green eyes smiling as if nothing was wrong.

Charlie turned the oven to 375 degrees Fahrenheit and then opened her coffee-stained cookbook with a tattered binding to page 650, as she had done countless times before. As she made the angel biscuits, one of Isaac's favorites, she heard Chris turn on the shower.

Charlie mixed the batter and rolled the dough out on the floured countertop, then cut it into circles with a floured wineglass. By the time she'd placed the angel biscuits into the oven, flour was all over her clothes and the floor. She set the oven timer for twenty-five minutes, cleaned up her mess, then walked to the bookshelf in the living room and picked up one of the numerous scrapbooks she had made for Isaac.

The scrapbook's cover was decorated with pictures from their trip to the United States Virgin Islands five years ago. One photo of Isaac was with his arms stretched out as far as he could reach, both hands making a peace sign. He was eleven, and there was a look of elation on his face as he had just earned his junior scuba diver license. In another picture, Isaac was lying on the white sand of Trunk Bay at the point where the waves met the beach. He lay half in the water, his green eyes and smile beaming from under Charlie's orange visor, which she'd put on him to keep his face from getting sunburned. Looking at the picture now, she could hear the rhythmic sound of the waves crashing and see Isaac smiling as he bodysurfed the waves near the beach. *He was truly happy that day—now he's dead,* Charlie thought. *He was my everything. . . . How am I to face living without him?*

When she opened the scrapbook, the first thing she saw was a drawing Isaac had made of a stick figure winking, wearing an enormous smile, his hands high in the air. On it, Isaac had written, Hi Mom, I Love Mom. Charlie smiled and turned the page. On the left page, she had pressed and glued two maple leaves. On the right, she had added a journal entry:

November 2009

Yesterday was Veterans Day and there was no school, so Isaac and I went to Oak Creek for the day. Isaac swam and played along the water, and I enjoyed playing with Isaac and catching some of the last rays of the sun before winter comes. We collected some leaves and Isaac found a baby scorpion! We threw rocks in the water and hiked for most of the day. At the end of the day, we hiked out of the canyon just as the sun was going down. When we got back to the car, I put the dogs in the back and got Isaac snuggled into his car seat. We had eaten dinner before climbing out of the canyon, so Isaac was content. He said he was happy to be back in the car all cozy and wanted to take a nap while I drove home. I said, "Okay, Honey. You sleep, and I'll get us home." I asked him if he had a good day, and he said, "I had a wonderful day, Mom," then he snuggled down for the ride. Before he went to sleep, he said, "Mom, I'm going to dream about you if I can." It doesn't get any better than that!

By looking at the date at the top of the page, Charlie figured that Isaac would have been eight years old. *Since the day he was born, I never had to worry about my heart—Isaac always kept it safe. Now everything is wrong.* She placed the journal back on the bookshelf, then went to the kitchen to make a second cup of coffee.

As the sun rose, she heard the usual Steller's jays screeching from the ponderosa pine tree in the backyard of their three-bedroom townhome in the heart of Flagstaff, Arizona. She took a handful of peanuts from an opened bag, walked out the back door to the porch, and put the peanuts in a round dish on the deck railing. As she breathed in the crisp air, she looked at the tall cottonwood tree and noticed it was beginning to leaf out. Its new bright-green leaves were a beautiful contrast against the morning sky. She glanced down toward the garden, where wild asters, blue flax, and scarlet-orange *Echinacea* were pushing their way up through the ground.

Spring was supposed to be a time of new life—of new beginnings—but Charlie was sure her life had ended on the day Isaac died: April 18, 2017. *He was my light. . . . Now everything's black,* she thought, walking back inside.

When the oven timer beeped, Charlie picked up a blue-and-yellow dish towel Chris had brought back from a vacation he'd taken to Portugal with his ex-wife. Opening the oven door, she felt a wave of hot air pour over her bare face and hands, and as she bent down to remove the golden-brown angel biscuits, her tears fell onto the searing hot oven door, hissed, and evaporated instantly. Charlie placed the hot biscuits on top of the oven and closed the door.

The high-pitched buzzing of hummingbirds fighting over the feeder outside the kitchen window drew her attention. She walked to the window and blankly watched them darting through the air. She imagined herself on a skiff far from land, stepping into the ocean, her dive weights securely fastened around her waist.

There would be no way to screw it up, and no one would ever find me.

Charlie imagined herself hidden in a watery grave, safe from having to face what lay ahead.

Her thoughts were interrupted as Chris walked into the kitchen. He poured himself a cup of coffee from his automatic coffee maker, added a splash of creamer, then sat at the kitchen table and opened his tablet. Isaac's death had left them both feeling defeated, and they had withdrawn into their own corners from exhaustion. Despite this, Charlie knew they still had each other's backs.

A confident, reserved man with gray-blue eyes and a winning smile, Chris had an athletic physique: one he'd earned from his love of downhill skiing and mountain bike riding. Although he wasn't insecure about having lost most of his curly blond hair due to premature balding, he regularly wore a baseball hat simply to prevent his fair skin from getting sunburned. Chris had received his master's degree in civil engineering from Iowa State University and was now employed by the City of Flagstaff as their stormwater manager.

Charlie glanced at him as he read the news through his black-rimmed glasses, thinking how he preferred his drip coffee over her espresso machine. Although he reluctantly admitted her espresso machine made better coffee, he still favored his. As an engineer, Chris enjoyed programming machines and then watching them carry out the tasks they were designed to perform. It gave him satisfaction knowing a fresh pot of coffee was brewing while he was in the shower and it would be ready for him by the time he got dressed and made his way to the kitchen. He was a man of stubborn habits.

Charlie sat down next to Chris and drank her coffee.

"Thanks for making angel biscuits, Mom. They smell great," Isaac said, sitting in his usual chair across from her. Having become younger when he died, Isaac was now seven years old—the version of himself when he'd been happiest. He was wearing a long-sleeved blue-and-orange plaid shirt, jeans, and hiking boots. Seeing his mom's tear-stained eyes, he was hoping to cheer her up.

Charlie stared blankly out the window while Chris continued reading the news. She was lost in memory, thinking back to last year when Isaac was fifteen. They'd all gotten up late that day because it was the weekend, and during breakfast, Chris had decided to go for a mountain bike ride. Isaac, feeling nostalgic about traveling, suggested that he and his mom go to the Phoenix airport to watch planes land and take off. It was a two-and-a-half-hour drive to the airport, but after some consideration, Charlie decided it would be an opportunity to cut loose from the day-to-day grind and have fun. After breakfast, she backed her blue Honda Fit out of the garage and waited for Isaac.

When he came out, he was wearing the new Icelandic sweater she had given him for Christmas.

They parked at the east parking lot near terminal 4. Inside, the shops and restaurants were bustling as they window-shopped. At one gift store, Isaac pointed out a penholder with a robotic-looking face made from repurposed metals, which he thought Chris would like for his desk. They bought it, then eventually made their way to the food court, where they ordered lunch from a friendly woman.

"The two of you look like two peas in a pod. He's your Mini-Me," the woman chuckled.

"Yeah . . . we're thick as thieves." Charlie smiled, nudging Isaac.

Isaac grinned and put his arm around his mom's shoulder.

"You even have the same smile," the woman said. "The only difference is the color of your eyes."

"He got his pretty green eyes from his dad," Charlie replied.

"I wish I had that kind of relationship with my daughter." The woman frowned, handing them their fish and chips.

Charlie and Isaac thanked the lady, then found a window seat where they could watch the planes take off and land, then speculate about where they were going and coming from. After lunch, they walked outside on a path landscaped with saguaros, prickly pears, and palm trees. While they were meandering down the trail, Isaac abruptly stopped and faced her. "Mom, the best thing about our relationship is that we're best friends! Can we stay best friends forever?"

Charlie would never forget those words—they completed her. Now, she sat at the kitchen table, wanting to die.

"Mom, thanks for making angel biscuits," Isaac repeated, trying to get his mom's attention.

Silence.

Isaac took a deep breath, placed his hand on the side of his face, and rested his elbow on the table.

Chris stopped reading the news, sipped his coffee, and sat his cup back on the table. He noticed Charlie crying and reached for her hand. "The angel biscuits smell good," Chris said, his voice dull . . . defeated.

Charlie dried her eyes, stood, and took two saucers from the kitchen cupboard. She placed an angel biscuit on each, took the gooseberry jam from the refrigerator, and sat back down. After spreading some jam on her biscuit, she started to take a bite, but then put the biscuit back down on her saucer.

"I need to understand what the hell happened and who's responsible!" Charlie said, trying to control her anger.

Chris looked at Charlie, and although he was trying to stay strong for her, he began to cry. "This is all so horribly wrong. It should've never happened, but if we don't find out why it happened, it will haunt us for the rest of our lives!"

"I think I can figure out if Isaac died due to medical negligence, but I'll need to get his birth records," Charlie said. Tears streamed down her face. Then, needing Chris to understand, she went into the details of Isaac's birth, not just the main facts as she had previously told him. "Ever since he was two and hadn't started talking yet, I've been worried about his delivery. It was close to thirty-six hours on Christmas Eve. . . . I think they were preoccupied. Then, when Isaac still wasn't talking by age five, I took him to a specialist who diagnosed him as a 'late talker': a bright child who talked late. So I held on to that explanation for as long as I could, but as Isaac got older, it was apparent that they were wrong. I thought about getting his records many times, but then I was concerned about how it would affect Isaac—he already had been struggling with his self-esteem. I just didn't know what the right thing to do was. . . . I should have known better!"

Chris shook his head and dried his eyes. "It's not your fault, but we do need to get those records. No matter what happens, remember, I'll always have your back—we're in this together."

"And I'll always have yours," Charlie promised. She made plans to go to the hospital later that day to request the records but first suggested they try to eat something, as the only thing they'd had the day before were some three-day-old leftovers.

As they ate their biscuits, Chris finished reading the news while Charlie stared out the window, watching the Steller's jays land on the railing and fly away with their peanuts. Charlie had first met Chris thirty-one years before when she was a freshman in high school. She was working at the soda fountain in the back of Don Wilson Drug in Idaho Falls when Chris came in, sat down on a red stool in front of the counter, and ordered a strawberry milkshake. He was a preppy, well-to-do senior with a wide grin like the Cheshire cat, which made her nervous because she was from the wrong side of the tracks. She blushed but maintained her composure as she added a large swirl of whipped cream on top of his milkshake, inserted a long red straw, and handed it to him with a flirtatious grin. He smiled back, then asked her out on a date. She fumbled for words, nervously accepted his invitation, and awkwardly handed him the icy cold stainless-steel tumbler with the leftover milkshake.

On the night of their first date, Chris picked her up in his white Impala with a light-blue stripe running down the sides. He opened the car door for her and made sure she was comfortable before closing it. At the drive-in movie, he went to the concession stand, returned with popcorn and refreshments, and asked her to join him in the back seat. They couldn't see the movie very well from there, but seeing the movie wasn't the reason he had taken her to the drive-in in the first place. She still couldn't remember what movie they'd seen, but she remembered that the back seat had been baby blue with a clear vinyl covering.

They dated briefly in high school, often sneaking in through the back door of his parents' house and heading to his upstairs bedroom, where they surrendered to their teenage hormones while his parents played bridge and drank cocktails with their friends. When his parents were away, he and Charlie raided their liquor cabinet, went upstairs with a few drinks, fooled around, and played chess. Later, when Chris went off to college, they went their separate ways.

"Is there anything I can do for you?"

Charlie didn't hear Chris. . . . She was lost in thought.

"Can I do anything for you?" Chris asked, reaching for Charlie's hand.

Chris's touch returned Charlie to the present. "No, but thanks for asking," Charlie said, wishing this nightmare wasn't their reality.

"Mom, it's going to be okay," Isaac said. "Trust me; we're going to get through this together."

Still, Charlie said nothing.

"I wish you could hear me." Isaac took a deep breath and stood to leave. He blew his mom a kiss goodbye, then walked out the back door.

—

As the door closed behind him, he entered the other side—a place where everyone goes after they die and is restored to perfect health. Isaac paused and took in the view of the Wood River Valley of Hailey, Idaho. Then, anxious to see his family who were waiting for him, he quickened his pace. As he walked down the old country road lined with a wooden fence and daisy fields, a large farmhouse with a red roof came into view.

2

THE GIRL OF HIS DREAMS
April 27, 2017

WHILE CHRIS WAITED for Charlie to return from getting the mail from the residential mailboxes down the street, he thought about all that had occurred to bring him to this point in his life. Before he reconnected with Charlie, he had been in a deep rut with his first wife and, after nearly three decades of marriage, had wanted out. Although he had still cared about her, he had grown sick of feeling alone and lonely. Living at opposite ends of their house, doing their own laundry, and sleeping in separate rooms was the straw that broke the camel's back. Their marriage was like an untended garden—the weeds had taken over. The roots of the invasive plants had slowly choked the roots of the delicate flowers, leaving only a few radiant blooms in their once-happy marriage.

Looking back, Chris felt that his ex-wife's focus had become the sport of dressage—horseback riding performed in competitions and exhibitions—and that he'd become second in her priorities. He felt this had become more evident after he'd been diagnosed with papillary thyroid cancer.

Chris had sat alone in the exam room, trying to digest what his doctor had told him. "You'll need a neck dissection to remove several lymph nodes along both sides of your neck and a total thyroidectomy. After the surgery, you'll have to undergo radioactive iodine treatment."

While recovering from his surgery at the Seattle Cancer Care Alliance, Chris started the low-sodium diet ordered by his doctor to prepare him for his radiation treatment. Adhering to the bland diet was unpleasant because one of his favorite things was sitting down to a delicious meal paired with a complementary drink. He enjoyed poring over recipes, mixing cocktails, filling the house with savory aromas, and following the recipe to a T. As a civil engineer, Chris treated recipes like holy blueprints—it was imperative to follow them to attain the proper outcome.

Two weeks later, he checked in a second time at the Seattle Cancer Care Alliance hospital for radiation treatment. His nurse took him to a small room, where she informed him that he would remain in his isolation room until his treatment was complete and his radiation level had dropped below 500 MBq, at which point he'd be able to be discharged. Visitors were permitted at a distance, but they had to remain behind the yellow tape mark on the floor outside his room.

While Chris made himself comfortable in his room, down the hall, a radiologist in a lead apron and gloves picked up a pair of tongs and carefully placed the four-centimeter-thick lead container encasing the radioactive iodine (I-131) capsule on a cart next to a cup of water. Then she wheeled the cart in front of Chris's room.

"You'll need to remove the lid and swallow the capsule," she said, stepping away from the radioactive cart.

Chris reluctantly walked to the table, removed the lid from the thick lead container, and paused as he looked at the capsule in his hand. *I hope this kills ALL the cancer left in my body.* He placed the capsule in his mouth and drank the water. *I guess I'll have to wait and see.*

Alone day after day, Chris lost a significant amount of weight due to severe nausea and a loss of appetite, causing him to become easily fatigued. He pictured his wife enjoying herself training her pony in their sun-drenched arena as his dirty food trays piled up in the corner of his isolation room. He sat on the edge of his bed, elbows resting on his knees and his hands on the sides of his face, wishing he could turn back the clock. He remembered when they first met. They often went out for dinner and shared a bottle of wine, but lately they spent more time apart than together. Not only was Chris alone in his isolation room, he felt alone in his battle with cancer. He wiped the tears from his gray-blue eyes, then, giving up, lay back down and cried himself to sleep.

After his radiation treatment, Chris returned home to their horse property near the Sammamish River, surrounded by quaint boutiques and wineries. Now that Chris could enjoy sinking his teeth into some real food, his friends visited and brought several homemade dishes to cheer him up. They commented on how pale and thin he was and offered their help. Gradually, Chris put on his lost weight and gained his strength back. Before long, he returned to his chores of mucking out the horse stables, mowing the pastures, and maintaining the outdoor arena.

Still, Chris was disheartened. Despite having tried for years to work out his differences with his wife, he felt their marriage was no longer about building a future together but about keeping up appearances, keeping financial tabs on each other, and assuming pretentious facades meant to camouflage their insecurities. But what troubled him most was that they retired to their separate bedrooms to sleep alone and dream alone.

Although Chris's life was not ideal, he still enjoyed his job and sports activities. He had a successful nineteen-year career working as a civil engineer for Snohomish County near Seattle, where he designed new culverts to protect the critical habitat of the Chinook salmon and other aquatic species of the Pacific Northwest and worked as a project manager, overseeing numerous culvert installation projects. And to escape the daily grind, Chris vacationed, usually alone, at his two favorite ski resorts, Grand Targhee Resort in Wyoming and Bald Mountain in Ketchum, Idaho. As a former ski instructor, Chris often outperformed younger skiers, screaming down the slopes while listening to blues rock and classic rock and roll. Chris also enjoyed mountain bike riding, and although he freely admitted his golf game needed vast improvement, he occasionally enjoyed working on his swing on the weekends.

One night, as Chris slept alone, he dreamed about a girl he'd known in high school, whom he had taken to a drive-in movie. When he woke, he had an overwhelming urge to contact her. He searched the internet, found her email address, and sent her a message: *I had a dream about you last night and was wondering how you're doing.*

What are you up to? I know it's been a long time, but I just wanted to say hi.

Although it had been over thirty years since they last spoke, Charlie replied without hesitation, and then they exchanged a few emails, braved the perils of talking to each other on the phone, and eventually made plans to meet. As they shared their stories, a wildfire ignited in Chris. The flame grew hotter, and he couldn't have extinguished it even if he'd wanted to—the wildfire had grown out of control. In less than a year, he divorced his wife; found a new job; moved to Flagstaff, Arizona; became friends with Isaac, who was fourteen at the time; and married the girl of his dreams.

Chris returned to the present when Charlie opened the back door, walked inside, and put the mail on the kitchen table. It had been a week since she had gone to the hospital and requested her and Isaac's medical records from the time they were both patients, back when he was born. She sat down and opened the manila envelope from the hospital.

"Four pages! Wouldn't you think there would be more than four pages if you were hospitalized for three days and had given birth?" Charlie asked, her voice hot with anger. "I specifically asked them for Isaac's COMPLETE birth records, including his fetal heart monitor strips, and there isn't even one in this envelope. I need those records because, as you know, I think Isaac suffered a brain injury during the delivery due to medical negligence and, as a result, developed seizures that ultimately killed him. It's so unfair—he was only sixteen!"

Chris shook his head, saying nothing.

"The only thing these records say is that I checked into the hospital at 08:00 on December twenty-fourth, and I had a baby boy at 20:03 on December twenty-fourth, 2000. They didn't even get the check-in time right. I called the midwife on the morning of the twenty-third, when I started having contractions, but she told me to wait until my labor pains were three minutes apart. That night, when they were three minutes apart, I checked into the hospital, but she said I could be having false labor pains and sent me home with some med and told me to come back the next morning if the labor pains continued through the night, which I did. That's when I checked in the second time on December twenty-fourth, at 08:00."

"I can't believe they let you stay in labor for a day and a half!" Chris said. "They're incompetent. They were probably too busy having fun because it was Christmas Eve and didn't realize Isaac was in trouble."

"Yes, and now Isaac's fucking dead!" Charlie said, coming unhinged. She stood and started pacing the kitchen floor, then steadied herself at the kitchen counter to keep her legs from buckling beneath her. Lowering her head, Charlie wept, her body trembling.

Worried about Charlie's state of mind, Chris attempted a little small talk to pull her back from the brink.

"I called my boss earlier today, and he said I've already used my week of bereavement time.... They won't let me have any more time off."

"It's so kind of the city to give you a whole week off," Charlie said sarcastically, wiping her tears. "One week ... that's what you get when your kid dies."

"Yeah, I'm very disappointed. They should have given me two weeks at the very least."

Charlie sat down next to him and explained what she thought had happened. "First, they should have delivered him much earlier, because after the last twenty-five hours of contractions every three minutes, the nurse rushed in and frantically said my son's heart was failing. She asked me to sign a consent form for an emergency C-section—that was the real giveaway that they screwed up. And secondly, we need Isaac's birth records, especially the fetal heart monitor strips, because they're the only records that actually show how Isaac's heart was doing throughout the labor. That's hard data that's not subject to someone's 'opinion.'"

Charlie stood and began to pace again. "I didn't know any better. I'd never given birth before, so I just had to trust the doctors and nurses. I didn't know anything was wrong. But when they did the C-section, they found that the cord had been wrapped around his neck twice, and he was being strangled the entire time." Then Charlie explained a medical term, knowing that wasn't Chris's area of expertise. "A hypoxic brain injury—a deficient oxygen supply to Isaac's brain—would explain his struggles: why he didn't talk until he was five and his severe learning disabilities." Chris was familiar with these challenges that Isaac faced, but then Charlie mentioned a couple that he wasn't aware of.

"I never told you this before, but Isaac only scored one to three percent in his peer group for reading and writing, which made school and homework incredibly hard for him, and people didn't get it because Isaac looked like a normal kid—he had no physical disabilities. Later, after he started taking seizure meds, he told me that was the first time his mind was quiet! Before that, he said there was a constant buzzing in his head, which made it very hard for him to concentrate. It kills me because I think all his struggles—all his suffering—were caused by medical negligence, including the seizures like the one that fucking killed him!"

3

ENTANGLED PARTICLES
The Other Side

THE SAWTOOTH MOUNTAINS to the west and the Pioneer Mountains to the east surrounded Isaac as he walked down the old country road toward the large red-roofed farmhouse near Hailey, Idaho. As he approached, he left the sunflower fields behind and entered a beautiful forest scattered with aspen, cottonwood, and ponderosa pine trees, where he heard the quiet rumble of the Big Wood River in the distance. When Isaac arrived at the farmhouse, he walked past a new 1957 Ford truck parked in front, then continued to the backyard to join the Williams family, who were sitting at a picnic table underneath a towering cottonwood tree.

With a slight gesture of hand, Isaac conjured a basket of Charlie's angel biscuits at the center of the table, then sat down next to his grandmother Hazel and his uncle Shane, Charlie's mother and brother. Hazel, now in her early twenties, had eyes that matched her name, loose brown curls, and a perfect smile. She was dressed in a white eyelet sweater, a cherry-red 1950s-style skirt, and black-and-white saddle shoes with bobby socks.

Shane, a handsome man in his late forties, had gentle brown eyes, but his mischievous smile revealed his true nature. He wore a bright vest over a long-sleeved white shirt and a black Stetson hat.

"How's your mom doing?" Hazel asked Isaac. "When you

crossed over, she spiraled into the darkness. . . . I'm worried sick about her!"

"I can't get through to her—she can't hear me," Isaac said, disappointed. "I'm worried she won't be able to find her way through the darkness. We were best friends, and losing me has devastated her."

"It's only been a little over a week since you crossed," Hazel said. "It sounds like she's in too much pain, and it's preventing her from hearing you."

"When people are overwhelmed with physical or emotional pain, it's hard to get through to them, let alone when talking to someone who's crossed over," Shane said. "People put up defensive walls to protect themselves, but this makes it very difficult to reach them in their time of need. Very few people can hear us when we talk to them."

"Maybe I should try something else . . . find a different way to contact my mom," Isaac said, his voice wavering. "It's difficult for me to think straight. I'm so worried . . . worried Mom might do something she'll regret."

"We understand that this is hard for you. . . . After all, it's your mom we're talking about," Solomon said, placing his napkin on his lap. "That's why we've all come together to help you."

Solomon Walker Williams, Isaac's great-great-grandfather, was sitting at the head of the table next to his wife, Ethel. He was a tall man with a white Western-styled mustache and dressed in a white-pearl Western shirt, Levi's, and boots. His family enjoyed his kind, unwavering disposition and was comforted knowing they could rely on him when the going got tough.

Ethel, a jovial, heavyset woman with white pin-curled hair, had a touch of the gift—she'd been able to communicate with the dead even when she was alive. She always wore a floral-patterned dress and laced shoes. Ethel loved making homemade pastries and caring for her family. She and Solomon had been raised in Tennessee and enjoyed Southern cooking. Their favorite foods included hominy, ambrosia, crab cakes, catfish with grits, and collard greens. They had met while attending Southern Baptist Sunday worship services and married shortly thereafter. They spent their lives raising their children and grandchildren together, and although they were old and gray, they were both spry.

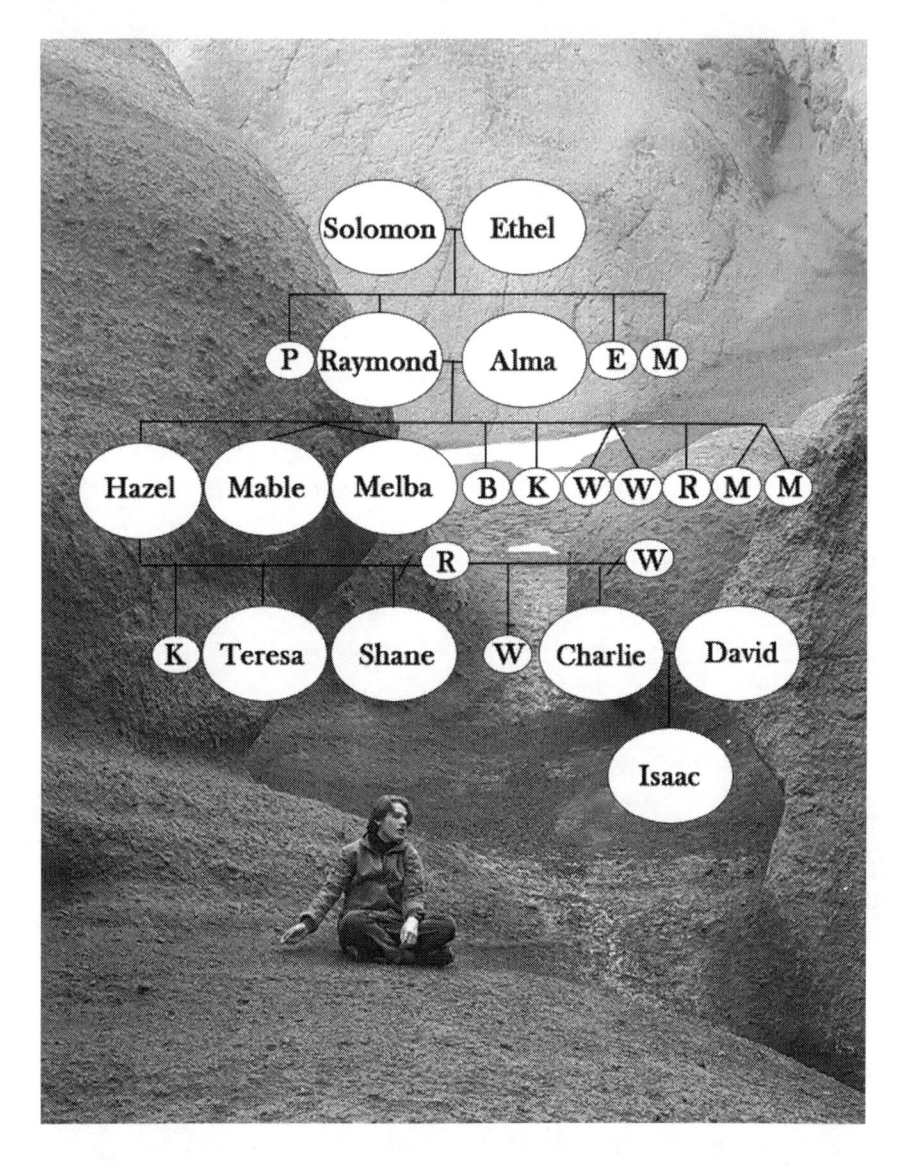

The picnic table was beautifully set with a patterned cotton tablecloth, pink Depression-era glass plates with a wheel-cut flower border, embroidered napkins, and polished silverware. A Fenton milk glass vase displayed a colorful mixture of wildflowers in the middle of the table.

Solomon and Ethel's son Raymond sat across from Isaac. Raymond was a handsome, rugged man dressed in a blue Western shirt and cowboy boots. His strong hands and brawny shoulders showed that he was a hardworking man. Sitting beside him was his wife, Alma, who was exceptionally beautiful with stunning dark eyes and a radiant smile. Their daughter Melba, in her early twenties, sat next to them and was the spitting image of her mother, except she wasn't soft-spoken. Like Shane, Melba was a mischief-maker who enjoyed playing tricks on people when they least expected it.

A small wooden hitching post lay between the picnic table and the Big Wood River, where Raymond's white quarter horse, Piute, and Hazel's brown quarter horse, Babe, were tied up and enjoying some oats. Raymond depended on Piute's quick maneuvering skills when working the cattle on his thousand-acre farm, and not wanting his horse to get spoiled, he forbade anyone else from riding him.

"When I lost Alma from throwing a blood clot following the birth of our third set of twins, I was heartbroken," Raymond said. "I not only lost my beautiful wife, but I was also overwhelmed with trying to take care of the farm and our ten children. I'd have lost everything if it weren't for my parents, who moved in to help me out. Thanks to Mom and Dad, we made it through those difficult times."

"Even though working the farm was difficult, it was a blessing in disguise," Alma said, reaching for her husband's hand. "You couldn't give up. . . . You had too many people counting on you."

"That's the thing," Isaac said. "My mom doesn't have anyone depending on her except Chris, and she knows he could get along without her if he had to, even though he might not want to. I have to find a way to let my mom know I'm still with her, so she doesn't give up and . . ."

"Being separated is harder for soulmates," Shane said, putting his arm around Isaac. "The two of you have shared so many lives together that it makes it very difficult for you to be apart."

"Now that I've crossed over, I know that we're soulmates and we have shared many lives together, but my mom doesn't know that!" Isaac said. "She and Chris believe death is the end . . . that I'm gone forever and she'll never see me again. I'm not sure my mom can carry that burden. If I can't make contact with her, she might . . ." Unable to finish his sentence, Isaac lowered his eyes and rested his face against his hand.

"It won't be easy, but I bet we can figure this out together," Melba encouraged him.

Shane nudged Isaac. "Even though you're an old and wise soul like Ethel, this is still difficult for you because it's your mom you're trying to save, but we're here to help."

"I appreciate it." Isaac took a deep breath and exhaled. "I can use all the help I can get."

"To be fair, making contact with the living is very difficult under the best of circumstances," Hazel added. "Most of us have tried—hence the countless mentions of various types of visions in religious texts throughout the world. But still, there are great barriers that prevent us most of the time. For instance, many cultures discourage the living from talking to the dead, and at times, countless people who communicated with the dead—seers, mediums, psychics, and clairvoyants—were considered witches and burned at the stake."

"Social stigma *is* a huge barrier," Ethel said. "People thought I'd plumb come off my rocker when I told them about seeing and hearing Alma shortly after she crossed over. She was—"

"I wanted to make sure all my kids were all right," Alma interrupted. "But once I knew you were there to take care of them, I felt reassured, and then I left."

"I knew you were just checking on your children, and I'm glad you knew I would look after your littl'uns," Ethel said. "And as a Southern Baptist, I'm familiar with scripture that advises people against speaking with mediums. However, being a medium myself, I understand that verse from a different perspective—as a warning to protect people. When a medium contacts those who've crossed over, they indirectly tap into the universal mind—the Akashic records—through us. We have unlimited access to it, but they don't, and it can be difficult to navigate. That's why it's best to consult with a skilled medium who can home in on the individual they're trying to contact."

"That's great advice for the living, but it's still unfortunate that some cultures consider talking to their ancestors as taboo. After all, many societies venerate the dead," Hazel said. "They talk to their ancestors, regularly offer them gifts, and seek their guidance, especially during difficult times."

"It's wonderful that Ethel could see and hear you," Isaac said, looking at Alma. "But my mom isn't able to do either. I need to find a way to get through to her!"

Shane pushed the brim of his black Stetson hat back. "The first written records involving dream telepathy came from the Greek philosopher Democritus, who theorized images could be transmitted by one person to another while they were dreaming. He was referring to two living people, but the fact is, those of us who have crossed over often reach the living through their dreams. Dreams can serve as a bridge to communicate with the living."

"Maybe I should try that," Isaac said, a little step in his voice.

"That's a great idea. Maybe she'll be able to hear you if you talk to her while she's sleeping." Melba took a bite of her angel biscuit with huckleberry jam. "Thanks, these are delicious."

"I'm glad you like them. They're my favorite," Isaac said.

"Speaking of scientific theories, I'm excited that scientists have recently proven Einstein and Schrödinger's theory regarding entangled particles," Melba said. "They theorized entangled particles act as one, even though there's no detectable connection between the two particles. And it turned out they were right!"

Seeing that some family members were confused, Solomon explained further. "The smallest unit of matter is an atom, which is made of particles. Einstein and Schrödinger theorized there was a connection between entangled particles, even though they couldn't detect one. Scientists have recently proved their theory correct by photographing two particles of light that were entangled. Using a beam splitter, scientists sent two entangled particles of light down a tube where, at a junction, they were split apart and then photographed. Although they had been separated, both entangled particles were positioned at zero degrees, and they looked like mirror images of a crescent moon facing each other, proving that they were somehow still connected. Then the scientists repeated the experiment but changed the orientation of one entangled particle to forty-five degrees, and its entangled twin instantaneously corresponded, matching its forty-five-degree orientation. Again, they repeated the experiment, orienting one entangled particle ninety degrees and one hundred thirty-five degrees, and the entangled twin instantaneously corresponded regardless of the distance between the entangled particles!"

"That would explain the connection people have with one another!" Isaac said. "Since we're all made of a zillion particles, then some of our particles might be entangled with particles of people we love. This would explain why one entangled person sometimes gets a gut feeling or premonition about their entangled loved one. They might share an invisible connection, regardless of how far apart they are. They remain connected through entanglement—not even death can separate them! This must be the case with my mom and me."

"That would also explain the special bond I share with Mable," Melba said, referencing her sister who was still alive. She smiled. "We're entangled twins."

"That's pretty awesome," Shane said. "But, Isaac, if you're right, then we could argue that we're all connected through entanglement—not just some of us."

"Yes, we're all one," Ethel agreed. "These theories—"

"Your grandfather on your dad's side had one of those entangled experiences and saved your dad's life when he was a young boy," Hazel interrupted, looking at Isaac. "Your mom told me that your grandfather was teaching a chemistry class when he suddenly dropped everything, told the class he had to save his son, ran from the classroom to the pond on the school grounds, and pulled your dad from the water, where he had accidentally fallen in and was drowning."

"I didn't know that," Isaac said, wide-eyed.

"It's a true story," Hazel said. "I'm sorry, Grandma.... What were you saying?"

"Oh, I was just going to say that these theories, combined with personal experiences, help people get closer to understanding that *dead* is a relative term," Ethel said. "This is important because it makes it more acceptable for people to communicate with those who have crossed over. In fact, receiving messages from the other side is a phenomenon as old as the hills—wise men recorded such events in the Bible. Our ancestors communicated with the living eons ago, the same way we do today."

"I tried many times to get in touch with my sisters after I passed, but I never succeeded," Shane said. "It's very helpful when the living are open to receiving a message. Making contact doesn't always happen, but it *does* make it a lot easier."

Ethel handed Isaac a jar of her homemade huckleberry jam. "I hope you like it. Since no one has ever successfully grown huckleberries, we used to handpick them from wild huckleberry shrubs, and picking the berries was sometimes dangerous—grizzly bears *love* wild huckleberries! Although we don't have that problem here in paradise, I still only bring it out for special occasions."

"Thanks, I'd love to try some." Isaac spread some on his angel biscuit and took a bite. "It's delicious. Sweet and tart at the same time." He handed a piece to Kéyah, his faithful red heeler, who was sitting beside his chair. "I love this dog; he was there to greet me when I crossed over."

"He sure was," Hazel said. "When we knew you were coming, we all gathered to welcome you over, and Kéyah was so excited to see you. He was barking and pacing around, making circles . . . anxious to see his master."

"You might not know this, but your dad gave Kéyah to your mom as a birthday present before you were born," Hazel said. "She gave him his name, which means 'land' in Navajo, because he was found on the Navajo reservation. I remember when Kéyah saved your life when you were just a small tyke—maybe two years old."

Anticipating one of Hazel's stories, everyone settled in.

> Since you didn't talk until you were five, your mom was a little high-strung about making sure she didn't lose you. She knew if she called you, you wouldn't answer back, which terrified her, so she always dressed you in a red shirt to make it easier to see you. It gave her a little comfort knowing that Kéyah, being a herding dog, saw it as his job to protect you. Everywhere you went, Kéyah followed.
>
> One day, when your parents were getting ready for a camping trip, your mom went to the garage to get the sleeping bags from your dad and, not seeing you, asked him where you were. As it turned out, he had thought you were with her. Realizing you were lost, they frantically ran through the house looking for you but couldn't find you. Then they started running across their ten acres, but still they couldn't find you! Your parents were terrified.

Out of desperation, your mom climbed the ladder to the top of the house, hoping she could spy your red shirt from that vantage point, but you were nowhere to be seen! As she stood there crying hysterically, she realized that if she could find Kéyah, she'd be able to find you. She hurried back down the ladder and started whistling as loud as she could, calling Kéyah's name. Your mom thought if she saw which direction Kéyah came from, at least she'd know which way to start looking. She continued whistling and calling, but Kéyah didn't come, because he didn't want to leave you. Eventually, Kéyah ran back to the house to see what she wanted, but your mom had her back turned, and she didn't see which direction he came from!

Not knowing what to do, your mom looked at Kéyah and said, "Kéyah, where's Isaac?" Not understanding what your mom was asking, Kéyah jumped into the open door of the car she had been packing for the camping trip. Your mom looked at him squarely and repeated, "Kéyah, where's Isaac?" This time, Kéyah jumped out of the car and took off running so fast your mom could barely keep up. Kéyah led her through the sagebrush and trees to where you were standing at the edge of your neighbor's swimming pool! Your mom knelt down, scooped you up into her arms, and burst into tears. Then she pulled Kéyah into her arms with you, kissed him on his head, and thanked him for saving your life!

"That's a great story," everyone cheered.

"Thanks, buddy," Isaac said, hugging his faithful dog. Kéyah wagged his tail, then laid his head down on his master's lap. "Kéyah saved me; now I need to save my mom. I think I'll try to reach her while she's dreaming tonight."

"That has been one of the more successful ways of communicating with the living," Hazel said in approval. "Some ancient Egyptians slept in special rooms designed for the purpose of receiving divine revelations in their dreams from a deceased relative. Many visions received in dreams are also recorded in the Bible, especially in the books of Genesis, Kings, Daniel, Acts, Numbers, Job, and Matthew. And many Native Americans believe they receive visions from their ancestors in their dreams. There are countless other examples of ancestors communicating with their loved ones in this way throughout history. It worked for all of them. . . . It might work for you."

Ethel agreed. "If you visit your mom while she's dreaming, she's more likely to hear you, since she won't be preoccupied with the troubles of the day. Go and visit her, but wait until she's sleeping soundly, then whisper your message in her ear."

"I will. And I know just what to say," Isaac said, smiling.

4

I MISS YOU
April 28, 2017

THIS IS ALL WRONG, Charlie thought, standing in the shower, her tears becoming one with the steamy water, then circling down the drain along with her will to carry on. *This is all wrong,* she repeated to herself. Not wanting to face the day, she stood in the shower a while longer, then reluctantly turned the water off and grabbed the towel from the sliding glass door.

"Since it's Friday, I'm taking half the day off," Chris said, taking his pajamas off. "What are your plans for the day?"

"I don't know," Charlie said, drying off. "I'll figure it out over coffee."

"Okay." Chris stepped into the shower and slid the glass door shut.

While Chris showered, Charlie dressed, fed Cobalt, Dexter, and Schmiggs, then scattered peanuts on the porch railing for the Steller's jays. Next, she made a cup of coffee and sat down at the kitchen table. She was making a to-do list when her ringtone, "The Man Who Sold the World" by David Bowie, began to play. It was her sister Teresa calling.

"Hey, what's up?" Charlie said, her voice flat and drained.

"I just wanted to see how you're doing today."

"If it weren't for Chris, I'm not sure what I'd do."

"I'm concerned about you. Do you think it would be helpful to take an antidepressant for a while?" Teresa asked with hesitation.

"Taking antidepressants won't make Isaac come back to life!" Charlie snapped, her voice instantly turning sharp.

"I know, honey, nothing will bring Isaac back, but it might help you get through the worst of it."

"I know you're concerned, but the only thing that will help is for ISAAC NOT TO BE DEAD!" Charlie said, trying to control her anger. Then she changed the subject. "How are you? How's the weather in Snowflake?"

Chris walked into the kitchen, got a cup of coffee, and sat down at the kitchen table. Charlie told Teresa she'd call her back later.

"Have you figured out what we need to do today?" Chris asked once she'd hung up.

"We need a few things from the grocery store, and I need to request Isaac's *complete* birth records," Charlie said, taking a sip of her coffee.

"It's April 28 . . . Arbor Day," Chris said.

"Then it's been ten days since Isaac passed. Do you want to plant some trees in his memory?"

Chris thought that was a good idea, so Charlie found the National Forest Foundation website on her phone, then opened a link that read: *$1 PLANTS ONE TREE*. "I'm going to donate five hundred dollars to plant five hundred trees," she said. "How much do you want to donate?"

"I'll do the same as you."

Charlie placed the order, paying the $1,000 from their joint account.

"That's a nice thing to do in Isaac's memory," Chris said as his phone rang. He answered it, occasionally nodding his head during the conversation, then hung up.

"What was that about?"

"Nothing . . . I need to sign some papers regarding a residential home built in the hundred-year floodplain. I can do it when I get to work."

Charlie looked out the window at the Steller's jays landing and flying away with their peanuts. "Do you remember the time when Isaac was eating breakfast and told us about his dream where I fed the birds so much that they grew fat and couldn't fly away?"

"Yeah, that made all of us laugh."

Charlie continued watching the Steller's jays, but she was remembering Isaac lying cold and lifeless at the funeral parlor. A wave of raw pain emerged as she recalled the funeral director calling and asking her to pick out clothes for Isaac's cremation, which seemed too horrible to be true. Charlie had stood hesitantly before Isaac's dresser drawer, then reluctantly picked out clothes to dress his cold body. She chose a pair of jeans, socks, and the Icelandic sweater he'd worn the day they went to the Phoenix airport to watch airplanes.

Charlie stared blankly out the window.

"What are you thinking about?" Chris asked.

Hearing his voice, Charlie returned to the present. "I was remembering when we had to go to the funeral parlor to say goodbye to Isaac before he was cremated."

"What a nightmare," Chris said, tears filling his eyes.

"When we walked into the funeral home, he was dressed in the clothes I had picked out for him and dropped off the day before. I remember putting my arms around him and pulling him toward me, but he was cold and rigid—he didn't move. I laid my head on his chest and broke down. I was hoping he'd start breathing and open his eyes." Charlie tried to control her breaking voice. "I was hoping he wasn't dead; I was hoping . . . but he didn't move. I remember horror settling in as I was forced to accept that he wasn't coming home with us—that he was *never* coming home with us—*that Isaac was dead*!"

Tears streamed down Chris's face.

"I placed my hands on his cold face, then ran my fingers through his hair and felt the stitches on both sides of his head," Charlie said, her voice filled with anger. "I was furious they'd done an autopsy. He died of a seizure, and the only thing in his system was his seizure meds, so I didn't understand why they had to cut him open. I wanted to scream, but I didn't. Then I saw his blue fingernails and picked up his cold hand. I laid my head back on his chest, knowing I'd never see his body again. I knew we were supposed to say goodbye, but I couldn't—I refused. I held his hand, looked at his beautiful face, and whispered in his ear, 'I'll never say goodbye to you,' and then we left."

"I don't know how we'll ever get through this."

Charlie grabbed Chris's hand as the sound of the garbage truck's screeching brakes down the street brought them back to the day's tasks.

"I need to put the trash out," Chris said, wiping tears from his eyes. Charlie nodded.

After regaining his composure, Chris put the trash out and dressed for work while Charlie got ready to go to the hospital to request Isaac's records and then take the dogs for a walk.

"Then I'll see you this afternoon," Charlie said.

"Okay, but I'm going for a bike ride after work; it helps me clear my mind."

As they walked to the garage, they triggered the motion sensor in the laundry room, turning on the light. Chris grabbed his jacket hanging on the wall, opened the door, and pressed the button on the wall to open the garage door. Their neighbor and house sitter, Nancy, waved as she and her dog walked by. On the other side of the street, a slender woman pushed her toddler in a stroller while her young daughter, dressed in a sweater and a lacy white summer dress, merrily skipped ahead of her mother. Songbirds chirped as the sun warmed the crisp morning air.

It doesn't seem fair that my son is dead and the rest of the world goes on living as if nothing happened, Charlie thought as she kissed Chris goodbye.

A few hours later, Charlie put a few things in her backpack, loaded Dexter and Cobalt into her Honda, and drove to the hospital. She opened the sunroof, cracked open the windows, and then made her way to the medical records department. She rang the bell outside the door, then heard someone approach the window. The same heavyset woman with short dark hair who'd helped Charlie previously pulled the blinds up and opened the window.

"How can I help you?" the woman asked.

"Yes, I'm sorry to bother you again, but I only received part of my son's medical records that I requested," Charlie explained. "On the Release of Information form, I specifically marked ALL birth records. Can you please get a COMPLETE copy of his birth records, especially his fetal heart monitor strips? I'm happy to sign whatever you need."

"What's your name?" The woman took her red-framed glasses

from the top of her head, placed them on the bridge of her nose, and sat down at her computer.

Charlie took a deep breath, trying to contain her frustration, and then exhaled. "My legal name is Charlotte Bynar, and my son's name is Isaac Calley."

"Oh yes, I remember you now. Just give me a couple of minutes while I look up your file," the woman said, typing on her keyboard. After a few minutes, she explained, "You've only received part of those records because the rest are stored at our medical records storage facility in Phoenix. Would you like me to request those records?" the woman asked, peering over her red-framed glasses.

"Yes! That's why I requested ALL his birth records in the first place." Charlie sighed. "How long do you think it will take to get them?"

"It just depends on how long it takes to locate them, but I'd guess you'll receive them in the mail in two to four weeks."

Charlie thanked her, and then the woman slid the window closed and lowered the blind.

Charlie walked back to her car, then drove to a trailhead off Old Walnut Canyon Road, where she often took Isaac and the dogs for a walk. She parked, let the dogs out, and grabbed her backpack. The dogs, recognizing the location, marked their spots, then took off barking down the dirt trail. Charlie put her phone in her back pocket, locked the car, then followed.

As the trail meandered through a ponderosa pine forest, Charlie noticed a colony of carpenter ants, stepped over them carefully, and continued toward a picturesque view overlooking Walnut Canyon.

Maybe if I walk far enough, I'll find Isaac somewhere along the trail. Maybe he'll be sitting on the fallen tree where we always used to stop to take a break and give the dogs some water, Charlie thought, even though she knew in her heart that "maybe" would never happen.

As she rounded a bend in the trail, she saw a young couple petting Dexter and Cobalt.

"Your dogs are adorable," the woman said as Charlie approached.

"Yeah. They're both very friendly, as you can tell."

"They certainly are," the woman said, smiling as she passed by. "Have a good day."

"Thanks, you too." Charlie whistled to Dexter and Cobalt, who were working the couple for as much attention as they could get.

"Have a good day" lingered in Charlie's mind. *That will never happen again.*

When Charlie reached the halfway mark, Isaac was sitting on the downed tree waiting for her, but she couldn't see him. She took her backpack off, sat down, and filled the dogs' water bowl. While the dogs quenched their thirst, Charlie took her phone from her back pocket and checked her messages.

She opened one from Chris: *I picked up the stuff we needed from the store and I'm heading out for a bike ride. Love you, Beautiful.*

Charlie replied, *I love you too, Handsome. I hope you have a good ride.*

Next, Charlie opened a message from Teresa: *I'm worried about you, are you all right? Is there anything I can do for you?*

Charlie wanted to answer that some things can't be fixed. That the love we have for other adults is calculated, but the love for a child bypasses all those conditions. People frequently get new wives and husbands, but you can't replace your kid—it's not the same. However, keeping her thoughts to herself, she replied, *Thanks for checking on me, but there isn't anything you can do.*

Despite their opposing political views, Charlie and Teresa had been there for each other through thick and thin, as their friendship mattered more. One year, Teresa sent Charlie a birthday card with a picture of two hillbillies dressed in overalls and straw hats with the caption: *DESTINY MADE US SISTERS, HEARTS MADE US FRIENDS*. Appreciating that perfect summation of their relationship, Charlie had put the card on the refrigerator decades ago, and it was still secured there by a rusty magnet.

Charlie continued scrolling her messages and opened the string of texts between Isaac and her. Since Isaac's death, she had continued to send messages to him on his phone. She scrolled back to the last message Isaac had sent her: ♥♥, two red emoji hearts with no text. She opened a new message to Isaac and attached a photograph of him standing in front of one of the Very Large Array radio antennae in New Mexico. The picture captured Isaac's sense of wonder as he gazed up at the giant dish against the blue sky. Charlie wrote, *I love you, Sweets. I*

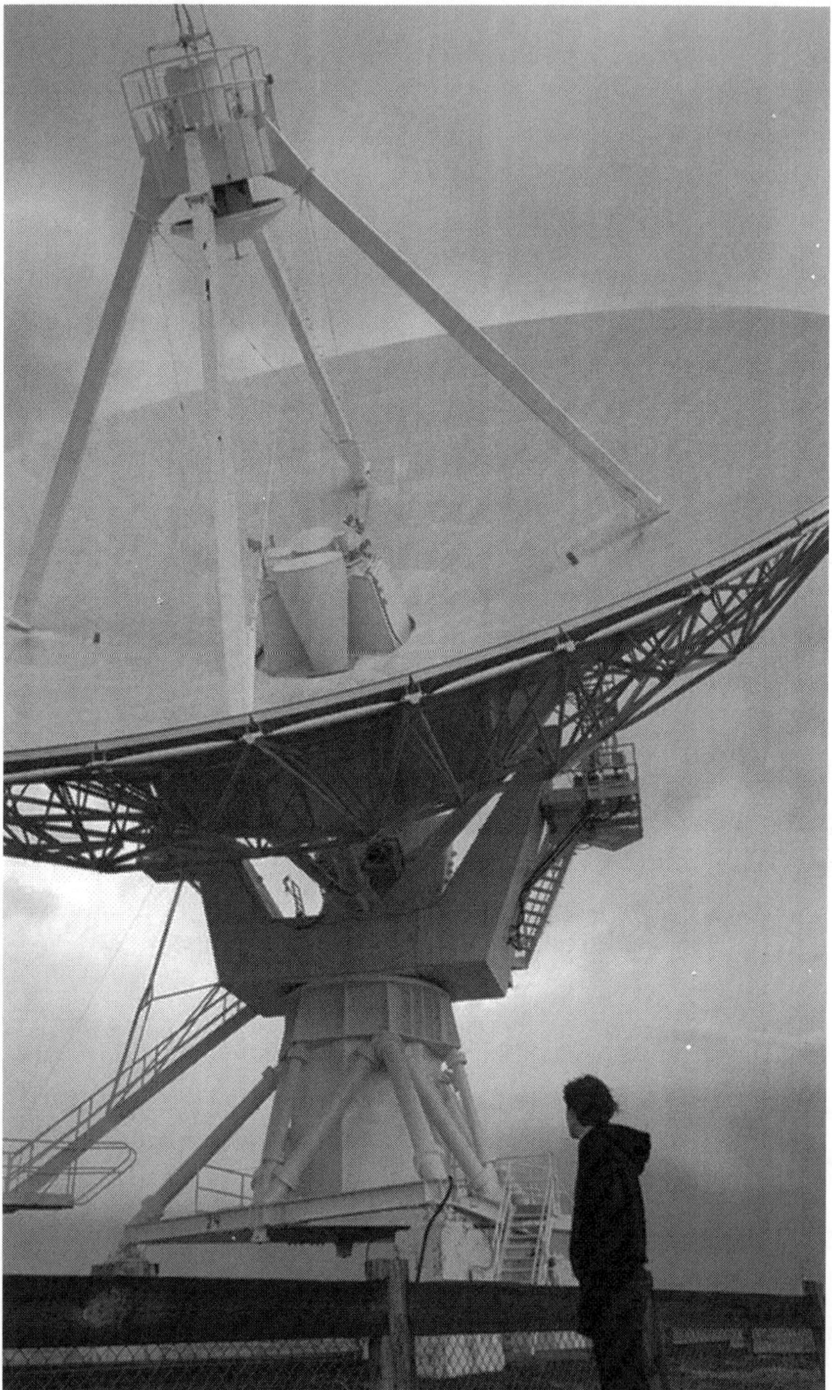

hope you're listening! FOREVER ISAAC ♥♥, then hit the send button, hoping somehow he'd receive her message.

On the downed tree nearby, Isaac smiled.

After they reached the Walnut Canyon overlook, Charlie, Cobalt, and Dexter turned and headed back toward the car. On the way, Charlie picked a small bouquet of wildflowers, wrapping the stems together with a long blade of grass. When they arrived home, Charlie parked in the garage. Excited to be home, Dexter and Cobalt pushed their way into the house, barking as they ran to the kitchen to meet Chris.

As Charlie hung up her jacket in the laundry room, she smelled dinner cooking. She walked across the hall and into Isaac's room, placed the wildflower bouquet among the stuffed animals neatly arranged on his bed, then walked to the kitchen, where Chris was cooking and drinking a glass of chardonnay.

"How was your bike ride?"

"It was good, but I biffed it," Chris said, showing Charlie the wounds on his shin.

"Looks like it hurts."

"Yeah, the trail has a couple of steep areas that are very rocky, and if you don't have the right momentum and keep your balance, then you eat it."

"Last time you rode that trail, you made it without falling," Charlie reminded him. "Hopefully, next time you come home, your legs won't be all scraped up. What's for dinner?"

"I picked up some salmon; I wanted to make you something special."

Charlie knew he was trying to stay strong for her, knowing she was barely hanging on.

"Oh, that was sweet of you," Charlie said, kissing him.

"I made rice pilaf and steamed broccoli to go with the salmon."

"It smells great." Charlie fed the dogs some dry kibble, then sat on a barstool at the raised kitchen counter to talk with Chris while he finished making dinner. "I saw the large red-and-black carpenter ants on the trail. I wish I had brought them some crackers or a piece of cheese, but I forgot."

"I always loved coming home after work. Every day, Isaac was excited to tell us some cool fact he had learned about ants," Chris said, taking a sip of his chardonnay. "I had always thought ants were just pests until Isaac told us how incredible they are."

"He certainly was fascinated by them," Charlie said. "I remember one year he put 'Queen Ant' on his Christmas list. Isaac always lit up whenever he talked about ants. What I'd give to see him smile like that again!"

"Me too," Chris agreed. "One of my favorite things Isaac explained to us was that ants use math. I still can't believe the Saharan silver ants have a pedometer inside their brains that counts their steps when they go out searching for food so that on their way back to their nest, they know how far to travel! And they turn in circles to clock the sun when they leave their nest to use it as a reference point to navigate back home." Reliving conversations they had with Isaac was a way for them to keep his memory alive, which helped them cope with their devastating loss.

"It's incredible, to say the least," Charlie exclaimed. "Another amazing fact Isaac told us was that ants are considered a superorganism. Every ant has a part to play, and no particular ant is in charge—they think collectively."

"I had always assumed the queen would be in charge, but that's not the case," Chris added. "I was surprised to learn the workers tell the queen where to go by dragging her by her mandibles—she basically serves the colony as an egg-laying machine."

"Yeah . . . I had no idea."

"Dinner's ready," Chris said, pouring himself another glass of chardonnay. "I tried a new recipe for the salmon. I hope you like it."

They sat down for dinner and Charlie tasted the salmon. It was perfect, crispy on the outside and tender and juicy on the inside. "Thanks for making such a nice dinner. It's delicious," Charlie said, concealing her true feelings. *Having such a nice meal when Isaac can't even breathe isn't right. I don't deserve to enjoy anything while he's dead.*

"I'm glad you like it."

"It was very kind of you," Charlie said. She told him about stopping by the hospital and everything the woman had told her. "She said we should receive the records in the mail in two to four weeks."

"Good, then we can figure out what happened," Chris said. "I hope they'll send *all* the records this time."

"Me too," Charlie agreed. "Thanks for being there for me and having my back. I know this is hard on both of us."

"I love you with all my heart," Chris said, tears falling from his eyes. "No matter what, we have each other's backs!"

"Absolutely!" Charlie said before changing the subject to something that had been nagging at her. "I haven't thought about it for a while, but I probably need to call work. They're going to wonder if I'm ever going to come back."

"It's only been ten days," Chris said. "And they said they had another nurse covering for you. . . . Give yourself a break! You shouldn't go back before you're ready."

"Yeah, maybe you're right," Charlie said, taking a deep breath. "I'm thinking about starting a foundation in Isaac's name. Since he's not here to do the work he wanted to do—sharing his love for ants—I wanted to try to do some of it for him. I can't keep him alive, but maybe I can keep his name alive. I know it's only crumbs, but it's all I have left. I don't know what else to do."

"I think it's a good idea," Chris said. "What should we call it?"

"I don't know . . . something about ants and Isaac's name."

As Chris drank his chardonnay, Charlie cleaned the kitchen, putting the dirty dishes in the dishwasher and the leftovers in a Tupperware container. When Chris was finished, he walked into the kitchen and put his arms around Charlie. "It's been a long day. Let's go to bed; we're both exhausted."

"Yeah, that's not a bad idea," Charlie agreed. "I feel like I'm swimming through quicksand. I don't know how much I can take."

Charlie put on her pajamas, got into bed, and Dexter and Cobalt lay down at the foot of the bed. After Chris had finished brushing and flossing his teeth, which he did religiously, he climbed into bed, curled up with Charlie, and they fell asleep.

As Chris and Charlie slept, Isaac stood watching them from the foot of the bed. First, Charlie's dreams were about random things, but later, she fell into a deeper sleep, where her mind was quiet. Isaac sat on the edge of the bed next to his mom, placed his hand on her shoulder, and whispered in her ear, "I miss you." Recognizing Isaac's voice in her sleep, Charlie automatically replied, "I miss you too," then suddenly woke up.

Charlie sat on the side of the bed, her heart pounding. *That was very strange. . . . I could swear Isaac was talking to me in my dream. . . . He said, "I miss you."* Unsettled, she got out of bed, made coffee, and sat at the kitchen table, wondering what had just happened.

After the sun rose, Chris got up and put on his bathrobe, poured himself a cup of coffee, and sat down with Charlie at the kitchen table.

"I had a dream about Isaac last night, but it wasn't like a normal dream," Charlie said. "Usually, dreams are like watching nonsensical silent movies, and part of my dream was like that, but then, in the middle of it, I heard Isaac's voice—his actual voice! I couldn't see him, but he whispered in my ear, 'I miss you.' It was as clear as day—I heard his voice. I told him I missed him too, and then I woke up." Charlie tried to hold back her tears.

Silence.

"I'm not going crazy!" Charlie said, detecting alarm in Chris's eyes. "I know it was Isaac—I heard his voice!"

Still, an uncomfortable silence hung in the air.

Charlie explained her dream again, hoping to convince Chris, but he wasn't swayed.

"What are your plans for the day?" he asked, trying to change the subject.

"I'm not crazy. I know what I heard!" Charlie took a deep breath and exhaled, then decided to let the topic go for now. "I'll probably start working on the foundation."

"Sounds good. I think I'm going to go for another bike ride. Hopefully, I won't come back with new battle scars."

Chris got up to go change his clothes. When he returned, he was wearing his biking clothes and cleats.

"Let me know what you find out about starting the foundation."

"Okay, hope you have a good ride," Charlie said, kissing Chris goodbye.

After Chris left, Charlie sat back down at the kitchen table.

Maybe I am going crazy. . . . Maybe it was just a dream.

5

THE TOP OF THE MOUNTAIN
The Other Side

IT WAS A BEAUTIFUL DAY on the other side. The Williams family sat around the picnic table under the eighty-five-year-old cottonwood tree, playing checkers, drinking fresh-squeezed pink lemonade, and eating apple cream tarts. A few fluffy white clouds drifted across the brilliant blue sky as the sunflowers covering the distant hills danced in the warm summer breeze. A robin flew down from the towering cottonwood tree and landed near Piute and Babe, where they were grazing near the Big Wood River, then tipped its head from side to side, listening for the movement of worms below the ground.

While Shane and Isaac played checkers, Shane's border collie, Hailey, grew restless and started barking and pestering Kéyah, who had been napping under the picnic table. Shane finished his apple cream tart, licked his fingers, then pulled a smooth, flat river rock from the front pocket of his brightly colored vest and slid it across the table to Isaac.

"After this game, would you like to go down to the river and skip rocks?" Shane asked. "We could take the dogs; they're getting restless."

"You mean Hailey's getting restless. . . . Kéyah was trying to take a nap," Isaac playfully clarified, picking up the smooth river rock and rubbing it between his fingers and thumb. "Sure, that sounds fun."

"I stand corrected." Shane grinned, jumping and capturing Isaac's last two checkers and winning the game.

Isaac rolled his eyes and put the river rock in the front pocket of his jeans.

"Good game," Shane said, shaking Isaac's hand, which was half the size of his. The difference between their statures was magnified when Isaac and Shane stood up to leave. At six feet, two inches tall, Shane stood two feet over Isaac, evoking an image reminiscent of Don Quixote and Sancho Panza, though Shane was not off his rocker, and Isaac was not rotund.

After saying goodbye to the rest of the Williams family, Shane and Isaac started walking down the small trail toward the Big Wood River while Kéyah and Hailey ran ahead, roughhousing and barking. On the way, Shane and Isaac stopped to pet Piute and Babe, then followed the trail through some sagebrush toward the riverbank. Shane picked a small piece of sagebrush, crushed it between his fingers, and inhaled the intoxicating scent.

"I love the smell of sage." Shane placed the crushed sage into Isaac's small hand. "It reminds me of when I was a young boy growing up in Hailey, Idaho."

"So that's why you named your dog Hailey," Isaac said, smelling the sage. "I can see why you like this. It smells like musky rain."

"Yep, that's how Hailey got her name," Shane said. "Musky rain . . . that's an interesting way to describe it."

Isaac smelled the sage again, then dropped it on the ground, and they continued down the trail to the river's edge and stood on the smooth, colorful river rocks polished by water and time. They stopped and listened to the quiet rumble of the river, enjoying the fresh, cool breeze on their faces. The Big Wood River was crystal clear, making it possible to see the beautiful rainbow trout swimming in its deep-running waters.

Kéyah ran up to Isaac and dropped a stick at his feet. Isaac picked it up and threw it down the riverbank as far as he could, and Hailey and Kéyah took off running after it, barking and splashing in the water.

Shane bent down and searched for a smooth, flat river rock. When he found what he was looking for, he placed the stone along the curve of his index finger, steadying it between his middle finger and thumb, then coiled back his arm and launched the stone across the river's glassy surface.

"Four skips. . . . That's pretty good," Isaac said, smiling. "When we were going to Canada, my mom, Chris, and I came down here to scatter some of your ashes."

"I know. . . . I was there." Shane smiled. "That was sweet of you guys."

"Oh, right. . . . Of course you were." Isaac grinned.

"Let's see what you've got."

Isaac pulled the river rock from his pocket and worked it between his fingers. *I hope I can beat Shane,* Isaac thought. He positioned the stone along the curve of his index finger, then sent it flying across the water's surface.

"Three skips. . . . Not bad, little man. Your mom and I used to come to this very spot when we were kids to play by the river."

Isaac directed his eyes toward the ground, fighting back tears.

Shane put his arm around Isaac's shoulders. "Let me tell you a story about your mom when she was seven . . . about the age you are now, and I was twelve. Your grandma Hazel, my mom, had five kids. Your mom was the youngest, and I was her only son. Since your mom was such a tomboy, we played together and sometimes got in trouble, which was mostly my fault. We called your mom Charlie because Charlotte was too proper for a girl who played in the mud and refused to wear dresses. Charlie and I used to come down here, and while I swam, your mom built mud pies on the riverbank because she was afraid of the water. . . . She didn't know how to swim."

Shane pointed to the top of Carbonate Mountain, where high school seniors had traditionally painted the numbers of their graduation years on the face of the mountain. "One time, your mom and I decided to climb to the top and touch the sixty painted in white. In order to reach it, we had to climb up the sheer face of the mountain, which is covered in loose shale. The bottom part was easy, but the higher we got, the steeper the mountain became, and the loose shale beneath our feet made us lose our footing, and we found ourselves sliding toward the cliff. Your mom managed to scramble off the shale to a large rock, but I was on another rock with about six feet of loose shale between us. The only way to get down was for her to somehow make it over to where I was. I reached out as far as I could toward your mom, and she inched over as far as she could and reached for my hand, but there was still about a foot between us—she was going to have to cross the shale just above the cliff!"

Isaac's eyes widened as he held his breath.

"She got up her nerve and managed to get hold of a small sagebrush growing on the side of the mountain," Shane continued. "But as she put more weight on the sagebrush, it gave way, and she started falling, but I grabbed her hand and pulled her to safety!"

"That sounds scary." Isaac exhaled, letting out a sigh of relief. "Now my mom's in another dangerous situation."

"She's entered a dark place, and you must try to guide her through it," Shane said. "On the mountain, your mom was facing physical danger, but now she's facing relentless sorrow—a formidable opponent for even the strongest individuals. This is a defining point in your mom's life. Either this situation will force her to find the wisdom she seeks, or she'll fall prey to the darkness."

"That's why before I crossed over, I left my mom a message in my journal: *Everything is a gift, even pain, and with these gifts, we pursue knowledge and eradicate hate*. I knew she'd be facing this nightmarish journey, and I hoped it would help give her the strength to overcome the challenges," Isaac said. "It seems counterintuitive, but sometimes pain can lead people to surprising gifts. I learned this from being a special needs kid. When you're ridiculed for your disabilities, it causes one to do a lot of soul searching. Physical pain is a warning sign to help prevent someone from injuring themselves, whereas emotional pain can force people out of their comfort zones and cause them to reevaluate their perspectives on issues they're struggling with. In doing so, they can find valuable insights, clarity of mind, and wisdom. In this way, pain is a bridge to obtaining those gifts. When people are content, they have little reason to reevaluate their perspectives. As a result, they're less likely to find the priceless gifts that are theirs for the taking. Although this concept is challenging, especially when we're in the eye of the storm, sometimes we learn the most from difficult journeys. . . . It's easier to appreciate once the storm has passed, but you already know this."

"Yes, but it helps us to reflect on these things," Shane said, skipping another stone. "People intersect many crossroads in their lifetime, and the crossroad your mom faces now will force her to either hold on to her preconceived view that death is the end or reevaluate it. If she chooses to hold on to her views, she will likely take her own life. But Charlie has one thing working to her advantage—love is greater than pain and darkness combined. Since her love for you is unwavering, hopefully, it will give her the strength she needs to reevaluate her views of death and obtain the wisdom she's seeking—that death is a transition, not an end. If she succeeds, Charlie will know that nothing can truly separate the two of you! She'll emerge from the darkness, able to find a renewed purpose in life."

"I agree," Isaac said, "but I need to get my mom on the right path. I sent a message to her when she was dreaming, but her self-doubt crept in and derailed my efforts. She's been sending me messages on her phone, which I love, but more importantly, the fact that she keeps doing this tells me she's holding on to the slightest chance that I'm somehow getting her messages. Since she received my first message while she was dreaming, I think I'll try again. Hopefully, it will help her overcome her doubt."

"That reminds me . . . let me tell you a fable based on Buddhist philosophy and explain how it relates to your mom. The obstacles she will face on her long and difficult journey are the five hindrances: doubt, ill will or adversity, sensual desire or self-indulgence, sloth or torpor, and restlessness." Shane walked to an old, weathered log overlooking the river and sat down on it. Isaac followed, sat beside him, and listened to his story.

> A wise raven flew over a beautiful valley, calling to all the animals that lived there that they could gain the knowledge and wisdom they were seeking if they met him at sunrise the following morning, at the foot of the mountain near the bridge that crossed over the river. When the sun came up the next day, a cottontail rabbit, a wild burro, a bighorn sheep, a bobcat, a red squirrel, a deer mouse, and three elk had gathered at the foot of the mountain to meet the wise raven. He was perched on top of a signpost with two arrows under a tall aspen

tree near the arched wooden bridge. The top arrow read: *KNOWLEDGE*, and pointed to the left. The bottom arrow read: *WISDOM*, and pointed to the right.

The wise raven smoothed his black feathers, asked the chattering animals to be quiet, and said, "Once you cross the bridge, you can take one of two trails. The trail to the left will lead you to profound knowledge. You will learn from Master Black Bear as he tells you about the time when he climbed to the top of the mountain and achieved the great wisdom that HE had been seeking. The trail to the right will lead you to wisdom, where you'll gain clarity of mind. The journey will be difficult, but the wisdom YOU SEEK awaits you at the top of the mountain."

Chatter broke out as the animals discussed which trail to take. Not wanting to take the difficult journey, the three elk decided they wanted to acquire great knowledge from Master Black Bear. But the cottontail rabbit, wild burro, bighorn sheep, red squirrel, deer mouse, and bobcat decided they wanted to find the wisdom each of them was seeking by climbing to the top of the mountain.

The three elk crossed the bridge, took the trail to the left, and followed it to a beautiful field of tall grass, where they saw Master Black Bear sitting next to a log, eating chokecherries. They lay down in the grass in front of Master Black Bear and listened to him tell his incredible story about the time when he climbed to the top of the mountain and gained the wisdom HE had been seeking.

The elk enjoyed Master Black Bear's story and gained a great deal of knowledge, but they now hungered for THEIR OWN wisdom. Realizing knowledge could be taught, but wisdom was gained through experience, the three elk thanked Master Black Bear, then headed back toward the trail that led to the top of the mountain.

Meanwhile, the cottontail rabbit, wild burro, bighorn sheep, red squirrel, deer mouse, and bobcat had crossed the bridge, taken the trail to the right, and begun their journey to the top of the mountain, each of them hoping to gain the answer to the question they held closest to their hearts. The animals followed the trail as it wandered through a grove of aspens, ponderosa pine, and cottonwood trees at the base of the mountain. Birds called through the forest, and the animals felt invigorated by the fresh mountain air. The trail turned and gradually climbed upward, where the animals reached a clearing in the trees with a view of the mountaintop far off in the distance. They stopped and gazed up at the mountain's peak.

"All we need to do is climb to the top of the mountain to obtain the wisdom we seek," the red squirrel squeaked. All the animals agreed except the deer mouse. He looked at his friends, then back up to the top of the mountain in the far distance, and considered the vast journey ahead. Overcome by self-doubt, he ran underneath a huckleberry bush, made a nest, and lived there the rest of his life, wondering what the answer was to the question he held closest to his heart.

The cottontail rabbit, wild burro, bighorn sheep, red squirrel, and bobcat said goodbye to the deer mouse, then continued up the trail and crossed over a large rocky area that ended at a grassy meadow. They crossed the meadow and followed the path to a shallow creek. The bobcat jumped from one rock to another, and the cottontail rabbit and red squirrel followed his lead. Not troubled by the water, the bighorn sheep waded through the creek, but the wild burro, not wanting to get wet, was overcome by adversity and refused to cross the water. He called out to his friends, who were waiting for him on the other side of the creek. "I don't want to get wet," the wild burro said. "I'm going back to graze in the grassy meadow." His friends wished him well, and the wild burro returned to the grassy meadow and lived there for the rest of his life, not bothering to find the answer to the question he held closest to his heart.

The bobcat, cottontail rabbit, red squirrel, and bighorn sheep continued up the trail to a large grove of aspen trees. As the animals walked through the woodland, they noticed the green aspen leaves shimmering in the gentle wind and their white trunks reaching upward toward the blue sky above. On the other side of the aspen grove, the animals entered a clover field with an array of colorful flowers. The cottontail rabbit jumped for joy. "I love clover; it's my favorite!" Overcome by self-indulgence, the cottontail rabbit forgot the question she held closest to her heart. She dug a burrow in the clover field and lived there the rest of her life.

The bobcat, bighorn sheep, and red squirrel said goodbye to the cottontail rabbit and continued up the trail to a rocky precipice overlooking the valley below. Hearing "caw-caw, caw-caw," the animals looked up and saw the wise raven flying high overhead; then they gazed at the top of the mountain and noticed how far they'd come. "All we need to do is climb to the top of the mountain to obtain the wisdom we seek," the red squirrel squeaked. The bighorn sheep agreed, but the bobcat looked out over the valley below, then back toward the mountaintop. Overcome by laziness, the bobcat decided the precipice was the perfect place to take a nap. The bobcat yawned, curled up on the rocky ledge overlooking the valley, and lived there the rest of his life, not putting forth the effort needed to answer the question he held closest to his heart.

The red squirrel and bighorn sheep said goodbye to the bobcat and climbed up past the rocky precipice into a beautiful deep forest of ponderosa pine and oak trees. The red squirrel eyed the abundant acorns in the oak trees and, overcome by her restless mind, put obtaining the answer to the question she held closest to her heart aside. She jumped from tree to tree, busily collecting acorns, and lived there the rest of her life.

The bighorn sheep said goodbye to the red squirrel, then climbed above the forest line onto a cliff of ragged rocks and loose shale just below the top of the mountain. Persevering in the face of great challenges, the bighorn sheep climbed upward, where she heard the bleating of her kid calling her. The bighorn sheep's heart quickened as she hurried her pace. As she reached the top of the mountain, the answer to the question she held closest to her heart came to her—she KNEW that her kid stood next to her, even though she couldn't see him. She KNEW that not even death could separate them. At last, she had clarity of mind and a peaceful heart. She and her kid raised their heads, called out triumphantly, and they lived there the rest of their lives.

Shane put his arm around Isaac as he started to cry. "I'm waiting for her on the top of the mountain," Isaac cried, his voice trembling. "But she doesn't know I'm here."

"That's not entirely true," Shane said. "As you said earlier, she sends you messages on her phone, which means somewhere deep inside her heart, she's still holding on to the possibility that you somehow still exist and she'll find you once again."

"You're right. . . . It's just difficult for me to see my mom struggling so much," Isaac said. "I wish she knew that the dead can communicate with the living through their dreams. Then she would know it was me and stop doubting herself. Thanks for talking, Uncle Shane; we make a pretty good team."

Shane smiled. "Like the deer mouse, your mom doubts her ability to walk the long, difficult journey ahead of her, but since you're her guardian angel and I'm your copilot, we can help her carry onward toward the top of the mountain."

Isaac wiped his tears. "I'll visit my mom again tonight when she's sleeping."

6

PLATITUDES
May 10, 2017

AFTER KISSING CHRIS goodbye, Charlie walked back into the house and started a grocery list. Worried about bumping into an acquaintance and being asked how she was doing, Charlie felt apprehensive about going out in public. She feared one of two ugly situations would unfold: If she bumped into someone who knew Isaac had passed, they might feel obligated to offer her a trite platitude to quell the social unease of dealing with someone who was grieving. Or even worse, if the person wasn't already aware of Isaac's passing, they might ask how he was doing and then want to learn what happened and press for details. Charlie would be forced to retell the events while trying not to break down in public. The stunned acquaintance would fumble for words, then offer a meaningless platitude of false hope: Time heals all wounds, tomorrow will be better, he's in a better place, or this too shall pass, which was all bullshit. Charlie understood that people meant well, but she wished they understood that it would be more helpful if they simply said sorry and asked if there was anything they could do to help. As a result, it was easier for her to stay home, away from the land mines she was forced to navigate in public.

But feeling obligated to help with chores, she pressed on with making her shopping list. She was nearly finished when she felt a migraine behind her eyes. Suddenly nauseous, Charlie ran to the bathroom, threw up, and then rinsed her mouth. Knowing caffeine and non-steroidal anti-inflammatory drugs were used to treat migraines, she made a cup of coffee, ate some chocolate-covered coffee beans, and took a couple of ibuprofen. Afterward, she lay on the couch for a couple of hours, then, wanting to delay going out in public, called her boss to touch base.

Charlie worked as a nurse in the cardiology department at the Winslow Indian Health Care Center on the Navajo reservation. She was proud that she had learned many Navajo words and phrases, which she used when caring for her patients. The Navajo language, Diné Bizaad, was notorious for being a formidable language to speak and translate. This was why the famed Navajo code talkers had been called upon to transmit secret tactical messages through military radios during World War II.

Spanish missionary Fray Alonso de Benavides first mentioned the Spanish word "Navajo" in *The Memorial of Fray Alonso de Benavides*, written in 1630. Benavides wrote, "Navajós are very great farmers, for that [is what] 'Navajó' signifies—'great planted fields.'" Today, the Navajo call themselves Diné, meaning "The People," and are proudly known for their silver and turquoise jewelry, sand paintings, pottery, and woven rugs designed with cultural symbols.

When the clinic's secretary answered the phone, Charlie asked to be transferred to Kay, the director of nursing.

"Charlie, how are you doing?" Kay asked. "I've been thinking about you. Is there anything I can do for you?"

"No, there's nothing you can do, but thanks."

"We're all thinking about you and sending our sympathies."

"I appreciate it," Charlie said. "Please tell everyone thanks for coming to the service and sending their letters. . . . It was very kind of them."

"I will," Kay told her. "Do you know when you'd like to come back to work? Some people find going back to work to be helpful. . . . It can be a good distraction."

"I don't know," Charlie replied. "How's Dr. V doing?"

"She's getting by. We have someone covering for you, but it's not the same without you on the unit. Dr. Villarino and her patients miss you."

"Maybe I should come back next week, but I'll need you to do me a favor."

"Of course.... What can I do for you?"

"I need you to email everyone and let them know I don't want to talk about Isaac's passing at work. It's too difficult. It'll be hard enough just coming back to work, let alone..."

"I understand," Kay said as Charlie's voice drifted off. "I'm sure everyone will respect your wishes. Should I tell Dr. Villarino you'll be back on Monday? That would be about a month of leave, and if you find you can't work, you can always take more time off."

"Okay, thanks. I guess I'll try to come back on Monday."

"I'll see you then," Kay said, then hung up the phone.

That's only five days from now, Charlie thought as she got off the phone. Hearing a knock at the front door, she put the shopping list in her front pocket. When she opened it, Isaac's father, David, was standing there with a book in his hand. Isaac's presence had always centered David, and now that Isaac was gone, he had lost his compass and didn't seem to know which way to turn.

Charlie invited him in.

"I can't stay," David explained, handing Charlie the book. "I just wanted to give this to you. In this book, *Biocentrism*, Robert Lanza, a medical doctor and scientist, explains from a scientific perspective that death is an illusion. I still think Isaac's with us, and eventually, we'll get to see him again.... At least, I hope so."

Seeing tears in David's eyes, Charlie hugged him. "That was very kind of you," Charlie said. "I'll try to read it."

"I better get back to work, but I thought this book might help you."

"Thanks, I appreciate it."

David wiped his tears, tried to smile, then turned around and left.

Charlie put the book on the kitchen table and grabbed her bag to leave. Hearing her keys jingle, Cobalt and Dexter ran down the hall to join her wherever she was going. In the garage, she opened the back door of her Honda and the dogs jumped in, then lay down on their dog bed. Before Isaac passed, he and Chris had always raced to call shotgun for the passenger seat, but there was no calling shotgun anymore, and Charlie had resentfully laid the back seats down to make more room for the dogs.

Charlie drove to the parking lot, where she opened the windows and sunroof for the dogs, and then walked into the busy store. As she got a cart, she noticed classic rock playing on the overhead speakers and took in the smell of freshly baked bread. Charlie pulled out the grocery list from her front pocket and began selecting items that she needed, starting at the produce section at the end of the store, then the dairy section. She then moved toward the beauty department. Seeing someone she had worked with decades before at a local coffee shop, she quickly backed out of the aisle.

I'll have to come back for the toothpaste after I get the bread.

As Charlie headed for the bakery, she saw a slender woman with her two kids near the glass case of freshly baked doughnuts. The woman's toddler sat in the shopping cart, content, eating Cheerios from the opened box. Another child, a young son, was standing next to her. The scene reminded Charlie of how she used to buy Isaac a doughnut whenever she went grocery shopping, just to let him know she was thinking of him. It had always made him smile.

As Charlie drew closer, she heard the woman arguing with her son.

"Can't I get a doughnut?" the boy cried, tears falling down his flushed face.

"No, they're not good for you," the woman insisted.

"But you never let me have any! Can't I just have one?"

"I told you no!" the woman snapped, grabbing her son by the arm and jerking him toward her.

Charlie took a deep breath, picked up a loaf of nine-grain bread, and placed it in her cart. As Charlie headed for the cereal aisle, the slender woman and her two young children passed her, the young boy looking back at her.

"You sure look handsome in your blue sweater," Charlie said.

The young boy smiled, wiping his tears.

Charlie turned into the cereal aisle. Seeing the Kellogg's Cocoa Krispies, she picked up a box, causing an upwelling of pain to surface. Staring at the happy elves against a chocolate-colored background, she remembered their last Christmas with Isaac. As a young boy, he had often begged her to get him chocolate cereal, and although she didn't mind getting him an occasional treat, she didn't want him to start every day with chocolate cereal. However, during their last Christmas,

Charlie had bought him a box of Kellogg's Cocoa Krispies, wrapped it, and placed it under the tree. When Isaac opened it, he was ecstatic. After opening the rest of his presents, Isaac sat at the kitchen table and ate a monstrous bowl of Kellogg's Cocoa Krispies. He was happy—and now he was dead.

The iconic guitar riff of "Hotel California," one of Isaac's favorite songs, started to play on the overhead speaker. The pain inside Charlie's chest erupted. Unable to maintain her composure, she dropped the cereal box and ran out of the store, leaving the shopping cart full of groceries in aisle eleven. After reaching the safety of her car, she closed the door and collapsed—feeling as though she were breaking into a thousand pieces. Isaac, sitting in the passenger seat, said nothing, knowing she couldn't hear him. After a long cry and wishing she were dead, Charlie regained her composure, decided she'd have to do the shopping some other time, then drove home.

On her way, she stopped to check the mail, hoping she might receive the paperwork she needed to create the foundation in Isaac's name while she was still waiting for his medical records from the hospital. She opened her mailbox to find a large manila envelope from the IRS.

When Charlie got home, she opened the manila envelope and pulled out the official document stating the IRS had issued an employer identification number (EIN) for Isaac's Ant Foundation. The only things required were two signatures. Charlie signed her name, then left the form on the kitchen table for Chris to sign when he got home.

I'll need to build a website for the foundation, Charlie thought, opening her laptop and searching for an online platform. Once she found what she was looking for, she started learning the tools for making a website. Although the work was time-consuming, it gave her something constructive to work on while she was biding her time.

While Charlie worked on her computer, Chris came home and sat down next to her at the kitchen counter.

"Hey, beautiful, what are you doing?"

"I'm building a website for the foundation. How was work?"

"A headache, like always—they won't give me the funding I need, and there's no more money until the next fiscal year. I don't know how

I'm supposed to get the job done without it." Chris stood up and got himself a beer from the refrigerator. "What did you do today?"

Charlie walked to the kitchen table and picked up the letter from the IRS. "I got the paperwork for the foundation today. I just need your signature as the vice president, and then I can drop it in the mail," Charlie said, not mentioning her shopping incident.

"Great, I'm glad we're making progress." Chris signed his name and sat down at the kitchen table.

"Me too." Charlie folded the form in thirds, placed it in the return envelope, and sealed it. "I made pizza. Are you hungry?"

"Sure, pizza and beer work for me."

Charlie took the pizza from the oven, cut it into slices, and placed it on the table with two plates. After getting herself a beer, she joined Chris.

"What's this?" Chris asked, picking up the book from the table.

"It's a book David brought by this morning. He said it's a scientific argument about death being an illusion, and he thought it might be helpful for us to read," Charlie said. "It sounds interesting, and I'm open to any theory that might provide 'evidence' that Isaac's still out there... that he's still with us in one way or another."

Chris took a drink of his beer. "I understand. I'd like to hear what the author has to say.... Let's read it together."

"Okay, that would be nice. I talked with my boss today, and she scheduled me to go back to work on Monday."

"Are you ready for that?"

"I don't know.... I don't want to, but I have to eventually, and I need the cash."

Chris nodded.

After dinner, Chris suggested watching a couple of episodes of *Mushi-Shi*, which Isaac loved and had gotten them hooked on. Charlie agreed, as it sounded like a nice thing they could do together.

A Japanese manga series, *Mushi-Shi* featured a mushi master named Ginko, a young man with white hair and one green eye, the other eye missing. He traveled around protecting people from supernatural creatures known as mushi. The series theme song, "The Sore Feet Song" by Ally Kerr, evoked a sense of melancholy in Charlie, as she felt she could have written the lyrics for Isaac. They were about how one person would go to the ends of the earth for another.

After dinner, Chris cleaned up while Charlie walked across the street and dropped the letter to the IRS in the outgoing mail slot for the residential mailboxes. When she returned, she sat with Chris while he had a second beer.

"So, what do we want to do with the foundation?" Chris asked.

"I thought we could donate ant colonies to museums and insectariums for them to use as exhibits. I also thought it would be nice to create separate endowments to help special needs individuals and to plant trees."

"How will we donate colonies if we don't have any queens?"

"We could go to the Painted Desert this weekend and see if we can find some honeypot colonies. If we do, we could collect some queens during their nuptial flight when the monsoons come and then grow the colonies," Charlie explained. "Isaac said the queens fly away from their parent colonies when the ground is wet so they can dig a founding chamber to start new colonies. We want the *Myrmecocystus mexicanus* species, the nocturnal honeypots, because they're yellow with black eyes. Since they're very showy, I think the museums and insectariums will be most interested in them."

"I'd love to go to the desert and look for ants with you, but then again, I'd go anywhere with you," Chris said, tears welling up in his eyes.

Charlie stood up and put her arms around him. "I love you, handsome. No matter what happens, I'm here for you."

"I know you are. I just wish Isaac was still here."

"Me too," Charlie said, trying to stay strong for Chris. This had become their new norm, one of them staying strong when the other was breaking down. "We're just going to have to help each other through this. . . . There's no other way."

When Chris finished his beer, they put their pajamas on, climbed into bed, then turned on the first episodes of *Mushi-Shi*. After they'd watched two episodes, Chris brushed and flossed his teeth, then turned off the light on his nightstand. They curled up together for a while, then rolled over to their separate sides of the bed and drifted off to sleep.

After a while, Charlie started dreaming about traveling to Africa with Isaac. In her dream, they were at a safari park with a large metal gate separating the visitors from the wild animals. On their way to see them, Isaac wanted to stop at the gift store to look for a stuffed animal he could add to his collection back home. As they looked around, Charlie grew impatient, eager to see what animals were on the other side of the gate. She told Isaac to stay in the gift store while she took a quick look, and she'd be right back. Happy to have a little extra time to browse the large selection of stuffed animals, Isaac said he wouldn't leave the gift shop. Charlie quickly went down the hall, looked through the large metal gate, and was shocked by the sight of wildebeests, hyenas, and giraffes all sunbathing around a swimming pool surrounded by white tables and tall, colorful beach umbrellas. The hyenas and giraffes were sipping cold drinks decorated with mini umbrellas while the wildebeests cooled themselves in the blue pool under the blazing Saharan sun.

Thinking the scene was truly bizarre, Charlie wanted to return to their hotel room to get her camera to take a picture. But first, she went back to the gift store and told Isaac what she had seen. Isaac looked surprised, then asked her if he could get something from the gift store. Charlie nodded, then told him to wait again while she went to get some money and her camera. As Charlie turned to go to their room, she heard Isaac's voice—not Isaac in her dream, but Isaac's actual voice.

"One of the reasons people sleep is to contact people on the other side."

Suddenly, Charlie woke up, her heart racing.

7

TIME: THE GREATEST FORCE
The Other Side

THOSE HILLS OVER YONDER sure are purty, Solomon thought, looking out the kitchen window while churning butter on the counter. He took the lid off the box-style butter churn, checked on the butter, and then put the lid back on. He continued turning the metal handle to rotate the paddle inside the wooden barrel, stirring the cream he'd separated from the milk that Daisy and Belle, the dairy cows, had provided the day before. He took a sip of coffee, then started singing "Go Tell It on the Mountain," an old gospel hymn he had learned from his parents when he was growing up near the Great Smoky Mountains in Tennessee. His parents had played musical instruments and sung at Southern Baptist revivals, and Solomon and his two brothers had later been in a trio and sung on the radio.

Through the kitchen window, Solomon saw Kéyah and Hailey roughhousing near the picnic table. Looking past the fenced haystack to the horse pasture, where Piute and Babe were grazing, he noticed that the rolling hills were brilliantly colored with arrowleaf balsamroot and purple lupine flowers, which bloomed every May. Beyond the rolling hills, the rugged Sawtooth Mountains rose effortlessly in the distance.

A milk jar filled with the same yellow and purple wildflowers stood on the kitchen windowsill. Ethel, who enjoyed their beauty and vibrant colors, had placed them there earlier that morning. Next to the wildflowers was a child's miniature green farm truck with a yellow wagon. Tweety, Ethel's small yellow songbird, chirped from a round metal birdcage hanging in the corner of the kitchen next to a white washbasin. Against the kitchen's back wall stood an old wood-burning stove and a crate filled with split wood and old newspapers. Lying underneath the table in the middle of the room was Charlie's dog, Buttercup, whom she had rescued as a pup from the side of the road. A tan-colored Lab mix, Buttercup was the gentlest of dogs, a quality that could be seen in her beseeching dark-brown eyes. Not much for horseplay, Buttercup was happiest when she was relaxing in the company of those she loved.

Once Solomon had finished churning the butter, he put it in a brown stoneware bowl and poured the buttermilk into glass jars while Ethel sprinkled a small spoonful of salt over the butter, mixed it with a wooden spoon, and tasted it.

"Ain't that the bee's knees." Ethel smiled. "I reckon all it needs is to be eaten."

"It sure is purty outside," Solomon said, putting the buttermilk jars in the refrigerator. "Shall we enjoy the fresh rolls and bread pudding you made this morning outside?"

"That's what I was fixin' to do." Ethel looked at everyone sitting around the breakfast table. "It'd be helpful if y'all set the picnic table."

Melba took a jar of cream and a pitcher of milk from the refrigerator, walked out the back door to the yard, and put them on the table. Hearing bleating coming from the small wooden pen nearby, Melba walked over to check on the crying lamb. He had cut his leg on some barbed wire and had needed to be separated from the flock while the leg healed. The lamb bleated repeatedly, wanting to return to the flock.

"How you doing, little guy?" Melba asked, looking at the sheep's injured leg. "It looks like Grandma's burdock salve is healing your wound. Only a couple more days, then you can rejoin the herd."

As she petted the sheep, she gazed out over the vast field behind their farmhouse, remembering the time when she had counted five black sheep as she and her dad were herding their band of sheep to graze near Rock Creek, where the family had a one-room cabin with a loft. Keeping one black sheep for every hundred was

Raymond's way of tracking how many heads of sheep he had at any given time.

The Williams family took turns, two people at a time, watching the sheep as they grazed the meadows in Rock Creek. One person slept on the cot near the small wood-burning stove while the other slept in the loft on a bed of straw. They kept their food cold in the stream near the cabin and used the stove to cook and stay warm. Melba remembered the night she had been sleeping in the loft and woke up from a horrific nightmare: a nightmare whose events would later come to pass. She quickly pushed the ghastly image from her mind.

Melba looked at the haystack and sleigh that stood surrounded by a wooden fence. During winter, Raymond and the kids loaded the horse-drawn sleigh with bales of hay and delivered them to the cattle out in the field. But during summer, the sleigh remained parked next to the haystack while their cattle grazed on their thousand-acre farm or on nearby Bureau of Land Management (BLM) land, for which Raymond had grazing rights.

Hearing Hazel and Shane talking while setting the picnic table, Melba returned to the present. She petted the lamb goodbye, then walked back to the picnic table and helped Isaac make room for the rolls Alma was holding.

Once the table was set, Hazel sat down and smoothed her red ruffled skirt. Shane and Isaac sat down next to her, and Raymond, Alma, and Melba sat across from them, and they all visited while waiting for Solomon and Ethel.

Inside, Ethel wrapped the butter in a large piece of wax paper, cut off a small wedge, put it in a milk glass butter dish, and handed it to Solomon. He opened the door for her as she picked up the bread pudding, and they walked out to the picnic table together.

Ethel set the bread pudding on the table, cut it into squares, and then took a seat next to Solomon, who always sat at the head of the table. Everyone chatted as they passed around the bread pudding and rolls.

After a while, Solomon wiped the milk off his mustache with his napkin. "I'd guess you were happiest when you were pretty young," he said, looking at Isaac and noting his young age. Everyone in the family enjoyed talking with one another, but they all were making a special effort to make their newest arrival, Isaac, feel welcome.

"Yes, I loved being with my mom when I was about seven. That was before all the troubles started, when I was bullied and publicly humiliated at school because I was in special education, which was excruciating . . . and then there were all the seizures! I did have one good friend at school—Django was someone I could trust," Isaac said. "But to answer your question, since we revert to the age when we were the happiest when we cross over, I chose a time when my mom and I spent endless days going on adventures, a time when we *both* were the happiest. I'm curious, Grandma. Why did you choose the 1950s?"

"Because I was the happiest in my early twenties, when I had my freedom," Hazel said. "I liked getting dressed up and going out to have fun, and even though the farm was a lot of hard work, it was still where we grew up together, and it gave us a sense of belonging. And since this is my heaven, I get to dress up and enjoy my family and the farm without all the hard work!"

"It's easy to see why you've made this place your version of heaven," Isaac said. "You have a wonderful family, and the Wood River Valley in the 1950s is beautiful. I'm happy we can be here together."

Hazel smiled and gave Isaac a little hug.

"Unlike you guys, I didn't want to revert to a younger age," Shane said. "I had learned a tough but valuable lesson just before I crossed over. I was going through a difficult time and had written this in my journal: *I'm like a monk who spends weeks creating a beautiful work of art in the sand, knowing the wind will eventually come and have its final say. Like the monk, I must remember it's the act of creating that gives you joy and connection to life, not the having. I am getting a powerful lesson: I have nothing. I own nothing, and nothing owns me. I can only choose to enjoy the moment and use the "now" to remember the God-ness in all things and everyone.* Shortly after I wrote that, I crossed over. I chose to stay forty-nine because I finally understood that everything was on loan, and I was free."

"That's beautiful," Melba said. "You know, this place—Heaven, Paradise, Jannah, Valhalla, the Other Side, or whatever you choose to call it—isn't so bad. We're free of bodily pain and injuries, and we get to be the age when we're the happiest—I kind of like it here."

"That's why I'm staying here for a while, but I plan to return to

Earth once I'm rested because I still have many lessons to learn," Hazel laughed. "I have a lot of knowledge from reading history, but I'm not as wise as Isaac and Ethel. They've gained a great deal of wisdom from all their past lives. I'm more of the new kid on the block—a young soul. And since wisdom is gained through experience and can't be taught, I'll need to go back."

"Don't worry. Even though we're all at different stages along our paths, we'll all complete our journeys and become part of the whole," Ethel said. "Like a raindrop making its way from a cloud to a stream to a river and finally becoming one with the ocean. Our souls remain singular and, at the same time, become one with the sea of energy of all that was, is, and ever will be—we're part of the whole."

"We return to the source from which we sprang," Solomon added. "But while we're here in high cotton, it's good to keep learning and help our loved ones on the other side who are facing difficult lessons. I wish they knew that it makes it much easier for us to receive their messages when they ask us directly for guidance. It makes it easier to help and possibly even to prevent them from making bad mistakes."

"But even if we get our message through to them, it doesn't always help, because people have their own free will," Shane added, then took a bite of his bread pudding. "As their angels, we can help guide them by giving them signs, insights, and intuitions, but ultimately, it's their decision what they do with that information. They can choose to heed the calling—advice we give them—or not. But whatever situation they're facing, trying and falling short is far better than not trying at all, because either way, their actions or inactions reveal their motives—their intentions—which, of course, they'll review after they cross over."

"Since I've shared many lives with my mom, I know she killed herself in her last life, so I'm worried she'll make the same mistake again," Isaac said. "She's not aware that the most valuable things in life are the nonphysical lessons we learn and take with us when we cross over. To hang on to life in the face of adversity is to realize there's still value in life's lessons. Taking your own life is a missed opportunity to receive those gifts. I hope she'll get my messages and be able to break free from this terrible cycle."

"If anyone can get through to her, it's you. Remember, you're her soulmate—two sides of the same coin," Hazel said. "And since—"

"That's it!" Isaac interrupted. "I need to remind my mom about one of our previous lives, when she was my older sister. Sir Chaloner Ogle, a relative of our family, had invited our parents to Coupland Castle to help him celebrate his victory over the terrible pirate Bartholomew Roberts. While the grown-ups were making a big to-do, we played hide-and-seek in the garden maze. Near the maze was an old wooden bench under a magnolia tree, where we stopped to take a break from playing. There, we found a coin that sort of resembled a yin-and-yang symbol. One side was white with a dark flower-shaped center, and the other side was dark with a white circle around the center. We wondered where it came from because we'd never seen anything like it before. In the end, my mom, who was my sister at the time, and I decided the coin represented two sides of one lesson, neither good nor bad, just two different experiences to learn from. Even more importantly, the coin symbolized that since we're two sides of the same coin, nothing can truly divide us—there's no coin with one side! We placed the coin under a large rock behind the bench for safekeeping. Somehow, I must remind my mom about that coin!"

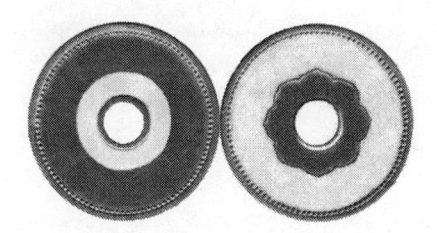

"That would be helpful, but I was also going to suggest that since she heard you the first time in her dream, maybe she'll be more open to hearing from you again," Hazel said. "I know she's furious about not getting the medical records yet. That, at least, is to our advantage—she won't take her own life while she's still fighting to defend you."

"I already delivered a second message to my mom when she was sleeping, and she knew it was me, but part of the issue is Chris," Isaac said. "When my mom told Chris about the first time I spoke to her in a dream, he thought she was losing it, which caused my mom to doubt herself. We'll have to wait and see what happens this time."

Hazel nodded. "Shortly after I crossed over, I visited your mom, but that was a long time ago and she's forgotten about it. Maybe, since you're getting through to her, she'll remember that and start putting things together. Hopefully, if she realizes we're still with her, she'll stop thinking about taking her own life."

"I hope so," Isaac said as Kéyah, who was lying next to him, sat up and placed his head on Isaac's lap. "I'm glad you no longer have cancer. It was tough losing you so long ago. It's wonderful to see you restored to perfect health."

Looking at Ethel, Melba picked a raisin from her bread pudding, held it between her fingers, and said, "Grandma, I love your bread pudding, but I always thought the raisins looked like little bugs. Of course, I've never eaten bugs, but I imagine the raisins are tastier." Melba smirked, then popped the raisin in her mouth.

"You're so silly," Hazel replied, rolling her eyes.

"At least I'm not ornery like you," Melba joked. "Do you remember when I was taking a nap in the haystack, and you found a bunch of baby mice and put them on me while I was sleeping? You liked to have scared me to death. It serves you right that Charlie used to collect grasshoppers in a tin can and line them up along your arms and legs while you were napping on the couch," Melba laughed. "Ask me if I'm the least bit sorry for you."

Isaac laughed. "It sounds like my mom evened the score."

"Yeah, I guess I had it coming," Hazel admitted.

The Williams family continued to reminisce about funny stories until Isaac brought up a theory he had been working on.

"I've been thinking about something," Isaac said. "Energy is a potential—it remains dormant without time. Therefore, time is the greatest force in nature because, without time, nothing happens. And regardless of whether time is linear or nonlinear, as it is here, it doesn't matter. The point remains the same: No matter what order you put the past, present, and future in, without time, none of it happens!"

"Very insightful," Ethel said.

"And according to the first law of thermodynamics, energy can't be destroyed or created; it only changes forms," Shane added. "In other words, energy is recycled—the universe gives up nothing."

"Exactly!" Isaac exclaimed. "Energy is what energy does—it's defined by what it's *doing*! But for energy to *do* anything, time must pass.

Therefore, time governs energy. Look at the big bang. . . . Everything didn't materialize from nothing. It started with an incredibly dense point of matter bound tightly together, and given *time*, that matter expanded outwardly due to the laws of nature."

Shane laughed. "So if time didn't exist, we would still be locked away in that dense ball of matter?"

"That's one way of looking at it," Isaac said, smiling.

"Well, as you know, abstract thoughts are sometimes difficult for people to grasp," Shane said. "People prefer finite ideas. They're easier to understand, and having all the loose ends nicely wrapped up makes people feel more comfortable . . . more in control. Certain. It makes them feel less vulnerable to the unknown. The infinite, on the other hand, makes them more likely to tie themselves into knots, trying to define that which cannot be defined rather than accept an unknown. Still, energy, space, and time aren't finite; they're infinite. They can't be wrapped up nicely in a box."

"But just for fun, let's say we could contain energy in a box . . . or in this," Isaac said, picking up an empty milk jar and tipping it sideways. "If energy were a liquid, it would pour from this jar and ripple through four-dimensional space-time—the three dimensions of space plus time—which of course won't happen, since it's not a liquid. However, since energy *does* follow a person's intentions, their actions *do* ripple through space-time. Therefore, it's best to be mindful of our actions, as they have a big impact on others."

8

THE DEEP END
May 13, 2017

CHARLIE WALKED INTO the spare room, where she created watercolor paintings on an old drafting table, and sat her cup of coffee on the desk, next to a green Seahawks blanket. The blanket was folded over to make a bed for Schmiggs, who enjoyed lying there and watching passersby from the window. Charlie opened the closet door and sifted through the greeting cards stacked on the second shelf, which she had received as gifts for donating to various environmental groups. She chose one with a picture of a giraffe superimposed on a light-green background with branches and oval-shaped leaves. The caption at the bottom read: *THINKING OF YOU*. Charlie found the matching envelope, closed the closet door, and sat down at the desk. Schmiggs jumped onto the desk and curled up on his bed, the green blanket a perfect match to his eyes. Charlie opened the card and wrote a letter with one of the Derwent Graphic 6H pencils she used for drawing compositions.

>Isaac,
>   I think of you all the time. I miss you so much that I can barely handle it. You came to me in a dream and told me, you whispered in my ear, "I miss you," and I replied, "I miss you too," then I woke up. I know you

are out there somewhere, and I can't wait to see you again. I had another dream three nights ago. I think we were in Africa, and I heard you say, "One of the reasons people sleep is so they can contact people on the other side," then I woke up.

Sending hugs and kisses always, Mom.

Charlie placed the card in the envelope, then wrote Sweets and drew a heart on the front. She walked into Isaac's bedroom, which she had kept the same as it was before he passed. The only difference was she had turned on his night-light next to his bed, just in case he came home. His bed was neatly arranged with the stuffed animals he had collected over the years. Charlie placed the card in the arms of one of the two teddy bears sitting on his bed, which she had given him for separate Valentine's Days. The other teddy bear held the dried wildflower bouquet she had placed there after she returned from taking the dogs for a walk.

Charlie stood by Isaac's bed, reflecting on his stuffed animal collection. A lover of all things Japanese, Isaac had studied their Buddhist philosophy and owned several figures from Japan. His favorites were the Sebastian and Ciel manga figures from the Black Butler series; a Pikachu geisha dressed in a red kimono with a red, black, and white umbrella; Ponyo, the goldfish princess; and Totoro, a gray-and-white character with a button nose, big round eyes, and a ginormous grin.

Next, Charlie remembered the time she had taken Isaac to Saint John, US Virgin Islands, in 2012 for spring break. They had camped on Cinnamon Bay's white sandy beach and completed their scuba diving course together. Charlie was so proud of Isaac for earning his junior open water diver license from the Professional Association of Diving Instructors (PADI) when he was eleven. After Isaac had finished his last open water skill—removing his mask and replacing it twenty-five feet beneath the ocean's surface—his instructor had congratulated him on earning his license. A look of pure joy came over Isaac's face as he raised his arms victoriously in the air. "Yes!" He'd beamed triumphantly.

It had broken their hearts when Isaac could no longer go scuba diving due to the seizures he started having when he was fourteen.

Charlie clenched her teeth, thinking that the seizures that killed him had likely been a result of medical negligence. When she told Isaac he could no longer go scuba diving—his favorite thing in the world—she'd tried to soften the blow by offering to take him on vacation anywhere in the world. Isaac chose Japan. Charlie and Chris saved their money, planned the trip, and then vacationed with Isaac for ten days in Tokyo and Kyoto during springtime to see the cherry blossoms at the Imperial Palace and the Buddhist temples.

Charlie had booked a table for three at the Skytree for their first night in Tokyo. On their way to dinner, Charlie, Isaac, and Chris gazed up at the brightly lit Skytree, the world's tallest freestanding broadcasting tower, standing an impressive 2,080 feet. The only man-made structures that were taller were the Petronius compliant tower, an offshore oil platform with a height of 2,100 feet, and the world's tallest building, Burj Khalifa in Dubai, which was 2,716 feet tall. Near the base of the Skytree, a quaint and inviting gift store called to them. Happily, they entered to see what treasures awaited.

Although Chris couldn't read the Japanese writing, 小豆大福 (azuki daifuku mochi), on the box of a traditional Japanese rice cake stuffed with sweet red bean paste filling, the images had apparently enticed his sweet tooth. He tucked the treat under his arm, then continued looking around. Isaac, always drawn to the plush toys, found Totoro and knew he had to add it to his collection back home. After they'd purchased the azuki daifuku mochi and Totoro, they made their way to the top of the Skytree for dinner. Although Isaac had traveled extensively throughout the world, on their flight home, he told Charlie their trip to Japan was his all-time favorite—a perfect vacation.

Next to Isaac's collection of Japanese figures in his room was an array of stuffed oceanic creatures: a whale shark, a humpback whale, a blue whale, and a green plesiosaur, all of them either Christmas or birthday presents, which Isaac couldn't keep separate, since his birthday was Christmas Eve. Many people resented having their birthdays near Christmas because the two occasions were often lumped into one, but Isaac didn't mind, as Charlie always made it a point to have two separate celebrations. Although others had their birthday celebrations at different times of the year, Isaac loved that his birthday was Christmas Eve because two parties were far better than one at Christmastime.

Isaac also collected crazy hats that he hung on his bedposts. A bright rainbow-colored octopus hat adorned the top-left bedpost with its long, dangling tentacles hanging down. Isaac and his best friend, Django, had bought matching hats when Charlie and Chris took them once to Six Flags Magic Mountain in Valencia, California. They spent the day riding scary roller coasters and eating junk food while the colorful arms of their octopus hats bounced on their shoulders and dangled down their faces. They went out for dinner in the evening, swam in the hotel's outdoor pool, and then lounged poolside with refreshing drinks—a perfect day.

On the bottom-left bedpost was a gray-and-white hammerhead shark hat that Charlie had bought for Isaac when they went to Monterey Bay when he was seven. They spent the weekend strolling around Old Fisherman's Wharf, where Isaac found the hat at a gift store. While there, Isaac had been gleefully accosted by a group of Japanese schoolgirls who thought he was the cutest thing they'd ever seen and wanted their pictures taken with him. All the schoolgirls had their black hair neatly styled and wore the same school uniforms: a white shirt, dark plaid skirt, and black socks and shoes. As they whispered in Japanese, they raised their hands to their faces, giggling. Not understanding a word they said, Isaac blushed as he posed with the schoolgirls while Charlie took photographs with their cameras, each girl wanting her own picture of Isaac to treasure when she returned home. After the photo session, the schoolgirls waved goodbye, giggling again as they departed. Charlie and Isaac continued down the boardwalk and found a restaurant on the pier where they ate clam chowder bread bowls as the gulls called while they soared in the light, salty breeze drifting off the ocean.

After lunch, they walked barefoot on the beach, collecting sand dollars and seashells. The following day, they went to the Monterey Bay Aquarium, where Isaac was fitted for a dry scuba suit before he joined an instructor-guided tour of the tide pool. Afterward, they explored the oceanic exhibits and petted the bat rays in their touch pool. Later that evening, they joined a sleepover party in front of the enchanted

Kelp Forest, an enormous twenty-eight-foot-tall aquarium. As they lay in their sleeping bags, they were mesmerized by the oceanic fish swimming through the illuminated *Kelp Forest*, then drifted off to sleep—a perfect weekend.

Now Charlie looked at Isaac's bed, remembering when she had commissioned her friend to paint Isaac's bedroom set when he was a preschooler. An artist herself, Charlie had wanted to give her friend his artistic liberties and so had only instructed him to paint the bedroom set with a wide variety of animals, leaving the rest up to him. The end table and dresser drawer featured various animals in a forest. A sentinel, a green-eyed wolf painted on the footboard, watched over Isaac as he slept. Having forgotten what was painted on the headboard, Charlie removed the pillows to find TWO MAJESTIC BIGHORN SHEEP ON THE TOP OF A MOUNTAIN with a crescent moon emerging from behind some wispy clouds in the night sky.

Chris walked into Isaac's room and put his hand on Charlie's shoulder. "What are you doing?"

Reality rushed in. "I was just thinking about all the places Isaac got his collection of stuffed animals from." Charlie picked up the stuffed Totoro. "Do you remember when Isaac got this in Japan?"

"Yeah, that was a great trip. What's that in the bear's hands?"

"I wrote Isaac a letter."

Chris looked concerned, then his expression softened. "Do you want to go to the Painted Desert and look for those honeypot ants you were talking about?"

"Sure," Charlie said, recognizing that it was the last weekend before she had to go back to work. "Should we eat breakfast, then go? We could take the dogs and let them run around."

After breakfast, Chris and Charlie drove an hour north to the edge of the Painted Desert, an arid badland where the sedimentary rock had eroded away, leaving steep mountains marked by horizontal bands of lavender, rust, charcoal, and mustard. They turned off US Route 89 North onto a dirt road, then drove to a remote location where they could spend the day looking for the honeypots. Thanks to Isaac, Charlie knew that this ant species had acquired its name from a specialized class of workers known as repletes, which serve the colony as food-storage vessels. The repletes hang from the ceiling, where the workers engorge them with nectar until their abdomens swell to the size of small grapes. Later, during winter or when food is scarce, the repletes feed the stored nectar to the members of the colony by regurgitation.

After Charlie had parked, Chris opened the hatch of her Honda Fit and grabbed his backpack as Dexter and Cobalt jumped out and took off running. Then Charlie locked the doors, and they wandered into the serene landscape of the Painted Desert. As they meandered, they scanned the ground, looking for a specific type of anthill.

Chris bent down as he eyed one hill. "Is this one?"

Charlie walked over to take a closer look. "No, I don't think so. The mound isn't big enough and the hole is too small, but let's check." She grabbed a twig and stuck it down the hole. A troop of tiny black ants came running out, attacking the twig. "Nope, these are *mimicus*; they're the diurnal honeypots," Charlie said. "Nice try, but let's keep looking."

Charlie and Chris kept searching, finding many more *mimicus* colonies before stopping to eat a snack. Charlie whistled to the dogs and poured a bowl of water. When they arrived, they lapped up the water, then took off again.

"Yesterday, I started making a list of fun ant facts for the website," Charlie said as she layered a cracker with cheese.

"Sounds like a good idea. Do you remember Isaac showing us those crazy-looking turtle ants that use their heads as a doorstop to prevent predators from entering their nests? Did you put that one on the list?"

"No, I forgot to add those. Thanks for reminding me," Charlie said. "I remembered Isaac mentioning that leaf-cutter ants are the oldest known farmers, so I looked it up. Apparently, they've been farming fungus for about sixty million years!"

"Well, they certainly started farming way before people did," Chris said, taking a long drink of water. "Do you remember him showing us the video of the Saharan silver ants? To survive the desert heat, they can run more than one hundred times their body length in one second—that's mind-blowing!"

"Indeed!"

After they'd finished their snack, Chris zipped up his backpack and wandered off. After a while, he called out.

"Hey, Charlie, I think I found the honeypots we're looking for." He put his backpack on the ground.

Charlie walked over to Chris and knelt down to take a closer look.

"I noticed an anthill fitting your description out of the corner of my eye," Chris said. "So I walked over to the mound, picked up a blade of dry grass, and slid it down the opening. I jiggled it repeatedly, but it seemed the nest had been deserted. I started to leave, but when I glanced back at the anthill, I saw a few yellow ants attacking the blade of grass I had left at the entrance of the nest!"

Charlie knew the nocturnal honeypots were reluctant to come out during the day, but the disturbance had apparently caused a few workers to surface to defend their colony.

"Holy cow, those are the ants we're looking for!" She beamed. "You found the first nocturnal honeypots!"

"Woo-hoo!" Chris grinned from ear to ear and threw his hands high in the air.

"Hold that pose." Charlie pulled her phone from her back pocket and took his picture.

"I need to tag this location," Chris said, unclipping his Garmin from his belt. He saved the location, then labeled it "HP."

They were excited! Now that they knew what they were looking for, they were able to find five more nocturnal honeypot colonies by that afternoon and saved their locations on Chris's Garmin.

"Now, all we need to do is wait for their nuptial flight during the monsoons, and then we can collect a few queens!" Charlie said.

Chris smiled. "And since I'm the stormwater manager, it'll be easy for me to track the rainfall."

They walked back to the car, loaded the dogs, and headed in the direction of the San Francisco Peaks on the distant horizon.

As Charlie drove, she began to cry. "I had another dream about Isaac the other night. Most of the dream was normal like before, but then I heard Isaac's voice again in the middle of the dream. He said that dreams are a way to communicate with people on the other side."

Chris said nothing. He just patiently listened while Charlie explained how her dead son had been talking to her in her dreams. But his silence confirmed Charlie's suspicion—*he thinks I'm going off the deep end!*

9

THIN ICE
The Other Side

"WHAT DO THE TEA LEAVES say this morning?" Isaac asked, walking into the kitchen, where Ethel was leaning over the kitchen counter, peering into an empty cup of tea. As she studied the tea leaves, a stream of sunshine cascaded in through the kitchen window, cheering the room.

"It's a time of unity . . . the family coming together to help each other receive messages and understand their gifts," Ethel said. "It's a time for the *possibility* of new beginnings. I say 'possibility' because, as you know, one must *choose* to walk the steps to a new beginning to receive their gifts."

"That sounds perfect because I was going to see if we could get everyone together to help me with a predicament I'm in," Isaac said. "On the one hand, I'm hopeful because I've been able to get a couple of messages through to my mom in her dreams. On the other hand, Chris thinks my mom's losing it because she's hearing voices from her dead son."

"That's because they're not aware that Charlie has a touch of the gift handed down from me, her great-grandmother. She can connect to those who've crossed over on rare occasions, even if she doesn't know it yet." Ethel rinsed the tea leaves out of the cup and set it aside. "Let's get everyone together, and we can talk it over with some coffee and doughnuts."

"That'd be great."

"I'll make some coffee if you can ask Solomon to round everyone up," Ethel suggested. "I saw him out back a while ago."

"Sounds like a fine idea," Isaac said, walking out the kitchen door, where Kéyah was patiently waiting for him.

Kéyah followed Isaac as he walked to the side of the house, where he found Solomon splitting wood. He was wearing his black Stetson hat and a black Western shirt and was singing one of his favorite gospel hymns, "Shall We Gather at the River," in his beautiful tenor voice.

When Solomon saw Isaac and Kéyah, he stopped singing and buried his ax in the stump he used as a chopping block.

"I'd like to get everyone together to help me with a situation I'm in with my mom and Chris," Isaac said. "Ethel's making coffee, and she asked me to have you round everyone up."

"Sure, let's go ring the dinner bell," Solomon said. "Besides, I could use a break. I'm thirsty from chopping all this wood."

As Solomon and Isaac walked to the corner of the house, where an iron triangle dinner bell hung, they noticed a flock of white doves landing in the old cottonwood tree. Solomon rang the bell, which echoed over the land. The white doves took flight, circled, and then landed back in the cottonwood tree. Their silhouettes were brilliant white against the cerulean-blue sky.

"I reckon that'll do the job," Solomon said. "Let's go in. . . . I want to hear what's troubling you."

As Solomon and Isaac walked into the kitchen, Kéyah lay down outside on the porch to nap in the morning sun. Solomon hung his hat on the coat rack and washed his hands while Isaac helped Alma set the table with coffee and cake doughnuts rolled in cinnamon sugar she had made earlier that morning.

As the family gathered around the kitchen table, Melba and Hazel came in, looking a little winded.

"What's going on?" Melba asked. "Hazel and I were across the river in the tree house, shooting the breeze."

"Isaac has something he wants to talk to us about," Ethel said.

After washing up, Hazel and Melba joined everyone at the kitchen table.

"Tell us what's on your mind," Solomon said, looking at Isaac. "Maybe we can help."

Isaac explained to them everything he'd said to Ethel. "All of this is making Chris uneasy," he said in summary, "which fills my mom with uncertainty. If not for that, I think she could overcome her doubt and listen to her heart. I think this because she wrote me a letter about the two messages and placed it on my bed."

"It's wonderful that you've gotten through to your mom," Hazel said. "I've been worried sick about her, but I also understand why Chris feels apprehensive. . . . His connection to you isn't the same as your connection with your mom. He's only getting the messages secondhand, never directly, which is why he questions what your mom tells him. Perhaps the best way to deal with this situation is to get a message directly to Chris, so he understands from firsthand experience."

"That's what I was thinking," Isaac agreed, "but there are a few obstacles in my way. One, Chris thinks like an engineer—if he can't measure it, it doesn't exist. And two, he drinks alcohol and smokes marijuana, which cloud his mind. Since these substances block my ability to get through, it's going to make getting a message to him rather challenging. People often numb their pain with drugs and alcohol, but they're not always aware that they're also numbing their ability to feel pleasure, excitement, and love. Substances don't selectively dull emotions—they dull them across the board. When you live life fully, you have front-row seats to both pain and pleasure, which honestly sounds a little rough. The key is to take one step back—to not identify with the mind or body—and then experience those emotions while remaining unattached to them. That way, a person can experience life fully without suffering and also gain the clarity of mind to choose wisely. Of course, all that's easier said than done."

"Well said, little man," Shane said. "And yes, since Chris uses things that cloud his mind, it will be challenging to reach him. What about using a bird? You could deliver a message to Chris through one of our feathered friends. That might get his attention."

"I think it's worth trying, since other approaches won't work," Isaac agreed. "As for my mom, if I can continue to reach her through her dreams, maybe she'll stop doubting herself and break free from thoughts of taking her own life."

"I sure hope so," Alma said.

"Maybe if I remind her that I chose her to be my mom, she'll remember her premonition of having a young boy with messy brown hair before I was born. Maybe then she'll start putting things together," Isaac said. "The last time we were here together, we both faced difficult lessons, and since we knew we could count on each other when things got tough, we planned our next lives together. Now, I just need to remind my mom of those plans."

"It might work, but she's very depressed and not thinking clearly," Shane said. "But all you can do is try and go from there."

Isaac nodded.

"Even though it's going to be difficult to get through to Chris, it's still wonderful that Isaac's reaching his mother through her dreams," Ethel said. "Let's celebrate with a special dinner tonight."

"I'll pull some venison out to thaw," Raymond said, placing his napkin on the table. He walked to the freezer, took out two packages of venison wrapped in butcher paper, put them in the kitchen sink, and sat back down.

"Isaac, I have to tell you a funny story about my dad," Hazel said.

Isaac smiled, then took a bite of his doughnut.

"When I was growing up, your great-grandfather Raymond and us kids used to feed the cattle during the winter, and the deer would come down from the mountains to eat the hay. If my dad needed meat to feed our family, he'd poach a deer, but once, he was photographed by the Fish and Game officers from a helicopter and taken to court. During the court hearing, the Fish and Game officers showed the photograph of my dad as evidence. He was wearing his hat and coat and had a deer draped over Piute's rump. His attorney argued that the man on the horse could be any man because the photograph had been taken too far away to identify the rider. When the Fish and Game attorney asked my dad about the photograph, he said, 'That's a fine-looking man on that horse, but it sure ain't me!' Later that evening, the judge came over to our house for what Dad called a 'wild beef dinner'!"

Everyone roared with laughter, then continued giving Raymond, who had a shit-eating grin plastered on his face, a hard time about his comment to the judge.

"Leave it to Raymond," Alma said, leaning over and kissing him on the cheek. "But I have to agree. . . . He's a fine-looking man."

While the others visited, Solomon walked to the wooden crate filled with split wood, put a couple of pieces in the old wood-burning stove, and closed the door. Smelling the sweet-salty aroma from a simmering pot on top of the wood-burning stove, he opened the lid to find pinto beans cooking with a large piece of pork from a pig that Raymond had butchered and cured with a brown sugar and salt rub. Solomon breathed in the aroma, placed the lid back on, and sat down beside his granddaughter Hazel.

"Seeing you, standing there in your black shirt, reminded me of when my house was set on fire in the summer of 1971," Hazel said, looking at him. "I woke up suddenly in the middle of the night and heard fire crackling outside my bedroom window! It was a hot summer night, so I had the windows open; otherwise, I might not have heard the fire burning until it was too late. I ran outside to see what was happening and saw a man dressed in black. He was standing next to our black Lab, Smokey, on the dirt road in front of our house. I ran to him but couldn't see his face, because it was too dark. I turned around to see what he was looking at and saw the shed and the house on fire. I gasped, 'Oh my God, my children!' The man told me everything would be all right, but I needed to go back into the house and get the kids out, which I did, and then the fire truck arrived."

Hazel took a deep breath, then continued. "After I got all the kids out of the house, I asked the firefighters where the man dressed in black was, but they said they hadn't seen any man dressed in black. The firefighters put out the fire, which I was grateful for, but I remember being upset because the water would ruin all the new furniture my neighbor gave us, since the windows were open when they sprayed the house down. After the firefighters left, I went inside and found something very strange. Nothing inside the house was wet, and I never saw the man dressed in black again. It was as if he had vanished into thin air. It just dawned on me that you might have come to help me and the kids in our time of need."

"Yes, my dear child; it was me." Solomon placed his hand on Hazel's. "I came to help you and the kids."

Tears welled up in Hazel's eyes. "Thanks, Grandpa, you've always been so kind."

"You're welcome, sweetheart. I was happy to help."

Then Hazel's expression hardened. "I despise the memories of that old house ... that shack. When it was finally torn down, we found out it had been insulated with newspapers and magazines," Hazel said, her voice wavering. "Although I had five kids and we were as poor as church mice, I always kept the house clean. I had a yellow vanity, a dresser, and a bed in my room, but since I had nowhere to hang our clothes, I ran a metal pipe along one side of the room and hung a shower curtain on it to make a closet. That's where I kept all our clothes and blankets."

Hazel wiped her eyes, then continued. "The kids shared one bedroom that didn't have a door. Bunk beds made of scrap wood were anchored into the wall at one end of their room. The two older girls slept on the top bunk bed, and the two younger girls slept on the bottom. We didn't have a ladder, so the older girls had to step onto the bottom bed, then the dresser, and finally into the top bunk. Shane's bed was on the other side of the room near the back door. We used a white owl in the mudroom during winter so we didn't have to go out into the cold to use the outhouse." Hazel paused, trying to control her breaking voice. "My husband used to mistreat Shane because he wasn't *his* son, and as a result, Shane sometimes wet the bed, which infuriated him."

Hazel buried her face in her hands as tears streamed from her eyes. "That bastard took hold of Shane's neck and dunked his head in the bucket of pee for wetting the bed. I screamed and yelled at him to stop and started hitting him as hard as I could until he left the house, but later that evening, he came back drunk and beat me unconscious. I found out later that Teresa had run to the neighbors' house to get help, and I was taken to the hospital, where they said he cracked my skull and I was lucky to be alive." Hazel cried, taking Shane's hand. "I'm so sorry, honey. I never meant for him to hurt you. I tried to stop him, but he got so mean when he was drinking. . . . Please forgive me."

"Mom, I forgave you long ago," Shane said, squeezing her hand. "And besides, it wasn't your fault! I know you tried to protect me, but to set the record straight, Teresa gathered all of us kids up and took us to Fern's house to get help, but she refused to believe her son would hurt his wife, let alone beat her unconscious. It was easier for Fern to turn a blind eye than confront the painful truth that her oldest son, Bill, whom she had worked so hard to raise, was a mean wife-beating alcoholic. When Bill showed up at her house, he took us back home, but you were still unconscious. That's when Teresa went to our neighbors to get help."

Hazel shook her head. "I didn't know that. What gets me is he never said he was sorry. He just walked out like a coward and went off chasing some other skirt. And speaking of his other women, I was furious when I found out he had named Charlie after one of his old girlfriends, Charlotte," she said bitterly. "I still hate him for being so mean and leaving me to raise all you kids by myself."

"Mom, you would never have gotten an apology from him for all the terrible things he did," Shane said. "For one, he doesn't remember most of it, because he was blacked out from drinking, and two, he had such low self-esteem, he couldn't apologize, out of self-preservation."

"What do you mean? I don't understand," Hazel asked, wiping her tears. "Why couldn't he apologize? All he had to do was say he was sorry and stop drinking. It's not that difficult! But he did neither; he just abandoned me and all you kids."

"It's harder than you think because we're talking about two different kinds of apologies; one stems from guilt and the other from shame. Let me explain. Suppose I accidentally spilled coffee on Ethel's favorite tablecloth. I'd immediately apologize for my mistake and wash it to make sure it didn't leave a stain," Shane said. "This type of apology is simple because it only draws into question a single accident. I'm guilty only of making a mistake. But things get much more complicated when an apology draws into question someone's self-worth. Then we're talking about shame—the feeling that *I am bad* rather than *I did something bad.*"

Shane took a drink of his coffee, then continued. "People who do the worst things often don't apologize, because it requires them to face their actions, which causes them to question their self-worth. To avoid that, they turn a blind eye to their actions and superficially prop themselves up by blaming others because if they face their actions, their low self-worth places them on thin ice. The fear of falling through and drowning in profound shame and self-loathing causes them to deflect their responsibility out of self-preservation. It's easier to blame others or abandon the situation altogether than face their actions. That's why Bill never said he was sorry and why he abandoned you and all of us kids."

For a moment, they could have heard a pin drop.

"I'm going to need to think about this," Hazel said, shaking her head.

"As hard as it sounds, it's best if you can forgive him even without ever receiving an apology," Shane said. "It also helps to consider his background to put things into context. Bill was the oldest of Fern's seven boys, and although she did her best to raise them after her husband abandoned her for another woman, the boys still got into their fair share of trouble, primarily with drugs and alcohol. And since the boys had no father figure, they basically had to raise themselves while their mom worked long hours as a housekeeper at the Moritz Hospital in Sun Valley to provide for her boys. Because she barely made enough money to cover the mortgage on her two-bedroom house and feed the boys, Bill started working at the Liberty Gem Mine digging ore when he was old enough while his younger brothers trapped small animals, taxidermied them, and sold them to earn extra money. I still remember some of their disfigured animals: a badger, pheasant, bobcat, and a red fox, which were mounted on the walls in the living room and the boys' bedroom. I'll never know how seven boys slept in that tiny room, but it gave me an eerie feeling thinking about all the dead animals staring blankly into the night, watching over the boys as they slept—their glassy eyes askew. And the chemicals they used to taxidermy those unfortunate creatures caused the house to smell putrid. Ghastly. They were used to it, but it burned my lungs every time I walked into that tiny house. Ironically, the guns that killed the dead and dusty animals were mounted on the wall next to them."

Shane took a bite of his cake doughnut, licked the cinnamon sugar off his lips, and then continued. "Fern kept everything her grandchildren ever gave her. She pinned some of her favorite drawings in the hall next to her bedroom and above her kitchen table. She stored the rest in her bedroom until the boxes reached the ceiling, leaving only enough room for her to walk to her bed and closet. I remember Fern sitting in the kitchen at her small wooden table with claw feet, drinking orange tea. During Christmas, she played the record *The Little Drummer Boy* as the snow fell. In summer, she let her chickens roam the yard to scratch around the elderberry bushes, chokecherry, and apple trees. Even though they were surrounded by the beautiful mountains in the heart of the Wood River Valley, they lived their own private hell. Understanding Bill's background might make it easier to forgive him."

"I'm not sure I understand," Hazel said, holding back her anger. "You're saying I'm supposed to forgive him even though he never said he was sorry?"

"Yes, not out of respect for him, but out of respect for yourself. Don't let any person or situation make *you* into someone *you don't want to be*!" Shane said. "Hasn't he taken enough from you already? Let him carry the burden of his actions when he crosses over. . . . They're not yours to carry, and holding on to them only robs you of your happiness. If you can forgive him, knowing he will own his actions during his life review when he crosses over, it will set you free from the heavy burden of being judge and jury."

"And being judge and jury is equivalent to trying to rein someone else's horse. It never works, and it only puts you at risk of falling off your own horse," Ethel added. "All we need to worry about is reining our own horse, knowing others will be responsible if they find themselves waist-high in cockleburs. You can't make people do the right thing. Sometimes, they need to get caught up in the cockleburs to learn their lessons."

"Again, I hear what you're saying, but . . ." Hazel shook her head. "I don't know. . . . I'm just going to have to think about this for a while."

"I agree with Hazel," Melba snapped. "I know we're supposed to forgive people for their trespasses, but some things are impossible to forgive!"

"I understand," Shane continued. "Forgiving others can be exceedingly difficult, especially regarding something very painful that's happened to you or a loved one. Take your time to think about it, and if you want, we can always talk about it later."

"Grandpa, would you sing some hymns while Melba plays the piano to cheer us up?" Hazel asked. "I love hearing you sing. It always makes me happy, and I could use a little cheering up right about now."

Solomon finished his coffee. "Sure, I'd be happy to. Shall we gather around the piano?"

Everyone got up from the kitchen table, went to the living room, and sat around the oak player piano Raymond had bought one year for Christmas. When the kids arrived home from school one day, Raymond had been seated at the piano, pretending he was playing it. Everyone was thrilled, and from that day on, the Williams family spent many evenings learning to play the piano and singing songs. On top of the piano was a sweet-potato plant, its green and purple leaves reaching in all directions.

Melba opened the lid of the music bench, rummaged through the sheet music and player piano rolls, found what she was looking for, and then sat down on the bench in front of the piano. Solomon glanced at the sheet music Melba had placed on the music rack, then took his place at her side. As Melba played "Tennessee Waltz," Solomon joined her, singing in his beautiful tenor voice.

10

THE SILVER LINING
May 15, 2017

CHARLIE SAT in her car in the parking lot, apprehensive about clocking in for work. She had gotten up at 5:00 a.m., taken a shower, and dressed in blue scrubs with a long-sleeved turtleneck underneath to cover the tattoos on her forearms, which she and Isaac had designed when he was six. She slipped on her nursing clogs and clipped her badge to her collar. Then she placed her scissors and pens in her cargo pocket and laid her black-and-silver stethoscope around her neck. Before leaving for work, Charlie had sent Isaac a text message and photo, and then she drove to Winslow with the sun in her eyes.

I hope no one tries to talk to me about Isaac. If they do, I'll probably lose it.

Finally, Charlie took a deep breath, exhaled, and got out of her car. As she walked toward the door carrying her backpack, she saw one of her coworkers, causing her anxiety level to spike.

Her coworker greeted her. "Charlie, it's so good to see you. Welcome back."

"Thanks, it's good to see you too." *They must have gotten the email from Kay,* Charlie thought, her anxiety level decreasing.

Charlie's coworker swiped her badge on the security pad, opened the door, and they walked in and went their separate ways. As usual, Charlie arrived early to prepare the cardiology department before the patients checked in for their appointments. She turned on the lights, then tried to log in to her computer, but her password had expired. *I'll have to call IT later and have them reset my password.* Charlie got up from her desk and pulled the curtain fixed to a track on the ceiling, separating the echocardiography exam table from their work area. Next, she put the folders of the patients scheduled for echocardiograms on her desk, turned on Dr. Villarino's favorite seventies rock station as background music, and then walked down the hall to clock in, but her access was denied due to her expired password. *Dammit, I should've known.* Charlie walked back to the cardiology department.

Suzanne, the echocardiography technician, arrived for work, hugged Charlie, and gave her a small bag of chocolate-covered coffee beans with a card. As tears welled up in Suzanne's eyes, she apologized. "I'm sorry. . . . Give me a few minutes while I pull myself together." She walked behind the curtain and turned on the ultrasound machine.

An awkward silence lingered in the air.

Charlie sat the bag and card down on her desk, noticing it was 8:01. She called IT, reset her password, then walked down the hall and clocked in. On her return, she picked up the first patient's folder from her desk, pulled up the patient's chart on her computer, and wrote down his medications at the bottom of his chart. Charlie pulled back the curtain and handed Suzanne his chart. "He's here for cardio clearance for shoulder surgery. He has heart failure and is taking a diuretic and a beta-blocker, which I wrote down for you. I'll go get his vitals and bring him back," Charlie said, leaving the room.

She walked down the hall to the nursing station, where Dr. Villarino's scheduler, Ashley, stared at her computer while typing. When she looked up and saw Charlie, she jumped up, ran around the counter, and gave her a big hug.

"It's great to have you back," Ashley said. "I've already called your first patient. He's waiting for you to take his vitals."

"Okay, thanks," Charlie said, walking toward the vitals room.

She pulled back the curtain, where Mr. Peshlakai, an elderly Navajo gentleman, sat wearing a blue-and-white Western shirt, Levi's, a large silver belt buckle with an image of a man riding a bucking bronco, and a tattered brown cowboy hat.

"*Yá'át'ééh abiní,*" Charlie said, pulling her blood pressure cuff from her front pocket. *Hello, good morning.*

"*Aoo'.*" Mr. Peshlakai smiled, rolling up his sleeve. *Yes, it is.*

Having worked at the clinic for over two years, Charlie knew the Diné Bizaad word *aoo'* translated into the English word *yes*, but the Diné also used the term broadly as an affirmation. Charlie placed her blood pressure cuff around Mr. Peshlakai's left upper arm, pumped the bulb to fill the cuff with air, then listened with her stethoscope as she released the pressure by turning the valve on the sphygmomanometer. She then wrote down Mr. Peshlakai's blood pressure, removed her stethoscope from her ears, and placed it back around her neck.

"*Haanít'éh?*" Charlie asked. *How are you?*

"*Yá'ánísht'ééh, ahéhee',*" Mr. Peshlakai answered in Diné Bizaad, then switched to English. "I'm fine, thank you. You're pretty good. You know more Navajo than my grandkids."

"Just call me Navajo Charlie," she joked. "Your blood pressure is a little high. Have you taken your meds this morning?"

"Yes, but I always get nervous when I have to see the doctor," Mr. Peshlakai replied, "especially when I have to have tests done. I'm worried I might not pass. I need to get my shoulder fixed. . . . It hurts all the time."

"I understand. Let's go to the exam room."

"*Aoo',*" Mr. Peshlakai said. *Okay.*

They walked to the cardiology department, where Suzanne started his echo and requested a bottle of "vitamin D," the slang for Definity, a contrast agent used to enhance images during echocardiograms. Charlie drew a bottle of Definity into a syringe and connected it to Mr. Peshlakai's IV. Suzanne and Charlie looked at each other, nodded, and then Suzanne counted down, "Three . . . two . . . one." Charlie pushed the Definity into the port, then rapidly chased it with a ten-milliliter saline flush. The Definity microbubbles, ranging between 1.1 and 3.3 microns, entered Mr. Peshlakai's bloodstream, then his heart. "Much better," Suzanne said, working feverishly to capture the images she needed before the contrast agent passed through Mr. Peshlakai's pulmonary system, where he would breathe it out within minutes of it having been injected.

"Thanks, I got what I needed," Suzanne said enthusiastically, then asked Charlie to look at the ultrasound video she had captured of Mr. Peshlakai's beating heart. It showed his mitral valve opening and closing rhythmically with a swishing sound, *lub-dub, lub-dub, lub-dub.*

"It looks like little hands clapping," Charlie commented.

"Yeah, I can see that," Suzanne agreed. "Did you know the average heart will beat approximately three billion times by the time a person turns seventy years old?"

"Wow, that's impressive!"

"Good morning," Dr. Villarino said, pulling the curtain back to hug Charlie. "We're so happy to have you back. We've missed you."

"Good morning, Dr. V. I've missed you too. I'll get your first patient ready for you," Charlie said, keeping the conversation work-oriented.

Charlie walked Mr. Peshlakai across the hall after his echo to room 26, where she asked him to have a seat, and then went to the waiting room and called her second patient, Mr. Nez, a proud medicine man who wore his long white hair in braids. While Suzanne began his echocardiogram, Charlie walked down the hall to warm her coffee in the microwave. When it beeped, she took her coffee and started walking back toward the cardiology department when one of her coworkers stopped her in the hall.

"I'm so sorry to hear about your son," her coworker said. "I know how you feel. I just lost my uncle last week. He had a heart attack, and his wife and three daughters are so upset! He was only sixty-one, and they didn't see it coming."

Charlie's heart began to race. "I'm sorry for your loss," Charlie said, biting her tongue and quickly excusing herself. "I need to get going; Dr. V's waiting for me to get her next patient."

"Okay, it's good to see you back at work."

Charlie politely dismissed herself, then continued down the hall. *I'm sorry, YOU DON'T FUCKING KNOW HOW I FEEL! Losing your uncle, who lived a full life—had the joys of falling in love, getting married, having three kids, and watching them grow up—IS NOT the same as losing your only child! Isaac never got to go on a first date, fall in love, graduate from high school, live on his own, have kids, or have a career! His life was taken from him when he was only sixteen! IT'S NOT THE SAME!*

Charlie ran to the restroom, shut the door, and sat on the closed toilet seat, then burst into tears. After she was finally able to regain her composure, she went to the cardiology department, sat her coffee down at her desk, and checked in with Suzanne. Not needing Definity, she had finished the second echocardiogram early. Once Mr. Nez put his shirt back on, Charlie walked him to room 27, went to the waiting room, and called her next patient. As she returned with her third patient, Mr. Peshlakai was leaving with a smile on his face.

"*Ahéhee', shik'is. Hágoónee',*" Charlie said. *Thank you, friend. See you later.*

"*Aoo',*" Mr. Peshlakai chuckled. "Dr. V. says my heart's good. I get to have my surgery!"

Charlie gave Mr. Peshlakai two thumbs-ups, then took her next patient to the echocardiogram exam table, where she helped him get ready for his exam. Charlie and Suzanne smiled at each other as they fell into their familiar routine.

At noon, when they took a thirty-minute break, Charlie took her lunch from her backpack and sat in an empty patient room to avoid talking with her coworkers. Nurse practitioner Mrs. Wilson, who had just come out of the physician's office, saw Charlie sitting alone and walked in to express her condolences. Charlie's heart sank, as they previously had challenging conversations about their opposing religious views. After Charlie had told her she wasn't religious, Mrs. Wilson had made it her mission to convert her—to save her from the fiery pits of hell and damnation.

"I heard about your son," Mrs. Wilson said. "I'm so sorry for your loss. I can't imagine what you are going through."

Anticipating conflict, Charlie felt her heart racing. "Thanks. I appreciate your kindness," she said, hoping to end the conversation.

"God bless you," Mrs. Wilson continued. "I hope it comforts you knowing it was God's plan to call your son back home."

"First of all, God did not bless me! He killed my only son—my only child!" Charlie erupted, scorn in her eyes. "And secondly, that's a pretty fucked-up plan, if you ask me!"

"I'm sorry you feel that way." Mrs. Wilson paused a moment, then left the room.

What Mrs. Wilson failed to understand was that the silver lining she offered was not the life buoy she intended it to be. Her words were rather like asking a drowning man if he wanted a ham and cheese sandwich—it was the last thing a drowning man needed.

Charlie closed the door and broke down as a floodgate of sorrow opened and washed over her. *Why can't people just leave me alone like I asked them to? I know she means well, but she knows I'm not religious. She should be respectful toward me and my point of view and leave me alone instead of constantly pushing her agenda—especially now!*

After lunch, Suzanne, Dr. Villarino, and Charlie finished seeing the rest of their patients, and then Charlie clocked out and drove home. When Charlie arrived, she put her scrubs into the washing machine, put on a pair of Levi's and a T-shirt, and then checked her email while sitting at the kitchen counter. An email from the hospital stating that they would not be sending a complete copy of Isaac's medical records, as they were required to hold them for only seven years, made her livid. Charlie got up from her computer and started pacing the floor. *They're giving me inaccurate information either because they don't know better or because his records incriminate them. Either way, I need to find some way to get Isaac's records. I remember reading somewhere that pediatric records have to be kept longer than adult records.*

Charlie sat back down at her computer and was researching Arizona law, hoping to find out how long medical records had to be retained, when Chris got home from work.

Chris sat his satchel on the couch and kissed Charlie on the cheek. "Hi, beautiful; how was your first day back at work?"

"Not great, and the hospital infuriates me!" Charlie said. "They said they're not going to give me a complete copy of Isaac's birth records, because they're only required to keep his records for seven years. I don't think that's the case, so I'm trying to look it up."

"What the hell," Chris exclaimed, walking into the kitchen to make himself a mojito. "As I said before, you have my complete support. While you're looking that up, I'll make some chicken and corn on the cob on the grill. When it's ready, I'll let you know, and we can have dinner outside on the deck."

"Thanks, handsome; that would be great."

Chris grabbed his mojito and everything he needed to make dinner, then went outside to the lower deck. Dexter and Cobalt followed, then lay down under the patio table, shaded by an orange umbrella.

While Chris made dinner, Charlie searched Arizona law and found just what she was looking for—the Arizona Revised Statute 12-2297 Retention of Records.

11

NOT CRAZY AFTER ALL
May 15, 2017

HAVING FOUND THE ARIZONA Revised Statute 12-2297 Retention of Records, Charlie felt hopeful. She clicked on the statute and read the following:

> A. Unless otherwise required by statute or by federal law, a health care provider shall retain the original or copies of a patient's medical records as follows:
> 1. If the patient is an adult, for at least six years after the last date the adult patient received medical or health care services from that provider.
> 2. If the patient is a child, either for at least three years after the child's eighteenth birthday or for at least six years after the last date the child received medical or health care services from that provider, whichever date occurs later.

That should get their attention, Charlie thought, copying the statute and pasting it into the body of her reply email to the hospital. Then, anticipating that the hospital would still drag its heels, Charlie searched for regulations that would encourage them to deliver Isaac's records to her in a timely fashion. On the US Department of Health &

Human Services website, she found "Individuals' Right under HIPAA to Access their Health Information," which read:

> Individuals' Right under HIPAA to Access their Health Information:
> Timeliness in Providing Access
> In providing access to the individual, a covered entity must provide access to the PHI requested, in whole, or in part (if certain access may be denied as explained below), no later than 30 calendar days from receiving the individual's request. See 45 CFR 164.524(b)(2).

Charlie copied this, added it to her email, and then informed the hospital that she expected to receive a COMPLETE copy of Isaac's birth records, including his fetal heart monitor strips, within thirty days. She sent the message, then walked outside to have dinner with Chris.

"Good timing," Chris said, taking the chicken off the grill. "Could you grab me a beer?"

"Sure."

Charlie went to the kitchen, took a Heineken from the refrigerator, then returned outside to the lower deck, and Schmiggs followed. Charlie sat down under the orange umbrella, where she, Isaac, and Chris once enjoyed playing chess and having dinner in the cool evening breeze.

Chris brought the platter to the table, placed a piece of chicken and an ear of corn on each of their plates, and sat down. Taking his keys from his pocket, he popped the lid off his Heineken with a shark-shaped bottle opener and took a long guzzle.

"Thanks, that hits the spot," Chris said, putting his keys back in his pocket.

Charlie leaned over and kissed him, tasting the beer on his lips. "Thanks for making dinner. I found what I was looking for." She explained what she'd found and what she'd written to the hospital. Her voice rose in anger. "I don't want to be an ass about it, but I want those records!"

"I don't see how they can get out of it now. After all, they're your records, not theirs," Chris said. "The way I see it, you asked them nicely and you got four pages. They've forced you to play hardball! That's on them, not you."

"It still infuriates me that they're forcing me to fight so hard to get MY records, but apparently, they're not going to play nice," Charlie said, shaking her head.

Cobalt nudged Chris's arm with his nose, begging for a treat. Chris cut two small pieces off his chicken breast and gave one to Cobalt and the other to Dexter. Schmiggs jumped onto the table, his bright-green eyes smiling as he meowed in his raspy voice. Chris placed a piece of chicken on the platter and Schmiggs eagerly ate it, then begged for more.

"I was thinking about the strange dreams I've been having, and I remembered something from when my mom passed," Charlie said. "She came to visit me shortly after she died."

Chris took a drink of his beer, saying nothing.

"After having two open-heart surgeries, my mom said her next heart attack had better kill her because she didn't want to live through that experience again, and she got her wish—her third one killed her. After her second open-heart surgery, I had to help calm her down in the recovery room because she tried to yank the vent out of her throat, and they had to tie her down. It was awful seeing her like that, writhing in pain."

Charlie took a bite of chicken, then continued. "About a year later, I got a phone call from Shane early in the morning. He had walked to Mom's house to check on her and found her dead in her living room chair. Before she died, Mom was concerned that I didn't believe in an afterlife and tried to convince me, but I never changed my views. A couple of weeks later, I was in my kitchen, and I sensed her sitting at the kitchen table. I couldn't see her, but I knew she was there. I was a little surprised but not afraid. I didn't know what to do, so I just kept doing the dishes. Later that day, I was driving with Isaac in the back seat, and I sensed my mom in the passenger seat. Still, I didn't know what to do, so I just kept driving. The following day, the same thing happened—Mom was sitting at the kitchen table, and before I knew it, I just started talking to her out loud. I told her I knew she was there, and I understood what she was trying to tell me: There's life after death—that death is not the end. Then I told her I loved her and, now that I got her message, there was surely something else she'd rather be doing, and she was free to go. After that, I never heard from her again!"

Chris looked intrigued but said nothing.

"Have you ever had anything like that happen to you?"

"No, I haven't," Chris said, taking a drink of his beer.

"There've been a lot of paranormal activities on my mom's side of the family," Charlie said. "Mom told me her grandmother Ethel died twice. The first time was at the Moritz Hospital in Sun Valley, where I was born. The Williams family had left the hospital room to mourn in the hallway after she was pronounced dead and covered with a sheet. As they tried to console each other, one of the nurses entered the room where Ethel lay dead and screamed. Everyone ran into the room to find Ethel sitting up in bed! My aunt Wilma, who was pretty young at the time, asked her grandmother why she didn't stay dead. She replied, 'The Lord wasn't ready for me.' Ethel got better and went home, but about six months later, she was sick again. The night before she died, she asked my aunt Wilma, 'Who's that man standing at the foot of my bed all dressed in black?' My aunt Wilma looked around and told her nobody was standing at the foot of her bed, but her grandmother Ethel insisted, 'It's the Angel of Death—he's come to take me home!' That night, Ethel died peacefully in her sleep. Of course, I wasn't there, but that's the way my mom told the story."

The topic clearly made Chris uncomfortable, but she could see he was still interested.

"My mom had also spoken of a 'man dressed in black' when our house was on fire. Since Solomon had died years before Ethel, and they'd been married close to sixty years, I think her 'Angel of Death' must have been Solomon coming to take her home," Charlie said. "My mom said her grandparents were 'angels' when she and her siblings were growing up. Ethel would warm their blankets by the fireplace downstairs, since that was the only heating in the farmhouse, then take the blankets upstairs and put them on their beds before they went to sleep. And I remember Mom telling me she and her brothers and sisters would run down the hill when they got off the school bus, and Ethel would always have fresh pastries waiting for them. Mom said they devoured her biscuits, molasses cookies with raisins, rice pudding, or whatever she had made before changing their clothes to go out to do chores. The only thing Mom didn't like was Ethel's eggs with syrup. My mom said she didn't like her 'hen berries' sweet."

"What are hen berries?" Chris asked.

"I know . . . right? Apparently, when my mom was growing up, they used to call eggs hen berries."

"I've never heard that one before."

"Yeah, me neither. Anyway, all these stories got me wondering what percentage of people have had similar experiences, and I found some interesting information." Charlie took her phone from her back pocket. She opened the 2009 report "Many Americans Mix Multiple Faiths" by the Pew Research Center, scrolled two-thirds of the way down the page, and showed it to Chris. It read: "Roughly three in ten Americans (29%) say they have felt in touch with someone who has died."

"I would have never guessed that," Chris exclaimed. "That's almost one in three people who say they've been in contact with someone dead!"

"I was surprised too," Charlie said. "And a man named Peter Fenwick, a neuropsychologist and former senior lecturer at King's College who's known for his near-death studies, says that deathbed visitors are common and usually involve first-degree relatives or spouses. He also said deathbed visions echo the person's 'cultural background' and have been reported throughout history. What really surprised me was that he thinks the brain is a filter . . . that it filters out the greater whole, leaving only a tiny piece of what we refer to as our world and everything in it. And at the time of death, your consciousness separates from your brain, no longer needing the filter, and you merge with the cosmos—the whole—and become aware of all that is, was, and ever will be."

Chris looked surprised as he took a sip of his beer.

"It reminds me of the reticular formation in our brains," Charlie said, pressing on. "One of its functions is to filter out repetitive and meaningless stimuli so the brain can focus on more important things. It's a necessary function because our brains are constantly bombarded by input from our environment, so the brain filters out what it determines to be meaningless information. But Fenwick says our whole brains function as filters, leaving only a tiny piece of the greater whole for us to interpret. Perhaps it's necessary so that we can focus on the tasks at hand . . . the lives we lead."

"That's an interesting concept," Chris said, clearly a little lost for words. "But I had no idea that one in three people would say they've been in contact with someone dead. I've never experienced anything like that, but a number like thirty percent tends to get your attention."

"Guess I'm not crazy after all . . . or if I am, so is one-third of the population!" Charlie said, when it occurred to her that she'd been doing all the talking. "But enough about that; how was your day?"

"It was difficult. One of my employees asked how I was doing, and I could tell by the way they asked me that they were expecting me to have processed everything and moved on," Chris said. "The same thing happened when my mom died of cancer. People expect you to get over it and move on within a certain amount of time. . . . I never understood that. It's only been a month since Isaac died. . . . Why would I want to get over losing him or my mom? I loved my mom. She always helped me with homework and taught me how to overcome my difficulties with reading, and even though she was the first woman pharmacist in Idaho, she gave up her career to raise her two adopted kids—my sister and me. People don't understand that you and I wake up to the same day Isaac died over and over again. Every day starts the same—Isaac's still dead, and even though Isaac wasn't my son, he was still my good friend, and I loved him. I finally had a little family. . . . Now it's all gone."

Charlie grabbed Chris's hand, seeing tears in his gray-blue eyes. "We don't have to move on. We're the only ones who know what we're going through, so we're just going to have to figure it out together, one step at a time. And in the meantime, we can work in Isaac's name to make him proud."

Chris agreed, wiping away his tears.

"Let's go inside; it's getting dark," Charlie said. "I wouldn't mind going to bed early. I have to get up at five for work, and I'm already tired."

"Me too. I feel so beat up."

Chris scraped and put the grill away while Charlie went inside and put the dirty dishes in the dishwasher. They put on their pajamas and went to bed, then Chris started crying.

"I wish Isaac were still here," Chris said, wiping his tears and crying. "I miss him."

"I wish he was still here too."

Charlie and Chris curled up together and cried themselves to sleep as Isaac watched at the foot of the bed. Once he saw that his mom's mind was quiet, he showed her an image of him reading in front of the class and his classmates making fun of him because he had a difficult time reading. He wanted her to know he was free from that pain and suffering. Next, he showed her a scene of her dropping him off at a friend's house, but as Charlie backed up to leave, Isaac came running out, saying, "Mom, I chose you." Then he jumped into the car, and they drove off together.

Charlie beamed, then she woke up. *I wish I could have stayed asleep. A few minutes with Isaac, even if it's only a dream, is far better than being awake and him being dead.*

She looked at the clock: 4:10 a.m. Deciding it was pointless to go back to sleep, she got up and wrote Isaac another letter before getting ready for work.

This time, she chose a card with the word *PEACE* written on the front of the card, but an image of an Adélie penguin replaced the letter *A*. She sat down, opened the card, and drew a line through the caption: *PEACE ON EARTH & GOODWILL TO ALL*, then wrote down her dream and ended the letter by saying, I have no intention of living until I die. At some point, I will come looking for you.

12

SUMERIAN TABLETS
The Other Side

THE SCENT OF SUMMER drifted in the air as three ravens cawed loudly from where they were perched on the hitching post between the Big Wood River and the towering cottonwood tree. Shane and Hazel were returning home from a walk along the riverbank with Hailey when they spotted Isaac sitting at the picnic table with his face buried in his hands. Kéyah sat next to him with his head resting on Isaac's lap. A folded piece of paper lay before Isaac, gently moving in the breeze. As they drew near, Kéyah ran to greet Hailey, and Isaac dropped his hands, seeing Hazel and Shane approaching.

"We were just coming back from a walk and saw you sitting here," Shane said as they sat down on the opposite side of the picnic table. "You look upset. . . . What's wrong?"

"I talked to my mom last night when she was sleeping, but it didn't go as intended. Now I'm not sure what to do."

"What happened?" Hazel asked.

"First, I explained how painful life was for me by showing her an image of me at school, which she understood. Then I tried showing her that I chose her to be my mom, but she misinterpreted my message to simply mean that I loved being with her, which I do, but she missed my main message—that we chose this life together. What's worse, she wants an answer to her question of whether or not I still exist. She thinks one way to find out is to come looking for me by taking her own life, which is exactly what I'm trying to prevent! Now I'm not sure what to do, but contacting her through her dreams is no longer an option. It's only making her want to come looking for me."

Hazel looked concerned. "I didn't see that one coming."

"Me neither," Isaac replied.

"It's not all bad," Shane said. "Your mom wants confirmation that you still exist, which is better than thinking that's impossible. Knowing and believing are two different things. Knowing is directly observing that something is true, whereas believing is blindly accepting something as truth. Your mom needs to *know*. . . . She's not satisfied with blind acceptance. And although she's been researching both science and religion, neither one has answered her questions: Are you still out there somewhere, and will she ever see you again?"

"We need a new plan that will *prove* to your mom that you still exist and you're still with her," Hazel said. "She also needs to understand that she still has things she must accomplish in her life and that when she crosses over of *natural causes*, she'll be with you again. That will give her the strength she needs to carry on."

"I have an idea," Shane grinned. "Since Charlie feels neither science nor religion has answered her questions, maybe it would be helpful for her to see a reputable psychic medium who can show her that you're alive and well and helping her from the other side. Nancy, your mom's neighbor, is familiar with Allison DuBois, a psychic medium who doesn't live far from your mom. Maybe you could influence Nancy to visit Charlie and Chris and have her suggest seeing a psychic medium and mention Allison by name. I think Charlie might see her because Allison is world-renowned, and Charlie's searching for the best information she can find to answer her questions."

"That's not a bad idea," Isaac agreed, then looked at Hazel. "The good news is my mom told Chris about Ethel dying twice and about the time you visited my mom after you crossed over."

"That's good," Hazel said. "She's starting to put things together."

"She also told him about other paranormal experiences in our family and some statistics about people having contact with the dead. It's caused him to reconsider his views about death and the dreams my mom's been having. I worry about both of them for different reasons.

Since I'm my mom's only child, she feels like her future is gone. . . . All her plans have been erased. She's alive but not happy. Chris's dreams of having a little family have been crushed, but I know he wouldn't take his own life. He still enjoys skiing, biking, cooking, eating, and golfing, and even though he's in a rough spot, he still has things he looks forward to, unlike my mom. There's nothing she enjoys. . . . Living is a burden for her. There are only two reasons my mom doesn't take her life. One, she feels it wouldn't be fair to Chris, and two, she's fighting to get my medical records to hold those responsible for causing my brain injury accountable for their actions."

"You're talking about anhedonia—the inability to feel happy," Shane said. "But your mom will be able to find some happiness if she knows you're still with her and she'll eventually see you again. We just need to find a way to make that known to her."

Isaac agreed.

"What's with the piece of paper?" Hazel asked.

"My mom wrote a poem," Isaac said, handing it to Hazel. "She hasn't shared it with anyone, not even Chris."

Hazel unfolded the piece of paper. It read:

THE FIELD OF SORROW

> I have a friend I've never met
> he walks the field of sorrow.
> I told him,
> build what is important
> around what is essential.
> He inhaled his pain.
> It paralyzed him.
> He walks no more.
> Darkness is everywhere.
> It's in the water.
> The fish are dying.
> The songbirds sang no more.
>
> I have a friend I've never met
> he swims the river of sorrow.

His top hat floated
downstream as the
river of sorrow
claimed the man,
pulling him under.
He swam no more.
Darkness is everywhere.
It's in the valley.
The animals are dying.
The flowers bloomed no more.

I have a friend I've never met
she walks the field of sorrow.
The woman held
the boy's broken body
cold, rigid, blue fingernails.
Her heart cracked open
as she fell to the ground.
The boy breathed no more.
Darkness is everywhere.
It's in the mountains.
The trees are dying.
The songbirds sang no more.

"What a mournful poem," Hazel said, wiping her tears. "I hate to see my daughter in so much pain and misery."

"Me too," Isaac said. "Ever since I can remember, my mom has loved the arts. Her favorites were the classics . . . Steinbeck, Orwell, Van Gogh, Vermeer, Hemingway, and so many others. Mom often painted while I sat with her and did my homework, and sometimes, after dinner, we would listen to books on tape. My mom taught me a lot about art, but I was a little surprised. . . . She's never written poetry before."

"Some of the most important works of art were the great epics," Hazel said.

"What are the great epics?" Isaac asked.

"They're very long poems written on clay tablets at the time language was first invented," Hazel explained. "Around 3200 BCE, in the city of Uruk, the Sumerians changed civilization forever when they invented cuneiform—the first written language, which was perhaps the most important development of ancient civilization. The Fertile Crescent was a crescent-shaped region of fertile land during the Mesopotamian era that arched around the northern edge of the Arabian Desert from the Nile Valley in Egypt to the Persian Gulf. It included the Tigris and Euphrates Rivers and the important Sumerian cities of Uruk, Nineveh, and Babylon. This area was also called the Cradle of Civilization because it's the origin of writing, agriculture, the wheel, long-distance trade, and the domestication of livestock, horses, and wheat. The Sumerians were also the first to divide day and night into twelve hours, and each hour into sixty smaller units that people now refer to as minutes.

"Before the written language was invented, the Sumerians used to pass information down from generation to generation through storytelling, and of course, the stories varied depending on the storyteller," Hazel continued. "Later, after the invention of writing, those stories about their rituals, history, laws, scriptures, hymns, and myths were written down on clay tablets and baked in kilns, turning them into stone. Again, there are many variations of the stories depending on who wrote them down, but the important thing was that the stories were preserved because they were literally written in stone."

"Wow, that's fascinating!" Isaac said.

"It certainly is," Hazel agreed. "One of my favorite epic poems is the *Atrahasis* epic from around 1700 BCE. It's a story about Enlil, king of the gods, and Enki, god of wisdom, and as you know, I never miss an opportunity to tell a good story."

> Before time, when the gods lived in the sky and on the earth below, the older, higher-ranking gods who preferred to live a life of luxury and leisure forced the younger, lower-ranking gods to do all the work required to keep the universe in order. Enlil, king of the gods and keeper of the tablets of destiny, forced the lesser gods to work in his fields, but they grew tired of tilling the soil and planting crops, so they revolted,

saying they shouldn't have to work so hard since they, too, were gods.

Enki, god of wisdom and fresh water, proposed making lesser creatures, called humans, to work the land and plant the fields. Enki suggested that the humans would have the same bodies and faces as the gods, and they would also speak the same language, have intelligence, and have similar relationships to those of the gods, but the humans would be powerless and not live very long. After gaining permission from Enlil, Enki had his wife, Nintu, kneaded the blood, body, and intelligence of the god We-llu, who volunteered to be sacrificed, into some clay. Then Nintu created seven men and seven women from clay and shaped their bodies and faces like those of gods.

Enlil and the other gods then forced the humans to plow their fields, make their food, adorn them with lavish gifts of gold and silver, weave their clothes, sing hymns to them, build them shrines and temples, and pray to them. The humans couldn't protest, because the gods held power over them. The humans believed that if the gods felt they were well cared for, they might be merciful and make the men heroic in battle; the women would bear many children; and the people's crops would be bountiful. But if the gods felt they had not been sufficiently cared for, they might become angry or irritated and cause horrible plagues, droughts, famines, and floods to punish the humans.

The humans multiplied, and soon there were thousands of people, and they grew loud. Unable to tolerate the noise, Enlil sent droughts, famines, and plagues upon the people to decrease their numbers, but the humans asked Enki for help, since he had conceived them. This he did, in secret. Enlil, not understanding why the population of the people had not decreased, decided to destroy all of them in a great flood. Again, Enki chose to help the humans. He traveled to the earth below and told Atrahasis of Enlil's plan, then told him to build a great ark and place two of every animal into the ark to save them. Atrahasis did as instructed by Enki, and when the great flood came, it destroyed all life on Earth except Atrahasis and the animals on the ark!

"That's quite a poem . . . more like a story," Isaac said.

"Yes, the great epics were stories written as poems," Hazel explained. "The creation story and the great flood story are very old and have been told throughout the ages. Because these stories were first passed down from generation to generation through oral tradition, they're much older than when they were first written down. Parts of the great flood story have also been told in the *Epic of Gilgamesh* from about 2000 BCE and the story of Noah's ark in Genesis from around 900 BCE."

Shane added, "Since the beginning of time, people have expressed themselves through art. Writing stories down helps people bring order to the chaos as they try to understand their place in the world and universe."

"True, and before the written language was invented, people left their marks in other ways," Hazel continued. "The oldest recorded art was from people who lived during the Stone Age era, dating back two hundred thousand to five hundred thousand years ago. In the Stone Age, people pounded half-circle dome-shaped holes called cupules into stone to leave their mark. Some impressive cupules are still preserved in the Daraki-Chattan cave, in central Madhya Pradesh, India. And in the Hohlenstein-Stadel cave in Germany, they found a lion-man sculpture with a man's body and a lion's head dating back to 40,000 BCE. It's the oldest known representation of a supernatural being. Another preserved artifact of early civilization, and one of my favorites, is the Chauvet Cave of Southern France. Engraved and painted on its walls are lions, horses, bison, reindeer, rhinos, and other animals, dating back to 30,000 BCE. I love reading history. . . . Not only is it fascinating, but it's my way of paying respect to our ancestors. Throughout time, people have struggled to understand their place in the world. Nothing has changed—we still have all the same questions."

"Everyone has to find their own way, but eventually, all roads lead to Rome—the other side," Isaac said. "And since we all are one, what one person does to others, he does to himself, and vice versa. As the Zen master Thích Nhất Hạnh said, 'We are all leaves of one tree.'"

"I love that," Hazel said, handing Charlie's poem back to Isaac. "I wouldn't be surprised if your mom continues to write to process her grief like our ancestors did. But I'm afraid I've gotten us a little off track. . . . What's your plan for getting your mom to see Allison DuBois?"

"I think I'll pay a visit to Nancy."

13

QUEEN ANT MELBA
July 14, 2017

A LIGHT RAIN SPRINKLED down as Charlie drove home from work. She was relieved it was Friday. She needed a break from wearing the mask she hid behind at work so she could fall apart and decompress. As she got closer to home, the light rain became a monsoon, and the brooding dark clouds north of Flagstaff piqued her interest. *It looks like it's pouring down where we tagged the nocturnal honeypots. Maybe they'll fly tonight!* Charlie thought, impatiently driving home. *Chris will be anxious to leave as soon as I get there.*

In anticipation of this night, Charlie and Chris had driven to the Painted Desert and checked the honeypot colonies before and after work every day for the past three weeks to see if the ants were ready for their nuptial flight—the mating flight when mature male and female alates, winged ants, fly from their parent colonies after a heavy rain, mate on the wing, and start new colonies. For the past several weeks, Chris and Charlie watched the male and female alates emerge from the colony's entrance, determine that the conditions were not optimal for their nuptial flight, then return down the opening of their nest. When she and Chris had checked the honeypot colonies that morning, there had been no activity. They had been waiting for the right conditions, and maybe tonight would be the night.

When Charlie arrived home, she parked her car in the driveway and quickly went inside.

"If we hurry, we can get to the honeypots before it gets dark," Chris said, looking at his phone. "The radar shows a large red cell right over their location." He told her he had already packed some water and sandwiches, and he offered to get the dogs in the car while she got ready.

Charlie quickly changed, grabbed her jacket, and jumped into the driver's seat. As she backed out of the driveway and headed toward the Painted Desert, Chris unwrapped a peanut butter and jelly sandwich and handed it to her.

"Thanks, my blood sugar's crashing. I needed to eat something."

"I knew you'd be hungry." Chris smiled. "It's a real toad-strangler out there, so I bet you're right. . . . They're going to fly tonight!"

"Toad-strangler?" Charlie questioned, taking a bite of her sandwich.

"You've never heard that before?"

"Can't say that I have."

"It means a very heavy rain . . . so heavy that the toads will either be forced from their burrows or drown."

"Nice terminology, especially from a stormwater expert like yourself," Charlie joked, raising one eyebrow. "If the queens fly tonight, we'll need to let them mate during the night; otherwise, they'll be sterile. We want fertile queens, so we'll have to go back tomorrow morning and collect a few."

"This heavy rain will give the queens a better chance at starting their new colonies," Chris said. "But it's no wonder only a few survive . . . so many things have to go right."

Charlie agreed. "I've been reading a lot about ants because we'll need to know how to take care of them. And you're right. For a queen to start a new colony, she first needs a decent amount of rain, which we have. Then, the alates fly from their parent colonies and mate on the wing. Afterward, the males die, and the queens rip off their own wings and dig a hole deep into the ground, where they start their new colonies. The wet ground enables the queens to dig their founding chambers and prevent their eggs from drying out and dying. As the eggs develop into larvae, the queen feeds them by regurgitating the small food reserves she has stored in her body. When the larvae are ready to pupate, the queen covers them with dirt, enabling them to spin a silk cocoon around—"

"Wait a minute," Chris interrupted. "Ants spin silk cocoons?"

"Yes! I didn't know that either," Charlie said. "Like caterpillars, ants spin silk cocoons and go through metamorphosis inside the cocoon, but instead of a butterfly, a tiny worker called a nanitic emerges. Once the nanitic's exoskeleton hardens, which takes about three days, it leaves the founding chamber searching for food to feed the queen before she dies of starvation!"

"That explains the article I read. It said only one in several thousand queens will live to start a new colony."

"Well, at least this rain will help."

Lightning cracked, illuminating the water tank decorated with a black-and-white image of a Navajo elder and young boy, which marked where they needed to turn off Highway 89.

"We should—"

Thunder boomed, followed by more lightning.

"We should be there in about fifteen minutes," Chris said. "And it's a good thing. We only have about forty-five minutes before it's dark."

"I hope we get to see the queens fly!" Charlie turned onto the dirt road, then sped through a mud puddle to make the biggest splash possible. When they arrived at their location, she pulled over and parked.

"Let's leave the dogs in the car," Chris said. "It's very muddy outside."

"Good idea."

They walked over to the first colony Chris had marked on his Garmin but didn't see any workers or alates. Then Charlie noticed the alates of a diurnal species emerging from their colony's entrance, buzzing their wings and taking flight.

"Chris, look at these girls. They're starting their nuptial flight. Maybe our nocturnal honeypots will do the same. At least I think it's a good sign!"

"It's a great sign," Chris agreed. "But we're losing light by the minute. Let's split up so we can check more colonies before it's dark. If you could keep checking the colonies around this area, I'll go check that colony I found across the field. Call me on your phone if you see anything, and I'll do the same."

"Okay, sounds good."

Chris quickly headed across the field, and Charlie checked the nocturnal honeypots they'd marked in her area. She had just found another diurnal colony starting their nuptial flight when her phone rang.

"I found the colony I was looking for, and the queens are coming out and buzzing their wings—I just saw one take off!" Chris said, his voice filled with excitement. "You need to get over here now!"

Charlie ran across the field, and when she reached Chris, they marveled as they watched the gold-colored queens buzz their wings and then take flight. A few minutes later, it was too dark to see, but they were thrilled to have seen a few of the queens take off just as the sun set over the serene desert.

Charlie was excited. "I can't believe it! We *actually* saw some of the queens take off, and it's awesome knowing they're flying all around us even though we can't see them."

"That was cool watching them fly away into the night," Chris agreed, taking a flashlight from his backpack. "I'm happy tomorrow is Saturday. We have to come out first thing in the morning and see if we can find some queens."

As they started walking back to their car, Charlie stopped Chris and kissed him as lightning bolts lit up the distant horizon.

Chris grinned, and then they held hands and walked back to the car.

As Charlie started driving home, they saw something bouncing on the road. Charlie stopped the car, and they peered at the object through the windshield but couldn't make out what it was. Chris got out of the car to have a closer look, and Charlie put the car in park, then followed behind him.

Chris knelt in the car's headlights. "It's a toad!"

"A toad?" Charlie questioned. "This is the desert . . . There aren't any toads out here!"

"Well, it's still a toad," Chris laughed. "I told you it was a toad-strangler."

"I can't believe it. I guess desert toads only come out after a real toad-strangler!"

Chris picked up the hefty toad, placed it in a mud puddle on the side of the road, and they got back into the car and drove home.

In the morning, they got their gear ready and drove an hour back to the same location, but this time, they let the dogs out to run because most of the rain had soaked into the ground. On their way across the field, Charlie looked down, noticing a small mound of freshly piled dirt around a small hole in the ground. She knelt and saw a honeypot queen come to the surface, drop a clump of dirt off at the hole's entrance, and then go back down.

"Chris, I think I found a queen!" Charlie said. "Come and check this out."

Chris knelt, watching the queen repeat the same action.

"I think you're right."

"I don't know what to do. I'm afraid to dig her up. I don't want to kill her accidentally."

"I'm going to give it a shot." Chris opened his backpack and pulled out a small trowel and a small plastic container with a moist cotton ball they'd prepared earlier that morning.

"Okay, I'm going to stay out of your way. Hopefully, I can find a queen I can just pick up off the ground," Charlie said, walking away and scanning the ground.

—

After Chris saw the queen come to the surface, drop off a small pile of dirt, and head back down the hole, he carefully removed the dirt from around the entrance, causing the queen to hide at the bottom of her tunnel. And although Chris couldn't see him, Isaac smiled as he stood beside him, watching Chris remove the dirt little by little.

"I got her!" Chris yelled. "I've got the queen!"

Charlie ran to Chris and saw the beautiful honeypot queen in the small plastic container.

"Oh my gosh. You did it! You got the first queen!" Charlie said, pulling out her phone. "I've got to take your picture."

Chris carefully screwed the lid on the container, placed the honeypot queen in the backpack, then stood with his hands high in the air, smiling from ear to ear while Charlie took his picture, and then they hugged and kissed each other.

"That's awesome. I'm so proud of you, handsome!"

"Thanks, beautiful, that was so much fun, but these trowels are not very good. We need to go back home and get a couple of shovels."

"Okay, let's go," Charlie said, whistling for the dogs. "We can be back in a couple of hours, and now that we know what we're looking for, it will be much easier."

When they arrived home, Chris went inside with Dexter and Cobalt while Charlie put two shovels in her car. Then Charlie went inside to find Chris standing in the kitchen, looking at the golden honeypot queen.

"Do you remember Isaac telling us that the oldest queen lived twenty-eight and three-quarters of a year—almost thirty years?" Chris asked. "I think he said it was a *Lasius niger* in a German lab."

"Yeah, I remember that," Charlie said. "It's crazy that this queen might live longer than both of us!"

"Yes, wouldn't that be something?"

"What would you like to name her?" Charlie asked.

"I don't know. I hadn't thought about it. Why don't you name her? You're better at that sort of thing."

"Okay, I'd like to name her Queen Ant Melba, after my aunt who was abducted from her home, beaten, raped, and then left on the train tracks to die," Charlie said, her voice rising with anger. "It could be our way to honor her and keep her name alive."

Chris shook his head. "I remember you telling me that horrific story. It was so terrible. . . . I still don't understand why that monster only got eight years!"

"Me neither! Apparently, when he got out, he killed another woman and is now serving a life sentence," Charlie said. "What makes it even worse is that when Aunt Melba was a teenager, she and her dad were at Rock Creek watching over their sheep, and she woke up from a nightmare in hysterics, saying she was going to be murdered! Her dad told her to calm down . . . that it was only a dream, but she knew otherwise!"

"She dreamed about it before it happened?" Chris grimaced.

"Yes, she said she saw it in a dream!" Charlie said. "There are no words to convey the horror of what happened to her. It was unspeakable, and it devastated her six children and our extended family."

"That's one of the worst things I've ever heard." Chris handed the golden queen to Charlie. "I think Queen Ant Melba is a great name."

"Let's place her in one of the small formicaria I made and put her in Isaac's room on top of his dresser drawers where it's quiet."

"Good idea," Chris said. "While you do that, I'll make breakfast, and then we can head back out."

Charlie prepared the small formicarium, a specialized ant dwelling, and carefully placed Queen Ant Melba inside her new home, then set it on top of Isaac's dresser.

After breakfast, Charlie and Chris started heading back to the Painted Desert but stopped to get their mail on the way. As Charlie drove, Chris sifted through the envelopes. "We have a letter from the Arizona Corporation Commission addressed to Isaac's Ant Foundation," Chris said, opening the envelope. It read: *We are pleased to notify you that the Articles of Incorporation for the above-referenced entity HAVE BEEN APPROVED.*

"That's great news! Now we can work in Isaac's name through the foundation," Charlie said. "I also finished its website, so I'll add these credentials to make it official."

"Everything feels so difficult right now," Chris said, putting the letter back in the envelope. "But at least we've collected our first queen today, and we're making progress on the foundation."

"It's good to get things done because it gives us something constructive to work on while dealing with the medical records situation, but it doesn't fix the problem—Isaac's still dead," Charlie said. "And speaking of problems, I've decided I'm going to look for a new job. I don't want to work with someone who insinuates that Isaac's burning in hell because he . . . *we* aren't religious—we don't practice the same religion as they do. Isaac was kind to everyone, and I'm sick of her trying to save me. Even though she means well, it still boils my blood that she's always pushing her agenda. Besides, who can say who's right when the definition of God varies depending on a people's culture? Perhaps all views are right, given their perspectives, but to me, that's not what matters. What's important is how we treat one another—it's really very simple: Be kind and tolerant of others. In any case, I can't take working there anymore. Maybe if I find a new job in town, where nobody knows me, it will be easier, and I won't have to commute. I could just do my job and call it done."

"That's an unacceptable work environment," Chris said. "You shouldn't have to put up with that. You're a great nurse, and it would be easy for you to get a job in town. You should start looking as soon as possible!"

"Thanks. I appreciate you having my back. You're a damned good friend. You believed me about the medical records when no one else did! For that, I'll always be grateful."

Chris grabbed her hand and squeezed it as they continued down the road. When they reached their destination, they let the dogs out again, grabbed their backpack and shovels, and walked to the area where they'd found Queen Ant Melba. Charlie walked onto the top of a small hill, found more than a dozen small piles of dirt that looked like what they were searching for, and called Chris over to have a look.

"Looks like you hit the jackpot." Chris laid his shovel on the ground and took a few containers prepared with moist cotton balls from his backpack.

After Chris showed Charlie his technique while digging up the second queen, they both started collecting honeypot queens. They had seven more by noon, and not wanting to take more than they needed, they packed up and headed back toward the car. On the way, Charlie saw dozens of newly mated *Pogonomyrmex barbatus* queens, known in lay terms as harvester ants, busily digging their founding chambers. They collected eight harvester queens to add to their collection, then drove home.

Working together, Charlie and Chris placed the queens in their formicaria, lined them up on Isaac's dresser, and then went to the kitchen for a beer. As they were sitting at the kitchen table, Charlie noticed the 2017 calendar hanging on the wall.

"Let's mark this date on the calendar so we can track the age of the queens and how long it takes them to have their first workers." She got up and wrote Queens inside the July 15 square of the calendar.

"Here's to collecting queens," Chris said, holding up his beer.

"Long live the queens." Charlie smiled, clinking her bottle against his.

"Are you hungry? I'm thinking of making grilled cheese sandwiches for dinner," Chris said, walking to the kitchen. "It's easy, and I'm tired from running around all day."

"That's fine," Charlie said, getting up from the kitchen table and sitting on a barstool at the kitchen counter to talk to Chris while he cooked. As she drank her beer, she checked her email and found she had an email from the hospital's legal department, which had been handling her requests since her last email. She opened the email, read it, and then summarized it for Chris.

"The hospital says they've found Isaac's birth records, which they'll send in the mail, but they're still looking for Isaac's fetal heart monitor strips. At least I'm making some progress."

"I guess playing hardball is paying off. At least Isaac's records will help us figure out what happened," Chris said, finishing his beer. "Keep pushing, and hopefully, you can get Isaac's fetal heart monitor records as well."

Charlie nodded.

Hearing a knock on the front door, the dogs started barking.

"I wonder who that could be," Charlie said, getting up to answer the door. She pushed the dogs aside, looked through the peephole, and saw Nancy. Charlie opened the door and invited her in.

Nancy stepped inside and closed the door behind her, then handed Charlie a card. "I came by earlier, but you guys were gone. I wanted to give you this card from Deb and me, and for some reason—I'm not really sure why—I also wanted to mention that over the years, when I've been in difficult situations, I found it helpful to see a psychic medium. I know you're struggling with losing Isaac, and I thought this might help you too. If you choose to see one, Allison DuBois is great."

"Thanks, that's very kind of you," Charlie said. "I've never considered that, but I'll think about it. I'm not really sure what to do. We're just trying to figure things out one day at a time."

"I understand, and just to let you know, everyone in the neighborhood is thinking about you guys. We're all so sorry for your loss," Nancy said. "I know you like your privacy, so I won't keep you. I just wanted you to know we were thinking about you guys."

"Thanks for the card; it's very kind of you."

"Let me know if there is anything we can do for you." Nancy opened the door and stepped outside. "We're here if you need anything."

"Thanks, I will. Please tell Deb hi," Charlie said, waving goodbye.

14

GUILT AND SHAME
July 22, 2017

A SEALED RED-AND-WHITE cardboard box of dark secrets labeled *TRACKED* ★★★ *INSURED* sat on the kitchen table as Chris and Charlie discussed their weekend plans over eggs and toast.

"I checked the queens in their formicaria while you were making breakfast," Charlie said. "It's been a week, and all the queens are doing fine, except one of the honeypots is dead. I think she was one of the queens I collected because when I dug one up, I had a feeling I had accidentally broken one of her legs. I feel bad, but at least all the other honeypot and harvester queens are doing well."

"That's a bummer, but we're complete rookies, so we should probably give ourselves a break." Chris took a bite of his eggs and toast. "Do you have any plans for the day?"

"I need to go through the box of medical records from the hospital to look for indications of any medical negligence. If I find any, I need to follow up with the hospital. I feel like it's a shitty little box of nightmares that conceals the story of how Isaac died. I don't want to open it—it's going to be extremely painful."

"That sounds difficult, but now that you've forced their hand, you can't give them any slack. Unfortunately, it looks like you'll have to keep pushing to get the fetal heart monitor strips," Chris said. "While you're doing that, I think I'll go for a ride to Fisher Point. That way, I'll be out of your hair, and you'll have all the time you need to look over Isaac's records."

After breakfast, Chris dressed in his biking gear and returned to the kitchen. "I should be back by this afternoon," he said. "I hope you can figure out what happened, and if the hospital is responsible, we'll hold them accountable."

"Either way, I still need to know what happened for my own sake—I have the right to know!" Charlie said.

Chris kissed Charlie goodbye, and she wished him a good ride.

After he was gone, Charlie picked up the dirty dishes from the kitchen table. As she was doing so, she noticed that Isaac's seat was covered in dust. She stood there for a minute, unable to address her feelings, then left Isaac's chair covered with dust and sat back down at the kitchen table. She opened her phone and sent Isaac a text message with a picture of Chris and him in downtown Tokyo with their hands high in the air, grinning from ear to ear. In the background were skyscrapers covered in anime characters and Japanese writing. The message read: *FOREVER ISAAC* ♥♥. After Charlie sent the text, she heard Isaac's phone ping in his bedroom, where she kept it charging. One more message was added to the scores of unopened messages from his mom.

Trying to delay opening the boxed-up nightmare, Charlie made another cup of coffee, then sat in front of her computer, wondering how many people die each year of medical negligence. She found an article by Johns Hopkins Medicine titled "Study Suggests Medical Errors Are Third-Leading Cause of Death in U.S.," released May 3, 2016. Their study analyzed the medical death rates over eight years and stated that more than 250,000 deaths per year are due to medical errors. The Johns Hopkins article also stated that the Centers for Disease Control and Prevention (CDC) does not classify medical errors separately on death certificates because the medical coding system was intended to maximize billing for physician services, not collect national health statistics. As a result, medical error deaths are not tracked or reported by the CDC, even though they account for 9.5 percent of all deaths in the United States.

Charlie shook her head, took a deep breath, and finally opened the foreboding box. As she looked through the medical files, she found the record of Isaac's cord blood gas values—two samples of blood routinely taken from the umbilical cord after every child is born. One sample was from the artery, carrying oxygen-rich blood from the heart to the body, and the other from the vein, returning oxygen-poor blood to the heart.

Charlie studied the cord blood gas values, knowing as a nurse that the "reference" noted on the left side referred to each lab value's "normal range." When lab values were out of the normal range, they were followed by an *H, L,* or *C* for high, low, or critical, respectively, as indicated at the bottom left of the lab report. Charlie also knew that *ART CB* on the top row stood for "arterial cord blood," and *VEN CB* along the second row stood for "venous cord blood." She placed Isaac's cord blood gas values in front of her, read the high, low, and critical values, and then researched what condition correlated with those blood gas values. The diagnosis indicated by Isaac's blood gas values was respiratory acidosis, which causes the pO2 and pH of the blood to fall below the normal range and the pCO2 to rise above the normal range.

Next, Charlie researched how respiratory acidosis affects newborns and found that it was a medical emergency, and if left untreated, it could result in death. She continued her research and learned that respiratory acidosis can be caused by umbilical cord compression, especially over a prolonged period of time, and that it can result in neurological deficits, including hypoxic brain injuries, cognitive delays, seizures, and permanent disabilities.

Charlie's blood ran cold as she reread Isaac's pO2, ART CB, which stated the amount of oxygen that had been in his bloodstream. The CRITICAL value read: *9 C*. Charlie compared it to the normal range, 60–70, knowing the medical term for this condition was hypoxia. Her pulse quickened, her face flushing with anger as her heart sank. *Isaac's bloodstream had hardly any oxygen,* she screamed in silence. *He was suffocating the whole time! And since Isaac had the cord around his neck twice, the umbilical cord was likely being compressed, further decreasing his oxygen supply for a prolonged period of time!*

Charlie reread Isaac's pCO2, ART CB, which reflected the amount of carbon dioxide that had been in the bloodstream. The HIGH value read: *53 H*. Charlie compared it to the normal range, 26–40. Rage coursed through her. *Since Isaac was being suffocated, he couldn't breathe out the carbon dioxide that was building up in his bloodstream.* Next, she looked at Isaac's pH, ART CB again. The LOW value read: *7.26 L*. She compared it to the normal range, 7.35–7.45. Reading Isaac's lab values caused Charlie to become irate. Livid. Her heart broke, and she was filled with anger and hostility. She wanted revenge. She got up and started pacing the floor. *They fucking killed my son,* Charlie thought. It was becoming clear to her that Isaac had sustained a hypoxic brain injury at birth, one that had caused his cognitive delays, his seizures, and ultimately, his death.

Charlie sat back down and continued her research. She read that perinatal asphyxia remains a common cause of death of a fetus during labor. Furthermore, many newborn deaths can be avoided if a fetal heart rate monitor is used to alert staff to intervene at the first signs of distress—irregular heart rate and rhythm and non-reassuring prolonged heart decelerations.

Charlie shuffled through the putrid box and found a document titled *OB ADMISSION ASSESSMENT* and *MEDICAL SCREENING EXAM* and another document containing a vitals plot and vital signs

BLOOD BANK

TEST NAME BLOOD BANK ORDER
reference
units
collect time
12/24/00 20:15   SEP RPT

CORD GASES

TEST NAME	INSPIRED O2	PH, ART CB	PCO2, ART CB	PO2, ART CB	O2 SAT, ART CB	BICARB, ART CB	BASE EXCESS
reference		7.35-7.45	26-40	60-70		19-30	-10--2
units	O2		mmhg	mmhg	%	mEq/L	
collect time							
12/24/00 20:16	21	7.26 L	53 H	9 C	6	23	-4

TEST NAME	INSPIRED O2	PH, VEN CB	PCO2, VEN CB	PO2, VEN CB	O2 SAT, VEN CB	BICARB, VEN CB	BASE EXCESS
reference		7.35-7.45	40 - 50			19 - 30	
units	O2		mmhg	mmhg	%	mEq/L	
collect time							
12/24/00 20:16	21	7.34 L	36	23	37	19	-6

SPECIAL INSTRUCTIONS   collected   comments   CORDBLOOD FOR DIRECT COOMBS

0359-5191   12/24/00 20:15   12/24/00 22:22   completed

with a section below titled *ADDITIONAL INFORMATION*. She placed the papers in front of her and read the first document, which clearly stated that she had been at the hospital at 18:30 on December 23, 2000, with contractions every two to three minutes with "variable decelerations" noted. Still, they had sent her home, the midwife saying she could be in false labor. Next, Charlie read the nurse's note in the *ADDITIONAL INFORMATION* field on the second document, which she had charted later that night. It read: *02:27 24 Dec, TS,–NOTIFIED PHYSICIAN OF FHT'S DOWN IN THE 100'S WITH A COUPLE OF UC'S. ORDER TO SEND PT HOME.*

That proves that when I checked in at six thirty on December twenty-third, Isaac's fetal heart tracing already showed irregularities in heart rate and rhythm during uterine contractions. But he wasn't delivered at the first signs of distress; they waited for another twenty-five and a half hours until the nurse ran in, saying Isaac's heart was failing; then they did an emergency C-section! He'd still be alive if they had delivered Isaac at the first sign of distress, which the fetal heart monitor would have recorded . . . but of course, they haven't sent me those records because they probably don't want me to see them! I need Isaac's fetal heart monitor strips to prove that the hospital was negligent in failing to intervene in a timely manner per protocol.

Charlie found Isaac's *LABOR AND DELIVERY SUMMARY*, *NEONATAL DATA BASE AND PROFILE*, and *PROVIDER ORDER SHEET* from the ugly box and placed them in front of her. Then she read Isaac's Apgar score at the bottom of the *LABOR AND DELIVERY SUMMARY* and *NEONATAL DATA BASE AND PROFILE*. It read: *6 at 1 MIN Totals and 8 at 5 MIN Totals*. Then she researched the Apgar score—which stood for *appearance* (skin color), *pulse* (heart rate), *grimace* (reflexes), *activity* (muscle tone), and *respiration* (breathing rate)—on her computer and found that a newborn with a score between 7 and 10 was reassuring, a score between 4 and 6 was moderate, and a score between 0 and 3 was low.

Next, Charlie looked at the *PROVIDER ORDER SHEET*, documenting she had checked in at 9:50 on December 23, 2000, thirty-four hours before Isaac was born at 20:03 on December 24, 2000, as seen on the *LABOR AND DELIVERY SUMMARY*, but they had charted, *Duration of Total Labor: 10:04*. One of the hospital's many errors had

THROUGH THE DARKNESS

VITALS PLOT

	24 Dec 0124	24 Dec 0206	24 Dec 0209	24 Dec 0214	24 Dec 0227
▼ HR (BPM) ◇ RESP (RPM) ▽ ABP_S (mmHg) △ ABP_D (mmHg) ⊲ NBP_S (mmHg) ▷ NBP_D (mmHg) ■ NBP_S (mmHg) ○ TempF (De-

0124 Dec 24
WT (kg) 52.1

200
160
120
80
40
0

	YESTERDAY Dec 22 00	TODAY Dec 23 00
IN	0	0
OUT	0	0
NET	+0	+0
Time		Weight (kg)
0118 Dec 24		62.1

VITAL SIGNS

TempF	98.3	98.7
TempC	36.8	37.1
Temp Mode	TY	TY
HR	68	64
RESP	18	18
NBP_S	117	113
NBP_D	73	80
NBP_M	90	91
Pain Source	SP BK	
Pain Char	I	

(TS- entries between all values)

Additional Information

Event	
0209 24 Dec, ●, * : PT STATUS GIVEN TO CRM
0227 24 Dec, ■, ▼ : NOTIFIED ▬▬▬ OF FHT'S DOWN IN THE 100'S WITH A COUPLE OF UC'S. ORDER TO SEND PT HOME.

been starting the "Duration of Total Labor" clock when she checked into the hospital the second time rather than on the previous day when the midwife sent her home.

Finding the doctor's *DISCHARGE SUMMARY*, Charlie looked at the indication for the C-section. It read: *Pitocin augmentation and amniotomy had been performed but there had been essentially no descent of the fetal head and no continued dilation beyond 6 cm. An internal fetal monitor catheter was placed, confirming adequate quality contractions with essentially no cervical change over an excess of six hours. At this point, a cesarean section was selected and discussed with the patient, and informed consent obtained. During this time also numerous deep variable decelerations of the fetal heart rate tracing were noted, which were also somewhat non-reassuring.*

Charlie wanted to scream. *You mean an emergency C-section was performed at the last minute because Isaac's heart was failing,* she thought, coming unhinged. *As for the decelerations, they were first documented twenty-five and a half hours before the C-section. You had plenty of time to intervene, but then again, doctors and nurses always cover their asses when they're documenting!*

Charlie felt nauseous. She wiped the tears streaming down her face and read from the *NEONATAL DATA BASE AND PROFILE: Birth Wt: 5 lbs 15.40 oz* and *Birth Length: 19.25*. She turned the page and read the *Delivery Comments: Nuchal cord x2*, which she knew meant the umbilical cord had been around Isaac's neck twice at birth. Charlie imagined Isaac fighting for his life as he tried to descend into the birth canal, even as the umbilical cord tightening around his neck prevented him. To make matters worse, Isaac was not only being strangled, but the umbilical cord, like a rope wrapped on top of itself, was also being compressed, causing an inadequate oxygen supply to his brain for a prolonged period of time. Charlie felt sick. She knew it wasn't the hospital's fault the umbilical cord had been around Isaac's neck. But had they been watching the fetal heart monitor, they could have delivered him at the first signs of distress—NOT twenty-five and a half hours later when his heart was failing.

Charlie found the doctor's *OPERATIVE REPORT* and read, *Baby was taken to warmer, cried and breathed spontaneously, weighed 6 lb.*

DELIVERY SUMMARY For Baby A

Mode of Delivery	*Primary C/Section*	Presentation	*OP*
Episiotomy	*No epis*	Laceration	*None*
Specimen sent to Lab	*Cord blood Cord gasses*	Cord	*NUCHAL CORD X TWO*
Previous C-section	Yes X No	VBAC	*No*
Membranes Rupture	*Artificial ROM*	Date	*12/24/2000* Time *1640*
Fluid characteristics	*Clear*	Placenta	*Manual*

STAGES OF LABOR

	mm/dd/yyyy		hhmm	
Onset of Contractions Date:	*12/24/2000*	Time:	*1000*	Onset of Regular Contractions
Onset of 2nd Stage Date:	*N/A*	Time:	*N/A*	Complete
Onset of 3rd Stage and Delivery Date:	*12/24/2000*	Time:	*2003*	Delivery
Placental Delivery Date:	*12/24/2000*	Time:	*2004*	Placenta
Duration of 1st Stage:		Duration of 2nd Stage:		
Duration of 3rd Stage:	*00:01*	Duration of Total Labor:	*10:04*	

INFANT DATA Baby A

APGAR SCORE	*6*	1 MIN Totals	*8*	5 MIN Totals		10 MIN Totals
Sex	*Male*	Baby Band #	*64350*			
Weight	*5* lbs	*15.40* oz	*2.705*	Kg		
Note						

15.4 oz, and received an Apgar of 8 and 9, then compared it to the LABOR AND DELIVERY SUMMARY.

This is bullshit! Isaac weighed 5 pounds 15.4 ounces, and his Apgar scores were 6 and 8—they can't even get that right! Charlie stood and began pacing the floor, remembering the day after Isaac was born. The doctor had visited them in their hospital room and then asked them over to his house for dinner once they were discharged from the hospital. Having never met the on-call doctor before, Charlie and David found this very odd but accepted his invitation, not wanting to be rude. A couple of weeks later, Charlie, David, and Isaac went to the doctor's house for dinner. Upon their arrival, the doctor took Isaac from David, looking at him with questioning eyes, then laid him on the bed in his spare bedroom. After a dinner of salmon, rice, and salad with the doctor and his wife, Charlie and her family left. They never heard from the doctor's family again.

It appeared now that Isaac had undoubtedly sustained a preventable hypoxic brain injury at birth and that this had caused him to struggle with disabilities throughout his short life. Although this was the information she had been seeking, it now seemed more than Charlie could bear. Isaac had had a severe speech delay, hadn't talked until he was five, had been bullied at school because he was in special education, had suffered from poor self-esteem, and was publicly humiliated when forced to read aloud in front of the classroom due to his reading disabilities. Then he'd developed seizures and died. Now, the thought of the medical staff dressed in Santa hats, merrily drinking hot chocolate and exchanging brightly colored Christmas presents as Isaac slowly suffocated hour after hour, caused a desire for retribution to come to the forefront of Charlie's mind.

Charlie sent the hospital an email asking them if they'd found Isaac's fetal heart monitor strips, and if so, could they please send her a copy? Then she walked into Isaac's room, curled into a ball on the floor, where he'd died, and fell to pieces.

I don't understand. Isaac had nocturnal seizures. He only had seizures just before going to sleep or just after waking up, but never in the middle of the day; otherwise, I would have never left him home alone. Still, I should have been there, Charlie thought, trembling. *Good thing I became a nurse to take care of Isaac. . . . A lot of fucking good that did me!* Then she recalled the day Isaac died. She had been leaving work, and as she started to drive home, she called David, asking him to check on Isaac because she had called him three times, but he wasn't answering his phone. David quickly went to Charlie's house and found Isaac face down on the floor. He wasn't breathing and had no pulse. David immediately started CPR and called 911, then called her back in terror, saying Isaac was gone. While Charlie was still on the phone with David, the paramedics arrived, took over CPR, and got a pulse. Charlie frantically hung up and called Chris, telling him to go home. When Chris arrived, the ambulance was speeding away with Isaac in the back, the sirens screaming and lights flashing.

Driving from work to the hospital had been all Charlie could do. The phone call had filled her with horror, causing Charlie's blood vessels to dilate. As her blood sank to her lower extremities, her face turned white and she lost blood flow to her hands, causing them to tingle and go numb, making it difficult to drive. Charlie kept one hand on the steering wheel by locking her elbow into place while she lowered the other arm down to force blood back into it. Once she could feel her hand again, she used it to steer the car while she lowered the other arm. She repeated the process over and over, and eventually, as her heart compensated for the low blood pressure, she began to feel both of her hands again. As she drove into town, she saw the ambulance run through the red light at the intersection and chased it to the hospital.

Charlie ran into the emergency department and forced her way back to the bay where Isaac lay unresponsive. She looked at David, who was standing on the other side of Isaac, and then saw Chris standing near the head of the gurney. Not wanting to get in the way, Charlie walked over to Chris, and they stood there paralyzed as they watched the medical team intubate Isaac, start a central line, and pump him full of cardiac medications to keep his heart beating. Then the medical team asked Charlie, David, and Chris to stay in the ER waiting room while they took Isaac to get a CT of his brain, but Charlie refused, insisting on going with them. David, Chris, and Charlie followed the medical team as they pushed Isaac's gurney into the elevator. They got off on the second floor and waited outside the door of the CT room. After the procedure, they took Isaac to a hospital bay where they continued pumping him full of cardiac medications while the doctor assessed Isaac's neurological function.

First, the doctor shined a penlight in Isaac's eyes, but his dilated pupils remained fixed. Next, the doctor brushed Isaac's cornea with a brush. Still, Isaac's vacant eyes remained fixed. It was then that Charlie knew Isaac was dead. She ran out of the room into an adjoining bay, where she stood immobilized by horror. Chris and a nurse ran after her, but Charlie refused to let them touch her. A few minutes later, realizing she needed to be near Isaac, Charlie rushed back into the room where Isaac lay dying. She lay beside him among the tangles of the ventilator hose and IV lines as David and Chris stood on opposite sides of the hospital bed, holding Isaac's hands.

Charlie lay there with her hand on Isaac's chest for over an hour. As she did, it slowly came to her what she must do—she had to let him go. She knew Isaac was already brain-dead—that he had died in his room and that the only thing that kept his heart racing at 140 beats per minute was the cardiac medication, which only prolonged the inevitable. Not wanting Isaac imprisoned in that nightmarish state, Charlie sat up and asked David if he'd agree to let Isaac go. David nodded, tears streaming down his face. Charlie left the room, found the doctor, and asked her to pull the cardiac medication and the ventilator, and moments later, Isaac was pronounced dead.

Now, Charlie lay on Isaac's bedroom floor, wanting to die.

Since I wasn't there to save Isaac, I should suffocate to death like he did. I could take his ashes with me and bury my guilt and shame in a watery grave at the bottom of the ocean.

15

NONLINEAR TIME
August 19, 2017

CHRIS FELT CONFLICTED as he drove to his second home in Sun Valley, Idaho. On the one hand, he was uncomfortable leaving Charlie home alone. It had been only four months since Isaac died, but her new job at the mental health clinic had scheduled her to work over the weekend, and she couldn't get the time off. On the other hand, he wanted to see the total solar eclipse that was going to occur in two days, and the location of his Elkhorn Village condominium just happened to be in the seventy-mile-wide pathway of its optimal viewing. It was a once-in-a-lifetime event, so Chris had reluctantly decided to go, and he planned to see the eclipse and play a round of golf while he was there.

As Chris drove, he acknowledged to himself that even if Charlie hadn't been scheduled to work, she still wouldn't have come with him. Idaho stirred up too many memories that she had, more or less, put to rest. Charlie's childhood in the Wood River Valley sharply contrasted with the lives of the vacationers who visited the world-renowned ski resort. She had merely survived, while they enjoyed reading Hemingway by the fireplace after a rigorous day of world-class downhill skiing, golfing, mountain biking, or fly-fishing. Chris understood why Charlie hadn't come with him, but he missed her and dreaded sleeping alone.

As he drove through the Wood River Valley, he passed the Hailey airport, which was lined with private jets, then continued down Main Street to the Bullion Street intersection, where he stopped, waiting for the red light to turn green. When he glanced to his left, he saw Carbonate Mountain and remembered the time when Charlie, Isaac, and he had gone there to scatter some of Shane's ashes in the Big Wood River. Shane's sudden death had devastated his sisters—Karen, Teresa, Wilma, and Charlie—whom he had tried to care for, often at his own expense. His sisters hoped his death had been a tragic accident and not suicide, but they were uncertain.

After scattering Shane's ashes, Charlie had shown Isaac and Chris the small red house on the corner of Bullion Street and Poulsen Road, where she grew up. In front of the house was a small creek, where Charlie used to catch the rainbow trout that got trapped under the bridge as the creek dried up in the fall. After catching them, she then returned them to the Big Wood River.

The light turned green, and Chris continued driving toward Sun Valley while remembering Charlie's stories about Big Charlie. After Charlie's dad deserted his family, Hazel had felt she needed someone to help her raise her five kids. She met Charles, a tall man with a shaved head and goatee who worked as a chef at one of the local restaurants in Hailey, and they were married at the Blaine County Courthouse in 1972. To eliminate confusion, everyone referred to the children's stepfather as Big Charlie and Charlie as Little Charlie. Big Charlie was an overbearing man whose insecurities played out in his mistreatment of Hazel and the kids.

One evening during dinner, Big Charlie had dished peas, mashed potatoes, and a piece of chicken onto Little Charlie's plate. Not wanting her peas to touch her mashed potatoes, Little Charlie separated them with her fork, which irritated him, so he mixed her peas into her mashed potatoes and then forced her to eat them. It caused Little Charlie to gag and throw up on her plate, infuriating him further. He screamed at her then, forcing Little Charlie to sit at the kitchen table until she finished eating *everything* on her plate.

After that, Little Charlie stayed away from Big Charlie as much as possible. Her favorite place to play was outside along the creek that ran in front of her house next to the Hailey City park. One summer, she befriended a stray cat living there. Throughout the summer, Little

Charlie snuck food from the kitchen and gave it to the thin gray tabby, and soon, they were fast friends. The cat waited for Little Charlie every day, purring and arching his bony back when she came to feed him and scratch his neck. As Little Charlie gained the cat's trust, he ventured closer to her house, but when Big Charlie saw the feral cat in the yard and learned that Little Charlie had been feeding him, he was furious. If there was any creature he despised, it was cats. They were notorious for following their own rules, and his inability to control them made him feel small. Inadequate. Big Charlie believed that a dead cat was a good cat and insisted that Little Charlie catch the stray so he could dispose of it, but she refused to betray her friend.

Big Charlie called animal control, and they came and took the stray cat away in a burlap bag. Little Charlie never saw her friend again, and for disobeying Big Charlie, she was forced to sit on her bed for two weeks. She was only allowed off her bed to go to the bathroom or eat at the kitchen table, and her bedroom door had to remain open so Big Charlie could look down the hall while watching TV to make sure she followed his orders. Little Charlie would get another week for disobeying him if she were caught off her bed, so she sat on the top of her bed for two weeks, counting the number of yellow and orange daisies on her seventies-style bedspread. She resented everything about Big Charlie, including sharing her name. Still, these events paled in comparison to the time he chased her sister Teresa around the house with a butcher knife and the time he beat her brother, Shane, unconscious in a fury of rage while drinking.

Chris's thoughts returned to the present day as he drove into Ketchum, passed Whiskey Jacques and the Pioneer Saloon, and then turned right on Fourth Street and parked at Giacobbi Square. He bought some groceries at Atkinsons' Market, then drove to the condominium he had purchased with his inheritance money from his mother—with the plan to spend his days biking, golfing, and skiing Bald Mountain after he retired.

Once inside, Chris put away his groceries and called Charlie.

"Hi, handsome. Are you there yet?"

"Yeah, I just got here. How are you? How was your first day at your new job?"

"I'm okay, but I don't like my job," Charlie said. "Yes, it pays more and it's in town, but I go through three security checks to my little cage, where I hand out meds all day. I feel terrible for the people I care for. Most of them have lived through nightmarish childhoods, and as a result, they have poor coping skills and have resorted to alcohol and substance abuse. I'm not sure this environment is the best place for me to work right now."

"It sounds depressing."

"It is, and to make it even worse, one of my patients had a seizure today. When I rolled him onto his side, I looked into his eyes, and his pupils were like saucers . . . like . . ." Charlie stopped, not able to finish her sentence. "It was all I could do not to lose it at work."

"Maybe you should keep looking for a different job?" Chris said. "I know they're going to start building a new rehabilitation hospital and a veterans' hospital in town soon, because I have to approve their stormwater permits. Maybe you should apply when they open."

"That's a good idea. Let me know when you hear more."

"Okay, I will," Chris promised. "I wish you were here so we could play chess and watch the eclipse together from the top of Dollar Mountain."

"That would be nice," Charlie said, then changed the subject. "By the way, during my lunch, I called an attorney about Isaac's medical records. Apparently, after a person dies, you can only argue a wrongful death case. I would have had to argue a medical negligence case while Isaac was still alive. The attorney also said there would be no direct evidence that the brain injury caused the seizures, because Isaac's seizures started when he was fourteen. That means the hospital is going to get away with causing Isaac's brain injury and, ultimately, his death," Charlie said, her voice trembling. "But I still want Isaac's fetal heart monitor strips, which the hospital says they're still looking for. I at least have the right to know what happened!"

Chris heard Charlie crying. "I can't believe they're going to get away with it. It's so unfair to Isaac! I shouldn't have left you while you're dealing with all this. Do you want me to come home?"

"No, it's okay. Stay there and enjoy the eclipse, but call me and let me know what it looks like from there. I'm sure your view will be better than mine."

"Okay, but if you change your mind, let me know."

"I will. When are you going to Dollar Mountain?"

"I plan to leave here by eight thirty on Monday morning and be there by ten, when the eclipse starts. I'll take my backpack so I can eat lunch while I watch the moon pass in front of the sun. It will be kind of cool because I'll be completely in the shadow of the moon."

"That'll be cool," Charlie agreed. "I plan to stay home and watch it from the deck. We can call each other and compare notes."

"Sounds good," Chris said. "I'm going to get off the phone. I need to order dinner and go pick it up. I haven't eaten since breakfast, and I'm starving."

"Okay, love you, handsome. I'll talk to you later."

"Love you too."

After hanging up, Chris called the Rickshaw, his favorite restaurant in Ketchum, and ordered Vietnamese caramel pork ribs with spicy Thai chilies and pork pot stickers with sesame-soy sweet chili sauce. After picking up his take-out order, he ate dinner on his back deck overlooking Dollar Mountain, remembering the time when Charlie, Isaac, and he had ordered takeout from the Rickshaw. Charlie and Isaac had stopped to visit him on their way to Banff, Canada, and after a fun weekend, they'd invited him to join them. Their favorite hike in Banff was to the Plain of Six Glaciers Teahouse, which had been built by the Canadian Pacific Railway in 1927 and was preserved in its original form, including no electricity. The kitchen was at the center of the quaint two-story log cabin, and the upper and lower decks were furnished with wooden tables and chairs painted in various colors. Visitors enjoyed eating lunch while taking in the stunning mountains as the prayer flags tied to the cabin's beams gently blew in the high mountain glacier air. While Charlie, Chris, and Isaac sat on the upper deck drinking coffee, eating biscuits with jam, and playing cards, the turquoise waters of Lake Louise shimmered at the trailhead far below. A Clark's nutcracker, accustomed to being fed by visitors, had landed on the railing, taken a piece of biscuit from Charlie's hand, and then flown away to a nearby tree, where he ate his prize before returning and begging for more: a perfect moment—a perfect day.

Now Isaac was dead, and Chris knew Charlie would never visit Sun Valley with him again, let alone live there.

On Sunday, Chris thought about selling his retirement home as he vacuumed and dusted, then went and played a round of golf at the Sun Valley Resort. After breakfast on Monday, he hiked to the top of Dollar Mountain, where a mob of people had already gathered. While the eclipse traced its path across the United States from Oregon to South Carolina, spectators stood wide-eyed in the moon's shadow as it covered the sun. The magnificent rays of the sun's corona sprayed outward from behind the brilliant-orange moon. As Chris gazed upward, he heard his phone ring.

"Hey, beautiful. I wish you could see this. It's incredible!"

"I'm so glad you're there to enjoy the eclipse. It looks pretty awesome even from here."

"It's really cool," Chris exclaimed. "And there are so many people with all kinds of glasses to view the eclipse that it's kind of crazy."

"That sounds fun," Charlie said. "I just wanted to tell you I love you, but I'm going to let you go so you can enjoy your awesome view. It won't last very long and we can talk later."

"Okay, I love you too. I'll call you later this evening."

—

Charlie stood outside on the back deck, watching the eclipse as the moon moved away from the sun and the sky gradually became brighter. She glanced down at the street, recognizing a woman and her two children she had seen a few months earlier. The woman pushed her toddler in a stroller as her young daughter, dressed in a red-and-white checkered dress, ran ahead to the mailboxes. Her ponytail, tied with a red ribbon, swayed from side to side. The young woman put her mail in the stroller's pocket, then turned around and headed back the way they'd come. They looked so lovely that it made Charlie feel sad. She went inside to the kitchen table and continued reading *Biocentrism* by Robert Lanza, picking up where she and Chris had left off a few weeks before.

Charlie read the text several times, trying to understand superposition, collapsed wave functions, and how physicists had photographed entangled particles reacting to each other even though the physicist had split them apart. She studied the figures that explained the setup and finally understood that the entangled particles were linked by some unidentified connection regardless of the distance between them. *I hope some of those invisible threads connect Isaac and me. Maybe this explains how Isaac sends me messages in my dreams.*

She turned the book over on the kitchen table, pulled up a barstool at the kitchen counter, and searched the internet on her computer for Robert Lanza's website. She read the cover of his second book, *Beyond Biocentrism: Rethinking Time, Space, Consciousness, and the Illusion of Death*. Feeling drawn in, she read a couple of articles by Robert Lanza: "There Is No Death, Only a Series of Eternal 'Nows,'" in *Aeon*, and "The True Nature of Death and Eternity," in *Psychology Today*.

After reading the articles, Charlie tried to fathom an infinite number of "now" moments in the universes and how they all exist simultaneously in a nonlinear fashion. Then she considered Lanza's idea that at death, our bodies die, but our consciousness simply moves from one "now" moment to another. *If I understand what Lanza is saying, Isaac's consciousness survived his death, and while he was alive, that was his collapsed wave function, but now he's returned to superposition—very intriguing.*

Charlie continued to read. Dr. Lanza backed his theories by quoting some of the great minds who came before him: "The human mind cannot be absolutely destroyed with the body, but there remains of it something which is eternal," wrote Benedict de Spinoza. "There's no way to remove the observer—us—from our perceptions of the world," said Stephen Hawking, who also said, "The past, like the future, is indefinite and exists only as a spectrum of possibilities." And Albert Einstein had written, after learning that his lifelong friend Michele Besso had died, "Now he has also gone ahead of me in parting from this strange world. That means nothing. For us believing physicists, the distinction between past, present, and future has only the significance of a however tenacious illusion."

Charlie felt a sense of cautious hope. Perhaps there was something to what all these great minds were saying. Maybe what they said was true.

Maybe she'd find Isaac along her path again, in some other "now" moment in nonlinear time.

16

THE QUIET OF THE STORM
December 7, 2017

SITTING AT HER COMPUTER while Chris was at work, Charlie continued looking through the photographs stored on her external hard drive. Four days earlier, she had looked through hundreds of pictures, and today, after completing three twelve-hour shifts in a row, she picked up where she had left off. As an artist, Charlie enjoyed photography, and she took numerous photographs of her subjects to use as references for her paintings. The result was tens of thousands of images securely stored in her photographic vault, a record of the main events in her life. The further she went back chronologically into the hard drive's files, the younger she and her loved ones became. She clicked the mouse, opening up one more frame into her past; it was a photograph of Isaac wearing a jester suit when he was eight years old.

Charlie had made Isaac's jester suit by painting aqua-green diamonds on a pair of forest-green pajamas. She then decorated the collar with mauve and blue triangles with small golden bells sewn onto the ends and made a hat to match. In the photo, Isaac's face was painted white with large fading blue diamonds painted over his eyes. He wore an almost imperceptible smile, and his eyes—the quiet of the storm. Charlie had painted a portrait of Isaac based on this photo, then hung it above Isaac's bed, where it remained.

After a moment of reflection, Charlie continued scrolling through the photographs, then stopped at a picture of Isaac dressed in a blue-and-orange plaid shirt, sitting in a small wooden chair, drawing pictures. One drawing was of a lizard with a curled tail, wearing roller skates while shooting fire from its mouth and deploying missiles from guns mounted on its back. Another drawing was of a flower. Isaac had written: I ♡ You Mom underneath it. Charlie had forgotten about the photograph, but when she saw it now, she instantly knew she wanted to paint a portrait of him sitting there, looking so innocent and beautiful.

I think I'll paint it in black and white. Life is full of color, but death is black and white—you're either dead or not.

As Charlie contemplated the painting's composition, she thought about Django, Isaac's best friend, who was devastated and had suffered dissociative blackouts ever since learning Isaac had died. Django said his blackouts came when he remembered Isaac having seizures. Whenever that occurred, he was no longer aware of his surroundings and couldn't remember what had happened during his dissociative blackouts. Later, Django told Charlie, "I see the world in color, but I *feel* in black and white."

Then Charlie thought of her old art professor, who had informed the class they were not allowed to use Ivory Black or Phthalo Blue paint, saying they weren't true colors. He'd suggested using French Ultramarine for Phthalo Blue and combining dark pigments to replace the Ivory Black. Although Charlie preferred French Ultramarine over Phthalo Blue, she considered black an essential tool that shouldn't be omitted from an artist's palette. The best result an artist could achieve using the professor's method was to arrive at varying degrees of muddy brown—a poor substitute for black as far as Charlie was concerned. After all, what color is the night sky? Preferring to make up her own rules, Charlie had dropped out of the course two weeks after it started.

Returning to the present, Charlie went to their spare room, put her coffee on the desk, and pulled a long rectangular cardboard box out from underneath her painting table. She took out a heavy roll of Lanaquarelle three-hundred-pound, cold-pressed watercolor paper, a type she preferred because she could apply many layers of paint without eroding its surface. As a result, her paintings had rich hues rather than the usual pastel colors often seen in watercolor paintings. Another quality Charlie liked about this paper was that the pigments didn't bleed; they kept a sharp line, allowing her to use the white of the paper rather than white paint. This was important, as she considered using white paint an admission of a mistake. White paint was only needed to cover up an error when starting with a foundation of white paper.

Charlie laid a clean bed sheet on the floor, unrolled the Lanaquarelle watercolor paper, and cut off three feet with a heavy pair of scissors. Then she laid the paper on her painting table, covered it with a thick canvas fabric, and secured it into place with two felt-covered one-by-fours and clamps to flatten it in preparation for her new portrait.

Placing the paper roll back into its cardboard box, Charlie

remembered standing in front of Van Gogh's 1887 *Self-Portrait* at the Art Institute of Chicago. Vincent's eyes looked directly at the viewer, his face gaunt and forlorn. He wore a white shirt under a brown jacket with a blue-trimmed lapel. His jacket looked brown, but on closer inspection, it became apparent that Vincent had painted it with small brushstrokes of dark-green and dark-red paint, which appeared brown only from a distance. His rust-colored beard and mustache were a sharp contrast to his pale face, and the background was a sea of small blue, green, and orange brushstrokes.

Charlie remembered looking into Vincent's eyes and sensing him looking back at her. He was in there . . . looking out through the eyes he had painted more than a hundred years ago! Somehow, his self-portrait embodied a part of him. Captivated, Charlie had stood mesmerized in front of the painting, feeling his presence through some unexplained connection. She remembered looking around to see if everyone else was experiencing the same thing, but the other patrons merely paused at Van Gogh's masterpiece, then moved on. It was an extraordinary encounter that she always remembered afterward but never understood.

Although Van Gogh is dead, a part of him is still alive in his paintings, Charlie thought. *Maybe I can give Isaac Van Gogh eyes—eyes that look into this world from the other side. That way, I can keep a little bit of him alive forever.*

Putting the paper roll underneath her painting table, Charlie returned to the present. She walked to the kitchen and checked her email, finding a message from the hospital that made her instantly livid. On November 3, the hospital had requested a thirty-day extension to continue looking for Isaac's fetal heart monitor strips. Last week, on November 30, they'd said they had found Isaac's fetal heart monitor strips but that the company that downloaded them was out of business, so the hospital was working with IT to print them. Now, a new email stated that they had only nine pages of the fetal heart monitor strips, with readings from 7:55 to 8:30 a.m. *It's been more than seven months since Isaac died. I've tried to give them time, but they just keep changing their story again and again.* Feeling stonewalled, Charlie considered various options. *The names of all the people who did this to Isaac are on his medical records. Maybe I'll—*

Too angry to reply to the hospital's email, Charlie paced the floor. Preferring to choose her vices so they didn't choose her, she picked up her small David Bowie notebook featuring the *Low* album cover. She turned to her to-do list, which she maintained in order to give herself a constructive outlet to work out her anger, grief, and frustration. She referred to the list whenever she felt worried about making choices she'd regret. Every time she checked something off the list, she imagined Isaac being proud of her. Charlie looked at her list of sixty-one things, then wrote down number sixty-two: Give Isaac Van Gogh eyes. Then she restarted at the top of the list, looking through it for something to work on while she curbed her vengeful thoughts.

The list read: Take the dogs for a walk; plant a tree; write a poem; forgive my dad; revisit the places I went with Isaac; go to some of the places I wanted to take Isaac before he passed, including having lunch at the Eiffel Tower; make Isaac's favorite dishes like angel biscuits; donate canned goods to the homeless shelter; go for a hike; research ants; create an endowment at CCC and NAU; give Django a new computer for school; make the green choice; pick up trash in the neighborhood; always clean up after yourself at hotels and restaurants; work out on the treadmill and floor exercises; leave a random coworker a Post-it note that will make them smile; work in the garden; build a bee box and bug hotel; go birding; volunteer; read a book; donate ant exhibits to insectariums and museums....

There, Charlie stopped short. *That's it. . . . I almost forgot. I need to order the new formicaria for the queens.* She got up to check on the honeypot and harvester queens.

After noticing that the larvae hadn't completed their life cycle in the last five months since they'd collected the queens, Charlie had contacted several experts online. They had suggested she place the queens in new formicaria made by Tar Heel Ants from Raleigh, North Carolina. As Charlie finished ordering the new formicaria, her sister Teresa called.

"Hi," Charlie said, her voice strained.

"I'm just checking on you," Teresa said. "It sounds like you're having a difficult day."

"I'm very frustrated with the hospital." Charlie filled her in on the newest email. "They're stonewalling me, and I fucking hate it!"

"That sounds frustrating; I wish there were something I could do," Teresa said. "Maybe watching a good movie would help take your mind off things?"

"Yeah, maybe that's not a bad idea. I'm too irritated to work on the foundation or on anything, for that matter," Charlie said. She thanked her sister, then suggested they reconnect in a few days.

"Okay, but text me tomorrow and let me know how you're doing."

"I will," Charlie promised.

Not knowing what else to do, Charlie took Teresa's advice, curled up in bed with Cobalt and Dexter, and scrolled through a selection of TV series, trying to decide what to watch while waiting for Chris to come home from work. At one point, she came across *Medium*, starring Patricia Arquette. She watched the trailer and was intrigued, not realizing Patricia Arquette was playing Allison DuBois, the psychic medium Nancy had mentioned. *I guess I'll watch this, since Nancy suggested I see a medium. Maybe I'll learn something.*

When Chris got home, Dexter and Cobalt jumped off the bed and ran to greet him. Charlie turned off the TV partway through the first episode of *Medium* and joined Chris and the dogs in the kitchen.

"Hey, beautiful, I've had a rough day at work. I thought we could go out to Hiro's for dinner." Chris cracked open a beer and took a long drink. "I'm hankering for some sushi and hot green tea."

"Sure; I guess it could be our late Thanksgiving dinner."

"I always loved that about you guys; you were never afraid to make up your own rules."

Charlie smiled. "One year, when I was in nursing school and didn't have time to cook a big dinner, Isaac and I went there for sushi because, one, Isaac loved Japanese food, and two, they're always open on Thanksgiving Day. After that, it just became our tradition."

"And Isaac thought it was great. You guys knew how to make little things like that so much fun," Chris added. "What were you watching?"

"*Medium*. It's about this woman who helps the police by talking with the dead. It seems kind of interesting," Charlie said. "Do you want to watch it together when we get back from dinner?"

"Sure, I'm game," Chris said, finishing his beer. "Let's go."

Charlie put on her jacket, and then they went out for a late Thanksgiving sushi dinner.

17

BORROWED TIME
The Other Side

RAYMOND STEADIED his stance, pulled his black Stetson hat down over his eyes to shade them from the bright sun, then placed his thumb against the toe of his horseshoe and raised it to the side of his face. He eyed the stake thirty-seven feet in front of him, lowered his arm down and back to gain momentum, then swung his arm forward and finally pitched the horseshoe. It flipped over as it glided through the air, landing with a solid clang around the stake.

"That's a three-point ringer," Ethel said, cheering her teammate.

Raymond tipped his hat and sent his second horseshoe flying through the air, landing a few inches from the stake.

"Nice job, Dad," Melba said. "But don't count your chickens before they hatch!"

Smiling, Raymond and Ethel stepped aside, allowing their opposing team, Hazel and Melba, to take their turn.

Melba raised her horseshoe near her face, concentrated for a moment, then sent it sailing through the air in a graceful arc, landing it directly on top of Raymond's.

"That's a dead ringer!" Melba exclaimed, doing a little jig.

"Great job, sis!" Hazel grinned, patting Melba's back.

Melba eyed the distant stake, then pitched her second horseshoe. Hazel and Melba held their breath as they watched the horseshoe sail through the air, land on its side, and come to rest against the stake, causing Melba and Hazel to giggle like schoolgirls.

"One point for us," Hazel called to Solomon, who was sitting at the picnic table keeping score.

Solomon announced, "Raymond and Ethel have twenty-one points, and you girls have twenty-three. You're in the lead, but not by much. I wouldn't let the horses out of the barn just yet."

Sitting next to Solomon, Shane and Isaac cheered for Hazel and Melba as the sun warmed their backs. Kéyah dropped a stick at Shane's feet. He picked it up and threw it toward the hitching post, where songbirds sang and fluttered about in the cottonwood trees, the delicate northern bluebells blooming along the riverbank under the clear blue sky.

Alma, standing in the kitchen wearing a wild rose–patterned dress with oxford shoes, took off her white ruffled apron and hung it up on a hook near the sink. Her short dark hair, loosely curled around her face, complemented her dark eyes. She picked up a fresh batch of dough gods, fried bread sprinkled with cinnamon sugar, walked out to the picnic table, and sat down with Solomon, Shane, and Isaac.

Melba, Hazel, Raymond, and Ethel took a break from their game to join everyone at the picnic table. The aroma caused their mouths to water, and the delicious taste brought happiness to everyone as they licked the cinnamon sugar off their fingers. After finishing their treats, they quenched their thirst with frog lemonade made with thinly sliced strawberries, lemons, and crushed ice.

Melba, Hazel, Raymond, and Ethel thanked Alma for the treats, then walked back to the horseshoe pit and started their next round while Solomon kept score, and Alma, Shane, and Isaac visited.

"Honey, were you able to get your mom to book a reading with Allison DuBois?" Alma asked, looking at Isaac.

"Not exactly, but I was able to get Nancy to suggest it might be helpful for her to see a psychic medium. She mentioned Allison specifically, but my mom has already forgotten her name because her mind is on other things." Isaac frowned. "Still, I'm hoping she'll remember her name because she started watching *Medium*, the television series based on Allison DuBois. I hope one thing will lead to another, and eventually, my mom will book a reading with her."

"At least she's heading in the right direction." Alma took a sip of her lemonade. "Since the living have free will, playing marionette-master has its limitations. They can choose to heed the calling, put it off, or dismiss it altogether."

"Definitely," Isaac agreed. "We can pull some strings, but ultimately, what they choose to do rests in their own hands. Things don't always go as planned, but I won't stop trying, because I have to save my mom!"

"Just keep at it. Hopefully, your mom will go see Allison eventually," Alma said.

"I will. I'm just impatient. Watching my mom struggle with so much pain is difficult for me." Isaac frowned. "I just want to fix everything right *now*, but I know I can't."

"Maybe you could play marionette-master with another person near your mom, like you did with Nancy. Only this time, you could influence an old friend or someone she bumps into on the street," Shane suggested. "If she hears the same suggestion from different people, she might get the idea that the universe is trying to tell her something."

"Charlie thinks it's impossible for her ever to be happy again," Alma said, "but all we need to do is help her realize you're still with her, and then she and Chris will be able to find some happiness despite the difficult challenges they're facing in life."

Shane put his arm around Isaac. "Like in the fable I told you, she'll smile from the top of the mountain, knowing you're standing by her side."

"Well, I must admit my mom is very stubborn. If anyone can climb to the top of the mountain, she can." Isaac grinned. "Let's see if watching *Medium* will lead her to Allison DuBois. In the meantime, I like your idea of influencing another person near her."

"It's a good idea," Shane and Alma agreed.

Hearing Melba giggle, Isaac, Shane, and Alma watched Hazel step up to the foul line, take her turn, and score three points.

"Alma, when we were growing up, Mom always told us how much she loved you," Shane said to his grandmother. "I remember her telling me you were always an angel and never raised your voice. She told me how you used to make mud dishes, then let them dry in the sun, and you'd play with them like you were having a tea party."

"I adored all my children." Alma smiled. "Being a mom was my greatest joy, especially when we stopped everything and made time to be together. It's not really what you do that matters; it's that you take the time to show your children that you care and don't get mad at them over frivolous things, like when my girls wore my dress shoes. I just smiled and told them they looked like Minnie Mouse."

Isaac laughed. "I can just see my grandma and Melba walking around in your high heels—they must have been adorable."

"They were," Alma agreed. "All those memories are the best moments in life."

"It's best to use time wisely because it can be fleeting. One second, you're walking down the railroad tracks, and the next second, you're looking down at your body. I didn't see that one coming!" Shane joked. "If you don't show your friends and family you love them, you might run out of time."

"And it's good to right your wrongs before it's too late," Isaac added. "People leave so many things unsaid and unfinished, then end up regretting it."

Just then, their attention was drawn to the game as Solomon announced the winners. "Melba and Hazel win forty-one to thirty-seven."

Melba and Hazel jumped up and down like schoolgirls.

Next, new teams replaced the first ones. This time, Solomon and Alma played against Isaac and Shane while Raymond kept score.

Solomon stepped up to the foul line, steadied his stance, and pitched his first horseshoe. It sailed through the air and circled the stake with a solid clang. Then Solomon pitched his second horseshoe, landing squarely on top of his first horseshoe.

"Woo-hoo, six points," Alma cheered.

Solomon tipped his head, then stepped back to let Isaac take his turn.

Isaac eyed Shane. "It looks like we're in big trouble, and I've never even played this game before.... We're going to get creamed!"

"Ya think!" Shane laughed. "We'll need all the help we can get, so you better use the junior foul line; it's closer. I'll show you how to pitch your first couple of horseshoes, and then you should be good to go."

Taking Shane's advice, Isaac stepped up to the junior foul line, and Shane demonstrated how to throw a horseshoe. Isaac then raised his horseshoe close to his cheek, eyed his target twenty feet in front of him, and pitched it, landing his horseshoe just before the sandpit.

"Not bad, little man. Just use a little more force so it lands inside the sandpit."

Following Shane's instructions, Isaac pitched his second horseshoe. It landed inside the sandpit, about a foot away from the stake.

"Good job," Shane encouraged him. "You'll get the hang of it in no time."

From the picnic table, Raymond announced, "Six points to Solomon and Alma."

They gathered their horseshoes from the sandpit, and then Alma took her turn as Shane and Isaac continued talking.

"About a week before I crossed over, I subconsciously knew I was going to die," Isaac told him. "I wasn't afraid for myself, but I was very concerned about my mom."

"Can you explain?" Shane asked. "I died suddenly from getting hit by a train, and it took me a while to realize I was dead. Clearly, you had a very different experience."

"Yes, I started having seizures when I was fourteen. One of my exit points could have been then, but I couldn't do that to my mom, so I lived on borrowed time as long as I could for her sake. But by the time I was sixteen, my time was running out, and honestly, I was ready to go because my life was very difficult," Isaac said. "Still, I was very worried about my mom. I faced two choices: I could either die in her arms or have a seizure in the middle of the day, when she wouldn't be home to prevent me from crossing over. I just couldn't die in my mom's arms. . . . I couldn't do that to her, so I chose to have a seizure in the middle of the day. I wanted to spare her the pain, but before I left, I sent her a text message of two hearts so she'd always know I loved her and she was my best friend. I felt terrible about leaving, but I was out of borrowed time."

"It was sweet of you to hang on as long as you could for your mom's sake, and I'm sure she'd really appreciate it if she knew," Shane said.

Isaac sighed. "But I wish my mom knew it wasn't her fault so she wouldn't feel guilty for not being there when I died. I planned it that way because I thought it would be better than dying in her arms, and as it turned out, both things happened. The paramedics restarted my heart after I crossed, so I was forced back into my body. The best part about that was I can still remember feeling my mom's heart beating as she lay next to me in the hospital bed . . . then she let me go."

"One day, you can tell her you meant to spare her by crossing over in the middle of the day, and it will be okay," Shane said. "Death can be heart-wrenching, but you did what you thought was best, and that's all you could've done."

Isaac nodded.

"Shane, it's your turn," Alma said, stepping aside. "I'm afraid I'm not very good at this game either. I barely got my horseshoes in the sandpit. I think Solomon's going to make all of us look bad!"

"Okay, Shane, we don't have any points," Isaac laughed. "It's up to you to save the game!"

Eyeing his target, Shane carefully pitched both horseshoes and scored two points.

"Way to go," Isaac said, high-fiving Shane.

"The score is six to two," Raymond announced.

Shane and Isaac retrieved their horseshoes, and then Solomon took his turn.

"Hey, Isaac, I have another game I like to play," Shane said. "The objective of the game is to get someone to laugh, and it has to be a real laugh . . . one that you can hear, not a smile—smiles don't count."

"That sounds fun. Who should we try to make laugh?"

"I think we should target Alma. She's been a doll, making those delicious pastries and lemonade for us."

"I'm in, but what are we going to do to make her laugh?"

"I have an idea." Smiling mischievously, Shane pulled a shiny gold coin out of the front pocket of his vest and showed it to Isaac. "Let's drop it on the ground near the sandpit and then try to get her to find it."

"That's a great idea!" Isaac grinned. "I think I'm going to like this game."

Shane inconspicuously dropped the coin about a foot from the sandpit, hoping Alma would see it the next time they returned to retrieve their horseshoes. However, after several more rounds of horseshoes and missed opportunities, it was clear that Isaac and Shane needed to step up their game. They were running out of time because Alma and Solomon were close to winning the game. The next time they were near the lucky coin, Shane purposely distracted Solomon while Isaac pretended to be preoccupied, tying his shoelaces. Seeing the others were busy, Alma knelt to gather the horseshoes and noticed something shiny on the ground.

"Look, I found a lucky coin," Alma said, picking it up. "God knows I need all the luck I can get. I haven't scored a single point yet!"

"What a lucky find!" Isaac smiled, eyeing Shane.

As Alma showed Solomon the coin, Shane whispered to Isaac, "Smiles don't count. She has to laugh so we can hear it."

"Dang it!" Isaac frowned.

As Alma stepped up to the foul line, she rubbed the lucky coin between her fingers, made a wish, and then put it in her dress pocket. Next, she raised her horseshoe near her face, eyed her target, and pitched her horseshoe. It arced through the air, turned over midair, and landed squarely around the stake with a solid clang.

"Woo-hoo, that's game point!" Alma laughed, pulling the coin from her pocket. "I think I'd better hang on to my lucky charm!"

18

UNDER WRAPS
March 27, 2018

WHILE DRINKING COFFEE, Charlie stood at the kitchen counter and cut an apple into half-inch squares. She then put six bottle caps onto a small cutting board, placed one apple square in each, and dabbed them with thin honey water, which soaked into the apple squares like a sponge. Next, she pulled a jar of small frozen crickets from the freezer, placed six of them into another bottle cap, and returned the jar to the freezer.

After getting ready for work, Chris walked into the kitchen and kissed Charlie on the cheek.

"I'm just going to feed the ants, but I'll be back in a minute," Charlie said.

"Okay, I'm going to get a cup of coffee and read the news."

Charlie walked into Isaac's bedroom and placed the cutting board on top of a piece of felt on Isaac's dresser. Knowing that the ants reacted adversely to the slightest movement, Charlie carefully placed everything on a piece of felt to reduce the vibration. She picked up the first bottle cap with her reverse tweezers, opened the lid to Queen Ant Melba's foraging area, and carefully placed the bottle cap inside. Immediately, the yellow workers, who lived solely on liquid food, started drinking the sweet honey water from the apple. Next, she tweezed a frozen cricket, placed it in the foraging area, and watched the workers drag it into the formicarium. The larvae, needing protein to develop into mature workers, eagerly munched the cricket.

After losing four of the honeypot queens over the last eight months, Charlie had continued feeding the other three, which she had labeled with Post-it notes attached to the side of each formicarium. The first was Queen Izzy, originally named by Chris as Queen Isabelle, though her name quickly morphed; the second was Queen Fern, named after Charlie's paternal grandmother; and the third, Queen Phoenix, had earned her name by rising from the ashes. While Charlie was raising the queens, one had died, leaving her workers queenless, whom Charlie continued to care for. Then, about six weeks later, Queen Phoenix's last worker died, leaving her to care for her brood: eggs, larvae, and pupae. Knowing Queen Phoenix would feed her brood until she emptied her food reserves, resulting in her death, Charlie took drastic measures to save her. Experts had warned her against introducing a queen to foreign workers, saying they would likely attack and kill her, but she knew Queen Phoenix and the queenless workers would die anyway if she did nothing.

Feeling trepidation, Charlie had connected the two formicaria. Immediately, and to her surprise, Queen Phoenix had walked into the adjoining formicarium and stopped in the middle of the queenless workers. The workers moved back, paused for a moment, and then cautiously approached Queen Phoenix, stroking her with their antennae. Then they started cleaning and feeding her, sealing the deal. The workers had adopted Queen Phoenix and would care for her and her brood.

After feeding her four honeypot colonies, Charlie fed the two remaining harvester colonies, Queen Hazel I and Queen Hazel II. Because harvester ants often lived on farms and were feisty, like her mom, she named them after her. She was careful not to make loud noises; although ants can't hear, because they don't have ears, they can feel the vibration of compressed airwaves that create sound. This can cause them to run around in panic mode. *If a tree fell and the only animals in the forest were ants, the falling tree WOULD NOT make a sound. For the tree to make a sound, there must be an animal in the forest with ears because sound is the interpretation of compressed airwaves on the eardrum. If a tree fell, the ants would feel the compressed airwaves as vibrations rippling through the ground, but the falling tree wouldn't make a sound.*

After Charlie fed the ants, she walked to the kitchen, placed the cutting board on the counter, and sat with Chris at the kitchen table. As the sun rose and warmed the chilly March air, they took some time to talk before he went to work.

"How are the queens doing?" Chris asked.

"Pretty good. Finally, the last six queens all have workers, and their numbers are growing. If they continue to do well, I'll look for museums and insectariums to donate the colonies to from Isaac's Ant Foundation."

"That sounds like a good idea," Chris said. "I wish more queens would have made it, but I'm glad the six colonies have completed their life cycles and produced workers. That's kind of cool, considering we were complete rookies!"

"The queens have been doing great ever since I put them in their Tar Heel Ants formicaria," Charlie said, eating a couple of chocolate-covered coffee beans from a pink Depression glass dish sitting on the table.

"I'm glad that worked. We were in trouble there for a while," Chris said. "Did you find out if all the workers are females?"

"Yeah, I did some research and found out that all the workers are daughters of the queen, and they'll defend her and the colony with their lives," Charlie said. "They're the quintessential team players—they put the well-being of the queen and colony above their own."

"That's cool. It sounds like people could learn a thing or two from the ants!"

"Well, there's a reason they've survived for more than 120 million years," Charlie said. "Which reminds me, I found this conference called the Invertebrates in Education and Conservation Conference, which is held in Tucson every year. It's a gathering of entomologists from across the nation, and I thought it might be helpful in regard to our work with the foundation. Would you like to go?"

"Yeah, that's a great idea. You know me; I'm game for whatever helps the foundation."

"Great, I'll make reservations later today."

Chris took a sip of his coffee. "How's your new job? Are you going to like being a rehab nurse better than being a psych nurse?"

"My new job is fine, except they asked me to be a house supervisor, which I'm reluctant to do."

"It sounds like they want to promote you. Why would that be a problem?"

"Many of our patients who've been admitted for hip replacements, strokes, and traumatic brain injuries are older," Charlie said. "They're stable when they leave the hospital, but older patients tend to have many other health problems, and I just don't want to be responsible for the floor when someone codes—I DON'T like it when people die on me."

Silence.

"I'm too angry and hurt to care about promoting my career at this point," Charlie explained, and then she brought Chris up to speed on the medical records situation. "After the hospital said they only had the fetal heart monitor strips from 7:55 to 8:30 in the morning, I kept pushing them. At the end of January, they told me they found the fetal heart monitor strips from 08:30 to 14:15, so I asked them to keep looking for the remaining strips from 14:15 to 20:00. Those strips were the most critical. Now it's been two more months, and I haven't heard back from them."

Chris shook his head. "That sounds very suspicious to me. Especially since the most critical strips—the last six hours—just happen to be the ones they can't find. Most likely because they show medical negligence on their end."

"It boils my blood," Charlie said, her pulse quickening. "I keep hoping they'll find the last six hours and give them to me."

"I wouldn't get my hopes up. . . . They're stalling for a reason," Chris said. "I also find it strange that they've made you go through their legal department rather than medical records. It all points to one thing—they're guilty of medical negligence and trying to keep it under wraps!"

"That's what I've suspected this whole time," Charlie agreed. "It's been a shitty little deal trying to get Isaac's birth records, and you're the only one who believed me. For that, I'll always be in your debt. Everyone else just thought I was looking for someone to blame."

"I watched Isaac struggle every day, and after you told me about the horrible delivery, I had a sinking feeling you were right. But, as painful as this is, I'm glad you've pushed them because their actions are very telling. They would have simply given you the fetal heart monitor strips if they had nothing to hide," Chris said, getting up to leave for work.

"And another thing I find telling is, since they printed the nine pages they sent me, why wouldn't they be able to print ALL the fetal heart monitor strips?" Charlie asked with anger.

"Like I said, their actions are very telling," Chris said, putting his coffee cup in the sink. "They're trying to keep those records from you for a reason!"

Charlie walked Chris to his car and they kissed goodbye, then Chris left for work. Charlie returned to the kitchen, picked up the breakfast dishes, and saw Isaac's chair still covered in dust. In frustration, she put the dirty dishes down, grabbed a dish towel, hastily wiped the dust off Isaac's chair, then put the dirty dishes in the sink.

Next, Charlie checked her email, opening one with the subject line *DAVID BOWIE PAINTING*. The sender wanted to know if she was the artist who had painted the portrait in the attached file, explaining the painting was part of David Bowie's archives and had been included in the *David Bowie Is* exhibition. The exhibition had opened at the Victoria and Albert Museum in London, had been traveling worldwide for the last five years, and was now at the Brooklyn Museum in New York. She opened the attached file and laid her eyes on the David Bowie portrait she had painted and sent to his record label more than thirty years ago. She couldn't believe it—the Brooklyn Museum had used her collage painting of David Bowie to advertise the exhibit! Stunned, she called Chris to let him know.

"I think we should go to the show," Chris said. "It's a once-in-a-lifetime event, and it's been a tough year. It might do us good to get out of the house."

"It's been the worst year imaginable," Charlie said. "It's almost been a year since . . . Maybe it would be good for us to get out of the house. I'll see if I can get the time off."

Charlie said goodbye to Chris, then opened an email from Coconino Community College (CCC). They were asking her to stop by to review the documents for Isaac's Ant Foundation endowment, which she'd created in Isaac's name. It gave scholarships to individuals with learning disabilities who were seeking a degree in science and who, despite their challenges, were putting their best foot forward. Charlie replied, saying she'd stop by later in the day.

Next, she opened an email from the hospital. It read: *Per Arizona Revised Statute (ARS 12-2297) fetal monitor strips are considered source data and are to be maintained for 6 years.*

Charlie's stomach hit rock bottom as she realized that she would never obtain Isaac's fetal heart monitor strips. She felt sick ... beaten up and filled with rage. Defeated!

He was only sixteen. His whole life was taken away from him, and now they're going to get away with their crime.

Charlie thought about the people responsible for the botched delivery listed on Isaac's birth records. Having little or nothing to lose, Charlie became desperate. Vengeful. *I could look up the midwife and the ancillary staff who were responsible, show them a picture of Isaac, and tell them what their careless actions cost him. I want them to know they killed my son. And since the hospital won't hold them responsible, I could!*

As Charlie considered her options, she looked up the doctor who had delivered Isaac and later had her family over for dinner. She knew he wasn't responsible; he had just been called in for an emergency C-section when Isaac's heart started failing. Still, Charlie would have liked to talk to him and ask him a few questions. Unfortunately, she learned he had already died of a heart attack.

Next, Charlie looked up the midwife and found she was working at the hospital in Tuba City on the Navajo reservation. *She probably lost her job in town when they did a case review of Isaac's delivery. It would be easy to find her and . . .*

At that moment, as a battle of conflicting emotions waged war inside her, she understood why someone who had experienced this kind of tragedy might resort to violence. But for Charlie, there was one feeling greater than her desire for retribution—her love for Isaac. Although she wanted those who had wronged Isaac to be held accountable, Charlie knew if she chose violence, it would forever tarnish Isaac's good name and make her as deplorable as the perpetrators. Fueled by love, Charlie quelled her anger, swallowed her pain, and sat back down on the barstool next to Isaac, although she couldn't see him.

I have to make Isaac proud. Doing the right thing is always the right thing to do!

19

FORGIVENESS
The Other Side

HAZEL TOOK HER favorite game, Scrabble, from the hallway closet, tucked it under her arm, and then went and found Melba standing at the kitchen counter, where she was painting her fingernails cherry red.

"It's going to be another beautiful day here in paradise," Melba said, looking out the window.

"It certainly is. Do you remember when we used red barn paint to paint our fingernails when we were growing up?"

"I sure do. We made good with what we had, but now I use cherry-red fingernail polish. . . . It's so pretty."

Hazel held out her fingernails, which were painted the same color. "I couldn't agree more."

Melba grinned. "What do you have there?"

Hazel showed Melba the Scrabble game. "I was wondering if you'd like to go outside and play a game of Scrabble at the picnic table."

"If you're ready to lose to your little sister," Melba joked, then blew on her nails to help them dry. Her long rhinestone earrings sparkled in the sunlight streaming in from the kitchen window. "I saw Shane and Isaac out there playing with Hailey and Kéyah earlier. Let's see if they'll play with us."

Melba and Hazel walked outside to the picnic table, where Shane was throwing sticks for Hailey and Kéyah.

"Where's Isaac?" Hazel asked, placing the game on the picnic table. "We wanted to see if you guys would like to play a game of Scrabble."

"Sure, that sounds fun. Isaac went to see his mom, but he'll be right back," Shane said, throwing a stick. Hailey and Kéyah both chased after it, barking at each other under the beautiful blue sky scattered with a few puffy white clouds. The new buds of the cottonwood tree were just beginning to open, and two gray squirrels squeaked at each other as they scampered up and down its trunk in the fresh mountain air.

"What's going on with Charlie?" Hazel asked.

"She just found out some bad news, so Isaac went to be with her." Shane sat down at the picnic table and opened the Scrabble game.

"We're all worried about her, but if anyone can get her through this, it's Isaac. I hope he'll find a way to erase her doubt and prove to her that not even death can separate the two of them," Melba said.

Just then, Isaac walked through the kitchen door and headed in their direction.

"It looks like we're playing Scrabble." Isaac placed a pink Depression glass dish full of chocolate-covered coffee beans on the picnic table and sat down. "My mom practically lives on coffee, and these are her favorites. Before I left her house, I grabbed some so we could enjoy them together."

"I love these," Shane said, popping a couple in his mouth. "But they can really get you wired."

"What are they?" Melba asked. "I've never had them before."

"Chocolate-covered coffee beans," Isaac said.

"We didn't have these when we were growing up," Hazel said, taking one from the dish. "Are they any good?"

Melba picked one up, popped it into her mouth, and crushed it between her teeth. "At first, the coffee bean is bitter, but then the smooth, sweet chocolate melts in your mouth." She took a few more from the dish. "I can see why your mom likes these."

"They're pretty tasty," Hazel agreed. "Thanks for bringing them."

"We should share them with Raymond, Ethel, Solomon, and Alma," Shane suggested.

"I already did," Isaac told him. "They were in the living room listening to the *Guiding Light* on the radio. I left some for them and came out to see you guys."

"How's your mom?" Hazel passed the bag of Scrabble tiles around so everyone could draw a tile. Isaac drew a blank, meaning he'd go first.

Isaac drew seven tiles, then passed the bag to Shane. "She's in a very difficult place right now. She just found out those responsible for my birth injury won't be held accountable. It not only broke her heart, but it also filled her with rage. She considered confronting them and, for a moment, thought about pursuing revenge, but then she decided that wasn't the right thing to do." Isaac placed his first word, TALLY, horizontally, landing the Y on a double-letter score.

"Nice job, Isaac. That's worth twenty-four points." Hazel took a piece of paper and a pencil from the Scrabble box and wrote down his score. "It's easy to understand why your mom's so upset. People want justice, especially for crimes committed against them or their loved ones. That's why we have laws." She played LEX vertically, placing the X on the triple-letter score. "That's worth twenty-six points," Hazel said, writing down her score.

"Yes, but is that a word?" Shane joked.

"It most certainly is; it comes from the Latin word for *law*." Hazel grinned.

"Speaking of laws, it seems justice wasn't served in Isaac's case," Melba said, contemplating a word to play. "The man who murdered me eventually landed in jail, where he's serving a life sentence. I'm sure that not getting the same justice makes losing you even more difficult and painful for your mom."

"Yes, it certainly has," Isaac agreed.

"Both of these deaths have been extremely difficult on our family," Shane said. "But, as hard as it may be to believe, these events provide an opportunity to learn critical virtues: compassion, empathy, forgiveness, humility—"

"If Charlie could hear you, she'd shudder," Hazel interrupted.

"I completely understand," Shane said. "Forgiving someone who murders you, in Melba's case, or accidentally kills an innocent child, in Isaac's case, seems impossible."

"Solomon and Ethel raised us as Southern Baptists and taught us to forgive our enemies. They often quoted the Bible: turn the other cheek; forgive, and you will be forgiven; and of course, forgive them for they know not what they do." Melba placed SQUINT vertically to connect with TALLY, landing the Q on a double-letter score.

"All the main religions encourage forgiveness," Isaac said. "The Qur'an teaches, 'Hold to forgiveness; command what is right; But turn away from the ignorant'; the Hebrew Bible, 'Who is a God like unto thee, that pardoneth iniquity, and passeth by the transgression of the remnant of his heritage? He retaineth not his anger for ever, because he delighteth in mercy'; and Buddha, 'When one gives birth to hatred for an individual, one should develop compassion for that individual. Thus the hatred for that individual should be subdued.'"

"Those verses are beautiful, Isaac. They also highlight another important point," Shane said, grabbing a few more chocolate-covered coffee beans. "Understanding leads to forgiveness, and forgiveness frees you from harboring contempt for others." He popped one of the beans in his mouth, then connected the word EXAM horizontally to LEX for thirteen points.

"What's missing is the *path* to forgiveness," Melba interjected. "I understand that forgiveness is a virtuous quality, but you might as well be asking me to cross a great chasm without a bridge. I need a way to reach the land of forgiveness—a bridge across the chasm of bitterness and hate."

"That's a great analogy," Shane said. "Let's look at these two horrible events separately to understand each situation better. Hopefully, that will show us what you're hoping to find. In Isaac's case, there were two crimes: First, the medical negligence that caused his brain injury and ultimately took his life, and second, the fact that those responsible weren't held accountable for their actions. They didn't intend to hurt Isaac, but they still did. And even though it was tragic, accidents are easier to forgive than acts with malicious intent because we've all made mistakes. Just as we want to be forgiven for our errors, we need to forgive others for theirs—we're more than the sum of our mistakes. Secondly, laws are only as good as they're written, and sometimes, crimes such as these cause laws to change. Unfortunately, that won't help Charlie. She'll need to learn to forgive without justice being served—one of the greatest challenges that exists, but one of her life lessons nonetheless."

Hazel reached for Isaac's hand. "I'm not sure I could do that, but I hope your mom can find a way."

Isaac nodded, squeezing Hazel's hand.

Shane continued, "The serial killer who brutally murdered Melba stabbed his two victims to death with a butcher knife on separate occasions. His motive was sexual assault, and he targeted women who lived near him in both incidents. It may seem impossible to forgive him for these hideous crimes, but it's easier if we separate the criminal and the crime. We can forgive the criminal and still hold him accountable for his crime. To forgive, we need to understand what caused him to be a serial killer with psychopathic traits. Psychopaths have abnormal brain functions, usually due to emotional, psychological, or physical brain injury. And since the brain is the seat of human emotions, those brain injuries affect their emotions, specifically empathy, remorse, and shame. The empathy zone of a psychopath's brain has been permanently silenced. Psychopaths have reduced impulse control or none at all, lack empathy, and are unremorseful and manipulative toward their victims to gain their objective. It's how their injured brains function."

Shane paused for a moment, then added, "The majority of psychopaths grow up in horrible environments. These children have often been tortured, repeatedly beaten, sexually assaulted, starved, or suffered from total neglect or were abandoned. Once innocent and naïve, these children are forced to become psychopaths out of self-preservation; as a means of survival, they shut down emotionally—they can't afford to think about anyone other than themselves. As a result, the empathic brain permanently turns off . . . the hallmark trait of a psychopathic serial killer. To ask a psychopath to care is to ask the impossible—*a man cannot offer what he does not have!* If a man fills his heart with hatred, he can offer hatred; if he fills his heart with kindness, he can offer kindness. It's similar for psychopaths; they can't offer empathy because they have none. That said, if you can think of him as a once innocent child who unfortunately grew up in an environment so horrible that it caused his mental illness, it might be easier to forgive him while still holding him accountable for his crimes. And when he crosses over, he will own his deeds because, as Isaac said, what you do to others, you do to yourself. He'll be restored from his illness, but he'll still own the debt of his action. This will place him with others with the same energy, as like attracts like. There, he won't have access to our dear Melba."

"It's also easier to forgive someone when we understand that we planned the events necessary for our learning before we were born," Isaac said. "Just as I chose my mom, she chose me as her son, and together, we chose these events to learn important lessons. Although my life was difficult, it taught me humility. I learned that all people are equal, including those with disabilities. If my mom knew that now, it would be easier for her to forgive my trespassers." Isaac played PUNISH to intersect with the S in SQUINT. "This seems like a fitting word!"

"It certainly does." Hazel wrote down his score of sixteen, then played FINK to intersect with SQUINT, simultaneously making a second word, KA, with the A in TALLY for twenty-eight points.

"Shane, what you said about separating the criminal from the crime has helped me step out of the role of the victim and look at the situation more objectively," Melba said. "I think I can forgive the man who murdered me while still holding him accountable for his crimes. It's clear to me now that all men are broken, and in truth, he's among the most broken of men. It makes it easier for me to forgive him when I see him as the utterly broken person he is."

"I'm proud of you," Shane said, squeezing Melba's hand. "You crossed the bridge to forgiveness. As difficult as it may seem, certain things must happen for us to encounter the life lessons we need to learn, and what's needed is different for everyone. But one of the keys to learning lessons is this: When you find yourself in a challenging situation, ask yourself what you can learn from that situation. What gift can it offer you? Whether that's forgiveness, courage, compassion, gratitude, caring for yourself, drawing healthy boundaries, or learning to trust yourself and the universe, it helps to know that there are things in play that you don't understand."

"For me, it's the gift of forgiveness," Melba said. "And if we can forgive these horrific crimes, it certainly makes it easier to forgive lesser crimes."

"I'm just glad he's locked up so he can't hurt anyone else," Hazel said. "In this case, the law served its purpose, but it's taken a lot of time for laws to get where they are now. Laws have changed over time, as Shane mentioned earlier. When the first cities were settled during the Mesopotamian era, the kings needed laws to govern their citizens. The laws in the Code of Ur-Nammu, written around 2100 BCE, stated, 'If a man commits a murder, that man must be killed'; 'If a man commits robbery, he will be killed'; and 'If a man knocks out the eye of another man, he shall weigh out 1/2 a mina of silver.' One mina of silver equaled sixty silver shekels in those days, and a person could buy five pounds of wool for one shekel. In other words, a man's eye was worth one hundred and fifty pounds of wool! Later, around 1750 BCE, when the Code of Hammurabi was written, some laws stayed the same, while other laws were changed to reflect the same punishment as the crime. The Code of Hammurabi stated, 'If the wife of one man on account of another man has their mates murdered, both of them shall be impaled'; 'If anyone is committing a robbery and is caught, then he shall be put to death'; and 'If a man put out the eye of another man, his eye shall be put out.'"

"If the punishment is equal to the crime, then it would seem you are no better than the criminal," Isaac said. "If you kill to right a wrong, then you have two wrongs, and two wrongs don't make a right, which I'm proud to say is why my mom decided against violence."

"I agree.... It's good to be mindful that every situation presents an opportunity we can learn from if we choose." Melba placed REPORT to connect to the P in PUNISH for eighteen points. "When something bad happens, we can choose a path of anger and violence or a path of forgiveness and generosity in the face of adversity. And when good things happen, we can take them for granted or learn to be grateful and giving to those less fortunate."

"Well said." Shane smiled, then added MENT to the end of PUNISH for a double-word score and thirty-four points. "Our free will indicates what we've learned and what we still need to learn by what actions we take."

As they continued playing Scrabble, the word maze gradually reached out to every corner of the board, and the tile bag eventually became empty. Finally, the only tiles left were the tiles on their racks.

Hazel ate the last chocolate-covered coffee bean, then played DAD on a double-word score for ten points. "That puts me in the lead, but only by two points."

"Do you remember all the times you put straw down the back of my shirt when we were doing chores? Well, it's payback time." Melba grinned, placing the letter I after the Q in SQUINT to make the word QI and connecting the H in PUNISHMENT to make a second word, HI. "That's worth sixteen points, and since we're out of tiles, I believe that makes me the winner!"

Hazel laughed. "Dammit, sis, I guess I had that coming!"

"You certainly did. You thought you had me after playing DAD, but I had other plans!" Melba smiled. "And speaking of Dad, I'm glad he asked for forgiveness before he passed. It seems there are two sides to that coin: asking for forgiveness and forgiving someone who has wronged you. And even though our dad waited until he was on his deathbed before asking to be forgiven for the terrible things he did to us when we were growing up, I was grateful he acknowledged his trespasses. It allowed me to let go of my hate and forgive him. Like weeds, hate is easy to grow and difficult to get rid of, and it's also a heavy burden to carry. Until I let it go, I didn't realize how holding on to my hate had weighed me down and caused me great suffering. And when I considered how difficult it must have been for him to take care of the farm and us kids, I wondered if I'd have done any better if I had been in his shoes."

"Sometimes people wait their entire life to find the courage to ask for forgiveness, but it's never too late. Doing so helps us resolve our guilt toward the person we hurt, and it also helps resolve our misgivings toward those who hurt us. If we do that, the misgivings and guilt won't follow us when we cross over," Shane said. "And forgiving ourselves makes it easier to forgive others because when we refuse to forgive ourselves, we also refuse to forgive others—it's two sides of the same coin."

Melba smiled. "There's something else . . . something wonderful. When Daddy owned his trespasses, they no longer owned him. He was free of the guilt and shame that had torn at his heart for so long."

"Owning his trespasses freed him from carrying their debts forward when he crossed over," Isaac said. "It was a gift he gave to himself, although he didn't know it at the time."

20

NEW FRIENDS
August 6, 2018

WHILE CHARLIE MADE coffee, Chris packed their suitcases in the car for their trip to the 2018 Invertebrates in Education and Conservation Conference (IECC) scheduled from August 7 to 11 at the Hilton El Conquistador Golf & Tennis Resort in Tucson, Arizona.

Charlie wrote a to-do list for Nancy, who would be caring for their pets while they were gone, then took some money from a tin can on the kitchen counter, paper-clipped it to the list, and texted Nancy to let her know they were leaving after breakfast.

Nancy replied, *Okay, safe travels.*

Next, even though Isaac had been gone for sixteen months, Charlie wrote him a text message: *I loved you, and for this reason, I wrote your name across the sky so that it may not be forgotten* ♥♥. She attached a photo of him hiking to the Plain of Six Glaciers Teahouse in Banff, Canada, then sent it, hearing Isaac's phone ping as he received her message.

Chris walked into the kitchen. "Is there anything else I need to pack in the car?"

"No, that's it," Charlie said. "A couple of days ago, when I asked Nancy to watch our place while we were gone, I remembered something about when she came over after Isaac passed. She suggested I see a specific psychic medium, but I can't remember her name. Do you remember?"

> I LOVED YOU, AND FOR THIS REASON,
> I WROTE YOUR NAME ACROSS THE SKY
> SO THAT IT MAY NOT BE FORGOTTEN.

"That was last year; my memory isn't that good." Chris shrugged. "I've never experienced paranormal activities like you've mentioned, so I don't know what to make of it. It all seems kind of crazy to me, but if you think seeing a psychic medium might help, you might want to try it. You have nothing to lose."

"I think seeing a *reputable* psychic medium might be interesting because I have so many questions unanswered by science or religion, but I don't know who to see.... There are a lot of charlatans out there. I guess I could ask Nancy what the person's name was, but I never seem to get around to it," Charlie said. "It would be great if I could see the psychic medium from the TV series *Medium* we watched, but I don't think that show's based on a real person."

"Yeah, I'm pretty sure it has to be based on a fictional character, because who can tell what happened to a victim just by looking at the photos from a crime scene?" Chris asked rhetorically. "We had better get going. I'll turn on the porch light, and then I think we're ready to go."

"I'm ready if you are," Charlie said, petting the dogs and cat goodbye.

As Chris drove, Charlie sat in the passenger seat, and they reminisced about some of the events that had taken place over the summer.

"I'm glad we went to the *David Bowie Is* exhibit in Brooklyn," Chris said. "That was so much fun! It was awesome how Bowie said he wanted to be a color TV rather than a black-and-white radio."

"I think he succeeded," Charlie said. "One thing that surprised me was how messy his handwriting was. Some of his lyrics had been crossed out, scribbled over, and changed to the point that you could barely read them."

"My favorite part was where they featured Bowie's blue-and-gold quilted suit as they played 'Starman.' I just stood there listening to it over and over again on my headset. . . . I couldn't get enough."

"I love that song, but I have to say my favorite part was Bowie's Berlin Trilogy. Those albums became part of me long ago, and whenever I hear them, they conjure up some deep-seated memories," Charlie said. "Those albums became larger than life, especially *Low* and *Heroes*."

"Of course the icing on the cake was seeing your painting displayed there behind protective glass," Chris said. "I wished Isaac could have been there. He'd have been so proud of you to see *your* painting in the Bowie exhibit at the Brooklyn Museum!"

"That was a perfect day, except there was one thing missing," Charlie said. "We keep taking steps forward, but it all seems empty without Isaac."

"The same was true about our trip to the North Rim," Chris added. "We sat in our nice wooden rocking chairs on the porch of our rustic cabin with cold drinks in our hands, watching the sunset over the Grand Canyon. Everything was perfect, except one thing was missing."

Charlie sighed. "And when we checked into our cabin, the lady at the front desk asked who the third person in our party was, because I made the reservations before Isaac died. I stalled, unable to answer her question, and you jumped in and said the third person couldn't make it. It all just seems so wrong."

"Even the hike from the North Rim to Roaring Springs would have been so much more fun if Isaac had gone with us. I miss having him around."

"Me too," Charlie agreed. "Isaac would have laughed at us for taking our ibuprofen with prickly pear margaritas after that hike—it was a ballbuster."

"If he'd been there, I'd have bought him a virgin prickly pear margarita so we could have all sat on the porch of our cabin and watched the sunset over the North Rim, but like you said, there's always an empty void we take with us no matter where we go."

Chris and Charlie continued reminiscing until they arrived at the Hilton El Conquistador Golf & Tennis Resort. When they checked in, the concierge informed them that their room had been upgraded to a suite with a king bed, a living area with a sofa bed, and a balcony, compliments of the resort. On the way to their room, they crossed through the outdoor pool and bar, which were still wet from the monsoon rains the night before. They entered building D and found their suite on the second floor, where Charlie and Chris placed their suitcases on the sofa bed, then walked out onto the balcony overlooking the pool with the Santa Catalina Mountains in the background. They took in the view, then Charlie went back inside to unpack and Chris followed.

"I think we should register for the conference after we get settled in," Chris suggested, unzipping his suitcase.

"Yeah, you're probably right. We also need to find out where to meet for the field trip in the morning."

After they'd finished unpacking, they went to the front desk and asked where they needed to register for the IECC. The concierge gave them directions to the conference center, where they saw numerous people dressed in insect and invertebrate paraphernalia. They registered for the conference, then stood in line to buy T-shirts. While waiting, they met Stephanie, a sassy, short-haired blond, and her son, Griffin, a cute, long-haired grade school boy outfitted with a glow-in-the-dark scorpion shirt, a butterfly net, and spy glasses. As they introduced themselves, Charlie read the name tag clipped to Stephanie's beetle-patterned shirt: *BEETLE LADY, ENTOMOLOGIST.*

"Hi, my name's Stephanie. I haven't seen you guys before. What brings you here?"

"We're here with Isaac's Ant Foundation, which we founded for my wife's late son," Chris said, knowing Charlie couldn't answer. "He had a thing for ants."

"Oh my gosh, I'm so sorry to hear about your son," Stephanie said, clearly noting the pain in Chris's and Charlie's eyes. "You've come to the right place. Like your son, we all have our favorite insects. I'm all about beetles, as you can tell," Stephanie said, straightening her shirt. "Zack, the guy over there goofing around, is mad about jumping spiders. Tad, the tall guy next to him, loves lady beetles, and Ginny, the lady with the tattoos, has a thing for walking sticks and scorpions. Don't worry; you'll fit right in."

Getting choked up, Charlie nodded to acknowledge Stephanie's kind words as Griffin ran past them, chasing a girl about the same age. The girl had long, wavy brown hair and was wearing a pink dress patterned with black spiders and spiderwebs. Griffin kept putting his butterfly net over her head, pretending to catch her, and then she'd duck out from underneath it and run down the hall. Griffin followed.

"I'm going to get you, Spider-Girl!"

Watching the beautiful children run around, full of life, caused mixed emotions for Charlie. On the one hand, she cherished the children's playful innocence, knowing how tender and fleeting it was. On the other hand, she felt an uncomfortable twinge of envy toward the parents whose children were still alive. Charlie resented having to live without the beautiful son who had been taken from her.

Zack drew Chris and Charlie's attention as he horsed around with his friend Tad, who towered over him at six feet, four inches tall. Charlie soon realized that Zack, a short, athletic man, had earned his reputation for having a personality similar to his favorite arachnids, the jumping spiders. He was playful, flashy, and always playing tricks on unsuspecting bystanders. Tad's stature was a sizable contrast to his favorite insect, the tiny red-and-black ladybug pictured on the back of his white T-shirt. The caption under the spotted ladybug read: *THE*

LOST LADYBUG PROJECT. The two men approached Charlie and Chris and introduced themselves.

"Hi, my name is Zack, and this is my friend Tad, but we call him Tiny for obvious reasons."

Chris laughed. "Hi, I'm Chris, and this is my wife, Charlie."

"You guys look like you're the new kids on the block," Zack said, grabbing Spider-Girl and Griffin as they ran by.

"Yes, this is our first time at the conference," Chris said.

"These two, Spider-Girl and Banana, are a couple of mischief-makers. You have to watch them because they're usually up to no good."

"Did you say Spider-Girl and Banana?" Charlie asked.

"They call me Spider-Girl because I'm crazy about spiders, but my real name is Freddie. The first spider I had was Rosie, a Chilean rose hair tarantula," Spider-Girl said. "We call Griffin Banana because his last name is Dole."

"And we call my mom Pineapple." Banana smiled and lowered his butterfly net over Spider-Girl's head. "I've got you now!"

Spider-Girl ducked out from Banana's butterfly net and ran down the hall. Banana chased after her, calling, "I'm going to get you!"

"Tad, I like your T-shirt," Charlie said. "Stephanie mentioned that you like ladybugs."

Tad nodded. "My favorite is the nine-spotted ladybug, which used to be found across most of North America, but they've almost disappeared in recent times. In 1989, New York State named them as their official state insect, but when people went out looking for them, they realized they were almost gone. The ladybug's history is a great story that gets people interested in conservation."

Dressed in a skirt and last year's IECC T-shirt, which revealed the colorful insect tattoos on her arms and legs, Ginny tapped Zack on the shoulder to get his attention. Zack turned around and hugged her.

"Excuse me, sir," the woman said from behind the counter, trying to get Chris's attention. She was holding up a navy-blue T-shirt featuring a huntsman spider with the IECC logo. "What size would you like?"

Chris handed her his credit card. "One small and one medium."

The woman processed the card, then handed it back with two T-shirts. "Enjoy the conference."

"Thanks, we will."

On the way back to their room, Charlie and Chris stopped at the indoor bar, where Chris ordered a rum and Coke, and Charlie ordered a prickly pear margarita to go. When they got back to their room, they sat on the outdoor deck, sipped their drinks, and listened to the grackles calling from the palm trees in the hot, humid air of the Sonoran Desert.

Later that night, after they'd been asleep for hours, Charlie woke up with a vicious migraine, ran to the bathroom, and threw up. Not having any coffee, she took a couple of ibuprofen, then lay back down, hoping the migraine would subside before their field trip. A few hours later, her alarm rang, and she turned it off.

"How are you feeling?" Chris asked. "I heard you in the bathroom last night."

"Much better." Charlie sat up on the side of the bed, taking stock of her condition. "I had one of my migraines, but it went away."

After getting ready for the day, Chris and Charlie returned to the same location where they'd registered for the conference and checked in for the all-day Bug-hemian Rhapsody field trip. This excursion centered on collecting insects and arthropods that would be exhibited later at various museums, zoos, and insectariums for public education on the importance of insect conservation.

Holding a manila envelope with a list of field trip participants, the addresses of the local hospitals, and a copy of the conference permit in his hands, Zack was goofing around—giving everyone nicknames like Ladybird, Spider-Girl, and Ant-Man while he called roll.

Charlie leaned toward Chris and whispered, "Apparently, Zack's leading the field trip."

"Looks that way," Chris agreed. "That will be great. He seems like a nice guy, and he's easy to talk to."

After roll call, Zack informed the group of the rules and regulations and the field trip route. "We will be making four stops along the Sonoran canyons and grasslands because they offer a great diversity of desert insects and arthropods. And since it's been raining, please remember to bring a jacket. You'll also need a pair of long forceps, as we'll be collecting desert centipedes and longhorn beetles from vicious long-spine cacti. If anyone gets stung, bitten, or attacked by the jumping cholla, we have a first aid kit in the vans."

"We'll be taking two vans," Tad added. "Zack will be driving one, and I'll be driving the other. After we take a group photo, you can get settled into either van. . . . We need to leave in the next ten minutes."

After the group photo, everyone piled into the vans and headed out of Tucson toward the desert at the foot of the Sierrita Mountains. At the edge of town, they stopped at a gas station to fill up and use the bathrooms. While waiting for everyone to finish using the facilities, Chris and Charlie stood outside the convenience store with Zack. Suddenly, a queen ant landed at Chris's feet and ripped off her wings.

"That's a queen," Chris exclaimed.

"Do you have a container to put her in?" Zack asked.

"No, I don't," Chris replied. "I think we came completely unprepared."

"No worries." Zack went and rummaged through a box in the back of the van, then handed Chris a small plastic specimen tube. "Here, put her in this."

"Thanks," Chris said. "I'm going to name her Queen Ethyl, since we found her at a gas station."

"Nice!" Zack laughed, placing Queen Ethyl in a cooler in the back of the van.

As they headed toward their first stop, Charlie and Chris quietly sat watching the lively bunch of entomologists cracking jokes. Then, just after they crossed a cattle guard, Zack saw some cow pies and immediately stopped in the middle of the road. Everyone grabbed their forceps, scrambled out of the van, and feverishly dug through the soft, fragrant cow pies, collecting dung beetles buried deep inside—like wild kids turned loose in a candy store.

"It's going to be a great day." Ginny smiled, placing her dung beetles in a plastic container and closing the perforated lid. "It looks like you guys are new to the group."

"Yes, we're complete rookies," Chris admitted. "But I'm sure you can guess that just by looking at us."

"Yeah, it's kind of obvious," Ginny laughed. "We have extra forceps and containers in the back of the van if you need them."

"That would be great," Charlie said.

Ginny placed her dung beetle in her bag. "I'll get them for you at our next stop. We're not going to be here very long."

"It's time to go," Zack called out to the group members who had wandered across the road into some tall grass searching for six- and eight-legged treasures.

Everyone piled back into the van and continued bouncing down the dirt road, telling jokes.

"Did you hear about the dung beetle that walked into a bar?" Zack asked, looking in his rearview mirror.

"No, we haven't," the group lied. "Why don't you tell us?" Everyone egged him on, knowing what he would say.

"A dung beetle walks into a bar, leans up against the counter, orders a dry martini, then asks, 'Is this stool taken?'" Zack laughed, and everyone joined in.

Ginny added, "A weevil walks into a bar and orders a dry martini, shaken, not stirred, and the bartender asks, 'Hey, buddy, why the long face?'"

Everyone roared, loud enough to shame a school bus full of kids.

As the van meandered down the winding dirt road, the jokes continued, filling the van with high energy and cheer, an environment Charlie and Chris were not accustomed to. The sharp contrast made them feel out of place, but knowing that kind and good-hearted people surrounded them was comforting.

They stopped along White House Canyon Road, and Ginny found a pair of long forceps and a specimen container for Charlie and Chris, then sent them to collect cactus longhorn beetles from the tops of jumping cholla cacti. As they were searching for the large black beetles, Spider-Girl and Banana ran up to them and asked them if they wanted to see a funnel spider.

"Sure," Charlie said. "What's a funnel spider?"

"I'll show you." Spider-Girl motioned for them to follow. When they arrived at the location, Spider-Girl crouched down and tossed a small pebble into a spiderweb. Immediately, an aggressive gray spider with two black stripes along its backside raced out from the silk tunnel to see what it had caught.

Spider-Girl grinned. "That's a funnel spider."

"Very cool," Chris said. "Hey, do you know why ants never get sick?"

"That's an easy one." Banana frowned, rolling his eyes. "They're full of ANTi... bodies."

"Well, if you're so smart, what do you call an ant that's good at math?" Spider-Girl asked smugly. Giving her the evil eye, Banana placed his butterfly net over her, but she ducked out from underneath it and took off running. Banana followed.

"Account... ANTs?" Chris guessed.

"Of course," Charlie agreed.

The next stop was at Box Canyon, where they collected praying mantises, plains lubber grasshoppers, and panther-spotted grasshoppers. Next, they traveled to Empire Ranch Road, where they stopped to eat lunch and collected vinegaroons, tarantulas, and giant centipedes that they found underneath old railroad ties. Afterward, they drove to Garden Canyon Road, where they gathered several different species of beetles, including one Hercules beetle and one orange velvet ant, which Charlie and Chris learned wasn't an ant at all but a wingless wasp.

When they arrived back at the hotel, everyone went to their rooms to freshen up in time to attend the opening presentation by the keynote speaker, Dr. Linda Rayor, from the Department of Entomology at Cornell University. As Charlie and Chris listened to her presentation about the benefits and costs of social huntsman spiders, which lived in groups rather than as solitary hunters, a little spark of light crept into their hearts.

21

EXPERT'S OPINION
March 23, 2019

CHARLIE ENTERED MR. CHEE'S hospital room, set the brakes of her mobile workstation, and greeted her patient.

"Yá'át'ééh abiní," Charlie said. *Hello. Good morning.*

"Aoo'," Mr. Chee replied. *Yes, it is.*

Charlie opened Mr. Chee's chart, checked off his medications as she placed them in a Dixie cup, and then handed them to him with a cup of water.

"After you take your meds, I'll change the dressing on your wound."

Mr. Chee grimaced. "Will it hurt?"

"I won't lie; it can be uncomfortable when I turn the wound vacuum back on, but most patients say it stops hurting once the suction comes up to pressure."

"I wish my leg hadn't gotten infected after the amputation," Mr. Chee said, frowning. "Diabetes runs in my family."

"I'm sorry. I'm sure this is very difficult on you," Charlie said, turning off Mr. Chee's wound vacuum. "I'll be as gentle as possible, and then it won't need to be changed for three days."

"Aoo'," Mr. Chee said. *Okay.*

"Neezgai?" Charlie asked, taking the old dressing off the wound. *Pain?*

"Ndaga'." Mr. Chee shook his head. *No.*

After Charlie had finished changing Mr. Chee's dressing, she asked him how he was doing.

"That wasn't too bad. It feels pretty good." Mr. Chee relaxed his tense shoulders. "My fear was much greater than the pain."

"That is often the case," Charlie said, unlocking the brakes on her mobile workstation. "Is there anything else I can get you before I go?"

"No, I'm going to take a nap. I'm tired from PT."

"Hágoónee'," Charlie said. *See you later.*

Charlie turned off the light and closed the door behind her. She walked to the nursing station, parked her mobile workstation at her desk, and took a drink of water from her Nalgene bottle.

The charge nurse, Lori, turned around in her chair and faced Charlie. "Are you going to the Traumatic Brain Injury Symposium in Phoenix tomorrow?"

"Yes. I hope to find an expert in acute hypoxic TBIs to see what their unbiased opinion of Isaac's history is. Maybe then I can stop wrestling my feelings, wondering if it's just me wanting to blame others for what happened to Isaac, as some have claimed."

"Oh, I hadn't thought of that, but it makes sense," Lori said. "I know your heart's broken over losing your son. Have you ever thought of seeing a psychic medium? It might be helpful."

"That's strange you say that," Charlie said. "That's been suggested to me before, and I'm starting to get the feeling that maybe I should go see one, but I don't know any with a good reputation. Do you have any suggestions?"

"I saw a psychic medium in Sedona who helped me when I lost a close friend. I can look her up if you'd like?"

"Sure," Charlie said, getting a Post-it note while Lori looked her up on her phone.

"Here's her contact information," Lori said, showing Charlie her phone.

"Thanks. I'll call her." Charlie wrote down the woman's contact information and put the Post-it note in the front pocket of her scrubs.

After work, Charlie drove home and put her dirty scrubs in the washing machine, and because she was tired and still needed to feed the ants, she forgot all about the Post-it note in her front pocket. She went to her bedroom, where Chris was drinking a White Russian and watching *The Big Lebowski*, put on her pajamas, and then went to the kitchen to prepare food for the colonies.

Chris turned the TV off and joined Charlie in the kitchen.

"How was work?" Chris asked, sitting down at the table.

"These twelve-hour shifts are tiring, but I do like having four days off every week," Charlie said. "I heard from the Cook Museum of Natural Science today. They want us to deliver Queen Fern in time for their grand opening scheduled for June seventh, 2019. That's only a few months from now. I thought we could deliver Queen Phoenix to Ginny at the Iowa State University's Insect Zoo during the same trip."

"I'm game. . . . You know me, beautiful. I'd be happy to go anywhere with you. I'm glad we're getting things done with the foundation." Chris took a sip of his White Russian. "It would be pretty cool if we could place two colonies during one trip, especially considering we had no idea what we were doing when we collected those queens almost two years ago."

"And we also signed our first endowment," Charlie added. "A part of me still wants those responsible for hurting Isaac to pay, but I think being generous in the face of adversity is the better way to go."

Chris agreed, then suddenly grimaced. "I feel a little sick to my stomach. I took one of my employees out for lunch at this new restaurant, and the food was pretty good, but—"

"Did you eat something that didn't agree with you?"

Chris held his stomach. "I don't know. . . . The fajitas were very spicy."

"That could be it, or maybe you're feeling run-down from skiing. Maybe you need to let your body rest," Charlie said. "I'll finish feeding the ants, and we can go to bed early."

"Yeah, I've been pounding it. I've skied forty-six days this year, but I don't think that's it. . . . I probably just ate something that didn't agree with me."

"Are you going skiing tomorrow?" Charlie asked, thinking his answer would indicate how sick he was.

"Of course." Chris grinned, then finished his White Russian. "I've already waxed my skis, and I'm going to wear my new Lange boots you got me for my birthday."

Charlie smiled, picked up the ant food she had prepared, and kissed Chris. "At least you're feeling good enough to go skiing, so it can't be that bad. It will only take me a few minutes to feed the ants, then we can go to bed. Hopefully, you'll feel better in the morning."

The following morning, Charlie got up at five, took a shower, and then went to the living room, where she picked up a book of matches to light a candle for Isaac, as she did every day. The candle sat on an ornately carved wooden urn containing Isaac's ashes. To the candle's right was a turtle made of two different-colored stones. The turtle's shell was made from a white-and-rust-marbled stone, and its body was made from a dark-gray stone etched with turtle scales. A smaller matching turtle was to the left of the candle. Charlie had bought them in a tourist boutique in the United States Virgin Islands when she and Isaac were vacationing. She now thought that the two turtles represented the undying love between a mother and her child and saw the lit candle as the eternal flame that burned between them.

In front of the urn was a shadow-box frame with a photograph of Isaac walking through a field of white daisies in Wyoming when he was six. Draped over the top was a necklace made of colored wooden beads she had bought for Isaac when they went to Belize with Shane. Inside the picture frame were a few of Isaac's favorite Native American animal fetishes: an orange hummingbird, a brown horned toad, and a shiny gray dolphin. Surrounding Isaac's picture were various treasures.

To the left was a bronze Egyptian cat curled up with his head resting on his paws and a three-legged clay pig from Chile, traditionally given to friends and family as a token of love and goodwill. To the right stood a miniature-sized vase decorated with two rust-colored parrotfish swimming through seagrasses, which they had purchased from a friendly woman near the Sittee River before taking a catamaran to Glover's Atoll. Inside the vase, Charlie had placed a small arrangement of dried flowers.

Other treasures included an ornate rocking horse from Montana; a small conch shell from Glover's Atoll; a wooden box puzzle in the shape of an iguana from Belize; two small crystal blocks with the Eiffel Tower engraved inside, which Isaac had brought back for his mom when he went to Paris with his dad; several five-hundred-million-year-old *Elrathia* trilobite fossils that Charlie and Isaac had excavated out of the ground in Delta, Utah; and a small flower-shaped box with a hinged lid that Isaac had painted in grade school. The box contained four handwritten notes from Isaac: I love you, I'll ♡ you forever, You make great lunches, and Let's go fishing.

The wooden urn, shadow-box picture frame, and treasures sat on the top of a small wooden table with a hinged lid that had belonged to Hazel before she died. Her Holy Bible was still safely tucked away inside its lavender crushed-velvet lining. It had the distinct smell that only old books have, and the page where the previous owners had written down their names had been torn out. Also neatly arranged inside the table were Isaac's small button-up denim shirt he'd worn as a newborn, four safety pins Charlie used to fasten Isaac's cloth diapers, and a collection of cards.

How long do I have to endure this? Every day is such a grind, Charlie thought, looking at the treasure collection. She struck the match, lit the candle between the turtles, and then went and sat at the kitchen table, dread filling her heart as she thought about what she was about to do.

Charlie then picked up her phone, called Isaac's phone, and recorded his voicemail greeting onto her phone. Once she was done, she logged into her phone service and canceled Isaac's phone, nearly two years after he had passed. *Isaac, I'll continue to send messages to you on my phone.* Charlie wept uncontrollably, feeling like she had just severed a link between her and Isaac. She buried her face in her hands as a river of sorrow washed over her.

Hearing Chris getting out of the shower, Charlie pulled herself together and dried her eyes, then made him a cappuccino, hoping to brighten his day. Once he was dressed, Chris joined Charlie at the kitchen table.

"Are you feeling better this morning?" Charlie asked, handing him the cappuccino. "I thought maybe you'd enjoy a special cup of coffee today."

"Thanks, beautiful." Chris took a sip of the cappuccino, then licked the foamed milk off his mustache. "Yes, I feel better than last night, but still not great. Maybe it's just a stomach bug or something."

"I'm glad you're feeling a little better," Charlie said. "My friend Bryce from work is picking me up soon. I'm catching a ride with her to the TBI symposium in Phoenix."

"When will you be home?"

"The symposium ends at four, so I should be home by six thirty,"

Charlie said. There was a knock on the door, and she got up to answer it. She greeted Bryce, then, leaving the door ajar, asked her to wait a minute. "I hope you have fun skiing," Charlie said, picking up her bag and kissing Chris goodbye.

"Love you. See you when you get home."

"Love you too." Charlie walked out the front door and closed it behind her.

Bryce, a speech-language pathologist, was a slender woman with long blond hair who had lost her brother to suicide. She and Charlie had quickly become friends after confiding in each other about losing loved ones to tragic events. Once they arrived at the neurological center, they checked into the symposium, picked up a pamphlet, and then settled into their seats in the auditorium.

As the first lecture, "Military Veterans with Traumatic Brain Injuries," began, Charlie and Bryce took notes as Dr. Welsh explained that many veterans who suffered traumatic brain injuries were not eligible for related services, because their injuries were not documented when they occurred.

The second lecture, "Acute Traumatic Brain Injuries," by Dr. Mahanti, started shortly after the first. Dr. Mahanti discussed at length the acute aspects of traumatic brain injuries due to hypoxia, resulting in blood values with an increase of pCO_2 and a decrease in pO_2 and pH. He added that many of these patients experienced neurological deficits, seizures, and cognitive delays.

Charlie's heart raced as she compared Isaac's medical records in her mind. After his lecture, Dr. Mahanti left the podium and walked down the auditorium aisle. Charlie quickly followed after him.

"Dr. Mahanti," Charlie called, catching up to him at the auditorium's exit.

The doctor turned around.

"Dr. Mahanti, do you have a few minutes to answer a couple of questions?" Charlie asked, catching her breath.

"Sure. How can I help you?"

"I have a scenario I want to run by you," Charlie explained. "Could a hypoxic brain injury occur if the umbilical cord was around an infant's neck twice throughout a thirty-four-hour labor? Especially if during that labor, there were deep non-reassuring decels over the last twenty-five hours, and then the medical team performed an emergency C-section due to the infant's heart failing?"

"Why wasn't the child delivered much earlier?" Dr. Mahanti asked. "Thirty-four hours is too long to keep a woman in labor, especially if there were signs of non-reassuring decels twenty-five hours before the C-section."

"It was Christmas Eve."

Dr. Mahanti shook his head, disdain in his eyes. "That should have never happened."

Charlie recalled the lab values that were burned permanently in her mind. "The arterial CO2 was fifty-three, and the O2 was nine. Under those conditions, would an infant sustain a hypoxic brain injury resulting in delayed cognition and seizures?"

"Yes. Those are critical values, especially given that the infant had the umbilical cord around his neck twice. That could have caused hypoxia due to strangulation and cord compression," Dr. Mahanti said. "Furthermore, the infant's brain would have been deprived of oxygen long before the infant's heart began to fail—the heart would be the last thing to go."

"Would those conditions cause late-onset seizures that started when the child was in their teens?" Charlie asked, her voice wavering.

"Yes, we continue to see secondary insults at varying stages," Dr. Mahanti said. "Why do you ask? It seems like you're asking from a personal experience rather than a clinical point of view."

"That was my son. At sixteen, he died from a seizure, and I needed to know what happened to him," Charlie cried, choking on her words. "Thanks for answering my questions."

Dr. Mahanti hugged Charlie. "I'm so sorry to be the one to tell you. Do you have any other questions I can answer for you before I go?"

"No, thank you. You've been very kind." Charlie averted her eyes as tears ran down her face. "I just need a few minutes to regain my composure."

"I understand. I'm so sorry for your loss," Dr. Mahanti said before he walked away.

After Charlie regained her composure, she returned to her seat and told Bryce what Dr. Mahanti had said.

"I'm so sorry!" Bryce hugged Charlie. "But I'm glad you finally know what happened to Isaac."

As they sat through the remaining lectures, Charlie didn't hear a word that was said. All she could think about was that what she had feared was true. All of Isaac's struggles—sustaining a hypoxic brain injury at birth, growing up with severe cognitive disabilities, being bullied at school, suffering from seizures, and dying—had been caused by careless hands. Furthermore, Charlie could do nothing to right this wrong, which caused her tremendous unrest.

Then Charlie remembered one particular incident. Isaac had had a seizure at bedtime nine days before he died. Early the next morning, he had walked to the kitchen and looked directly into her eyes.

"Mom, I'm not afraid to die."

22

LIFE LESSONS
The Other Side

"MELBA, LET'S GO COLLECT eggs for Easter Sunday," Hazel said, her voice filled with excitement and cheer.

"That sounds fun," Melba replied. "I hope you remember that I found the golden egg the last two years and won a quarter each time!"

"Yes, I remember! Last year, Dad hid the golden egg inside Grandpa's long-handled underwear hanging on the clothesline," Hazel laughed, picking up a wicker basket from the kitchen shelf, then lining it with a blue checkered dishcloth. "That was tricky of him, but there's no laundry on the line, so that trick won't work this time!"

"True, but I plan to use my sixth sense to find the golden egg," Melba said, opening the kitchen door.

Hazel and Melba reminisced about other Easter egg hunts on their way to the chicken coop, which had a large fenced area and housed three dozen white leghorns, Rhode Island Reds, and speckled Dominique chickens, plus a few snow geese and ducks.

Melba unlatched the door and stepped inside, and then Hazel followed behind her. While they searched for eggs underneath the hens, the clucking grew louder, and some of the hens flew from their nesting boxes and ran outside to the fenced area, making a big racket on their way out. After collecting an assortment of white and brown eggs,

Hazel and Melba walked out to the fenced area, where an old A-framed doghouse sat against the outside of the chicken coop. It was painted forest green and had a wooden shingled roof. Above the door, in white letters, read the name of Alma's faithful dog: BUSTER. After Buster received a new doghouse for his birthday, they had started using his old one for the geese and ducks.

Hazel gathered the geese eggs from the doghouse, and then they filled the metal trough with water from the river, which the geese and ducks used as a birdbath.

"Dad certainly loves his geese," Hazel said.

"He sure does," Melba agreed, latching the chicken coop. "It's cute how they follow him into the yard, honking and making a big fuss as they go."

"Yes, it's very sweet."

Hazel and Melba went inside and put the basket of Easter eggs on the kitchen counter.

Ethel put the geese eggs into the refrigerator to use later for cooking. "I think Solomon and Raymond plan to go fishin' after breakfast, so I made some hot cereal. Everyone can help themselves."

Hazel, who had a sweet tooth, scooped a spoonful of brown sugar on top of her bowl of hot cereal, then added fresh milk, raisins, and walnuts on top.

"Thanks, sis, that's just the way I like it." Melba smiled as she took Hazel's bowl of cereal from her. She sat down at the kitchen table with Shane and Isaac, who had already eaten and were drinking coffee. Isaac was drawing a picture as Shane read the 1950s comic strips while Buttercup slept underneath the table.

"Dang it, sis! You're always trying to get my goat." Hazel smiled, then made herself a second bowl of hot cereal and joined the others at the kitchen table.

Shane nudged Isaac and showed him the iconic Betty Boop with her exaggerated large head and black curly hair, looking coy. She had her fingers interlocked near the side of her face, and she was wearing a red miniskirt and tiny black high heels. Felix the Cat was walking on a strip of wavy piano keys, singing a song with small musical notes coming out of his mouth.

"Nice cat!" Isaac smiled, and then he showed Hazel and Melba his drawing of the daffodils and crocuses blooming outside underneath the kitchen window.

"That's beautiful," Melba said.

"You have the same eye for composition and detail as your mom," Hazel added. "Speaking of your mom, how's she doing?"

"She's struggling. I haven't been able to get her in touch with Allison, but I'm still working on it." Isaac frowned. "And she recently talked to a doctor who specializes in traumatic brain injuries, and he confirmed what she had suspected all along . . . that I suffered a brain injury at birth that caused my seizures and ultimately my death. My mom was thankful to learn the truth, but it also caused her a great deal of pain. It's very difficult for me to watch her struggle as she faces one of life's hardest lessons—learning to forgive a great tragedy without justice being served. It's a lesson she's likely to wrestle with for the rest of her life."

"I've been thinking about that—forgiveness—since our last conversation, and it occurred to me that our ability to forgive someone is directly tied to how we judge them," Melba said, walking into the kitchen with her bowl.

"What do you mean?" Hazel asked.

"When we judge someone, we don't see them for who they are. We see them as we've imagined them through our lens of judgment. It's a false image of who they really are, and if we only look for the bad in someone, that's what we're likely to find." Melba picked up the eggs that were still on the counter and started to wash them, one by one, so that they could be cooked for decorating. "If I see my killer only as a monster, it makes it difficult for me to forgive him, but when I see him as once an innocent child who is now a broken man, then I'm on my way to forgiveness."

"I see your point," Hazel said. "It seems that we've all been wrongfully judged, and every time it's happened to me, I've thought that if the other person only took the time to understand the situation from my perspective, they would no longer judge me the same way. Unfortunately, I've also wrongfully judged others," Hazel admitted, regret in her eyes. "It's easy to throw judgment at someone who's struggling down a difficult path, but walking that road is altogether a different thing."

"You just said it, sis. . . . Take the time to understand the situation from their perspective. In other words, be empathetic. Empathy is the cure for judgment, and not judging leads to forgiveness." Melba put the eggs on a towel to dry, then poured herself a cup of coffee and joined Hazel, Isaac, and Shane at the kitchen table.

"I'm not sure that will help my mom—is it possible to be empathetic toward someone who's simply careless? I suppose we can because to err is human, but it won't be easy for Mom to forgive those who were responsible, knowing it was a careless accident that ultimately killed me." Isaac sighed. "Even though it's been two years, I'm still worried about my mom. If it weren't for Chris . . . well, some people wake up one morning and decide they've had enough." He shook his head, not wanting to think about the worst possibility. "The good news is that Teresa has recently watched *Medium* and read that it was based on a real person—Allison DuBois. Now, I only need to get my mom to visit her. Maybe that will work."

"You're making progress; just keep at it," Hazel said. "Are you and Shane going fishing with Solomon and Raymond, or are you guys staying to help us get ready for Easter?"

"I think we'll stick around here," Shane said, answering for Isaac. "I'd like to decorate the Easter eggs, and I think Isaac wants to draw some pictures for Easter presents."

"Yeah," Isaac whispered. "This drawing of the daffodils and crocuses is for Ethel. Do you think she'll like it?"

"I'm sure she'll love it," Hazel grinned. "I remember one Easter, I cut out a cute little rabbit from a coloring book and used it as a stencil to make rabbit-shaped cookies. After they cooled, I decorated them with pink frosting, and the kids loved them."

"That was long ago, but I still remember those cookies," Shane said. "They were delicious!"

"Let's work on our sewing projects while we visit," Melba said.

"Good idea," Hazel agreed.

While Melba and Hazel went to the sewing room, Shane and Isaac cleared the dishes from the kitchen table, filled everyone's coffee cups, and sat back down. Melba and Hazel returned with their sewing basket and an arrangement of cattails, which they had sprayed with hair spray—to prevent them from fluffing—and then painted gold. They sat down, and while Hazel continued embroidering sweet williams on a table napkin where she had left off, Melba added tatting along the edge of a table runner with a shuttle.

"What were you talking about earlier?" Ethel asked, walking into the kitchen. She put the eggs on to boil, then fed Tweety. He chirped, sorting through the seeds, eating his favorites first. "I missed the conversation. . . . I was outside watering the daffodils and crocuses."

"We were talking about judgment and forgiveness," Melba said.

Ethel put on her apron. "That seems like a fitting topic for Easter. You know, the ego is very insecure. . . . It uses judgment as armor to protect itself. The ego judges others to shield itself from its own insecurities, which are based on fear. The ego, needing to be special, feeds on constant approval and needs enemies in order to be superior—it raises itself up by putting others down. . . . In other words, by judging others," Ethel explained, gathering the ingredients for piecrust. "People have a never-ending fear-based dialogue with their egos, which is a source of much unhappiness. They're afraid of not being good enough, being wrong, not being in control, losing their possessions, being shamed, being judged, not being smart enough, being ugly, being rejected, being destitute, being old and alone. And ultimately, they're afraid of dying."

"That's another thing that happened," Isaac said. "My mom recently remembered the time I told her I wasn't afraid to die. I didn't know it then, but those words really hurt her."

"Of course they did." Hazel reached for Isaac's hand. "Parents don't want to hear that their kids are thinking about dying, let alone that they're *not* afraid to die!"

"I know," Isaac said. "But at the time, I had become aware subconsciously that I was going to die, and I was a little surprised that I was okay with it, so I told my mom. Maybe that wasn't the right thing to do."

"Knowing what is the right thing to do isn't always easy," Shane said. "What you need to focus on now is getting your mom to visit Teresa so she can tell her about Allison."

"I agree," Melba said, finishing the tatting on one side of the table runner.

"You weren't afraid to die, but many people are because they identify primarily with their body and ego," Ethel said. "They're afraid to die because they don't want to let go of their worldly possessions, but hanging on to them sets them up for a difficult crossing. But when people know their soul is only temporarily residing in their bodies, it decreases their fear of dying. I was surprised the first time I died. I was free, looking down at my body in the hospital room. Everything was more wonderful than anyone could imagine—it was heaven. I remember having a life review, an account of all my actions and how they affected others, but then I was sent back because it wasn't my time."

"It must have been difficult to go back," Hazel said.

Ethel cut the flour with butter. "It was, but I wasn't afraid to die the second time, because I knew death wasn't the end."

"What are you making?" Alma asked, walking into the kitchen.

"A couple of piecrusts for you," Ethel said. "I figured you'd be itching to make your famous cherry pies for Easter."

"How did you know?"

"A little bird told me so," Ethel said, taking the eggs off the stove to cool. "The piecrusts will be ready for you soon, and the girls are finishing the dinner napkins and table runner for the Easter centerpiece."

"That sounds nice. I'll start the pie filling," Alma said, putting on her apron.

Just then, Raymond and Solomon walked into the kitchen after chopping and stacking firewood.

"What's for breakfast?" Solomon asked.

"There's hot cereal on the stove," Ethel said. "Are you guys going fishin' after breakfast?"

"Sure thing," Solomon said. "I hope we catch some trout for Easter dinner. I love them dredged in cornmeal and fried in bacon grease!"

"Well, if the creek don't rise by the time you and Raymond get home from fishin', we'll have everything ready for Easter dinner. All we'll need to do is fry up the fish when you get home, and after dinner, we'll have an Easter egg hunt."

After Solomon and Raymond ate breakfast, they grabbed their

fishing poles and a bucket of night crawlers from the refrigerator, then went to their favorite fishing hole on the Big Wood River, where the waters ran deep and calm in the shade of the towering cottonwood trees.

As everyone visited, Alma made two cherry pies and Ethel made coleslaw and ambrosia while Hazel, having completed her first table napkin, began embroidering another one with daffodils. Shane started decorating the hard-boiled eggs at the kitchen table while Melba added tatting to the second side of the table runner and Isaac finished a drawing inspired by Ethel's earlier conversation about fear. When he was finished, he showed it to everyone.

[A hand-drawn spiral of text depicting fears winding inward to a small stick figure at the center.]

"That's interesting, Isaac. I like how you've shown that people are sometimes imprisoned and isolated by their own fears," Shane said. "I was just thinking about our earlier conversation about ego, fear, and judgment and how they relate to the aikido philosophy. That's the Japanese martial art in which I earned my black belt. Based on Buddhist principles, the aikido philosophy is a balance between harmony, spiritual strength, and following a peaceful path. We do not engage in our opponents' attacks. We practice stepping aside, placing our opponent off-balance, and then using the attacker's momentum to facilitate their fall."

"Can you give me an example?" Isaac asked. "It would help me understand if I had a visual."

"Sure, let's say your sparring opponent rushes in to throw a punch. Rather than meeting them head-on with force, you grab and twist their wrist in such a way to force them off-balance and then use their momentum to cause them to fall to the ground and roll away from you. Using their energy against them is practicing a nonviolent approach toward your opponent. Does that make sense?"

"Yes, I understand," Isaac said. "That's a great philosophy and approach to dealing with conflict."

"It occurred to me that people could use the same principle toward nonphysical opponents," Shane said, placing an egg into the red dye. He had drawn two yellow hearts on it with a crayon, and as it soaked, the dye created a deep-red color around the two yellow hearts. "First, and most importantly, a person must recognize their opponents: ego, fear, and judgment. Otherwise, those opponents remain in control. But once a person is aware of their opponents, they can disengage and step aside. Simply acknowledging these behaviors sets them off-balance and facilitates their fall."

"Because engaging with your opponent only makes them stronger?" Isaac asked.

"Exactly. If you refuse to engage, the opponent has no leverage over you."

"I like it. Disengage and step aside." Isaac smiled.

Alma took the golden-brown cherry pies out of the oven, filling the kitchen with a heavenly aroma. Setting the pies on the counter, she looked out the window and saw Solomon and Raymond coming, their baskets heavy with rainbow trout.

23

LONG LIVE THE QUEEN
May 2, 2019

Hearing Charlie calling, Dexter and Cobalt ran through the laundry room to the garage and jumped into the back of her car. She closed their door, Chris got into the passenger seat, and they drove to the Painted Desert early in the morning to collect natural materials for the two ant exhibits they were scheduled to deliver by the end of May. First, they planned to install Queen Fern at the Cook Museum of Natural Science in Decatur, Alabama, before the grand opening scheduled for June 7, 2019, and then continue to Iowa State University's Insect Zoo to deliver Queen Phoenix.

When they arrived at their location, Chris opened the car's hatch, and Dexter and Cobalt took off running, barking as they chased after a jackrabbit. Chris and Charlie grabbed their coffee and backpacks, then walked into the serene Painted Desert, the sun lingering just above the horizon in the morning's chilly air. As the two meandered through the desert, Chris collected several small rocks that caught his eye.

"Look at these." Chris handed Charlie a few small light-yellow rocks that had been polished by the elements and time. "I think they'd look nice against the wavy sandstone we picked up last time we were out here. We should also try to find some of those lava rocks and desert grasses. They'd look nice in the foraging area."

"These are perfect, and we should also keep our eyes out for a small piece of twisted sagebrush." Charlie removed her backpack, pulled out a plastic bag, and placed the rocks inside. "All these materials will make a natural-looking exhibit. It will look great." She zipped up the backpack and put its straps around her shoulders. "After we arrange everything, we can scatter some of that beautiful rust-colored sand I collected from the Vermilion Cliffs to give it a natural feel."

After she and Chris had finished gathering the natural materials, Charlie whistled for Dexter and Cobalt, and they all walked back to the car. Charlie played Ratatat's album *Classics* as she drove home because hearing it made her feel that if she just kept driving, the road would eventually lead to Isaac. In Charlie's mind, she was always driving toward Isaac, but she never arrived at his intangible location. Instead, she always ended up at menial places like the grocery store, work, or home. Although she had gotten used to being disappointed, she still played the album to evoke the vision she held in her mind of meeting Isaac somewhere down the road.

"When we get home, do you want to clean up the garden?" Chris asked. "I could remove the leaves from the flower beds while you make some hummingbird food."

"Sure," Charlie said, giving a car on the side of the road a wide berth. "We're late taking care of the garden; we should have done it last month. I've heard the hummingbirds and felt bad because I haven't got the feeders up yet."

When they arrived home, Charlie hung the grasses they collected upside down in the garage to dry, and then they spent the rest of the afternoon working in the garden. Chris removed the winter's debris from the flower beds planted with wild asters, blue flax, and scarlet-orange *Echinacea* while Charlie cleared off the garden memorial stone, which read: FOREVER LOVED AND MISSED, ISAAC CALLEY 2000–2017. Next, Charlie straightened the engraved stone hanging on the fence, which featured an image of five songbirds singing on a tree branch. It read: *ISAAC'S GARDEN*. Finally, she placed the ant sculptures, made from repurposed metal, under the Apache plume so they appeared to be looking out from underneath its protective branches.

As Charlie worked, she reflected on what had happened over the past two years since Isaac died. Thinking of all of her and Chris's former plans—watching Isaac grow up, planning birthday and Christmas parties, helping Isaac get his driver's license, watching him graduate from high school, planning vacations together, being proud of him for getting his first job, and maybe having grandkids—she couldn't help but feel like they all had been erased. Deleted. Canceled. Although Charlie and Chris tried to be productive, it seemed to her that they were just going through the motions and not really living. They had lost the wind in their sails and felt like they were drifting.

That evening, Chris made salmon and asparagus on the grill while drinking a beer. It was a pleasant evening: The birds chirped, the weather was perfect, and the dinner was delicious, but there was always one thing missing.

Over the next two weeks, Charlie and Chris worked together to create two beautiful ant exhibits for Queen Fern and Queen Phoenix. Next, they painstakingly moved Queen Fern's colony into the first exhibit, using a paintbrush to transfer each ant, one at a time. Then, they carefully transferred Queen Phoenix's colony into the second exhibit. The repletes were the only ants left behind, but they couldn't travel, because they were so engorged with nectar that if Chris and Charlie attempted to take them cross-country, they would fall from the ceiling where they clung. If they fell, they could rupture, spilling the contents of their abdomens and potentially leading to mold and bacteria growing inside the new formicarium and killing the colony. Charlie and Chris decided it wasn't worth the risk, so they placed the repletes on a damp towel inside a plastic container and called their friend Rich, a professor from Northern Arizona University (NAU), where they had donated Queen Hazel I.

"Hey, Rich, this is Charlie. Are you interested in eating some repletes with your students and colleagues?" Although she felt bad about leaving the repletes behind and had no intention of eating any of the repletes herself, she knew it served no purpose to let them die a slow death.

"Absolutely! That sounds fun," Rich said. "When should I expect you?"

"I can be up there in about fifteen minutes if that works for you."

"Sure. We just ate lunch, so we'll have repletes for dessert!"

When Charlie arrived at NAU's School of Forestry, Rich opened the container and looked at the repletes, where they clung to a damp paper towel, moving their heads and antennae but so engorged with nectar they couldn't walk. He picked one up by its head and thorax, placed the nectar-filled abdomen in his mouth, then pinched it off. Rich looked surprised as the nectar spilled into his mouth. He licked his lips while still holding the squirming ant's body between his fingers.

"Very sweet," Rich said, placing the writhing head and thorax of the ant into the plastic container alongside the other repletes. "It sort of tastes like a sweet apple."

"That's because I feed them honey water and apples." Charlie felt bad for the dying ant but knew it would soon be out of its misery.

"Makes sense," Rich said. "You know, many Indigenous people, including some Native Americans and Aboriginal Australians, dig up colonies for the repletes—they're considered a delicacy. And in parts of Thailand, they fry the workers, pupae, and larvae, then sprinkle them on salads. They're nice and crunchy and provide a valuable source of protein. Let's share the repletes with the biology department just down the hall. They're going to love this!"

Rich and Charlie walked around the biology department, offering repletes along the way. Many professors, staff, and students were eager to taste the repletes, while others were squeamish and preferred being spectators. Some willing participants ate the ants the same way Rich had, but others ate the repletes whole. One student winced after crunching the body of a replete between her teeth. "At first, they're sweet, but when you bite into its body, it's very bitter." Once the plastic container was empty, Rich thanked Charlie for bringing the repletes, and they said goodbye.

In the morning, Chris and Charlie placed Queen Fern's and Queen Phoenix's exhibits into the back of Chris's Touareg on a cushion, secured them into place, then pulled the back cargo cover over the ants to provide shade from the sun during the long drive. Once they'd put their suitcases in the back seat and Charlie had texted Nancy to let her know they were leaving, Chris carefully backed out of the driveway and drove to the end of the street. Charlie briefly unbuckled her seat belt to check on the ants. To her surprise, they were calmly eating the pineapple she had placed in the foraging area.

"They seem to be doing pretty well. I thought they would be running around, but they're just eating," Charlie said. "Well, it's only one thousand five hundred sixteen miles to Decatur."

"Then we best get going!"

Chris drove from Flagstaff through New Mexico to Texas, where the giant windmills dipped their blades in and out of the fog that lingered just above the ground, like enormous white three-petaled daisies with their heads slowly turning in the soft breeze. Leaving the windmills behind, Charlie and Chris reached Amarillo by evening, where they checked into a hotel.

"Do you have any pets?" the clerk asked.

Chris inconspicuously winked at Charlie. "We left our dogs at home."

They opened the hotel room door, propped it open with a chair, and carefully moved the two ant colonies into the hotel room.

Early the next morning, they packed the ants back into the car, stopped at Starbucks on their way out of town, and headed for Oklahoma City. Although Chris simply enjoyed a good cup of coffee, Charlie needed the caffeine to prevent migraines from caffeine withdrawal. Whenever they were on the road, Charlie made a habit of making a mental note of the location of the Starbucks in each city so she knew where to stop on her return home.

Later that day, they stopped behind a gas station in Little Rock, Arkansas, to eat lunch. They left the car doors and hatch open to prevent the ant colonies from overheating.

"Corrie, from Cornell University, said she'd love to have Queen Hazel II." Charlie took a bite of her egg salad sandwich. "Should we donate that colony to her?"

"Absolutely! It would be awesome to have one of our colonies at Cornell University!"

Charlie agreed. "And Corrie's a nice person who's all about ants, so I'd feel good about them going there."

"It's great to keep adding to the list of things we've accomplished through the foundation," Chris said. "We've already planted two thousand trees and started our second endowment at NAU."

Charlie nodded, then cut the conversation short. "It's getting hot. . . . We need to get going and turn on the AC; I'm worried about the ants."

Charlie and Chris finished their sandwiches, then got into the car and cooled the temperature down to seventy degrees. Chris carefully avoided potholes while they enjoyed watching the landscapes change along Interstate 40. They crossed the Mississippi River into Memphis, where they took US Route 72 Alternate to Decatur, Alabama, and checked into a hotel.

Early the next morning, they left the ant colonies in the hotel room to make a quick coffee run but were dumbstruck to find out the coffee shops wouldn't be open until 10:00 a.m., since it was Sunday.

"I'm not sure this is going to work for me," Charlie complained.

"I'm not sure we have any say in the matter!" Chris took a deep breath, then exhaled. "We'll have to come back after delivering the colony to the Cook Museum."

Charlie sighed, and then they drove back to the hotel, loaded Queen Fern into the car, and drove to the Cook Museum of Natural Science to meet Sarah May and Eric. As they'd been instructed, they parked near the gate, and Charlie called Sarah May on her cell phone.

"Good morning, Charlie. Are you here?"

"Yes, we're in the parking lot by the gate."

"Eric and I will be right out to let you in."

Eric and Sarah May greeted Charlie and Chris in the parking lot, then held the bay doors open as Charlie and Chris carried Queen Fern into the insect area of the museum and sat the exhibit on the floor. As Charlie and Chris installed the ant colony, Sarah May called Brian and Leslie Cook, who kindly came to the Cook Museum of Natural Science to thank them for donating the colony to their museum. A couple of hours later, after finishing the installation, Sarah May showed Charlie and Chris some of the other insects that were on display.

"Did you know that praying mantises are the only insects that can turn their head one hundred eighty degrees?" Sarah May pointed to their exhibit. Next, she pointed to a blue beetle in the adjacent exhibit. "And the blue death-feigning beetles get their name from their behavior. When they feel threatened, they fall over on their backs and hold a feigning death posture until their predator leaves."

"And one of my favorite insects is the giant water bug," she continued. "The adults can catch and eat an animal up to fifty times its size. That's the equivalent of a person eating a hippopotamus in one sitting! The giant water bug pierces its prey with a sharp beak and injects paralyzing enzymes into its prey, which liquefies its internal organs.

Then it slurps out the juices like a milkshake. They have a snorkel-like breathing tube near the end of their abdomen that extends to the water's surface, which they use to breathe. They also trap air bubbles beneath their wings while submerged under the water's surface, which they breathe from small holes in their abdomens."

"Very cool," Chris said. "It looks like Queen Fern has a perfect forever home with you and your other insects."

"Oh, I almost forgot to tell you, Queen Fern is part of the Longest Reigning Queen Contest," Charlie said. "We started this contest to keep track of the age of the queens. We're trying to break the record of twenty-eight and three-quarters years for the longest-lived queen in captivity. She'll be two years old this year, so if you make her a special birthday cake made of fruit and insects with two candles, it will make a great photo and help you record the queen's age. The contest also helps ensure that everyone who receives a colony from us will do their best to take excellent care of their colony because they won't want to lose the contest to one of their friends in the entomology community."

"Celebrating the queen's birthday also provides a great excuse to throw a party," Chris added. "I don't know about you, but I'm always game to eat cake at work!"

"That sounds like a lot of fun," Sarah May agreed. "Count us in!"

After saying goodbye to Sarah May and Eric, Charlie and Chris drove to Starbucks, got two cups of coffee each, and returned to their hotel. They loaded Queen Phoenix into the car, checked out, and started the eight-hundred-mile drive to Ames, Iowa. As they traveled north from Nashville to Kentucky, they marveled at the mansions with thoroughbreds grazing on the rolling green hills, surrounded by white picket fences. Picture-perfect.

They passed through Saint Louis in the afternoon and arrived in Ames that evening in time for a late dinner. They picked up Thai noodles, went back to the hotel, and tried to recover from the long drive.

The next morning, Charlie and Chris stopped at Starbucks and then met Ginny at Iowa State University's Insect Zoo, where they delivered Queen Phoenix. As Chris and Charlie installed the ant exhibit, they visited with her.

"I'm so glad we met at the IECC," Ginny said. "And I'm thrilled to get this colony. Everyone loves the yellow honeypots!"

Charlie took a sip of her coffee. "It was great to meet you there.... Two things I've learned about insect people are that they're very kind and eccentric!"

"Yeah, we're a different breed," Ginny agreed.

"This heating cable will help the colony produce more workers," Charlie said, plugging in the heating cable attached to the bottom of the formicarium. "They use the heat as an incubator for their pupae. It helps speed up their development."

Ginny smiled. "That's a great trick."

"In nature, they put their pupae under rocks or just under the ground's surface because those areas naturally collect the heat from the sun and serve as a natural incubator," Chris added. "They're very clever."

"They certainly are," Ginny agreed. "Now that we've finished here, I'd like to show you around the rest of Iowa State University's Insect Zoo."

"That sounds fun," Chris said, smiling.

Ginny showed Charlie and Chris some of her favorite critters: Australian walking sticks, millipedes, hissing cockroaches, giant stag beetles, scorpions, and tarantulas.

Ginny picked up an Australian walking stick. "These guys are so cool. They make an odor that smells like butterscotch, and they trick ant colonies into taking their eggs into their nests and rearing them as their offspring! When the young walking stick leaves the ant colony, it molts and becomes an adult walking stick."

"Whoa, that's crazy that the walking sticks trick the ants into raising their young!" Chris exclaimed.

"I know, right?" Ginny said. "I love these guys."

Once Ginny had finished showing them the rest of the insect collection, Charlie reviewed the care instructions for the ant colony and told her about the Longest Reigning Queen Contest. After that, Ginny thanked them for donating Queen Phoenix, and they said goodbye.

Chris and Charlie stopped to pick up a bite to eat on their way out of town, then headed for Texas. While Chris drove, Charlie wrote a poem.

COFFEE WITH ANTS

A young woman sat drinking coffee with the ants.
One little yellow ant with small dark eyes
    asked the woman for a bite to eat.
The woman handed the ant a biscuit with raspberry jam.
The ant thanked the woman kindly, turned, and
    walked away.
The young woman remembered the blue jays,
    wondering if the boy had been right.
At daybreak, the birds flew down from the sky,
    perched in the trees, and begged for peanuts.
They filled their beaks, turned, and flew away.
The boy had been gone so long
    the woman wondered if he would ever return.
The little yellow ant with small dark eyes
    returned and asked for seconds.
The woman gave the ant a pot of honey and a
    cricket.
The ant thanked the woman kindly, turned, and
    walked away.
The woman finished drinking her coffee
    and noticed her hands had grown old.
Still, the boy did not return.

That night, Chris and Charlie stayed in Amarillo, and the following morning, Charlie drove the rest of the way home. When they arrived, they greeted Dexter, Cobalt, and Schmiggs and decided to unpack the car the next day because they were exhausted from their journey.

"That was a great road trip, but I'm happy to be home," Chris said. "It'll be nice to sleep in our own bed tonight."

"Indeed," Charlie said. "We just drove over thirty-six hundred miles. I'm beat!"

"Me too. I don't know if I'm just worn out from the long drive, but I feel a little sick," Chris said, lying on the bed and rubbing his stomach.

After a moment, he asked Charlie to come over. Then he took her hand and placed it on top of a hard mass just beneath the surface of his upper left quadrant.

24

KING SOLOMON AND SIR ISAAC NEWTON
The Other Side

SOLOMON PUT ON his black Stetson hat, buttoned up his jacket, and then picked up the cup of coffee Ethel had poured for him.

"Isaac, my dear boy, let's go for a walk down by the river."

Isaac smiled and put on his favorite light-brown jacket. "I love this coat. My mom got it for me a long time ago, and wearing it makes me feel a little closer to her."

"Your mom does the same thing." Ethel handed Isaac a cup of coffee, knowing how much he took after his mom. "She wears your jackets to keep your arms around her; it's very endearing. I hope you and Solomon enjoy this beautiful morning. It will do you both some good to get outside."

"Thanks, we will," Solomon said, opening the door.

Isaac and Solomon walked through the door, and Ethel kissed Solomon on the cheek, then closed the door behind them.

As Solomon and Isaac walked along the Big Wood River, the steam from their hot coffee left a faint fleeting trail behind them in the brisk morning air. The leaves of the towering black cottonwood trees were bright yellow against the blue sky, while red grasses stood out sharply against green shrubs. The bright-red and yellow disc-shaped leaves of the tall quaking aspens flittered in the wind like silver dollars.

Pine-scented air washed over Isaac and Solomon as they walked down to the riverbank, where the river quietly rumbled, and the rainbow trout swam in the deep, cold waters.

"You know, Grandpa, there are a lot of things... intangible things that can't be measured," Isaac said, stopping to take a sip of his coffee. "Just like the connections between entangled particles, our connections to our loved ones exist but can only be observed indirectly through our actions."

"You're absolutely right." Solomon pointed to a fallen tree not far from where they were standing. "Let's sit over there while we visit and enjoy our coffee."

Isaac and Solomon walked to the fallen tree and sat down, facing the Big Wood River. "Many things—especially the nonphysical—can't be measured or understood through science. Take the unseen forces of guilt and shame. You can't measure them, but they can drive people to destruction. The same is true about love. You can't put your finger on it, but it can cause people to move mountains. Just because something can't be measured doesn't mean it doesn't exist—science has limitations," Solomon said. "Still, science is a valuable tool because it helps people understand the world they live in."

"I agree, but that's the whole problem for my mom and Chris. Science can't prove that you and I are sitting here, but here we are nonetheless," Isaac said. "If science could prove that death isn't the end, it would eliminate a great deal of suffering."

"True," Solomon agreed. "But a lack of proof isn't all bad. It causes people to look for the answers beyond the physical—they have to listen with their hearts."

"I know you're right. I just wish it wasn't so hard on my mom, Chris, and everyone else. Unfortunately, sometimes life's lessons can be very difficult," Isaac said. "You know, Chris was always very kind to me. I'm glad we were able to spend a little time together. I quickly grew to love him as a true friend... someone I could trust. He loved good food and enjoyed making us special dinners and going out to different restaurants just for fun.... I loved that about him."

"I'm so glad the two of you were close," Solomon said. "I know Chris loves and misses you too."

"My favorite time with Chris was the ten days that he, my mom, and I spent together in Japan. We found this amazing restaurant in the Gion district of Kyoto, where we sat on the floor and placed our legs in a hollowed-out space under the table. The young woman who served us dinner was dressed in a silk kimono with cherry blossoms. She knelt on the floor near our table, bowed her head, and in a soft voice—almost a whisper—she took our order. She was beautiful, and the sushi was to die for—I was in heaven. Dinner was so delicious we went there twice," Isaac said, taking another sip of his coffee. "And there was this bakery in Tokyo called the Ginza Kimuraya that had been open since 1869! Since Chris and I both have sweet tooths, we went there at least three times. We figured they must be doing something right if they'd been around that long. They were famous for their sweet rolls filled with red and white bean paste, but the apple squares were my favorite."

"What are apple squares?"

"They are these wonderful pastries baked in the shape of a square, and when you bite into them, the sweet apple filling in the center fills your mouth . . . so delicious! It makes my mouth water just thinking about them, and the funny thing is, Chris and I almost got sick trying out all the pastries. . . . We went a little overboard."

"Those are fond memories." Solomon smiled. "I know you've been watching over Chris and your mom, but they have some challenging times ahead. Let me know if I can help."

"Thanks, Grandpa. I will. I can certainly use all the help I can get."

Solomon took a drink of his coffee. "As for science, man has made extraordinary advances in many fields despite its limitations."

"I agree. Science is a wonderful tool that can be used to gain knowledge, and knowledge empowers people to think independently."

"True. That reminds me of some stories about ancient beliefs regarding solar and lunar eclipses," Solomon said, pushing back the brim of his Stetson. "The Vikings thought the moon and the sun were being chased by two wolves, Hati and Skoll. Whenever either wolf caught their prey, an eclipse occurred. And the ancient Chinese believed eclipses were caused by a dragon eating the sun, and in order to save it, they had to make a lot of loud noise by banging on their drums. The Choctaw people had a similar belief. They thought a hungry black squirrel was eating the sun, and they also believed the way to save the sun from being devoured was to make a lot of noise. In many cultures, there used to be a good deal of banging on drums and making loud noises every time an eclipse occurred." Solomon chuckled, then his expression hardened. "But the Incas were more macabre. They worshipped the all-powerful sun god Inti and thought eclipses occurred because Inti was displeased. To appease Inti, the Incas made human and animal sacrifices. People now understand, of course, that a solar eclipse occurs when the moon passes between the sun and the earth, casting its shadow on Earth, whereas a lunar eclipse occurs when the earth passes between the sun and the moon, casting its shadow on the moon."

"That's a great example of how science has helped people," Isaac said. "Now they understand what an eclipse is, and there's no perceived need for human or animal sacrifices. People prefer things to be finite. Not having answers makes people uncomfortable, and this leads them to fill in the gaps in their knowledge with speculations, which can be dangerous and deadly. Science is a much better path."

"Yes, science has helped man for a long time," Solomon agreed. "Around 350 BCE, Aristotle used the term *natural philosophy* to refer to the study of nature, but during the sixteenth to eighteenth centuries, scientists, including Copernicus, Galileo, and Sir Isaac Newton, regarded the world differently and were central figures in the scientific revolution. The word *science* comes from the Latin word meaning knowledge. As scientists studied astronomy, physics, and mathematics, the scientific revolution caused a separation between the study of science and philosophy. As a result, *natural science*, using observation and experiments, eventually replaced *natural philosophy* and has greatly advanced man's understanding of the natural world he's been forever captivated and puzzled by."

Solomon picked up a flat, polished river rock and moved it between his fingers. "To further understand how science has shaped the world, we need to dig into the scientific revolution, starting with Ptolemy. He was an Egyptian mathematician and astronomer from around 150 CE who theorized that Earth, rather than the sun, was at the center of our solar system. Ptolemy was doing the best he could with the information he had at the time. Still, his error was recorded in Ecclesiastes 1:4–5: 'One generation passeth away, and another generation cometh: but the earth abideth for ever. The sun also ariseth, and the sun goeth down, and hasteth to his place where he arose.'" Solomon took a sip of his coffee, then added, "My father was a Southern Baptist preacher, so I grew up studying the Bible."

"Is that why people still refer to the sun as setting and rising?" Isaac asked.

"Yes, even though the sun is stationary at the center of the solar system, people once thought the sun went down in the evening and rose the next morning," Solomon said. "Some fourteen hundred years after Ptolemy theorized that the earth was at the center of the solar system, Copernicus challenged his theory, saying the sun was at the center of the solar system rather than the earth. At first, Copernicus's book, *On the Revolutions*, did not create controversy with the Roman Catholic Church, but things changed once Galileo confirmed Copernicus's theory using a telescope. Galileo was investigated by the Roman Inquisition in 1633 and found guilty of heresy. His book, *Dialogue Concerning the Two Chief World Systems*, was kept in the church's Index of Forbidden Books until it was released in 1835, and Galileo was put under house arrest and spent the last eight years of his life locked away in his own home."

"That's terribly unfair!" Isaac exclaimed.

Solomon nodded. "Although it took a while, in 1980, Pope John Paul II ordered that the evidence in Galileo's trial be reexamined. Later, Copernicus's remains were found in an unmarked grave and then laid to rest at the Archcathedral Basilica, and Galileo was reburied near Michelangelo's tomb in Florence's magnificent Basilica of Santa Croce. Now, Copernicus and Galileo are both celebrated scientists by the Roman Catholic Church," Solomon said. "Earlier, I mentioned that Copernicus, Galileo, and Sir Isaac Newton were all central figures in the scientific revolution. Now I want to tell you a little bit about Newton. He—"

"My mom named me after Sir Isaac Newton," Isaac interrupted, grinning.

"Yes, I know. The two of you have almost the same birthday. You were born on December twenty-fourth, and Sir Isaac Newton was born on the twenty-fifth."

"I didn't know that. That makes it even more special."

"Yes, it does," Solomon agreed. "As I was saying, Sir Isaac Newton was one of the leaders of the scientific revolution. He studied Galileo's and Descartes's mathematical ideas, developed them further into his own mathematical systems, and became one of history's greatest mathematicians. One fascinating aspect of his life that likely drove him to success was being abandoned when he was a small boy. His father died before he was born, and after his mother remarried, when he was three years old, she left him to be raised by his grandmother. Later, when Isaac was eleven, his mother came back into his life after her husband's death. But by then, he had already developed many insecurities."

"Abandoned children often see themselves as throwaway kids—not worth keeping, and as a result, they often have low self-esteem."

"That's true. But over his life, Sir Isaac Newton became very accomplished, especially for someone who probably felt like, as you say, a throwaway kid. But because of his past, he might have felt a need to prove his self-worth to himself and to prove to his mother that he was worth keeping!"

"Perhaps that was one of Sir Isaac Newton's life lessons," Isaac said. "Coming to believe he had worth."

"And his extraordinary contribution to humanity is a great example of how one person learning their life lessons can benefit so many others," Solomon said. "It's fitting that Queen Anne knighted Sir Isaac Newton in 1705, making him the first scientist to be honored with knighthood. After all, his law of universal gravitation explained why the planets orbited the sun at a certain distance and included the formula he developed to calculate the distance!"

"And he figured that out in the seventeenth century!" Isaac added.

"He was an exceptional man, and his story is a great example of why learning our life lessons is so important."

"I couldn't agree more."

Solomon adjusted his Stetson. "Have I ever shown you my favorite fishin' hole?"

"No, but I'd like to see it."

Solomon and Isaac finished their coffee and then walked along the riverbank, where they saw three quarrelsome magpies. One left with something in its beak, and the others followed, chattering as they flew away.

They continued to Solomon's favorite fishing hole under the yellow canopy of cottonwood trees and sat down on an outcropping of rocks overlooking the crystal-clear water. The leaf litter scattered on the ground was scarlet red, lemon yellow, and grass green—autumn in its full glory.

"This is where I always sit when I'm fishin' for rainbow trout."

"I can see why; it's beautiful here." Isaac sat down beside Solomon and picked up their conversation where they had left off. "You know, it occurred to me that science and religions are searching for the same thing—truth and understanding of our place in the universe. They're telling the same story, but from different angles, and therefore, they have different things to offer. Science gathers information through experiments, whereas religions gather information from stories handed down by our ancestors."

Solomon smoothed his thick Western mustache. "When I was growing up, my parents read me stories from the Bible and explained their important morals, which grounded me and gave me a sense of purpose and direction to lead my life. I'm grateful for the gifts the Bible has taught me and also for what science has taught us about physics, biology, chemistry, astronomy, and medicine. Through science and religion, we've gained a greater understanding of our place in the world and universe."

"True. We've also made mistakes, which are great learning opportunities," Isaac said. "It takes humility and courage—two of life's great lessons—to admit one's mistakes and correct them. As you said, the Catholic Church admitted its errors regarding Galileo, and now he and Copernicus are honored and revered scientists. Even great scientists like Ptolemy and Einstein have made errors. Einstein, one of the most brilliant minds known to man, once thought the universe was static . . . that it was a constant. Later, when Edwin Hubble discovered the universe was expanding, Einstein had to reconsider his theories."

"To err is human," Solomon said, working the polished river rock between his fingertips. "Like you, I have a namesake. My parents named me after King Solomon, one of the wisest men in the Bible, who is credited with writing the majority of Ecclesiastes, Proverbs, and some of Psalms. Many ancient wise men wrote in hieroglyphs, demotic script, and ancient Greek, like the various writing scripts found on the Rosetta stone. For centuries, our ancestors collected the most inspirational writing from the wisest men before assembling them into the Bible. The result was an incredible gift of wisdom that has been handed down to us. And the same can be said about other religious texts. The stories are different because they reflect different cultural backgrounds, but many of the texts convey similar morals."

Isaac agreed, then suggested, "Let's go get another cup of coffee and walk down Quigley Road. I'd like your help finding ways I can help my mom and Chris achieve their life lessons and navigate the difficult road that lies just ahead of them."

"That sounds wonderful." Solomon stood up, placed the flat river rock alongside his index finger, coiled back his arm, and skipped the stone along the glassy surface of the crystal-clear water.

25

ISAAC'S ASHES
August 15, 2019

STANDING IN THE SHOWER, Chris felt the lymph nodes on the side of his neck. *That doesn't feel right; they're larger than usual.* He got out of the shower and stood sideways in front of the mirror, looking at his swollen stomach. "I look like my mother did before she died," he muttered to himself. *It's a good thing I quit my job last month. I don't think I could make it to work the way I feel.*

Chris put on a pair of sweatpants and pulled a loose-fitting T-shirt over his swollen belly, then went to the kitchen, poured himself a cup of coffee, and joined Charlie, who was drinking coffee at the kitchen table.

"What are you doing?" Chris asked.

"I bought these small urn pendants, and I'm putting some of Isaac's ashes in them," Charlie explained. She sealed the pendant cork with a drop of superglue, pressed it firmly into place, and sat it on the table.

Chris picked it up. "Can I have this one?"

"Of course, that's why I made it." Charlie put some of Isaac's ashes in a second pendant while they waited to see the oncologist that Chris's GP had referred him to. His appointment was at nine o'clock that morning. "I'm worried. . . . I just wanted Isaac to be with us through these difficult times."

"That's a nice idea." Chris held the ceramic urn in his hand for a moment, then placed it around his neck and tucked it inside his shirt. "I'm scared. My mother died from cancer and . . ." He began to cry.

Charlie stood up, put her arm around him, and pulled him close. "You're not alone. You've had my back through all the horrible times with losing Isaac, and I'll have your back no matter what happens."

Charlie held Chris in her arms while he wept. They were dreading going to the doctor . . . worried about the prognosis. They were already emotionally tapped and didn't know how much more they could take.

"I need to get myself together," Chris said, drying his eyes.

"Would you like some eggs and toast?"

"No, I've lost my appetite. . . . Maybe just a piece of toast and jam."

After breakfast, Charlie drove Chris to the doctor and checked in for his appointment. As they waited in the lobby, he filled out the paperwork they gave him.

"Chris Kirkendall," a phlebotomist called from the opened door. Charlie and Chris got up and walked over to meet her.

"I'm Chris."

"I'm going to take you back for a blood draw," the phlebotomist said. "It will only take a few minutes, and then you can come back to the lobby and wait to see the doctor."

Chris and Charlie followed the phlebotomist to her workstation, where Chris sat down in a chair surrounded by empty blood collection tubes with various colored tops, tourniquets, and needles. Chris rolled up his sleeves, revealing his large, ropy veins.

"You're going to make our job easy this morning," the phlebotomist remarked. "You have the veins we all dream of."

Chris smiled. "Yeah, nurses always love me because I have great veins."

"I'll say." The phlebotomist placed a tourniquet around his upper left arm, then tapped his veins. "Here comes the prick." She punctured his vein and filled a handful of vials with various colored tops, then released the tourniquet, withdrew the needle, and put a piece of cotton over the site before securing it in place with a Coban wrap. "Thanks, that's all I need." She motioned toward the door. "You can go back to the waiting room. Your doctor's nurse will call you soon."

Chris and Charlie returned to the waiting room, where Chris continued filling out his forms. When he was finished, Charlie returned them to the receptionist, and a few minutes later, a nurse called Chris's name, and they followed her down the hall to an exam room. The nurse had Chris sit on the exam table while she took his vitals. "Dr. Mitchell will be in to see you in a few minutes," she said, then closed the door behind her. Apprehension hung in the air.

Chris tried to stay optimistic. He hoped that if he had cancer, it would be something they could treat, like the last time. Still, he felt an overwhelming sense of dread.

"This sucks!"

"It certainly does," Charlie agreed, hugging Chris from his side to avoid his swollen stomach. "But remember, we're in this together!"

Chris took his glasses off and wiped his tears on his shirtsleeve. "Thanks, beautiful. I love you with all my heart."

"I love you too, handsome. I'll always be by your side—you don't have to face this alone!"

There was a knock on the door, and Dr. Mitchell, dressed in a casual business suit, walked in holding a clipboard. He shook Chris's hand and introduced himself in a heavy Czech accent.

"I've reviewed your history. You had thyroid cancer more than a decade ago, and now you have a large mass on your upper left quadrant and enlarged lymph nodes on both sides of your neck."

Chris nodded.

Dr. Mitchell placed his clipboard on the counter. "I need you to lie flat on your back so I can examine your belly."

Chris lay down as Dr. Mitchell pulled out the footrest. "Are you comfortable in that position?" the doctor asked.

"I'm okay," Chris said, feeling anxious.

Dr. Mitchell palpated Chris's stomach, the upper region of his groin, armpits, and neck. "When did you first notice this lump in your abdomen?"

"About two months ago. It took a while for me to get an appointment with you because I recently quit my job. Charlie put me on her insurance when I quit, but my previous doctor wasn't on her plan. I finally got a new primary doctor who referred me to you. . . . My old oncologist is in Seattle."

"Are you in pain?" Dr. Mitchell asked.

"Not a lot, but I'm very uncomfortable with the pressure in my stomach."

Dr. Mitchell finished his examination, then asked Chris to sit up.

"I need to make a phone call to see if I can quickly get one of the lymph nodes removed from your neck so we can get a positive ID of what type of cancer this is," Dr. Mitchell said, urgency in his voice. "I don't mean to alarm you, but this could be very serious."

"Are you saying I have cancer?" Chris felt his shoulders grow tense.

"Yes, but some types are more easily treated than others, and before I can plan a course of treatment, I need to know which one you have. Let me make a quick phone call, and I'll be right back," Dr. Mitchell said, leaving the room.

Chris got down from the exam table, and then they sat on chairs across the room. They looked at each other in shock, knowing the oncologist would only work in haste if something terrible was wrong. Feeling defeated, Chris slumped his shoulders and lowered his head.

Charlie grabbed his hand. "I don't know what to say. . . . I'm so sorry!"

"I don't want to battle cancer AGAIN!" Chris sobbed. "I've already had cancer. What did I ever do to deserve this? THIS SUCKS!"

"It totally sucks," Charlie agreed, grabbing a tissue box from the counter. "I feel so bad for you."

After a few minutes, Chris regained his composure. "Let's see what the doctor has to say. Maybe there's a treatment for this kind of cancer. I've beaten cancer before; I can beat it again."

Charlie nodded, looking concerned.

Dr. Mitchell walked in, closed the door, and sat down. "I called Dr. Turrell, an ear, nose, and throat specialist. He said he could see you at two fifteen. Would you be able to see him then?"

The doctor waited for a reply.

"Yes, we can," Charlie jumped in, seeing Chris was on the verge of tears again. "Just tell me where to go, and I'll make sure we get there."

"Okay, I'll have my nurse set it up. Make sure you don't miss that appointment. It's critical that Dr. Turrell remove a lymph node to test as soon as possible!"

"I understand. We'll be there."

"Once Dr. Turrell removes it, he'll overnight it to the Mayo Clinic in Phoenix, where they will identify what type of cancer it is," Dr. Mitchell explained. "I'll follow up with you as soon as I have the results. In the meantime, get plenty of rest and try to eat to keep your strength up."

After the appointment, they went home, and Charlie made an early lunch, but Chris pushed it aside and made himself a mojito. Charlie grabbed a Heineken from the refrigerator, and they walked outside and sat beneath the orange umbrella. They wished they could avoid the elephant in the room, but they knew they couldn't.

Chris took a drink of his mojito. "Just what the doctor ordered," he said sarcastically. "If this type of cancer is like my thyroid cancer, it's fairly easy to treat, and I probably can get treatment here or in Phoenix. I've learned from experience that the best way for me to deal with cancer is to try to stay optimistic."

"Okay, I understand, but you're not alone like before. I'd never leave you to fight cancer by yourself," Charlie reassured him. "There's nothing more important to me than taking care of you."

"Thanks, beautiful. You mean the world to me," Chris said, tears in his eyes. "I just don't know how much I can take. First, we lost Isaac . . . and now this."

"I was thinking the same thing. It seems so unfair."

"There's no use trying to figure out what to do until we have the diagnosis, and honestly, I don't want to talk about it anymore." Chris sighed. "Let's talk about anything other than cancer. . . . CANCER SUCKS!"

Charlie and Chris made small talk until they left for their appointment. After Chris was checked in, they held hands in the uncomfortable silence of the exam room. A few minutes later, Dr. Turrell entered the room, examined one of the lymph nodes on Chris's neck, and asked them to check into the outpatient surgery center at five thirty for the excision.

Once they arrived, Chris was prepped for surgery and escorted to one of the bays of the operating room.

—

While Charlie waited, she felt conflicted . . . like she had been running away from Isaac's death for almost two and a half years while remaining stuck in the same place and time—the day Isaac died. Now, she also wanted to run from her current situation. She tried to read a magazine to take her mind off what lay ahead, but when that failed, she called Teresa and talked with her while pacing the hall.

Eventually, a certified nursing assistant came and took Charlie to the post-anesthesia care unit, where Chris was waking up but still groggy. The nurse in the unit explained to Charlie that Chris had been placed on two liters of oxygen because his oxygen level hadn't remained above 90 percent following the procedure.

Charlie held Chris's hand. "I'm right here, handsome. You're recovering from having the lymph node removed from your neck," she reminded him, helping him to orient himself. "And you're doing fine."

Chris slowly opened his eyes. "Hi, beautiful, it's good to see you." He squeezed Charlie's hand.

"Just rest, and once your vital signs are stable, I'll take you home."

"Thanks for taking care of me," Chris said, closing his eyes.

After watching Chris's oxygen level for over an hour and determining it wouldn't remain above 90 percent without supplemental oxygen, the post-anesthesia nurse called the doctor and received an order to release Chris home on oxygen. Once the oxygen tank and concentrator had been delivered, Charlie took Chris home and settled him into bed. She propped his legs up on two pillows to help relieve the pressure on his abdomen, which they had begun doing since he started retaining fluids. Cobalt and Dexter jumped onto the bed and lay down next to Chris.

"I won't be able to sleep with the noise from the concentrator, and since I work in the morning, I'm going to sleep in Isaac's room," Charlie said, holding his hand. She felt guilty about leaving Chris to sleep alone. "I'll be just down the hall. . . . Call me if you need anything."

"I will, and don't worry, I understand. Right now, I'm so tired I think I could sleep through just about anything," Chris said. "But there is one thing you could get me before you go to bed."

"Of course. What is it?"

"I need a bag of ice. I'm burning up."

Charlie made a bag of ice, put it inside a pillowcase, and gave it to

Chris. He lifted the covers and placed the bag of ice in the middle of his chest.

"Thanks, that feels great."

"Is there anything else I can get you?"

"No, but thanks," Chris said, petting Cobalt on the head.

Exhausted from the day, Chris quickly fell asleep.

At 5:00 a.m., Charlie got up and quietly took a shower, trying not to wake Chris, but as she dressed for work, she noticed he was awake.

"How are you doing? How did you sleep?"

"Pretty well at first," he said, "but then I woke up and had a hard time getting back to sleep. I got up a couple of times because I was burning up and needed more ice. And the pressure in my stomach is very uncomfortable."

"I'm sorry, handsome. I'm surprised I didn't hear you. I wish you would've called me. I'd have gotten up and made you another bag of ice," Charlie said. "Do you want me to call work and tell them I can't come in today? I can stay home and take care of you if you want me to."

"No, I'll be okay," Chris reassured her. "It's not difficult for me to get to the kitchen and make myself something to eat. I'm just going to rest, watch TV, and try to sleep. If I need something, I'll call you."

"Okay, but remember, I've already talked to my boss, and she said there's no problem if I need to leave early or take the day off." Charlie clipped her RN badge to her collar and placed her stethoscope around her neck.

"I know, and I appreciate it. I'll get up and have coffee with you before you go to work." Chris slowly got out of bed and walked to the kitchen table, pulling the twenty-five-foot-long oxygen tubing attached to the concentrator behind him. Once he sat down, Charlie gave him a cup of coffee. While they visited, she packed a lunch and made sure Chris had everything he needed before leaving for work. When Charlie's alarm on her phone rang, she turned it off and reluctantly kissed Chris goodbye.

Midway through the day, as Charlie was sitting in the break room eating her lunch, Lori, the charge nurse, came in and sat down.

"I'm so sorry about your husband. Did the doctors find out what's going on? How's he doing?"

Charlie quickly brought her up to speed.

"I wish there was more I could do to help," Lori said. "Was the psychic medium in Sedona able to help you with your loss of Isaac? Did you ever go see her?"

"No, I completely forgot," Charlie said. "What was her name? I think I wrote it down, but I must have misplaced it."

"Let me look her up." Lori picked up her phone and found the phone number on the website.

Charlie dialed the number and waited for the medium to answer, but it went to voicemail. As she was leaving a message, a blaring announcement was broadcast on the overhead speaker: "Code Blue to physical therapy, Code Blue to physical therapy, Code Blue to physical therapy."

After the emergency was resolved, Charlie worked hard to catch up on the work delayed by the Code Blue, then reported on the status of her patients to the on-coming nurses, clocked out a little over thirteen hours after she had clocked in, and drove home.

When she arrived, she changed her clothes and found Chris in bed, watching *Gunsmoke*. "How are you feeling?" Charlie asked, kissing him.

"I feel like shit, and I have no energy." Chris grabbed Charlie's hand and scooted over in bed, making room for her.

Charlie sat down next to him. "Did you get anything to eat today?"

"A little bit, but the pressure in my stomach makes eating very uncomfortable," Chris replied. "I missed you today. How was your day?"

"Just another day at work," Charlie said, not wanting to bother him with stories of other people's medical emergencies. "Did you hear from the doctor?"

"Yes. He called, and I made an appointment to see him tomorrow to go over the biopsy results."

"That was fast. . . . They have the results? What time is your appointment?"

"Eight in the morning."

"Let me make a quick call. I need to get the day off so I can take you to that appointment."

Charlie called her supervisor and, after a brief conversation, hung up.

Chris looked relieved when she told him she got the day off.

"Honestly, I'm glad you can go with me," he said. "I'm worried that tomorrow will be one of those dates forever etched in my memory." He squeezed Charlie's hand.

"Me too," she admitted. "I'm very worried, but we'll get through it, one step at a time."

Charlie made Chris another bag of ice, put it on his chest, and then curled up next to him, and they watched TV for a while before bed.

The next morning, Chris came into the kitchen wearing his old bathrobe and found Charlie already there, drinking coffee.

"Hey, handsome. Can I make you a cappuccino and a piece of cranberry hazelnut toast?"

"Sure, why not? That'd be nice."

Chris and Charlie talked over breakfast, then got ready for Chris's early appointment. Charlie helped Chris get comfortable in the passenger seat, put the oxygen tank behind his chair, and then Chris put the nasal cannula on. Before backing out of the driveway, Charlie put on one of Chris's favorite songs, "More Than a Feeling" by Boston. Chris loved it not only because it was a great song and because it was on the first record he had owned, but more importantly, because his mother, Edith, had bought the album for him to cheer him up one day when he was sick and had to stay home from school.

Chris smiled as the song began to play.

26

HOUSTON
August 17, 2019

CHARLIE PARKED at the front entrance of the cancer center because walking caused Chris to become short of breath and quickly fatigued. She unloaded the oxygen tank from the back seat, placed it on the ground, and then helped Chris to the lobby by giving him her arm to steady himself. She pulled the oxygen tank behind them with her other hand.

Shortly after 8:00 a.m., Dr. Mitchell's nurse called Chris's name and escorted Chris and Charlie back from the lobby to the same room they'd been in before.

Charlie and Chris sat beside each other as they waited for the doctor, the air in the room thick with tension. Chris placed his hand over the ceramic urn beneath his shirt. The only time he took off the pendant was when he went to bed, but every morning, he put Isaac's ashes back around his neck.

Dr. Mitchell knocked on the door, walked in, and firmly shook Chris's hand, his poker face telling them nothing about the biopsy results. He sat down and placed his clipboard on the desk.

"I received the pathology report from the Mayo Clinic," Dr. Mitchell said. "It's what I was afraid of."

Chris and Charlie braced themselves for what was coming.

"I'm so sorry to be the one to give you the bad news, but you have mantle cell lymphoma," Dr. Mitchell said. "This type of cancer is very aggressive, and it's in stage four. We need to start treatment as soon as possible."

Charlie's reasoning skills froze. She felt ill-equipped to react logically to what they were hearing—like a deer caught in the headlights.

"I don't understand! What does this mean?" Chris asked, his voice shaking. "What are we supposed to do?"

"Our facility can only administer outpatient chemotherapy. We're not set up to give inpatient chemotherapy," Dr. Mitchell explained. "You'll need to choose whether to have inpatient or outpatient chemotherapy, and then we'll need to start treatment as soon as possible."

"Which is best?" Chris asked. "Which one should I do?"

"I can't tell you which treatment plan to choose, but generally speaking, patients with this type of cancer have better outcomes with inpatient chemotherapy, which you could receive in Phoenix or at MD Anderson in Houston. Your choice may depend in part on your insurance." Dr. Mitchell took one of his business cards from the inside of his jacket, wrote his cell phone number and Chris's diagnosis on the back, and handed it to Chris. "Mantle cell lymphoma is a rare type of cancer. You'll want to research it before making a decision."

Chris took the card. "I don't know what to do."

Speechless, Charlie wrung her hands.

"You and your wife need to talk this over. Please call me in the next couple of days with your decision. Again, I'm sorry." Dr. Mitchell stood up. "Is there anything else I can do for you before I leave?"

"No." Chris's tense shoulders dropped in defeat.

Dr. Mitchell shook Chris's hand and said goodbye, leaving Charlie and Chris to pick up the pieces of their shattered lives. Not knowing what mantle cell lymphoma was, they didn't realize the gravity of the situation, but they knew the news wasn't good.

After they got home, Chris sat at the kitchen table, the oxygen tank clicking every time he took a breath as he stared out the window. Charlie turned on the concentrator, brought its long tubing to Chris, and exchanged it for the nasal cannula. Then she turned the oxygen tank off, put it by Chris's side of the bed, and went back into the kitchen.

"Is there anything I can get you?" she asked, trying to break the heavy silence.

"No, but thanks." Chris's voice was flat as he continued staring blankly out the window.

"Where's Dr. Mitchell's business card? I need to look up what type of cancer you have. I can't remember what he said."

Chris took it from his pocket and handed it to Charlie. She sat down in front of her computer, looked up mantle cell lymphoma, then opened a page titled "Mantle Cell Lymphoma (MCL)." She learned that, when treating MCL, the median time for chemotherapy to fail was less than eighteen months, and the median survival time was approximately three years.

Charlie's heart grew cold as terror struck. "I can't fucking believe this!" She showed Chris the information, then burst into a state of panic and started cursing and pacing the floor. "THREE YEARS! LESS THAN EIGHTEEN MONTHS! I can't FUCKING believe this!"

"Those are NOT good odds." Chris buried his face in his hands.

Seeing Chris begin to break, Charlie put her arms around him as the darkness settled around them. After a while, unable to bear the weight of the air, Charlie started pacing the floor again, then looked out the kitchen window and burst into tears.

Watching Charlie lose control of herself clearly made Chris uncomfortable. "Hey, beautiful, the best way for us to deal with this is to try to stay calm and optimistic."

Charlie turned around. "I understand what you're saying, but you're going to have to give me a few minutes to lose it before I can pull myself back together." She was wiping her tears and crying at the same time.

"I understand."

Later, after Charlie had regained her composure, she researched the leading specialists treating mantle cell lymphoma on her computer while she and Chris ate lunch. The profile of Dr. Wang from MD Anderson in Houston said that he was the mantle cell lymphoma program director there.

"Chris, look at this guy." Charlie showed Chris Dr. Wang's profile. "He's the leading specialist for mantle cell lymphoma and works at the best cancer center in the country. Let's try to get an appointment with him."

Chris agreed.

When Charlie called, the receptionist asked her for the patient's information and booked Chris for September 5. When Charlie asked if there were any earlier appointments, the receptionist explained that Dr. Wang's schedule was fully booked until then. Charlie confirmed their appointment and thanked the receptionist for his help.

"September fifth is almost three weeks out," Chris said anxiously. "I'm worried about waiting that long. Dr. Mitchell said we need to start treatment as soon as possible."

"Well, I've made the appointment, and we can cancel it if we choose to go another route," Charlie said. "But he's the leading specialist for mantle cell lymphoma at the most prestigious cancer hospital in the nation. Still, three weeks makes me uncomfortable too. Can you call Dr. Mitchell and ask what his opinion is?"

Chris called Dr. Mitchell, and they talked briefly.

"Dr. Mitchell said it would take two weeks to arrange for me to get inpatient treatment in Phoenix and urged me to keep the appointment with Dr. Wang at MD Anderson. He said one more week to get the best treatment possible wouldn't make a lot of difference in the long run."

"Okay, the receptionist in Houston said to plan to stay up to ten days on the first visit," Charlie said. "I'll arrange time off from work tomorrow."

"Thanks," Chris said. "I'm tired. I'm going to have a drink and sit outside. Will you join me?"

"Sure." Charlie walked to their bedroom and returned with the oxygen tank. "I'll take this downstairs so we can sit outside under the umbrella."

Chris made himself a White Russian, then they sat outside and talked about what lay ahead. They made reservations to stay at the Hilton Houston Plaza / Medical Center, a five-minute drive from the MD Anderson Cancer Center. Charlie insisted on driving them to Houston, and Chris reluctantly gave in but asked her to drive his car because the seats would be more comfortable for the twenty-hour drive. After they'd finished making their travel plans, they tried to recover from the horrible day.

—

As time wore on, Chris did his best to eat to keep his strength up and rest during the days because his night sweats kept him up during the nights. Meanwhile, Charlie tried to balance the demands of her job, taking care of Chris, looking after the animals, and doing the household chores. She continued to work full time in order to keep her health insurance. She was grateful she had chosen the high-deductible health care plan, which would cover 100 percent of the costs after their deductible was met. She knew cancer treatment would be expensive but felt relieved knowing that Chris could easily pay the deductible and that the remaining expense would be covered.

After the first week of waiting for Chris's upcoming appointment, Charlie proposed a plan to help the time pass more quickly. They were eating dinner when she made the suggestion. "What do you think about leaving two days early so we can deliver Queen Izzy to the Audubon Butterfly Garden and Insectarium in New Orleans before heading back to Houston for your appointment?"

A concerned look crossed Chris's face.

"It might be a good distraction for us while we wait," Charlie said. "All we're doing here is waiting around, watching the walls move in closer."

"I can't see a downside," Chris admitted. "But I just wonder if it's the right thing to do."

"I don't want to do anything you're uncomfortable with."

Chris thought for a minute, then it became clear that he'd made up his mind. "The sooner we can leave, the better," he said. "I don't see any reason not to go early."

"I have the next four days off, so we could transfer the colony tomorrow if you like."

"Fine with me," Chris said. "It'll be good to see Zack. He was so nice to us on our first field trip with the IECC. Remember when we stopped to collect vinegarroons? You were very upset at the time and went off to be by yourself, but he and I stayed behind and had a nice conversation about Isaac and his love for ants."

"That's why I want to donate a colony to him and the Audubon Butterfly Garden and Insectarium."

Chris smiled.

The following morning, Chris started to help Charlie transfer Queen Izzy and her colony into the New Orleans exhibit, but he quickly grew tired and had to lie down. While he watched *Gunsmoke*, Charlie finished transferring the rest of the workers. Then, using the utmost care, she moved Queen Izzy in with her daughters. They immediately started arranging their new home. Once Charlie was finished, she brought Chris a chocolate Häagen-Dazs ice cream bar, sat beside him in bed, and called the oxygen company. She ordered eight tanks for the two-day drive to Houston. They planned to use the concentrator while in their hotel rooms.

Charlie's supervisor had given her the next two weeks off, and her friend Sydnie, who was the director of physical therapy, had volunteered to take care of Cobalt, Dexter, Schmiggs, and the ant colonies while Charlie took Chris to Houston.

Finally, September 2 arrived. Sydnie came by in the dark hours of the morning to help Charlie load the New Orleans exhibit into Chris's car before she headed off to work.

"Be safe, and let me know where you are at the end of the day."

"I will. Thanks."

After Sydnie left, Charlie finished packing the car and checked on Chris, who was getting dressed after showering. Once they'd eaten, she helped Chris get comfortable in the passenger seat and laid the oxygen tank on the floor behind him. Then Charlie went back into the house, scratched Schmiggs on the head, petted Dexter and Cobalt goodbye, and stood for a moment in front of the small table where Isaac's candle was burning. She paused, looking at Isaac's picture. *I don't know if you can hear me, but if you can, please help me. I'm afraid and don't know what I'm supposed to do. I miss you.* Then Charlie blew out the candle.

She got into the driver's seat, fastened her seat belt, and drove them the twelve hours from Flagstaff to Albuquerque, on to Amarillo, and finally to Wichita Falls, Texas. They made good time, only stopping to get fuel and buy lunch. Once they arrived in Wichita Falls, they checked into a hotel just off the freeway. Charlie helped Chris to their room and texted Sydnie to tell her where they were. Sydnie replied, saying everything was good on her end. Then Charlie made two trips back to the car to get the concentrator and their suitcases.

While Charlie unpacked, Chris ordered takeout from a Mexican restaurant down the street. Feeling happy that Chris had an appetite, Charlie picked up the order, and after dinner, they went to bed, but the night was not restful. Having terrible night sweats, Chris tossed and turned while Charlie got up to make ice bags from the ice dispenser down the hall.

The next day, they drove through Dallas, Shreveport, and Baton Rouge to New Orleans and checked into the Hilton New Orleans Riverside, where they had dinner at Drago's Seafood Restaurant.

"It's nice to sit down and enjoy a well-prepared meal after such a long drive," Chris said, sipping his bourbon and water. "The spinach dip appetizer and this lobster Marco are delicious. I'm glad Zack recommended this place."

"Me too. I've never had fried catfish before. . . . I'm surprised how good it is." Charlie felt grateful that Chris was enjoying a nice dinner out. To her surprise, Chris ate everything on his plate and even made room for a small piece of her catfish. The dinner was a welcoming reprieve from the persistent and inescapable darkness that was looming over them.

Chris was tired the following morning, so he decided to rest at the hotel while Charlie delivered Queen Izzy to the Audubon Butterfly Garden and Insectarium. When she arrived, Jayme, the director of animals and visitor programs, met her to help carry the ant exhibit inside. He explained that Zack wasn't able to join them, as he had a personal issue that he needed to take care of. Once Queen Izzy was safely placed in their lab, Charlie reviewed the care instructions, and Jayme gave her a quick tour of the facility. Then Charlie cut her visit short, explaining that Chris wasn't feeling well and she needed to get back to him. The crew thanked her for the colony, told her to give their best to Chris, and then said goodbye.

After Charlie returned to their hotel room, she relayed the crew's best wishes, packed the car, and drove Chris to Houston, where they checked into the Hilton Houston Plaza / Medical Center. While Chris watched TV, Charlie unpacked and lit a small votive candle she had brought. Then she took a small photograph of Isaac walking in a field of daisies from the pocket of her bag, kissed the photo, and propped it up next to the candle.

Chris checked the hotel directory and saw they had an outdoor pool and bar.

"I know I probably shouldn't be drinking, but I'm going to anyway," Chris said defiantly. "Besides, one drink isn't going to kill me, but this cancer might."

Not knowing how to respond but understanding that he felt conflicted about drinking prior to being treated for cancer, Charlie followed Chris's lead. "Let's have a drink together at the outdoor bar. We can watch the sunset over the high-rises. Hopefully, a drink will help you relax.... Maybe you'll sleep better tonight."

Early the next morning, Charlie drove Chris to the hospital. She parked on the eighth level of the garage, and they took the elevator to the third level, where they walked across the sky bridge to the main building of MD Anderson Cancer Center. Next, they took elevator A to the second floor and checked Chris into the lab. After the phlebotomist drew close to a dozen vials of blood, they went to the cafeteria and ate breakfast, then took elevator B to the sixth floor, where they checked into the lymphoma and myeloma center to see Dr. Wang.

As they waited, they looked around the room. The sight of the pale and lethargic patients filled their hearts with apprehension and dread. Some patients were slumped over with scarves tied around their heads while others were so thin that they were chronically cold and shivered underneath blankets. Several other patients sat in wheelchairs with their IVs connected to infusion pumps, which were making a repetitive sound like a muffled car engine trying to turn over but continuously misfiring—personifying the patients' withered appearances.

Charlie and Chris looked at each other with fear in their eyes and remained silent as they overheard some other patients talking.

"The night sweats are the worst," a woman in a red scarf said, looking at a gaunt man sitting across from her.

"That and not being able to eat," the gaunt man replied. "The chemo makes me nauseous, and I've lost my appetite. I'm tired and worn out most of the time."

Then Charlie and Chris saw a nurse walk out the double doors and announce Chris's name. They followed her to the exam room, where she asked Chris a battery of questions, charted his responses, and took his vital signs. After she'd finished, she asked Chris to sit on the exam table and then left the room. Chris and Charlie sat quietly, waiting for the doctor. Finally, they heard a knock on the door.

"Hello, my friend," Dr. Wang said, shaking Chris's hand. He wore a casual business suit and had a strong Chinese accent. "I'm Dr. Wang, and you must be Chris."

"Yes, and this is my wife, Charlie."

"Nice to meet you." Dr. Wang's eyes smiled at them from behind his black-rimmed glasses. "I'm worried about you, my friend. I need you to lie down so I can examine the tumor in your belly."

Chris lay down on the exam table, and Dr. Wang pulled out the footrest and then palpated Chris's stomach and the lymph nodes on his neck. "This is very concerning. I'm going to admit you to the hospital and start you on chemotherapy right away! The first round of chemotherapy will take three days. You'll need to come back in twenty-one days for the second round. Can you do that?" Dr. Wang asked, having Chris sit back up.

"Yes, we can," Chris said. "Am I going to survive this?"

"I'll do my best to kill the cancer," Dr. Wang said. "Now, I must hurry and put the orders in to have you admitted! My nurse will come in and tell you what to do."

Dr. Wang shook Chris's hand, said goodbye, and left. A few minutes later, the nurse came in and explained the lengthy admission process. That afternoon, Chris was checked into his private room at MD Anderson Cancer Center and started on chemotherapy.

Having a sweet tooth, Chris asked Charlie to see if she could find him some candy.

Charlie took the elevator to the second floor, where she found a gift shop next to a Starbucks, where a long line of doctors, nurses, and patients waited to place their orders. Inside the gift shop, she found saltwater taffy and chocolate-covered nuts, as well as a navy-blue T-shirt with white lettering that read: *CANCER SUCKS*. Charlie took the T-shirt off the rack and walked to the counter. As the cashier rang her up, she noticed Charlie's tattoos on her forearms.

"I love your tattoos!" the cashier said. "I think those are the sweetest tattoos I've ever seen."

"Thanks. I got them when my son was six years old," Charlie said, paying the cashier and wishing her a good day.

Charlie returned to Chris's room and gave him the bag from the gift store. He was pleased about the sweets but rolled his eyes when he saw the T-shirt. Still, he ended up wearing it for the next two days. Charlie stayed with Chris until late in the evening, then went to the hotel room to sleep.

The next morning, on her way to the hospital, Charlie stopped at a red light and glanced over at a family in a silver-rose Lincoln Town Car. A teenage boy dressed in a pressed white shirt and tie sat in the driver's seat, smiling at what appeared to be his father in the passenger seat. The man, also dressed in a pressed white shirt and tie, was talking to the boy. A young girl and a beautiful woman, both wearing floral-patterned dresses, were sitting in the back seat. The woman smiled as she brushed the young girl's long brown hair. The whole scene seemed so idealistic—a painful contrast to where Charlie and Chris stood in the eye of the storm.

27

TWO REASONS
The Other Side

TRYING TO ANNOY ISAAC, Shane kept nudging him with his elbow as they sat drinking coffee after a late breakfast of bacon, eggs, and toast, but Isaac didn't give in to him. He continued drinking his coffee and reading one of his favorite books, *Of Mice and Men*, by John Steinbeck.

"You've already read that book several times," Shane said, getting up and pouring himself a second cup of coffee.

"I know," Isaac said. "But it's a great book, and I remember reading it with my mom. She loved the classics. She said they revealed important truths about the human condition."

Across the kitchen table, Solomon took a sip of coffee. "One of my favorite stories about the human condition is *Moby Dick*, by Herman Melville. It's a story of being driven mad by the desire for vengeance. Ultimately, all of Captain Ahab's efforts are meaningless—the vast ocean swallows him and the *Pequod*, leaving only the screeching gulls soaring overhead . . . calling—"

"Calling as they had done for the last five thousand years," Ethel said, smiling while finishing Solomon's sentence for him.

Solomon leaned over and kissed her on the cheek.

"I know how much you love that book," Ethel said. "One of my favorites is *Candide*, by Voltaire. It epitomizes his philosophy—'Perfect is the enemy of good.' Candide travels the world from end to end in his pursuit of finding all things *perfect*. As a result, he suffers terrible calamities, only to realize there is no *perfect* . . . that *good* is tending his garden at home."

"I agree that many books become classics because they embody some important truth about a person or humanity," Shane said. "In Ahab's case, his thirst for revenge was his undoing—not a path I recommend for anyone! As for 'good,' I think it's a *good* time to go swimming! It's so beautiful outside. Let's go swimming, and you can continue reading your book this evening."

"Better yet, let's take a picnic down to the swimming hole," Ethel said. "We can sit and enjoy the sun by the towering cottonwood trees while you and Isaac swim."

Shane nudged Isaac again. "Yeah, Isaac, let's go do some cannonballs."

"I can see it's going to be one of those days." Isaac smiled and rolled his eyes. "Shane's already up to no good, and the day's just begun."

"If you ask me," Melba said, "Shane's usually up to no good. It's just his MO."

"Melba, that's like the pot calling the kettle black!" Ethel laughed. "You're just as bad as he is . . . maybe even worse. I do believe you could start an argument in an empty house."

Shane was smug. "Yeah, Melba, you could start an argument in an empty house!"

Melba gave Shane an evil eye.

"You two make yourselves useful," Ethel said, shaking her head. "Help me get things ready for the picnic. I already have macaroni salad in the fridge, but if the two of you would slice the watermelon and put it in that large container we bought from our neighbor's Tupperware party, that would be helpful. While you're doing that, I'll fry up some chicken, and we'll be ready to go."

"I do believe Isaac's onto something," Hazel said. "Relaxing on a blanket under the cottonwood trees and reading sounds nice to me. I'll get my book from my nightstand and change into my riding clothes. I'm sure Dad will want Piute and Babe to carry the picnic supplies down to the swimming hole like they did the last time."

"You bet your bottom dollar," Raymond said, then finished his breakfast.

"There's something wonderful about the relationship between the rider and their horse. If you have a close connection, you can read each other. I think that was partly why Babe and I won the rodeo-queen contest together." Hazel smiled. "Another fond memory I have of Babe is from a time when she and I were rounding up cattle. We were traversing down a steep gorge when the ground broke out from underneath her feet, and we started sliding down the slope! But Babe didn't spook. She just gently rolled over me, and neither of us was hurt. Any other horse would have become frightened and could have seriously injured or killed me, but not my Babe—we understand one another."

"That's exactly right," Raymond said, putting on his riding boots. "Your horse becomes your friend . . . a trusted partner when working a farm."

When Hazel returned from collecting her book, she and Raymond went to the barn to bridle and saddle Piute and Babe while Solomon pulled the ice trays from the freezer and filled a thermos with iced tea.

Feeling mischievous, Melba discreetly grabbed a couple of ice cubes, casually walked behind Shane, and dropped them down the back of his shirt. Shane jumped up from the kitchen table, hollering, trying to shake the ice out.

"Good one!" Isaac laughed.

"Dang it, Melba," Shane said. "You know what they say about payback!"

"If you think I'm afraid of you . . . you're wrong! I'm not. Not even the slightest!"

"You just wait," Shane moaned. "Sooner or later, I'll find a way to get you back."

"Sounds like it will have to be *much* later." Melba smirked. "Right now, I'm helping pack things up for the picnic."

"I almost forgot," Ethel said. "Shane and Isaac, can you get the picnic blanket and tablecloth from the sewing room and take them to Hazel and Raymond? They can roll them up and tie them behind their saddles."

"Sure." Shane narrowed his eyes and looked at Melba. "Just you wait."

He and Isaac went to the sewing room, found the blanket and tablecloth, and went to the barn, where Raymond and Hazel tied them behind their saddles. Melba brought the picnic food to the barn and put it inside Piute's and Babe's saddlebags. Then Raymond and Hazel mounted Piute and Babe and headed down the trail to the swimming hole. Hailey and Kéyah ran ahead, barking and roughhousing along the way.

The rest of the Williams family enjoyed walking along the riverbank to the swimming hole, taking time to enjoy the fall colors shimmering in the sunshine. Partway there, Shane realized he and Isaac had forgotten their swimming trunks. So they ran back to the house, put them on, grabbed a couple of towels, then raced back to catch up.

Once Raymond and Hazel arrived at the swimming hole, Raymond untied the quilted blanket and laid it on the ground next to an old fallen tree trunk. While he was doing this, Hazel placed the food on the red-and-white checkered tablecloth, and then they took Piute and Babe down to the river's edge to quench their thirst. Hazel took two large, juicy apples from Babe's saddlebag and gave one to Piute and the other to Babe. The horses shook their heads as juice ran down their lips, apples crunching between their teeth. Hazel rubbed the bridge of Babe's nose while Raymond patted Piute on his back, and then they walked the horses to a post under a tall cottonwood tree and tied them up. Hazel took her book, *The Good Earth* by Pearl S. Buck, from Babe's saddlebag and sat down on the quilted blanket. She opened the book where she had placed a yellow ribbon and continued to read where she had left off.

After the Williams family arrived, they settled in to enjoy their picnic. The women sat on the blanket while Raymond and Solomon sat down on the old tree trunk facing the swimming hole. Alma pulled out a set of pillowcases from her sewing bag and continued embroidering the floral pattern where she had left off. The songbirds sang as the family enjoyed lunch and the cool breeze drifting off the river.

A while later, when Shane and Isaac arrived, Shane walked to the edge of the deepest part of the river, took a deep breath, and jumped in cannonball style without hesitation, causing a great splash. A moment later, he surfaced, looking exhilarated. Hailey and Kéyah barked enthusiastically, then jumped into the water and swam toward him.

"Isaac, come in. The water's great!"

"Is it cold?" Isaac asked reluctantly.

"It's not bad," Shane fibbed, shivering. "Jump in. . . . You'll get used to it."

Isaac looked at his family, comfortably basking in the warm sun. "I don't know why I let Shane talk me into these kinds of things, but he always does." Isaac set his towel down and stepped up to the edge of the swimming hole.

Knowing Shane was most likely telling a white lie, Isaac paused, trying to gather his nerve as the rest of the family cheered him on to take the big plunge into the chilly water.

Isaac took a deep breath, jumped in cannonball style, and surfaced with a look of surprise.

"Not bad, little man." Shane smiled and high-fived Isaac as they trod water.

"You said the water wasn't bad," Isaac groaned. "It's downright freezing, if you ask me." Then, a moment later, he smiled and asked, "Do you want to do a cannonball at the same time and see how big a splash we can make together?"

"You're on!" Shane grinned and climbed onto the outcropping of rocks, then gave Isaac a hand out of the water. They stood side by side, and Shane counted down. "Three . . . two . . . one." Shane and Isaac jumped into the air together, tucked their knees to their chests, and hit the water with a big splash!

The Williams family cheered.

After several more impressive cannonballs, Shane surfaced, looking at something cupped in his hand. "Melba, come and see what I found," he said, treading water.

"Do I look like I was born in a barn?" Melba laughed. "I'm not falling for one of your tricks."

"Suit yourself." Shane shrugged his shoulders and showed Isaac he had nothing in his hands. "She didn't fall for it. Let's get out and have something to eat."

Shane climbed onto the outcropping of rocks and gave Isaac a hand out of the water. They dried off, wrapped their towels around their shoulders, and joined the picnic.

"Isaac, what's the latest news about your mom?" Hazel asked, putting her book down.

"Well, you know, I was hoping Mom would look up Allison DuBois when she and Chris watched *Medium*, but she missed that connection because she didn't realize the show was based on a real person. I still haven't figured out how to get my mom to visit Teresa so she can tell her about Allison DuBois." Isaac frowned. "But I did get her to call a different psychic medium and leave a message. My mom's surrounded by a wall of pain, which makes it difficult for me to get through. I'm worried about Chris too. I need to help him and my mom, but her walls are even harder to get past now that he's sick. I don't know what to do. . . . If I could reach her, it would help both of them."

"It's not your fault, Isaac. Your mom's been through a lot, and as a result, she's just not quite making the connection," Hazel said. "Rather than trying to get your mom to visit Teresa, you might try to get Teresa to ask your mom to visit her. . . . I think you'd have better luck approaching it from the other direction."

"I should have thought of that," Isaac said. "That's a great idea. I'll give it a try."

"It's hard to think clearly when you're upset and worried. After all, it's your mom you're trying to save, but that's why we're here to help," Hazel reassured him.

"Getting Mom to visit Teresa won't be easy, because she won't want to leave Chris's side," Isaac said. "Plus, she has very little time on her hands with all she's trying to manage. Still, it might work because my mom will be reluctant to say no to her sister. And if Teresa tells her about Allison DuBois, hopefully, my mom will *finally* go see her! If my mom sees Allison, it will change her and Chris's lives."

"Most people dismiss or ignore the signs we send them because society generally frowns upon talking to the dead," Hazel said. "When this happens, it can be helpful to work through a loved one, a friend, an acquaintance, or even a pet of the person we're trying to contact."

"Good advice. In a way—" Isaac stopped suddenly, his attention caught by something the others couldn't hear. "Chris is calling me. He's having a reaction to the chemotherapy," Isaac said, his voice filled with alarm. "I need to go."

"Can I go with you?" Shane asked. "I knew Chris when we were in high school together. I was one grade ahead of him."

"That would be great, but we need to go now. We'll let you guys know how Chris is doing when we get back."

Traveling instantly by thought, Isaac and Shane, now dressed in street clothes rather than their swimming trunks, stood next to Chris's hospital bed at the cancer center.

Chris writhed in pain, twisting and arching his back, his heart racing as he fought for every breath. He was experiencing tachycardia and severe respiratory distress caused by the chemotherapy drug rituximab. The hospital had given him rituximab three weeks earlier during his first round of chemotherapy, but at a slower rate, which he tolerated. This time, they'd doubled the infusion rate, causing Chris to go into acute heart and respiratory failure.

Isaac placed his right hand over Chris's heart and closed his eyes. As the medical equipment alarms blared, Chris clutched his pounding heart, placing his hand on top of Isaac's hand as he gasped for breath.

Calm came over Isaac as he remained motionless, holding Chris's hand over Chris's heart. After a moment, Isaac opened his eyes.

"He's going to be all right," Isaac said. "Although Chris wants to cross over now, it's not his time, for two reasons. First, he still has two vital life lessons he needs to learn, and second, I need him to stick around for my mom's sake. She's not strong enough yet to walk this road on her own."

Shane placed his hand on Isaac's shoulder. "Nice work, little man."

As Chris's hospital room filled with the medical emergency team, Isaac and Shane stepped aside and stood on the other side of the room. Then a slew of doctors, nurses, and ancillary medical staff worked to gain control of the chaos and stabilize Chris following his near-fatal reaction to the chemotherapy drug.

"It's a good thing Charlie isn't here," Shane said. "She'd be beside herself."

"She'll hear about this in the morning when she comes to visit. For now, she's sleeping, and I'm glad she doesn't have to witness this," Isaac said. "It's better that she sees Chris after he's stabilized."

Isaac noticed a well-dressed middle-aged woman with short, curly brown hair standing behind the emergency medical team as they feverishly scrambled to rescue Chris. The woman put her hands together over her chest, then closed her eyes. After a few minutes, she opened her eyes, lowered her hands, and noticed Isaac and Shane standing against the far wall. As she walked over to them, Isaac greeted her.

"Hi, my name is Isaac, and this is my uncle Shane."

"Yes, I know who you are. My name is Edith. I'm Chris's mother. It's so nice to meet both of you. Thanks, Isaac, for being one of Chris's true friends. He really loves you."

"And I love him," Isaac said. "Chris was always very kind to me. . . . I'm glad to be here for him in his hour of need."

While the emergency medical team worked, Isaac, Shane, and Edith sat on chairs on the other side of the room and continued their conversation. Doctors, nurses, and respiratory therapists rushed in with a defibrillator and crash cart, racing to stabilize Chris. They placed a non-rebreather mask on him, hung a bag of IV fluids, and gave him one milligram of epinephrine every three to five minutes per the orders of the doctor who was running the Code Blue.

"It hurts me to see my son going through this. I wish I could remove him from this situation, but things must run their course." Tears welled up in Edith's gray-blue eyes.

"Yes, and although he doesn't know we're here helping him right now, he will someday." Isaac reached for Edith's hand. "Chris told me how much he loved you and how you were always there for him. It broke his heart when you passed from cancer. . . . He was only twenty-four years old, and he never stopped missing you!"

Shane reached for Isaac's and Edith's hands. "Let's send Chris some strength and guidance."

They all lowered their heads and closed their eyes, bringing calm to the chaos as the rapid response team stabilized Chris.

A couple of hours later, the doctors making rounds entered Chris's room, but, seeing that he was peacefully sleeping after a close call with death, decided to return later.

Relieved that Chris was finally sleeping peacefully, Edith, Isaac, and Shane walked to the side of his bed to say goodbye. Edith kissed Chris on his forehead, thanked Isaac and Shane for helping her son, and left. Isaac and Shane held Chris's hands, said goodbye, then left him comfortably resting and went to visit Teresa.

—

Teresa had long been a restless sleeper, and she often lay awake in the dark, her mind reliving previous events. When she was sleeping, she frequently tossed and turned, and many of her dreams were filled with anxiety about trying to accomplish a specific task and not succeeding. But this night was unusual. Teresa was sound asleep beside Rory, her husband of thirty-five years. On their last anniversary, they had sat next to each other at the kitchen table, drinking coffee, and agreed it seemed longer than thirty-five years. They raised their cups to each other, then continued reading the morning news.

As Teresa slept, Isaac leaned over her and whispered something in her ear. Then Shane and Isaac sat down beside her. After a few minutes, Shane nudged Isaac. "Let's go back to the swimming hole and finish our picnic. We can let them know how Chris is doing and tell them we met his mom . . . and maybe I can get even with Melba!"

28

SISTER TERESA
January 16, 2020

AT THE SOUND OF CHRIS PICKING UP their leashes, Cobalt and Dexter jumped off the bed and barked as they ran to the front door. Chris fastened the leashes to their collars and then handed Cobalt's to Charlie, as his constant pulling was too strenuous for Chris to manage. Then they set out for their evening walk around the block.

"I don't want you to worry about me going to Houston by myself," Chris said. "I'm just going for a blood draw and a follow-up with Dr. Wang. Once he makes sure I'm tolerating the trial meds he put me on since the last round of chemo stopped working, I'll come right back home. Besides, you went with me on the first three trips for chemotherapy and then on the first flight to Houston, when Dr. Wang put me on these new meds. I promise I'll be fine."

Charlie looked at Chris in concern. "I know you don't want to pay for two tickets every time you have to go to Houston for the next six weeks, but I'm worried about you traveling by yourself. It's only been three months since you went into cardiac arrest."

They held Cobalt and Dexter back as the dogs barked and tried to cross the road to greet a golden retriever who was pulling a woman by his leash on the other side of the road.

"If I were still on oxygen, it would be a different story. But since the chemo partially shrunk the tumor, I have more energy and I'm stronger than before," Chris said. "Honestly, don't worry. I'll call you on the way, and I'll be back before you know it."

"Okay, but you have to promise me you'll let me know where you are at all times," Charlie insisted.

"I promise."

Charlie took Chris to the airport early the next day, they kissed goodbye before Chris checked in through security, and then she left.

Once Charlie got back home, she made coffee, sat in front of her computer, and opened the children's book she was writing, *Charlie and the Rainbow Trout*, which she'd started in Houston while waiting for Chris to be released from the hospital. Charlie had always wanted to write this story, which was based on true events that happened when she was a young girl. She continued working from where she had left off.

After a while, she heard her phone ping. Charlie checked her messages and opened Teresa's text to find a GIF of a cup of coffee repeatedly winking and then yawning.

Charlie replied, *You know me too well!*

What are you up to? Did Chris leave for Houston this morning?

Yes, I dropped him off at the airport this morning, and I'll pick him up in two days.

You should come and visit me for the day.

Charlie was in the middle of replying when her phone rang.

She answered. "Hey, girl, what's up?"

"I took the dogs out for a walk, and now I'm making your favorite oatmeal chocolate chip cookies. I was hoping you'd come and see me today," Teresa said, a little sugar in her voice. "I'm worried about you, and it would probably do you good to get out of the house for the day."

"I was working on my kids' book, but . . . did you make the cookies with coconut oil?" Charlie asked, not wanting to disappoint her sister.

"Yes, of course. Just the way you like them. Will you come and see me?"

"Those are the best cookies," Charlie admitted. "Just let me wrap things up, and then I'll be on my way. I should be there before noon."

Charlie saved the changes she had made to *Charlie and the Rainbow Trout*, fed the dogs and cat, and then drove to Snowflake, Arizona. After a two-and-a-half-hour drive, she turned onto the road that led to Teresa's house. The cold January winds had blown the snow away, leaving only a skiff of snow pellets in the troughs of the corrugated dirt road.

—

Teresa's pack of dogs grew louder as Charlie approached her sister's house. The dogs were dear to Teresa, as they reminded her of a time when her six kids had been young and naïve—a simpler time when they were grateful for the small things and never judged her. The rescued mutts followed her everywhere she went, enthusiastically wagging their tails and smiling, filling Teresa's emptiness after her six children left home. Like everyone, Teresa had made mistakes, but she had dedicated her life to caring for her children and husband the best she could. After years of looking after her family, she often felt she had nothing left to give, but she was always kind and went out of her way to help others, asking for very little in return. Teresa's husband, Rory, a nuclear engineer who worked contract jobs at different nuclear power plants across the country, was gone half the time. They each lived two lives, the one they shared and the separate one they lived when Rory was away working hard to provide for his family.

Hearing the commotion, Teresa came outside and waited while Charlie parked her car outside the fence, walked through the gate, and closed it behind her to ensure that the dogs remained inside the fenced two acres of Teresa and Rory's forty-acre parcel. Then Teresa met Charlie and gave her a warm hug.

"Thanks for coming," Teresa said. "It's so good to see you. Come inside. I just pulled the last batch of cookies out of the oven."

As Teresa opened the front door, the aroma of the oatmeal chocolate chip cookies wafted over them. "Wow, those smell great," Charlie said, then made her way through the pack of dogs to the kitchen table.

Teresa handed Charlie a cup of coffee, put a plate of warm cookies on the table, and sat down with her. Sadie, Teresa's spry deer head Chihuahua, jumped up into Charlie's lap, begging for attention. Teresa and Rory had bought her at the senior center for eighty dollars—twenty dollars less than the asking price.

Charlie took a bite of a cookie while petting Sadie. "It was sweet of you to make these; they're my favorite."

"That's why I made them." Teresa dunked a cookie in her coffee, then took a bite.

Alice, Teresa's medium-sized black dog with a narrow face and sharp white teeth, pushed her nose against Charlie's arm from underneath the table. Charlie reached down and patted her on the head.

"How's Evil Alice?" Charlie asked the friendly dog.

Alice wagged her tail, grinning.

Alice had earned her nickname, Evil Alice, when she once bit Charlie, mistaking her for an intruder. Unwilling to let Teresa live the incident down, Charlie had playfully called her Evil Alice ever since.

"How long will Rory be gone for work?" Charlie asked, petting Alice and Sadie.

"He'll be gone until the end of February, and then he'll be home for two weeks before going back to work." Teresa motioned toward the hall. "Should we work on a puzzle while we catch up? I've already started one in the other room."

"That sounds nice."

After they finished their cookies, they took their coffee into the spare room, where a brightly colored puzzle lay scattered on Shane's old dining table, which Teresa had kept after he passed. Trying to regain some of the innocent childhood she never knew, Teresa enjoyed doing puzzles, especially those with pictures from children's classic stories like *The Tale of Peter Rabbit* or other images that depicted a slice of good old-fashioned life. Charlie picked up the box, looked at the cheery picture of beautifully decorated cupcakes, and put it back down.

Teresa sat down and started putting together the red and white pieces she had already gathered while Charlie walked around the table, picking up all the green and white pieces she could find.

"I'm glad you came," Teresa said. "I'm very worried about you.... You seem so down. You're not going to do anything ... ?" She broke off for a second. "I mean, first you lost Isaac, and now Chris has cancer. I just don't want you to ..."

"Well, I will admit I've thought about it. It's been over two and a half years of pure misery since Isaac died, and I still have nightmares about him all the time. In one I had the other night, I was very upset because I hadn't talked to Isaac in so long, so I went to David's workplace to get Isaac's phone number from him. But when I got there, he said he didn't have it either. Then I started screaming and woke up." Charlie shook her head. "And now it looks like my husband's going to die on me as well. The chemotherapy has failed, so they put him on these trial drugs, and I don't know how well they will work. I'm worried. . . . They don't call them trial drugs for nothing."

Teresa listened patiently, as always. Listening and helping others was one of her greatest gifts, especially for those who were struggling with a difficult situation.

"Honestly, what do I have to look forward to? Nothing," Charlie said. "There's absolutely nothing I enjoy. Nothing makes me happy. Other people have the luxury of watching their kids grow up and have grandkids, but I'm a childless mother. They still have hopes and dreams, but that's all been taken away from me. And watching other people enjoy their families, knowing I'll never have one, is . . . It's just easier for me to be alone and withdraw from everybody. I'd probably be okay if I knew Isaac was still out there. I could find out by going to look for him, but that wouldn't be fair to leave Chris alone, so I just try to do my best for his sake."

"It wouldn't be fair to me either," Teresa said. Tears dropped onto her red and white puzzle pieces. "That would devastate me."

Charlie reached out and grabbed Teresa's hand. "I'm sorry, you're right. You've always been there for me. Ever since we were little kids, you've reached out and pulled me up every time I've fallen down."

Teresa wiped her tears with her hands.

"I would have never made it through all the horrible times without your help," Charlie said. "I'll always be in your debt for saving my ass."

"You would have made it, but I'm glad I could help."

"No, you *don't* understand," Charlie pushed back. "You've been looking out for me ever since we were little kids, and you still do, even today. It's always bothered me that you and Shane bore the brunt of Big Charlie when we were growing up. . . . He was so horrible."

"He was a real bastard. I remember that Big Charlie put our dog, Wallabee, and all her puppies in a burlap bag and threw it over the bridge into the Big Wood River," Teresa said, petting Mia, her one-eyed rescued mutt, who was sitting on her lap. "There were plenty of difficult times when we were growing up, but life's taught me not to dwell on the things I can't change and to be grateful for the fond memories I have. It's harder to remember them, but there were some good times as well."

"Good point. . . . You were always the wise one."

"I remember hearing the sound of Mom working the pedal on her Singer sewing machine while she sat up late at night, making us pajamas for Christmas. Every year, she bought flannel material when it was on sale at the Merc, and then she'd stay up late, making us new pajamas in time for Christmas. I remember one year, she made Shane a pair of blue-and-green plaid pajamas, which he loved. Another year, she made Wilma a white-and-pink nightgown and Karen a yellow one with small pink rosebuds," Teresa reminisced. "And Mom used to ask us what kind of cake we wanted for our birthday, and one year, I told her I wanted a pumpkin pie, so she made me a pumpkin pie with candles, and I got a *big* box of crayons . . . the one with sixty-four colors and a sharpener, which I had always wanted."

"Oh, that was sweet of Mom."

"Do you remember when she used to take us to Broyles Pharmacy for a drink at the soda fountain while we waited for Karen's prescription to be filled?"

Charlie shook her head.

"Since Mrs. Broyles liked Mom, she always gave her extra coupons so we could all have a soda while we waited. I can still hear the bell above the door jingle as we walked into the pharmacy. We knew we couldn't buy anything, but we still liked to look at the gifts in the toy department. One year, Wilma found a stuffed orange rabbit that she fell in love with and didn't want anyone to buy, so she always hid it before we left the pharmacy. Whenever we went back, Wilma took the orange rabbit from her hiding place and played with it until we had to leave. One day, when we went to the pharmacy, the orange rabbit was gone. Wilma was heartbroken and cried about it all day, but when she opened her Christmas present, she found her long-lost stuffed orange rabbit inside. Wilma was beside herself. She held the bunny to her chest and wouldn't let him go! Mom had asked Mrs.

Broyles to set it aside and bought it for Wilma when she had saved enough money."

Charlie smiled. "Oh my gosh, that's so cute! I remember that photograph of Wilma holding the stuffed rabbit, but I never knew the story behind it."

Charlie's phone pinged. She picked it up, looked at it for a moment, and informed Teresa that Chris had made it to Houston and had checked into the hotel. Charlie replied, put her phone in her back pocket, and then continued a conversation they'd touched on earlier while talking on the phone.

"I've told you this before, but I keep thinking about these dreams I've had where Isaac's talking to me," Charlie said. "I don't know if it's just my imagination, if I'm going crazy, or if Isaac's out there in some other dimension trying to get ahold of me. On two separate occasions, when I mentioned this to other people, they suggested I see a psychic medium. Maybe the universe is trying to get my attention by bringing it up again and again. Anyway, I started looking into different psychic mediums, but I don't know any with good reputations—there are a lot of charlatans out there. One of my coworkers suggested seeing this psychic medium in Sedona, so I finally scheduled an appointment with her. I figured I have nothing to lose at this point."

"Why don't you go see Allison DuBois?"

"Who's Allison DuBois?"

"She's the psychic who inspired the TV series *Medium*, which you and Chris watched together."

"Oh, I didn't realize Patricia Arquette played a real person," Charlie said, a spark of interest rising in her voice. "And I certainly didn't think I could go see her!"

"I think she lives in Phoenix. Let's look her up."

Charlie and Teresa looked up Allison DuBois and read that psychologist Gary Schwartz had studied her at the University of Arizona. Upon further reading, they discovered Allison DuBois had an excellent reputation and was booking appointments for readings.

"I really want to see her." Charlie scrolled through Allison DuBois's website and clicked the button that read: READING AND EVENTS. "Should I book a reading?"

"I don't think you'd regret it," Teresa encouraged her. "Even though it's expensive, it'll be worth it. If you don't make an appointment, you'll always regret not having gone to see her."

Charlie agreed and scheduled a thirty-minute "Life Questions" and a thirty-minute "Mediumship" in-person reading for March 5 in Scottsdale, Arizona.

"I can't believe I get to go see her in two months!" Charlie said, her voice filled with excitement. "And she's just down the road. I can drive to Scottsdale, see her for the reading, and be back by the afternoon to take care of Chris. I'll keep my appointment next month with Tarra, the psychic medium in Sedona, since I've already scheduled it, and she seems really nice. But I'll be very curious to see what Allison has to say."

"Me too," Teresa said. "You're not going to regret this. You'll have to call me afterward and tell me everything she says."

"You'll be the first person I call," Charlie promised, then looked at her phone. "Let's work on the puzzle a little more, and then I should head home before it gets too late."

"Okay, sounds good."

Teresa's gray tabby cat, Albert, stood up from where he was sleeping on his perch in the corner of the room, stretched, turned around, and then lay back down.

"He's so cute," Charlie said, then brought up her own cat. "You know, Schmiggs has been extremely affectionate lately. He usually sleeps at the foot of the bed, but lately, he's been coming to the head of the bed, insisting I pet him. He pushes his nose against mine, so I move over to make room for him. He lies down next to me, purrs in his loud, raspy voice for a while, and sleeps there all night. It's not his usual behavior." She held her palms up, a gesture of confusion. "I don't know what's up with him."

29

AN OLD SOUL
February 6, 2020

THE STUNNING GORGE of Oak Creek Canyon dwarfed Charlie's Honda as she drove down the switchbacks from Flagstaff to Sedona. The snow that had fallen earlier that day caused a stillness to settle over the land and created a beautiful contrast between the white-dusted trees and the streaked red cliffs towering high above. At the bottom of the ravine, a half-frozen creek babbled quietly under a canopy of oak and sycamore trees.

Familiar with the winding canyon road, Charlie wasn't bothered by the sheer cliffs. As she banked from side to side, she mentally prepared herself for the reading with Tarra, the psychic medium she was scheduled to meet in less than an hour. *I'm going to hold my cards close to my chest,* Charlie thought, making a hard left around a hairpin turn. *I don't know if psychic mediums can ACTUALLY see into the future and TALK to the dead or if they're just telling us what we want to hear. It seems far-fetched and kind of crazy, but then again, maybe priests and other religious figures who've claimed they had visions were talking to the dead the same way psychic mediums claim they can. Either way, at this point, I have nothing to lose. I'm just going to try to keep an open mind. Maybe she'll be able to help me understand if Isaac is still out there somewhere and if he's been talking to me in my dreams. And maybe she'll be able to tell me how Chris is doing and if he'll be okay.*

As Charlie rounded another hairpin turn, her blue notebook, containing a list of seven questions she intended to ask Tarra, slid to the end of the passenger seat and almost fell to the floor. Charlie reached out and pushed several photographs back into the notebook, then tucked it underneath her right hip. As she drove, she thought about her questions.

At the bottom of Oak Creek Canyon, she entered Sedona, where she crossed through streets lined with new-age gift stores, restaurants, and art galleries. She continued down State Route 89A to West Sedona, where she turned right at a grocery store and drove into a residential area. Charlie found the address she had scribbled down on a piece of paper and parked in the driveway of a two-story green home. With her blue notebook in hand, she walked to the back door as instructed and knocked on the sliding glass doors. A middle-aged woman dressed in a brown blouse and jeans entered the room. She smiled, brushed her wavy brown hair away from her eyes with her hand, and opened the sliding glass door.

"Hi, I'm Tarra," the woman said. "You must be Charlie."

"Yes. Thanks for making time to see me."

"My pleasure. Please come in and have a seat." Tarra motioned toward the table in the middle of the room. As Charlie entered, she noticed several framed prints of various religious figures hanging on the wall and several African masks and figurative sculptures arranged around the fireplace at the far end of the room.

She sat down at the table, and Tarra sat beside her with her iPad. Tarra handed Charlie a water bottle and explained that she'd record the reading, then send it to her in an email the next day. After a few minutes of small talk, Tarra clicked the record button on her iPad.

"The following mediumship reading, dated February sixth, 2020, is for Charlie. It's so nice to meet you."

"It's nice to meet you too," Charlie said, opening her notebook to her list of questions.

"Have you always gone by Charlie rather than Charlotte?" Tarra asked. "You seem like you're a bit of a tomboy."

"Yes, I've always gone by Charlie."

"Okay, if you're ready, I'd like to start by calling the ancestors." Tarra took a sip of water.

"Yes, I'm ready."

Tarra closed her eyes and lowered her head. "I call upon the holy ascended masters and all the ancestors and ask their permission to look into the book of life, the Akashic records, so I may help guide Charlie on her journey. I thank all of Charlie's guides and teachers for making this opportunity possible. I now call upon Charlie's loved ones who support her on her life's journey. Please enter one by one, by name. I give thanks to all of you for letting me help Charlie in this way."

Tarra paused. "I have a message from your teachers and guides. When you go into the heart—not the body's heart, but the heart deep within your soul—you'll accept that things truly are as they should be, and you are not alone. We, your guides and teachers, are with you and have been with you since the beginning and will remain with you beyond your last breath. Many stand behind you to be your backbone, strength, and foundation. When you're tired, we will hold you up. We walk with you so you may feel the sunshine upon your skin. Know that you can call upon us at any time. All you need to do is ask us for our guidance. Now it's time for you to release your tears upon the land so the flowers may bloom."

Charlie, maintaining her poker face, remained silent.

"Your guides tell me you're a male soul in a female body, which explains why you go by Charlie rather than Charlotte. They said you need to learn how to receive. Like a man, you're good at doing but not very good at receiving. To learn the values of both sides of the coin, we must experience the two sides—giving and receiving. Taking care of others and being taken care of are two sides of the same coin—there's no coin with one side. The two sides of the coin are opposites and complement each other perfectly. By experiencing both sides, we can complete that lesson. Your guides say you're good at giving but not receiving. . . . You might want to work on that," Tarra suggested.

"I understand," Charlie said. *There's no coin with one side,* Charlie repeated in her mind, feeling a sense of déjà vu. *That rings a bell, but I can't quite place it. It seems like I've heard that somewhere before.* Then Charlie imagined a coin: One side was white with a dark flower-shaped center, and the other was dark with a white circle around the center, similar to the yin-and-yang symbol. *It seems like I've already seen this coin somewhere before. . . . It has something to do with a castle and a beautiful garden. There was a young boy and—*

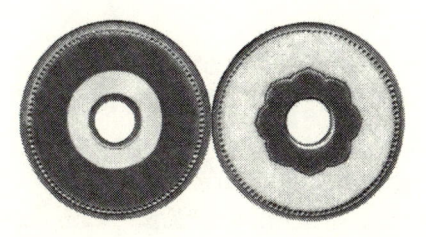

"Your intuition is right on the money," Tarra said, interrupting Charlie's train of thought. "But you need to listen to it more closely. When you have a gut feeling about something, don't dismiss it. The first thirty seconds is your intuition, but then your rational brain kicks in and tries to override it. You must try to remember this and trust your gut feeling—your intuition."

Charlie nodded. *My gut tells me Isaac's reaching in from the other side to let me know he's STILL with me.*

After they'd talked for more than ninety minutes, Charlie referred to her list and asked her first question.

"Do we have past lives, and if so, are they connected to lessons? If we're here to learn lessons, are we ever done at some point, or do we just keep coming back forever?"

"We come back to experience and learn new things, but we're not forced to," Tarra said. "We might choose to take a break and then return to learn a particular lesson. Or we might come back with a loved one to help them through an especially challenging lesson. We rely on the people we have the strongest relationships with to help us get through the most difficult lessons."

"That makes sense. If you're going through something hard and painful, it seems like you'd want your soulmate to come back with you. . . . Is there such a thing as a soulmate?" Charlie said, asking her fourth question.

"Yes, there are soulmates, and you'd certainly call on them for the most difficult lessons."

"Can a soulmate be your kid?"

"A soulmate can be your husband, wife, sister, brother, child, or even a friend."

Charlie smiled, then asked her second question. "Why are some people's lives so hard and painful?"

"It goes back to the two-sided coin. The opposite sides are needed to complete the lesson. Some lives seem very difficult, and others seem relatively easy, but both pose different lessons. If a person needs to learn self-respect, they might return and have an abusive relationship with a family member who pushes those boundaries. That situation encourages individuals to stand up for themselves and draw healthy boundaries. But if you come back to learn compassion or empathy, living a life of luxury can cause a person to be complacent, and therefore, they might live their whole life without learning their lesson. An *easy* life might set a person up for a more challenging lesson than a *difficult* life. They might get so caught up in their life of luxury that they see no reason for soul searching, and as a result, they never learn their lessons. Imagine an individual driving down the road, seeing a repeating sign—*LIFE LESSON . . . LIFE LESSON*—but they pay it no mind; they just keep driving! Hopefully, they'll make a U-turn; otherwise, they've missed their exit—their opportunity to learn an important lesson."

"Make a U-turn. . . . I like it. I don't want to miss my opportunity to learn *my* life lessons—I really need to figure this out!"

"That's why you're here," Tarra said. "Remember, all things are as they should be. It's a difficult concept . . . *especially* in the face of adversity. But in the end . . . all things truly are as they should be."

"I'll have to think about that," Charlie said, struggling with Tarra's words. "How can you see into the future?" Charlie said, asking question number three. "How does that work?"

"Time is linear here, but it's *not* linear on the other side. This allows mediums to see things differently."

"That's another one I'll have to think about," Charlie said, puzzled, then asked question number five. "I was going to ask you if there are 'old souls,' but I think you already answered this question at the beginning of our session when you said Isaac was an old soul in a young body . . . that the reason he was wise for his age was because he's been around a long time."

Tarra beamed. "Oh my gosh, he's an incredibly bright light. There's something very special about his soul—there really is."

Charlie's heart wanted to burst, but she held back her pride, and then asked Tarra her sixth question. "Are there people of all races and religions on the other side?"

"Of course there are, but you already know that. Ask your inner heart, then listen for the answer. What does it say?"

"Okay, I'm just asking because some people say otherwise, but I get it. . . . I need to listen and trust my gut feeling—my intuition," Charlie said. "My intuition tells me we're judged by our deeds, not by our race, religion, or any other superficial label when we cross over."

"You're getting the hang of it. Just don't let your mind overrule your intuitions."

"Okay, I'll work on that." Then Charlie asked her last question, number seven. "What happens if you don't complete your life lesson, because you took your own life?"

"First, it's important to note that all people with suicidal thoughts have some element of disease, and they should seek help. The brain, like any other part of the body, can become ill, be it physical, mental, or emotional. Secondly, many suicides are not true suicides; they're accidents due to substance abuse or something like that and, therefore, are treated differently, because their intentions matter. But to answer your question, you know that U-turn we just talked about?" Tarra asked.

"Yeah."

"In the case of suicide, they're so ill that they're not in their right mind, and there's no option for a U-turn. The individual has gone too far down a wrong road, and after they cross over, they must return to a previous point in their soul journey—a starting point before they took the wrong exit."

"Good to know. Thanks so much for everything." Charlie stood up to leave. *I'd better think twice about jumping in the ocean. . . . I don't want to take the wrong exit down a dead-end road.*

"You're very welcome," Tarra said, standing up. "Thanks for coming, and have a safe journey home."

Tarra and Charlie hugged and said goodbye.

Feeling anxious afterward, Charlie drove down the street, parked in a grocery store parking lot, and called Teresa.

"Hey, girl. How was the reading?" Teresa asked. "Where are you? Are you still in Sedona?"

"I'm sitting in the parking lot of some grocery store, but I'm a bit freaked out from the reading. I was hoping we could talk before I head up the switchbacks."

"Why, what did she say?"

"I can't tell you everything right now, because I need to get back to Chris, but she said a few things I don't want him to hear."

"Like what?"

"First, I asked if she could tell me anything about my husband and handed her his picture. It was the picture of Chris in the victory pose with his hands high in the air after he collected our first queen. He was grinning and was very happy. Tarra looked at the photo for a minute and then said she felt like his and my relationship was more like a brotherly-sisterly relationship than a husband-and-wife relationship and that I was taking care of him. It made me feel bad because it was more or less the truth. The thing is, ever since Chris got sick, he's become a very restless sleeper, so I've slept in Isaac's room. I just became his caretaker, and that, with already losing Isaac . . . I don't know, I just . . . anyway, she said he was happy in the photo, but he's not happy now, and she didn't feel a lot of 'oomph' or 'fire' in him. Then I asked her about his health. Tarra told me his health wasn't great, that his kidneys were weak, and she kept saying she felt like I was taking care of him. That's when I told her Chris had cancer."

"I thought you said the tumor was in his spleen."

"I did, so I don't know what that's about, but I know the new meds he's on can be hard on your kidneys; maybe that's it," Charlie said. "She also said he's not really living. . . . He's just sort of existing. Tarra told me he needs to come to terms with . . . that he needs to not be afraid of crossing over to the other side, because she couldn't see his future past fourteen months from now! When Tarra said that, my heart sank. I felt paralyzed by—"

"What are you saying?" Teresa interrupted. "Was she saying . . . ?"

"Tarra told me I needed to have a conversation with Chris about him giving me a sign when he crosses over! She said I was holding a torch for him to help him get to the other side. She also said there would be a lot of driving in the near future."

Teresa stammered, "I . . . I don't even know what to say. . . . That's horrible; I'm so sorry. . . . Fourteen months to live? How did she know you were taking care of Chris and that his health was so bad?"

"I have no idea! Only a few people know Chris has cancer. We've kept it under wraps!"

"You can't tell this to Chris," Teresa insisted.

"I know; I won't. It's just so horrible. I don't know what I'm going to do."

"Me neither," Teresa said. "Did she say anything about Mom?"

"Tarra said Mom's happy that she's gone and she enjoys sitting around with a group of girls . . . sort of like a clique, and that they visit most of the time, but she also said Mom and Isaac had been spending time together as well," Charlie said. "I almost forgot . . . at the beginning of the reading, she asked me if I knew a person named William, Walter, or Bill, so I told her that Mom's maiden name was Williams. She said, 'That's it—there are many people from the Williams family coming through.'"

"I can just see Mom sitting around visiting with a bunch of women. It must be her sister Melba and the rest of the Williams family," Teresa said. "And you know, Walter is very close to Walker . . . as in Solomon *Walker* Williams, and Bill is short for William."

"Good point. I didn't think of that. Oh, and remember I told you about Schmiggs being really affectionate?"

"Yes."

"Tarra said Isaac's been working through him to comfort me . . . that Isaac sits on the corner of my bed when I'm sleeping!"

"They can influence animals?"

"Apparently," Charlie said. "I thought that sounded a little crazy and sweet at the same time."

"Did you ask her if our pets are on the other side?"

"No, I should have. That would have been a great question," Charlie said. "But Tarra said Isaac wants me to keep traveling and that he'd go with me. She said I gave him a lifetime of adventures in his short sixteen years because, on some soul level, I knew he wouldn't be around very long."

"I told you the same thing," Teresa said enthusiastically. "You guys traveled more in his sixteen years than most people do in a lifetime! Did she say anything about Shane?"

"Tarra said Shane didn't know what happened after he died. He just kept saying, 'HOLY SHIT, HOLY SHIT,' over and over, but eventually, he came to terms with the fact that he had died," Charlie said. "She said Shane is some sort of teacher on the other side."

"I knew Shane didn't kill himself. It was an honest accident . . . a stupid accident, but an accident nonetheless," Teresa said bitterly.

"Sometime after Shane was killed by the train, I came to the same conclusion," Charlie said. "No one pays their taxes and then stands in front of a train on purpose. Besides, I went to the spot where Shane was killed and waited for the train. I heard it, and then it came barreling around the bend only a few seconds later. There was hardly any warning, and since Shane was walking down the tracks with his back toward the oncoming train, listening to the Moody Blues on his *noise-canceling* headphones, he simply couldn't have heard the train."

"I hate to even think about it," Teresa said. "Did she say anything that didn't make sense to you?"

"Tarra mentioned that Chris thinks about numbers and the budget a lot, which is true, but she thought it might be connected to a new job that will require a lot of traveling. I think the traveling has to do with Chris and me going back and forth to Houston because it's obviously not a new job—he's too sick to work. Tarra said she saw me teaching a small group of people and told me my nursing career would 'fall away.' She said that everyone in my life either leaves or dies because I'm supposed to learn about loss and death to help others deal with these issues. I don't know what she meant by all that, but I've read that psychic mediums say talking to the dead is like playing charades with them. The person on the other side tries to convey a message, and the psychic medium tries to interpret their message. . . . They don't always get it right, or they might only get it partially right."

"Playing charades with the dead is an amusing thought." Teresa laughed. "If that's what it's like, I can easily see how the psychic mediums might interpret some things wrong. The fact they get any of it right is bizarre!"

"I agree. It's strange at best!" Charlie said. "I need to get going and check on Chris. I'll call you tomorrow and tell you the rest."

"Okay, drive safe."

Charlie hung up her phone and headed back up the switchbacks. Driving in the dark, she tried to remember where she had seen the two-sided black-and-white coin. She couldn't quite put her finger on it. Then a thought came to her: *Soulmates! That's it—Isaac and I are soulmates—we're two sides of the same coin, and since there's no coin with one side, we can never be divided!*

When she arrived home, she found Chris in the kitchen making goulash. "Hey, handsome, how are you doing?" Charlie hugged him and sat down at the kitchen counter to visit while he finished making dinner.

"Better, thanks to the new meds. I think they're working." Chris stirred the ground beef as he drank his beer. "While you were out, I took the dogs for a walk on the Arizona Trail."

"Wow, that's great! I'm so glad you're feeling better. How's your energy level?"

"Some days are better than others, but I feel a little stronger today. It was really nice to get outside with the dogs." Chris smiled. "How did the reading with the psychic go? What did she have to say?"

"I still have my doubts, but the reading was definitely interesting. Tarra told me there had been some sort of loss and depression around me . . . something hard on me emotionally and mentally. Then she added that an anniversary involving the number three was coming up."

"It's close to three years since Isaac passed."

"I know! After she said that, I showed her a picture of Isaac standing in the Bamboo Forest in Kyoto and told her he had died close to three years ago," Charlie said. "She looked at his picture and was taken aback, saying there was something exceptional about him—that he was an incredibly bright light."

"Well, he certainly made my life brighter." Chris sighed, then took a drink of his beer.

Charlie nodded. "Tarra told me Isaac is still with us. All we have to do is call on him, and he'll be able to hear us! She said nothing could have prevented Isaac from passing . . . that he could have left when he was fourteen when the seizures started, but he stayed as long as he could until he ran out of time. She said he was sorry for causing us so much pain."

"It wasn't his fault he died!"

"I know. That's how I feel, but Tarra said he felt responsible," Charlie said. "Apparently, according to Tarra, Isaac's been traveling and listening to music.... He likes Frank Sinatra."

Chris looked surprised. "Frank Sinatra?"

"Isaac loved the oldies. He always said our music tastes were the opposite of what they should be. He liked listening to the golden oldies, while I liked listening to what Isaac called the 'new noise.'"

Chris added the noodles to the pot of boiling water. "He was funny that way.... I remember him listening to 'El Paso' by Marty Robbins."

"I remember that too. Tarra told me Isaac hated school because it was excruciating for him... that he preferred to learn by traveling."

"I'm so glad we took him to Japan. That was a great trip. Did she say anything about me?"

"She knew you were sick and that we had been doing a lot of driving," Charlie said, figuring out how to answer the question. "Tarra said you thought about numbers and the budget a lot, but we mostly talked about Isaac and the messages I received from him in my dreams. I wanted to know if they were really from him or if I was just imagining things."

"You seem to get messages from him, but why can't I?"

"I asked her that, and she said there are many different things that can prevent messages from getting through to the person they're trying to reach. Sometimes a person has a wall of pain or guilt up so high that it gets in the way—they can't break through the emotional barrier. Also, if a person is taking medication, doing drugs, or drinking, it can make it difficult to get through because their mind is clouded. If that happens, sometimes the person on the other side might try to get a message through by flickering the lights, moving objects around, or working through animals," Charlie explained. "Tarra said Isaac will be coming through as a hawk, so we're supposed to keep our eyes out for one."

"A hawk?"

"That's what she said. Tarra also told me another way those on the other side can deliver a message is by going through someone in the proximity of the person they're trying to reach. Apparently, the dead can influence a person to say a word or a phrase that means something specific to the person they're trying to contact."

"Didn't you say your mom used that trick on your sister Wilma after she crossed over?"

"Oh, you're right. I forgot about that," Charlie said. "After my mom passed, Wilma's Alzheimer's patient looked up at her while taking her medication and called her Muffin Bird, the nickname my mom used to call Wilma when she was just a little girl. It's a *very* obscure nickname, so the only logical explanation is that it had to be my mom. Tarra said it's a good idea to decide on a word or a phrase you will use to let your loved ones know you've crossed over safely to the other side."

"If you pass before me, what word or phrase will you use to let me know you've crossed over safely?" Chris asked.

"I don't know." Charlie fumbled, unable to ask him the same question. "But we should think of something."

Five days later, on Tuesday evening, after Chris and the dogs had gone to bed, Charlie lay in Isaac's bed, trying to follow Tarra's instructions for the meditation she'd given her. Charlie was to imagine herself walking in a garden to a bridge, where she would meet the person she wanted to talk to from the other side, filling in the details as she visualized the scene. The bridge was the meeting place, representing the halfway point between the living and those who had crossed over.

First, Charlie closed her eyes, recalling the day's events in a backward succession to clear her mind, as Tarra had suggested. Then, she imagined herself walking through a Japanese rock garden with meticulously pruned bonsai trees, rock sculptures, and a wooden bridge arching over a tranquil pool with koi and water lilies. As Charlie walked toward the bridge, she saw a silhouette of a figure standing in the middle of the bridge, feeding the koi. Her heart quickened, and she hurried her pace—hoping. As Charlie stepped onto the bridge, the young boy turned and smiled at her. Charlie ran to him and threw her arms around her son.

"I've missed you so much," Isaac said. His eyes sparkled, green like emeralds.

"I've missed you too!" Charlie replied, almost crushing Isaac with her arms. "I've come to ask you to give me a sign . . . something I will know is you to make walking this path easier. If it's possible, can you please give me a sign?"

Suddenly, Charlie was drawn from the tranquil Japanese rock garden as Schmiggs jumped onto her chest, looking at her with his emerald-green eyes. She petted Schmiggs, and then he lay down beside her, and they fell asleep. Sometime in the night, Charlie woke and saw the laundry room light on. Its motion sensor had been triggered even though everyone was asleep.

30

FOREVER ISAAC
March 5, 2020

STANDING IN FRONT of her closet, Charlie ran her eyes up and down the clothes rack, ambivalent about what to wear over her T-shirt. It was cold outside, and since she'd be driving to Scottsdale to see Allison DuBois, she wanted a second layer to keep her warm in the cold morning air. Her eyes perused her sweaters, hoodies, and long-sleeved shirts and landed on a purple-and-white plaid shirt, but it didn't seem like the right thing to wear—nothing seemed like the right thing to wear. Still, she kept looking. Then her eyes landed on Isaac's gray-and-maroon hoodie. *That's the perfect thing.* Charlie took it from the hanger and zipped it up over her T-shirt.

She walked to the living room and lit the candle at Isaac's altar, noticing particularly the strand of small wooden beads draped around his picture frame. She picked it up, made a double loop, and placed it around her neck. On her way to make coffee, she stopped and kissed Chris on the cheek as he read the news at the kitchen table.

"When is your reading with Allison?" Chris asked.

"One o'clock. I'm a bit nervous. I just don't know if she can give me the answers I'm looking for."

"You mean if Isaac's still with us or not?"

"Yeah . . . I think if I truly knew he was still out there, and it was just a matter of time before we saw him again, I'd be okay."

"I used to think death was the end, but now I'm not sure," Chris said. "With all the strange things that have happened: the lights flickering five times in the living room when we were talking about Isaac, the laundry room light turning on by itself, and your dreams, it got me thinking. Maybe death isn't the end.... Maybe there's something else. I don't know; I'm still on the fence."

"Exactly. That's why I want to talk to Allison," Charlie said. "My first reading a month ago was interesting, but I'm still not sure. But since Allison is world-renowned, I'm hoping she can give me the missing pieces I need to understand what's been happening."

"I'll be curious to hear what she says."

"What are you going to do while I'm gone? I should be home around dinnertime."

Chris took a sip of his coffee. "I'm feeling pretty good, so I'll probably take the dogs out and then watch some old Westerns. I'll make something for dinner, and you can tell me about the reading when you get home."

Chris walked Charlie to her car and kissed her goodbye. Then Charlie traveled two and a half hours south to Scottsdale, where the streets were landscaped with saguaro, ocotillo, and prickly pear cactus. She found Tom's address, parked underneath a palm tree, and waited for her appointment. Just before 1:00 p.m., a blue four-door car drove into the driveway and parked in the garage. Charlie became anxious as she recognized Allison sitting in the passenger seat, talking to the driver, a middle-aged, dark-haired man. *That must be Tom, the astrologer who works with Allison,* Charlie thought. She took a few minutes to settle her nerves, then knocked on the front door.

Tom introduced himself and shook Charlie's hand. "I'll show you to the guesthouse, where Allison is waiting for you. If you need anything, I'll be in the kitchen just inside the main house."

Charlie followed Tom past the swimming pool to a quaint guesthouse. Tom opened the door, introduced Charlie to Allison, and left. Allison was a slender woman of medium build with long brown hair and a streak of highlighted bangs on her left side. She was dressed in leather sandals, jeans, and a baby-blue sweater. Her friendly disposition made it easy for Charlie to relax.

Allison asked Charlie to make herself comfortable on the couch while she sat at a wooden desk, where she had placed a box full of sharpened pencils and a blank notepad. Charlie opened her bag and placed Isaac's leather-bound journal on her lap. Tied to its yellow ribbon were a lock of Isaac's hair and Isaac's timepiece, which he had bought in Japan. Charlie opened the journal to her list of questions, then placed Isaac's lock of hair and timepiece on the adjacent page.

"First, I want you to know that when people die, they still appear the way they looked when they were alive, but they revert to a time when they were the happiest," Allison explained, picking up her notepad and placing it in her lap. "They keep the physical qualities they identify with, so if a person was always complimented on their blue eyes, they would come through with those same blue eyes. Or if a person was a dancer and had great legs, they would still have those same great legs—they keep their physical makeup when they come through. And beauty is more important to women than men." Allison laughed. "Women tend to revert to a younger age than men . . . to an age when they were the most beautiful and free."

"That's funny."

Allison chuckled. "Yes, women tend to be a little vainer than men."

Looking at the open page of Isaac's journal, Charlie asked her first question. "Are people who have died still with us? Shortly after my son died, I had these dreams where I swear I could hear him talking to me, but now that hasn't happened for some time."

"Yes, they are. But I need to help you get rid of the pain. People put up a wall of protection around themselves to try to prevent them from experiencing more pain," Allison said. "But the wall can prevent those on the other side from getting through. I need to help you dismantle the wall so he can get through. Sometimes, they'll go through other people if they can't reach you."

Charlie then asked, "Do they also use your pets? My cat's been acting very strange."

"Yes, they can work through animals. Animals know when they're around, and just like your loved ones, your animals will wait for you when you cross over."

"Oh, that's sweet."

"Animals also revert to a younger age," Allison said, smiling.

Charlie returned the gesture, then put on her poker face. "Are we here to learn lessons, and if so, what are people supposed to learn from having a brain injury or cancer?"

"When good people die, it can inspire others to spread their goodness through their death," Allison said. "When a bad person dies—nobody cares."

"What about accidents? When someone has a near-death experience, and they see their bodies from above . . . wouldn't that mean they're in two places at the same time?" Charlie asked.

"In those situations, the outcome is not decided. Some deaths are set in stone, like my dad's was, but others are not—they have various exit points."

"That's very interesting," Charlie replied, then, feeling a sense of urgency, asked one of the questions on her list. "Why do some people get cancer?"

"Cancer is very different. Cancer erodes your soul. It feels like electricity . . . like pinpricks, and cancer repels other people."

"Can you tell me about my husband? He's struggling with cancer."

"Okay, questions on husband," Allison said. "I don't need the year, but I need the month and day he was born."

"December fifteenth."

"Okay, I just need to say this because people who take care of people with cancer . . . they absorb that sick energy, and it can drain you."

"Yes, I'm exhausted."

"If someone you loved has died and your husband has cancer, then your loved one on the other side is probably trying to keep your husband here so he can learn his lesson before he dies," Allison said. "The reason your loved one has died is they've already learned their lessons. Everyone has a different reason for being here."

"So you're saying we need to figure out what lessons we need to learn?"

"Yes, but sometimes we're kept around for other people to help them out." Allison picked up a sharp pencil. "I'm going to write down the impressions I have around your husband, and then I'll share them with you, so here we go."

Allison took a deep breath, exhaled, and then started drawing circles on a clean piece of paper on the notepad resting on her lap. Charlie listened to the graphite of Allison's pencil, busily drawing circles. She paused to write something down, and then continued drawing circles.

"One thing I'm worried about is it's in here," Allison said, patting her chest. "His breathing . . . it will affect his breathing. Are they watching to see if it's spread to his lungs?"

"It's everywhere."

"His lungs are being highlighted. That will be something he will be fighting or what may take him out. He's afraid of leaving you, which is predominantly the reason he tries to stay . . . and he's fighting like hell. He's holding on with everything he's got," Allison said, still drawing circles. "When I tap into his energy, it makes me feel very tired. It's hard to breathe. Little by little, he's slipping away, and he will get to a point where he won't have to fight anymore. Since he is a Sagittarius, he has eleventh-hour luck. If anyone can beat the odds . . . it's a Sag. He's probably already beat the odds along the way, which is a positive for him."

Charlie tried to digest what she was hearing as Allison took another deep breath, exhaled, and continued drawing circles. "His dad is being highlighted. Has his dad already passed?"

"Yes."

"His dad is either a soft place to fall, or they have unfinished business."

"They probably have unfinished business. When Chris's dad died, they were on bad terms."

"His dad might want to apologize. . . . They're emotional-based beings," Allison explained. "It feels like he is fighting an uphill battle. . . . That's what it feels like."

"I need to know if he's going to make it or not," Charlie said, trying to keep her composure as her voice wavered. "I feel terrible saying this, but I'm really struggling. I shouldn't be complaining—I'm not the one who's sick."

"I understand. . . . When I tap into his energy, it feels like he will be able to go on his own terms, and he will go quickly," Allison said, snapping her fingers. "It's going to come out of nowhere, which might make you feel unsettled. You'll think he's okay, then out of nowhere, it hits, and he'll be gone . . . but going quick is better for him. I just don't feel like this is something he can beat. . . . He's just buying himself time right now."

"We're going to Houston in a couple of weeks for a CT to see if the trial drugs are shrinking the tumor," Charlie said while Allison continued drawing circles.

"Six months stands out, connected to your husband. I just don't feel like these drugs are going to work the way you want them to. I'm just telling you this so you can mentally prepare yourself. The drugs will change the cancer, but I don't think they will do enough to save him," Allison said. "This is your thing together. . . . You're both trying to save his life. You'll do everything you can, so when you look back, you'll be able to say you did everything you could for him. But when he passes, he won't take the cancer with him."

Charlie was horrified by what Allison was saying, but at the same time, she didn't know how much stock to put into Allison's ability to see into the future. She replied with a follow-up question.

"Are you saying when people die, they no longer have the injury or disease that killed them?"

"Absolutely!" Allison exclaimed. "I've brought back children who couldn't walk because of a physical disability, and they were climbing trees! You're restored when you cross over. When your husband dies, he will go back to a younger age. It feels like a six-month prognosis, so make sure you do things with him now . . . make memories together."

"We were planning on going to New York, but then COVID hit, and his white blood cell count is very low, so I'm worried about his exposure."

"COVID is making it really difficult," Allison agreed. "Do you have any other questions about your husband?"

Charlie looked at her list of questions. "I think we've answered them all. My next question is about the person I lost."

"Okay, who am I bringing through? Who were they to you?"

"My son, Isaac."

"I'm so sorry." Allison turned the notepad over to a clean page. "What was his birthday?"

"December twenty-fourth."

"That's the same birthday as my mom and dad."

Charlie smiled but said nothing. . . . She was nervous about what was going to happen—if Allison would be able to connect with Isaac.

"I'm going to connect with your son, and I'll share with you what he has to say afterward." Allison took a deep breath and exhaled. She busily started drawing circles and writing things down for four minutes, stopping only once to get a new sharp pencil.

"When I tap into his energy, he's very easy to like," Allison said. "The first thing he said was 'My mom was my best friend.' . . . That was the first thing he wanted you to know."

Charlie burst into tears, putting her hands to her face, unable to reply. *That's EXACTLY what he'd say if he were here!*

"He said, 'She always encouraged me. . . . My mom was always in my corner,'" Allison said, drawing more circles, and then she began to laugh. "He said he tried to get you to wear his shirt today."

Charlie was dumbfounded. "I HAVE IT ON!" Charlie exclaimed. She wiped her tears and grabbed the collar of Isaac's gray-and-maroon hoodie. "THIS IS HIS SHIRT!"

Allison laughed. "You guys *were* best friends."

"Absolutely," Charlie said, smiling and crying at the same time. She moved the fabric of Isaac's hoodie between her fingers and thumb. *That's got to be Isaac! I just put his jacket on this morning—there's just no other way!*

"He talked about camping. . . . That's his version of heaven. He relives those memories to feel close to you. He referred to himself as a free spirit in life. I feel like he was very unique . . . his own guy. He didn't try to be like other people, and he said, referring to you, 'My mom's not like other moms.' He thought you were much cooler!" Allison chuckled.

"Oh, that's so sweet of him."

"He's talking about tattoos. It feels like two people memorialized him through tattoos."

Charlie pushed up the long sleeves of Isaac's hoodie to show Allison the tattoos of Isaac's three-month-old handprints on her forearms. On Charlie's right forearm was Isaac's left handprint. Beneath it, it read: *FOREVER*, and on Charlie's left forearm was Isaac's right handprint. Beneath it, it read: *ISAAC*. As Charlie put her arms together, Allison read the caption: *FOREVER ISAAC.*

"Oh, okay . . . so he knows you did that. Is there someone else with the same tattoo? Oh wait, that's funny because I wrote matching under the word tattoos. It's not someone else—it's you. . . . You have the matching tattoos! I've never had anyone say 'matching' with tattoos before."

"Yes, I have the matching tattoos."

"Oh, that's so sweet." Allison smiled. "I asked him how he felt around the time he died, and he showed me that his head felt confused . . . like he couldn't think. He just felt kind of out of it. He wants you to know that he was not in a lot of pain . . . more of a feeling of being confused."

"He died from a seizure and I'm really struggling," Charlie said, choking on her words. "He was my best friend and . . . and some relationships are stronger than—"

"It's a soulmate thing," Allison interjected.

"Yeah, I think so. I don't understand why Isaac had to suffer his whole life and then die!" Charlie said, her voice turning sharp and angry.

"Often, we don't get those answers until we die," Allison said, drawing circles on her notepad. "He referred to your cell phone as his phone. Is your screen saver a picture of him?"

"Yes." Charlie picked up her phone and showed Allison a picture of Isaac standing in the Bamboo Forest in Kyoto. Allison took Charlie's phone, looked at the picture, and handed it back to Charlie.

"He says your phone is his phone."

"Okay. Good to know," Charlie grinned, realizing Isaac had received all the text messages she had sent him.

"This is a sidenote about the time he died," Allison said. "He said he was so sorry. He had to watch the effects it had on you, and he felt really bad. He said he didn't want to go."

Charlie nodded, unable to reply.

Allison laughed. "He says, 'Let's go on a road trip. . . .' That's another version of his heaven. See, to him, his life with you isn't over."

"I can do that?" Charlie asked. "Losing him . . . it's a hard life for me."

"The world lost color for you when he left," Allison said. "But yes, he wants you to go on a road trip, and he'll go with you. Just bring a picture of him and think of him, and he'll go with you."

"Does this mean I can still travel with him and stay connected?"

"Yes, absolutely."

"When I'm painting, I ask him to help me," Charlie said. "I imagine he's leading the way, and all I need to do is follow."

"About your painting . . . he says you're painting a picture of his soul."

Charlie looked surprised. "I'm painting a portrait of Isaac!"

"He says it's a painting of his soul."

"Oh, that's so sweet of him!"

Allison smiled. "He's completely vibrant and can do anything you ask of him."

"I feel like I can walk the steps. . . . I just need Isaac to lead the way."

"Here's what I can tell you," Allison said. "Until your husband has run his course, you can't move forward, because your husband's passing has something to do with what path you will take. At that time, you will have to concentrate on yourself. You will either do more art or write about these events."

Lost for words, Charlie listened.

"He says, 'Nice necklace.'"

"Are you serious?" Charlie exclaimed. "I just put this necklace on this morning! I had them wrapped around his ashes, and . . . when we were in Belize, we bought them for a buck. I can't believe he said, 'Nice necklace.'"

"He's a bright light—he's what people think of as an angel, and he's capable of helping you with whatever you need. He's got a lot of energy. He was very kind, and he'll wait for you," Allison continued. "And you loved him more than most parents seem to be able to love their children—you have that soulmate connection. I must say, you've packed more into your son's sixteen years than most parents pack into a lifetime!"

"Indeed, he was my travel buddy. We went everywhere together."

"He's holding an owl feather. Do you know what that's about?"

"No, I have no idea."

Allison laughed. "Maybe he's saying he's the wise one."

Charlie laughed with Allison. "I really don't know anything connected to owls, but I just started birding, if that counts."

"Yeah, I don't know. . . . There's something with birds . . . something symbolic to him," Allison said. "He says, 'What's up with my room?'"

"I sleep in Isaac's room because I find it hard to sleep with my husband and the dogs," Charlie said. "Ever since my husband got cancer, he doesn't sleep well and often reads during the night. And since I work as a nurse, I need to sleep, so I started sleeping in Isaac's room. He's probably still in his room with me."

"He is," Allison assured her. "At night, he sits at the end of the bed with you. . . . He's still with you."

"My husband and I started a foundation in my son's name. Isaac loved ants, and rightly so. . . . The more you learn about ants, the more fascinating they are. To make a long story short, we now grow ant colonies in his room and donate them to museums and insectariums. It's something my husband and I do to honor my son."

"Oh, I love that. It's so quirky. He says you need to be careful because the ants are going to get loose!"

"One of the things—"

"Oh, just a second," Allison interrupted. "I can't hear you, because he's playing that song by Frank Sinatra. It's about a little ant and a rubber tree plant. Isaac's playing that song in my head." Allison laughed.

"Frank Sinatra? That's funny," Charlie said, remembering Tarra had also mentioned that Isaac was listening to Frank Sinatra.

"He's rolling up his sleeping bag. . . . He's like, 'Let's go.' He says you need the fresh air under the stars."

"I loved camping with him. We took long road trips and camped along the way. It was great fun."

"You still can. Take a picture of Isaac, and he'll go with you." Allison urged her. "He says he likes breakfast. What was his favorite thing for breakfast?"

"Angel biscuits."

"Make him some angel biscuits, and he will enjoy them with you. See, their version of heaven isn't complete until we're there with them, so they wait for us."

"If I just knew he was there. . . ."

"He says, 'I'm right next to you, but you can't hear me. We're going to get through this together,'" Allison said.

"We're going to get through this together." I like the sound of that!

"He can only make new memories with you or other loved ones," Allison explained. "He can live vicariously through you, so if there is somewhere you didn't get to take him, you can go, and he'll go with you. That's the only way he can experience something new. Through you or with someone else he loves."

"Then I had better get out there and get some things done," Charlie said. *When he was young, his smile was my smile. Now that's reversed— my smile is his smile.* "I heard him say 'I miss you' when I was asleep, then I woke up."

"One of the easiest ways he can communicate with you is when you're sleeping... in your dreams, when your mind is quiet. Your walls go down when you're asleep," Allison explained. "He's still your buddy ... he's still with you ... he's not going anywhere. He loves other people, but *you're* his person."

Charlie felt overwhelmed with cautious elation, realizing that only Isaac could convey the information that Allison had told her. Only Allison could hear and see him, but Isaac was there, talking to her through Allison.

Charlie asked, "Do soulmates share multiple lives together?"

"Soulmates have many lives together. They keep coming back and finding each other over and over again until they're done coming back." Allison started laughing. "He says, 'My mom has a silly side; she just doesn't show it to many people.' He also says one of the reasons he loved you so much was you treated him as an equal."

"He's my guy."

"You'll have a spiritual journey when it's just you on your own, and you'll be very busy helping other people. Isaac would have helped other people, but since he can't, you will. It will involve your computer and helping parents who have lost their kids. You will help them by answering their questions. It's probably what you are doing now. You're trying to figure out what death is."

"I'm trying to figure out how to deal with death."

"This is your classroom.... You need to go through this. You're learning so you can help other people. This is happening for a reason."

"It reminds me of a photo I took of Isaac standing in the rain in Japan," Charlie said. "We had just had the best dinner in the Gion district of Kyoto and were heading back to our hotel. Isaac was walking ahead of me, and the streetlights were reflecting in the water on the road. I asked Isaac to turn around to take his picture. I feel like he's still standing there in the rain ... waiting for me to catch up to him."

"That sounds like a possible book cover," Allison said. "He says, 'I'm not going anywhere.' He's going to wait for you and help you cross over.... You and Isaac could write a book together."

"I'll have to think about that," Charlie said, puzzled. "When Isaac was eight years old, he asked me what the greatest force in nature was. I thought about it, then told him maybe a supernova was the greatest force, and then explained what a supernova was. Three days later, he came to me and told me he had the answer. I asked, 'The answer to what?' Isaac replied, 'The greatest force in nature is *time* because, without time, nothing happens!' I stood there dumbfounded."

"Wow, that's so big and brilliant of him. He was an old soul," Allison said. "It's the biggest force in our world but not theirs. Time is different on the other side."

"Yeah, he was an awesome kid."

"I'm going to break my connection with him and send him with you," Allison said. "He's not going anywhere.... He's going to wait for you and help you cross over."

Charlie and Allison stood up and said goodbye, and then Charlie walked to her car and sat in the driver's seat, still stunned by the reading. It took her a few minutes to gather herself, and then she called Chris.

"Hey, beautiful. How did the reading go?"

"It was incredible!" Charlie said. "I have so much to tell you when I get home, but I wanted to let you know that Isaac's still with us, and he's watching over us through these difficult times!"

31

LUNCH ON THE PIER
March 18, 2020

CHARLIE AND CHRIS had traveled the twenty-hour drive to MD Anderson Cancer Center in Houston so many times over the last six and a half months that the route had become ingrained into their memories. They no longer needed maps, having worked out all the stops along the way, and they had become familiar faces at the hotel where they stayed halfway through the drive.

While Chris drove the first four hours from Flagstaff toward Houston, Charlie worked on her children's book, *Charlie and the Rainbow Trout*. When they reached Pie Town, New Mexico, the streets were deserted—not a soul to be seen—not even a stray dog roamed the streets of the abandoned town.

"I remember stopping here with you and Isaac when we went to the White Sands National Park," Chris said, sounding nostalgic.

Charlie looked up from her writing and glanced out the window. "Every time we pass through here, I think of that day we stopped to get a piece of pie. You and Isaac both had apple-and-green-chili pie, which sounded terrible to me. I played it safe and ordered the good old-fashioned blackberry pie. As it turned out, yours was far better than mine."

"Isaac was always a good sport about trying new foods." Chris glanced at the Pie-O-Neer restaurant. Its hand-painted wooden sign,

PIES, creaked and flapped in the wind. Another red-and-white sign hung on the front door: *CLOSED*. "It looks like they went out of business."

"This place is nothing more than a ghost town," Charlie said, "but I still remember asking Isaac to stand under that sign so I could take his picture. . . . I can still see that image of him in my mind."

"I remember flying kites with Isaac at the White Sands National Park sand dunes and digging a hole down to the cool sand below the surface during the heat of the day. We buried Isaac up to his neck, and then I drew a heart in the sand on his chest." Chris's voice was breaking. "I miss that kid."

Charlie reached over and laid her hand on Chris's leg as they drove out of Pie Town, leaving the abandoned streets behind. Then they traveled through the Datil Mountains and dropped down into the windswept grasslands near the Plains of San Agustin, where the Very Large Array spread its great arms across the landscape and stood like a beacon, listening to the sky.

I remember coming here with Chris and Isaac. The sky was filled with stormy clouds, and it started to rain as Isaac and I stood in front of the radio dishes, but we didn't care. We just stood there smiling in the rain as Chris took our picture. More images passed through Charlie's mind. *And I remember being here with Isaac when he was only two years old and again when he was about seven. We went to the visitor's center and used the small radio dishes to send each other secret messages. He whispered, "I love you, Mom," and I whispered back, "I love you too, sweets." Life doesn't get any better than that.*

Chris pulled off the road into the radio telescope viewing area, and they got out of the car and ate a snack while marveling at the rows of radio telescope dishes. After eating, they hugged and switched seats.

Charlie drove them to Socorro, stopped to fill the car with diesel, and then headed toward Las Cruces. As they passed the exit for Hatch, New Mexico, Charlie told Chris about the time she and Isaac had stopped there on their way to Carlsbad Caverns.

"When Isaac was about five, we made this game up that we played on road trips. We decided if the great universe really loved us, it would direct us to a place where we could stop and have a milkshake," Charlie said. "It was just a silly game, but it gave us a break from the road and was a great excuse to stop for ice cream. We loved the adventure as much as reaching our destination. Part of the game was scoring the milkshakes on a scale from one to ten. As part of our duty, we took it upon ourselves to enjoy our fair share of milkshakes in our quest to find *the* best milkshake on the road."

"I'm sure he loved that game."

"Isaac loved it as much as I did—we knew how to have fun," Charlie said. "Well, in Hatch—the town we just passed—there's a restaurant called Sparkys that advertises 'world-famous shakes.' Of course, we had to stop to see if what they claimed was the golden truth. We were surprised by all the fun, iconic fast-food statues surrounding the building when we got to the restaurant. There was a Colonel Sanders figure sitting on a wooden bench at the front door of the restaurant. One of his arms was resting on the back of the bench, and he was missing his right foot. I took a picture of Isaac sitting on the bench, and it looked like Colonel Sanders had his arm around him. On the corner of the building was Ronald McDonald waving, and on the roof were several characters from A&W holding a root beer in one hand and a hamburger in the other. We walked in, found a nice little table by the window, and ordered two chocolate milkshakes. To our surprise, they *were* the best milkshakes we'd ever had!"

"I loved that about you guys," Chris said. "You always took the opportunity to make those little things count, like when you guys used to dance together in the kitchen."

"Yeah, I'm glad we did because . . ." Charlie paused, choking down her pain, then continued. "After finishing our milkshakes, we hit the road and drove to Carlsbad Caverns. We had so much fun walking down the long, winding trail into the heart of the caverns. . . . We were mesmerized by all the formations along the way. But Isaac's favorite thing about the Carlsbad Caverns was the bats. We watched the four hundred thousand bats fly out of the cave just before sunset, and an employee of the park service handed out photographs of bats to people who donated five bucks to their Adopt-A-Bat program. Since Isaac had fallen in love with the bats, we donated five bucks, and Isaac was given a photo of one of the zillion bats, which looked just like all the other bats. Before we left, we bought a plush bat puppet from the gift shop. He loved it and made it soar through the air, flapping its wings in the car as we drove home."

"I can see why Isaac had so many stuffed animals in his room."

Charlie nodded and kept driving until she stopped at the last Starbucks on the east side of El Paso. There, she bought six shots of espresso to go so she could make coffee the next morning in Fort Stockton, the halfway point between El Paso and San Antonio. The first time she and Chris had traveled their new route through Texas, they'd painfully learned there was no Starbucks or decent coffee on that eight-hour stretch. Knowing Charlie couldn't afford to get a migraine from caffeine withdrawals while driving the endless roads of Texas, they always made an espresso pit stop before heading into the land void of good coffee. They did the same thing going the other way, always stopping in San Antonio before heading west.

Charlie and Chris woke at five the next morning and headed for Houston. By the afternoon, they arrived at the Hilton Houston Plaza / Medical Center, checked in, and went upstairs to the outdoor bar to have a cocktail on the deck. While they watched the sunset over the bustling city, they enjoyed margaritas.

"I keep thinking about everything Allison and Tarra told you. It's all very strange. I don't know how much of what they said is true, but they both told you details only Isaac would know," Chris said, puzzled.

"Indeed!"

"Here's to Isaac." Chris smiled and raised his drink.

They cheered, then sipped their margaritas.

"I feel pretty good. I'm hoping for a good report from Dr. Wang."

"Me too, handsome."

As they enjoyed their cocktails, Charlie checked her email on her phone and opened an email from her insurance. Shaking her head, Charlie showed Chris her statement from the previous month.

"I used to question whether or not you had chosen the right kind of insurance, but I don't anymore," Chris said. "I remember the bill was over ninety thousand dollars for three days when I had that adverse reaction to one of the chemo drugs."

"And we've been coming here since September, and now it's March. . . . That's more than six months," Charlie said. "If I hadn't chosen a high-deductible plan that covered everything after the seven-thousand-dollar deductible, we'd have been screwed."

"You've saved me in more ways than one." Chris raised his glass.

"Here's to you, beautiful."

"You're sweet, handsome. I'm just glad it's allowed us to get you the best care possible." Charlie reached for Chris's hand. The next day was Friday, and Chris was scheduled to have a blood draw in the morning, followed by a CT. But his appointment with Dr. Wang to review the results wasn't until Monday. "Maybe after the CT, we could get out of town and have lunch in Galveston on the pier," Charlie suggested. "And maybe on Saturday, we could go to the Houston Museum of Natural Science."

"That's not a bad idea. I don't want to sit in the hotel all weekend; that will get old. We might as well go do something fun."

"Okay, so lunch in Galveston tomorrow?"

"Sure, I'd like to get some seafood." Chris smiled. "You know me. . . . I love seafood. And if you don't mind, I'll let you drive so I can have a few drinks."

"No worries. I'd be happy to drive."

On Friday morning, Charlie and Chris went to MD Anderson Cancer Center, put their COVID-19 masks on before entering the building, and checked Chris into the lab department. After his blood draw, they went to the third floor and checked into Diagnostic Imaging, feeling hopeful the CT images would show that the two new trial drugs, acalabrutinib and venetoclax, had shrunk his tumor.

An hour and fifteen minutes later, Chris walked out the door of the Diagnostic Imaging department.

"What took you so long?" Charlie asked him. "It seemed like you were in there longer than the last time."

"I had to get the CT done twice," Chris said, grinning. "The first time, I had Isaac's ashes around my neck, so Isaac and I got CT'd together!"

"Oh, that's kind of sweet."

"Let's go to Galveston; I'm starving."

"I think I found the perfect restaurant. Jimmy's on the Pier is right on the water, overlooking the ocean."

Chris walked toward the elevator. "Perfect. It'll be good to get out of MD Anderson and out of Houston, for that matter—I'm sick of this place."

"I'm sure you are, but you never complain." Charlie pushed the down elevator button. "I wouldn't be nearly as good of a sport as you are. The chemo, IVs, blood draws, CTs, MRIs, transfusions, pneumothorax, adverse reactions, and bone marrow aspirations all had to hurt. Not to mention all the paracentesis procedures you've had to remove the bloody fluid from your peritoneal cavity."

"That's why we're getting the hell out of here!"

"Exactly!"

After a ten-minute walk through the hospital maze, they reached the parking garage.

Chris held out his hand. "I feel okay right now, so I'd like to drive there, but you can drive on the way back, if you don't mind."

"Sure, that's fine." Charlie opened her bag and handed Chris the keys.

Leaving Houston gave them a sense of freedom. They knew it was only temporary; still, they clung to the feeling for the rest of the day, knowing reality was waiting just around the next bend. In Galveston, they parked at Jimmy's on the Pier and walked into their gift shop. Spotting the stairs leading to the upper deck, Chris motioned Charlie to follow him. The salty breeze drifting off the ocean greeted them as they reached the upper deck of the outdoor restaurant and bar.

Chris pulled up a barstool at a small round table facing the ocean at the far end of the restaurant, and Charlie sat next to him. A waiter came over. Charlie wasn't drinking, but the man took Chris's order and returned a few minutes later with a tequila sunrise with an orange slice and a blue-and-white striped paper straw.

Chris took the orange slice from the rim of his glass, crushed it, and then stirred it into his tequila sunrise. "This is more like it," he said, picking up the menu.

"I'm going to have the crab cakes," Charlie said. "My mom loved crab cakes, and every time I have them, I think of her."

Chris took a sip of his tequila sunrise. "And I'll have the shrimp with fries."

Once Charlie and Chris had laid down their menus, the waiter returned and took their order. As they were waiting for their lunch, Charlie and Chris discussed their plans for the next couple of days. Charlie felt grateful as she watched Chris relax under the white canopy of the restaurant, taking in the ocean breeze. She knew he was enjoying himself because she caught little glimpses of his gold teeth in the back of his mouth, which were visible only when Chris flashed his Cheshire cat grin.

"You know, handsome . . . you look pretty cute sitting there in your baseball cap, enjoying your tequila sunrise."

Chris smiled and took a deep breath of the salty, humid air. Charlie could see his tense shoulders relax.

As the waiter brought their lunch, the gulls called from the blue skies above, and although Charlie knew she wasn't supposed to, she couldn't resist the urge to feed them some of her french fries. The calling of the gulls tapped some deep-seated feeling of freedom within her that she chose not to resist. Once the waiter left, she placed one french fry on the white deck railing, and a gull immediately swooped down and flew off with his prize. Charlie put a few more french fries on the railing, and a small flock of gulls flew in, snatching up the french fries in their yellow beaks. Some gulls flew away while others landed on the railing, calling for more. As Charlie gleefully fed the birds, she and Chris listened to the sound of the waves crashing on the beach and watched other gulls sailing in the warm ocean air. As they soared, the midday sun illuminated their white wings and tails, causing them to shine brightly against the clear blue sky. It was a fleeting moment of happiness that they savored, knowing it wouldn't last.

After lunch, Chris enjoyed a second tequila sunrise, and then they drove along the ocean road to Kelly Hamby Nature Trail Park, where Charlie parked. Chris was too tired to walk down the boardwalk to the beach, so they continued driving down the road to Surfside Beach, then turned north toward Houston.

On Saturday morning, they went downstairs and ate breakfast at the hotel restaurant, and then they went to the Houston Museum of Natural Science. As they entered the *Alfred C. Glassell, Jr. Hall*, they were overcome by an enormous moon suspended from the ceiling. They learned that the glowing sphere was a replica of the moon but half a million times smaller. They gazed upward at the brilliant moon as they walked in circles, studying its impact craters.

Next, they walked down the hall to the *Herzstein Foucault Pendulum*, where an enormous golden pendulum swung just above the floor from a sixty-foot cable. The pendulum appeared to be gradually moving, but in fact, this was an illusion caused by the earth moving underneath it. As the earth rotated throughout the day, the pendulum knocked down small wooden pins that stood on the floor in a large circle around its center. Charlie and Chris waited with the rest of the crowd, anticipating the fall of the next wooden pin, and once it was toppled, they moved on to the next exhibit.

Chris and Charlie walked down the hall and entered the *Morian Hall of Paleontology*, where they marveled at the trilobites and dinosaur fossils but were truly astounded by the massive crinoid fossil. Numerous crinoids were securely anchored to a common piece of wood, their long, ropelike stalks gracefully swaying as if they were still moving freely in the ocean current. At the top of each column was a fan-shaped cluster of feathery arms the crinoids used to gather food long ago.

Chris gazed up at the enormous fossil. "That's amazing."

"I love how the motion of the crinoids moving with the ocean current has been forever frozen in time."

"The plaque says crinoids are sometimes called sea lilies, but they're actually animals dating back eighty-five million years!" Chris added. "And there are still many species alive today. I'm glad we came here.... This is a great museum."

"Me too. Do you want to go see the minerals and gems next?" Charlie asked, taking hold of Chris's hand.

"Sure, I think that exhibit is upstairs."

After walking through the stunning *Cullen Hall of Gems and Minerals* collection, Chris and Charlie entered the *Lester and Sue Smith Gem Vault*. Their jaws dropped as they gazed at the jewels before their eyes. Some of their favorites were the platinum tiara with a 42.4-carat emerald centerpiece, the 2,765-carat Australian boulder opal, the Tahitian platinum necklace with black pearls, and an elegant platinum brooch with a 168-carat yellow sapphire center stone surrounded by green diamonds.

After leaving the museum, they drove to the bustling Rice Village and parked in front of Prego, a family-owned restaurant specializing in modern Italian cuisine.

Chris opened the car door for Charlie. "I love this place."

"I know you do, handsome. It's your favorite restaurant in Houston."

They walked to the back of the restaurant and sat down at their favorite booth against the redbrick wall. The waiter greeted them with a basket of assorted bread and olive oil, then took Chris's wine order.

When he returned with Chris's chardonnay, he took their order and then left to place it with the chef busily working in the kitchen.

"You're such a foodie," Charlie joked.

Chris dipped a piece of hearty bread in the olive oil. "I know I am, but I really enjoy a nice meal paired with the right drink. I couldn't decide whether to get the sea bass or the fettuccine, so I ordered chardonnay instead of pinot grigio—chardonnay would go nicely with either."

"I'm just glad you're feeling better!"

"Me too."

While they chatted about their morning, Chris savored his grilled Mediterranean sea bass with tomato, avocado, and spinach, and Charlie enjoyed her mushroom risotto. Once they'd finished half of their entrees, they asked the waiter to box the rest to go so they could save room for dessert. A lover of all things chocolate, Charlie ordered the double chocolate cake. Chris ordered the vanilla bean panna cotta, having greatly enjoyed its exceptional flavor and silky-smooth texture the previous time they'd dined there.

Sunday morning, Chris was tired and wanted to relax in the hotel room, but later that afternoon, they went to Houston's Hermann Park and fed the ducks.

Charlie got up at six on Monday morning, took a shower, and then got coffee from Starbucks in the hotel lobby while Chris took a shower. Once Chris was ready, she handed him his coffee, and then they drove to MD Anderson. As they walked in, Charlie carried a teal-and-white checkered package in her arms. They checked in and drank their coffee while waiting to find out the result of the CT.

After Chris was called, they followed Dr. Wang's nurse to the exam room, where she asked Chris a battery of questions before telling him Dr. Wang would be in shortly to see him.

Charlie got up, handed Chris the teal-and-white package, and sat back down.

A few minutes later, Dr. Wang walked in, smiling. "Good morning, my friends. . . . What do you have there?"

"It's a gift for you," Chris said. "We bought it while we were in Japan years ago."

"Oh, so nice of you, but you didn't need to do that." Dr. Wang grinned and removed the wrapping paper, revealing a painting of two golden koi fish swimming up a waterfall toward enlightenment. "It's beautiful, but you really didn't need to give this to me. It's a very generous gift."

"I know you're Chinese, not Japanese," Chris said. "But I still wanted to give this to you because it reminds me of the struggle I face every day. You're always here, helping me swim against the current. If it weren't for you—I'd be a dead man."

"I'm going to hang it in my office, and I will think of you when I see it," Dr. Wang said. "I have good news, my friend—you're in remission!"

Chris looked surprised. "I am?"

"Yes," Dr. Wang said. "The new medications, the acalabrutinib and venetoclax, are shrinking your tumor."

"Does that mean I can go skiing?"

"No!" Dr. Wang said, looking clearly shocked and even a little exasperated. "As I told you earlier, these medications increase your risk for bleeding, so you need to be careful."

"So if I hit a tree, I should hit it straight on." Chris laughed.

Dr. Wang looked at Chris, then at Charlie.

"He won't listen to me." Charlie made a dismissive gesture with her hand. "I've tried. He's going to do whatever he wants."

Dr. Wang looked at Chris sternly. "I can't tell you what to do, but you must be careful."

"I'd much rather die skiing than lying around in bed waiting for the vultures to circle," Chris said, flashing his signature grin.

Dr. Wang nodded reluctantly. "Thanks for the beautiful gift. Now I must go." He shook Chris's hand before leaving.

Obviously, Allison was wrong about the trial drugs not working! Charlie thought, feeling a great sense of relief.

32

ISAAC WAS HERE
The Other Side

SEATED ON AN OLD, weathered log underneath a budding oak tree, Isaac and Shane watched Charlie gather light-colored river rocks and place them in a pile on the gray sandbar overlooking the small pool at Kinder Crossing. Although Charlie had her down jacket on over a long-sleeved T-shirt and a sweater, the cool air caused her cheeks to flush. Still, she carried on with her task.

Isaac petted Buttercup, who was sitting beside him. "This was one of my favorite places that Mom used to take me when I was the age I am now . . . when I was the happiest. That's why my mom came here today. April nineteenth is the third anniversary of my crossing."

"It's no wonder you guys loved coming here. With the beautiful reflections of the water dancing on the red rocks towering above the pool . . . it's a perfect place to spend the day."

"Yeah . . . Mom used to pack a lunch with some of our favorite treats, and then we would spend the hot summer days playing in the water and feeding the minnows," Isaac reminisced. "It was an all-day adventure. First, we drove an hour east of town and parked at the Kinder Crossing trailhead, and then Mom would let Buttercup and Kéyah out of the car, and they'd run ahead of us as we hiked down the canyon through the tall ponderosa pine trees into Kinder Crossing. After Buttercup and Kéyah crossed, we adopted Dexter. The first time we took him down here, he got lost and we couldn't find him. I can still hear my mom's voice echoing through the canyon as she frantically called Dexter's name, but we couldn't find him. Luckily, when we got back to the car late that afternoon, he was lying by the car waiting for us. I was so happy to see him! On our way home, Mom would stop in Happy Jack to get ice cream, and then I usually fell asleep and woke up as she carried me to my bed and tucked me in for the night. . . . Those were perfect days."

"I remember when you got Dexter; you were crazy about him."

"I loved him so much. He slept with me every night. . . . He was my snuggle buddy."

Shane and Isaac watched as Charlie knelt down and cleared away the twigs and fallen debris from the sandy area in front of her, then started neatly arranging the light-colored stones she had gathered.

"I know today's a difficult day for your mom," Shane said. "But I'm happy she no longer wonders whether or not you're still with her."

"Yes, *finally*, she received my messages!" Isaac grinned. "I'm so happy that my mom is no longer considering taking her own life! And knowing I still walk with her, she's found a new direction and purpose."

"That knowledge has renewed her strength and settled her troubled heart and mind," Shane said, then his expression became pensive. "Which reminds me, I have something that's been troubling me, and I want to clear it from my conscience. Do you remember the time when I came here with you and your mom?"

"Yes."

"I want to apologize for scaring you. It wasn't right of me to dive underwater with you on my back. You couldn't swim, and it really scared you. It also made your mom very angry with me . . . and rightly so."

Isaac nodded.

"We all thought your mom treated you with kid gloves as you were growing up, but now I understand things differently. She explained to us numerous times how difficult things were for you and how you were struggling with learning disabilities, but we all brushed it off, thinking she was just being overly protective. Now I know she was trying to shelter you from more harm because she knew how much you were suffering. We were wrong and your mom was right. I'm sorry I scared you, and I'm sorry I made your mom mad at me."

"Thanks for your apology; I appreciate it. It's sometimes easier to dismiss ugly truths than believe them," Isaac said. "As for the swimming, I know you weren't being mean. You were just being mischievous. . . . It's your nature."

"Yeah, but sometimes my 'mischievous nature' gets me into trouble," Shane said, with a look of regret. "Ultimately, that's what led to my death. It was foolish of me to walk down the train tracks with my headset on—that was just reckless of me. At least your mom learned from Tarra that my death was an accident. That was the worst part . . . my sisters questioning if I had intentionally killed myself—I wasn't a suicide looking for a train!"

"I'm glad she knows that now. It gave your sisters peace of mind," Isaac said. "I remember a couple of the messages my mom sent me on her phone that had photos from Kinder Crossing. One was a picture of me wearing my goggles and eating a sandwich while I played with little plastic dinosaurs in the grass over there." Isaac pointed to a grassy area across the water. "And another photo was from when I was younger—maybe five years old, because my hair was much lighter, almost blond. We came here with your other sister Karen, and I remember sitting in the water, playing. I remember that feeling . . . a feeling of peace and happiness."

"Speaking of messages, it looks like your mom's writing the letter *T* with the stones." Then Shane shook his head. "No . . . it's not a *T*; she's making an *I* for Isaac."

"I bet you're right," Isaac agreed. "You know, Chris and my mom hiked into Red Mountain yesterday and took flowers to the last place I went with her. It's something they started doing on the first anniversary of my death. They made an altar with a small bronze Buddha statue at the center, then arranged small white daisies and pink roses around it. Since my passing took place over two days, April eighteenth and nineteenth, Chris and my mom usually spend the eighteenth together, and then my mom likes to be alone on the nineteenth. That's why Chris is skiing today."

"It's good to see him smiling again. These last few years have been brutal on both of them, and battling cancer for the last seven and a half months has taken a real toll on Chris. I'm thrilled he's feeling good and enjoying himself," Shane said. "The Buddha statue must have belonged to me. Your mom probably kept it after I passed."

"That makes sense," Isaac agreed. "She wasn't a Buddhist, so she wouldn't have gotten it for herself, but since she had it and knew how much I loved the Buddha teachings, she must have decided it would make a nice centerpiece for the altar."

"I'm glad. That's perfect."

"She used to talk to the little Buddha, hoping he'd relay the message to me, but now that she knows I'm still with her, she talks directly to me. That makes it much easier for me to get her messages so I can help guide her along her journey."

"That's wonderful," Shane said. "It's not often we get a direct line with our loved ones!"

Shane and Isaac watched Charlie finish spelling Isaac's name in large capital letters on the sand, and then she started writing something beneath it.

"Once, my mom and I brought Max here. He was my best friend from grade school. We dug a hole, and Max buried me in the sand. That was fun, but most of the time, it was just me and my mom. She always brought a picnic blanket that we could sit on and have lunch, and then afterward, we waded in the creek with the dogs and had a great time." Isaac petted Buttercup as she nudged him again. "I miss my mom as much as she misses me."

"It will be good to see her again when she crosses over."

"I really look forward to that, but first, she still has many things to do."

Shane and Isaac watched Charlie place the last river rocks on her message, creating an earth-toned mosaic in the sand. When she was finished, it read: *ISAAC WAS HERE*. Next, she outlined a heart with lighter stones, then filled it with the remaining brown rocks.

After she'd finished her message, Charlie walked through the tall foliage to the creek above the sandbar, and Isaac, Shane, and Buttercup followed. She found a grassy area and lay down. Shane and Isaac knelt beside her.

Charlie closed her eyes, then whispered, "Isaac, I know you're here with me, and you can hear me. I wrote that message in the sand because I wanted everyone to know you were here. I'll try to make you proud of me so when I see you again on the bridge, I'll have earned your smile. Thanks for watching over Chris and me. I can walk the steps; I just need you to lead the way. I hope you're having a great time. Know I walk with you and always keep you in my heart. Please say hi to Mom and Shane for me. I won't ask for specific things, because I don't know what's best for me. I trust your guidance, and I'm trying my best to listen and follow your lead. Love you, sweets."

"Nothing better than that," Isaac said, putting his hand to his heart.

Shane nodded, a smile on his face.

Charlie kept her eyes closed for a few more minutes and then whispered, "Isaac, I hope you can hear the sound of the creek and smell the fresh air." Then Charlie opened her eyes; the cool breeze had flushed her face and hands. She got up and walked back to the rock mosaic as Shane, Isaac, and Buttercup followed. Charlie looked at the message one more time and then walked underneath the oak tree and put her backpack around her shoulder. She blew a kiss into the air, then started hiking out of the canyon and disappeared into the forest.

"Hey, Isaac, I think we should get back," Shane said sheepishly. "I think your grandma Hazel wants to talk to you about something."

"Okay, but it sounds like you're up to one of your good-for-nothing tricks."

"Me?"

"Yes, you!"

—

When they arrived, Isaac and Shane entered the farmhouse through the kitchen door.

"Surprise!" everyone said in unison.

"What's all this?" Isaac asked, taken aback.

"While you and Shane were out with your mom, we got things ready for a surprise party," Hazel said. "Look, I even made a special red velvet cake."

"That looks great . . . but why three candles?" Isaac asked.

"We're making a new tradition. This is your third graduation party," Melba said. "To your mom and Chris, it's the third anniversary of your death, but we're making it a celebration. When you crossed over, you had learned one of life's most difficult but important lessons—humility. So rather than it being a sad occasion, we're celebrating it as a graduation, and besides, we also wanted to celebrate Chris's remission and your mom's victory! She finally knows you're still by her side and always will be!"

Shane put his arm around Isaac. "Your mom made it to the top of the mountain!"

"I suppose you're right." Isaac grinned and returned the hug. "Are graduation parties similar to birthday parties? Do I get to make a wish before blowing out the candles?"

"Absolutely." Hazel smiled. "Let's light the candles so Isaac can make a wish."

As Shane took a small box of matches from his pocket, Isaac looked at the blue party banner with yellow letters that read: *CONGRATULATIONS, ISAAC.* The room was decorated with colorful balloons, and the table was set with a white tablecloth, pink Depression glass cake plates, and fruit punch, and the red velvet cake sat at the center of the table. The fluffy white frosting, sprinkled with shaved coconut, glistened.

Shane struck a match and lit the three candles. Isaac paused momentarily, then, realizing he had already received his wish, he blew out the candles. Everyone hugged Isaac, then sat down at the table while Hazel cut the cake. She placed the first piece on a plate, revealing two layers of scarlet-red cake between icy-white frosting, and handed it to Isaac, then waited for him to take a bite.

"It's delicious, Grandma," Isaac said, licking the frosting off his lips. "I can see why Mom always said this was your favorite cake."

Hazel cut the cake as everyone handed the pieces to the rest of the family. Lastly, she cut herself a piece and sat beside Isaac and Shane.

"Isaac, I'm proud of you," Solomon said. "If you hadn't tried so hard to reach your mom, she might have fallen prey to the darkness and taken her life. But you saved her, and as a result, Chris is also well on his way to learning one of his two life lessons—death is not the end. You not only saved your mom, but you've also profoundly changed Chris's life."

"She was always there for me." Isaac smiled. "Turnaround is fair trade."

Solomon raised his glass of punch. "Here's to Isaac, a job well done!"

"Hear, hear," everyone cheered.

"Thanks, everyone, but I couldn't have done it without your help!" Isaac said, raising his glass. "Here's to all of you!"

"Hear, hear," everyone cheered again, then began visiting as they enjoyed their red velvet cake.

"I'm so glad your mom went to see Teresa," Ethel said. "That's what eventually led Charlie to Allison."

"It wasn't easy, and things didn't go as planned a few times, but you kept at it until you succeeded." Hazel smiled. "You're just as stubborn as your mom, but it's paid off!"

Isaac put his hand to his heart. "I'm so glad they're both doing so much better. There were a few bumps in the road, but things rarely go as planned—people have their own free will, which continually changes their path. But my mom taught me an important lesson while I was still alive—if you keep taking steps toward your goal, then it's only a matter of time. And the thing is, sometimes the unplanned routes can be serendipitous. . . . They can offer unexpected gifts. It wasn't necessarily my intention for my mom to have a reading with Tarra, but it turned out to be very valuable in the long run. Tarra's reading was more of a big-picture approach. She explained to my mom how people were born into certain lives to learn specific lessons, how I had been living on borrowed time, and that all things are as they should be. Allison, on the other hand, conveyed specific details: That we were best friends, that I tried to get my mom to wear my maroon-and-gray hoodie, the matching tattoos, the necklace we got in Belize, and all the other details made it clear to my mom that I was talking to her through Allison. In the end, it worked out nicely because the two readings complemented each other."

Shane nudged Isaac, a twinkle in his eye. "I'm not sure if you're stubborn or just determined."

"The truth is the same either way." Isaac returned the nudge. "When you start something, it's good to finish it. As some Buddhists have said, 'There are only two mistakes one can make on the road to truth: not starting and not going all the way.'"

"I love that, but it's also good to remember that the darkest hour is just before the dawn," Shane added. "Don't give up on your journey when you meet an obstacle. When you're tired and worn out, the answer you're looking for is often just around the bend."

"True," Isaac agreed.

After everyone finished their cake, Shane retrieved a box from the hall closet that he'd stashed there earlier and sat it on the table.

"Anyone care to light some firecrackers?" Shane grinned, showing everyone his pile of smoke bombs, sparklers, Roman candles, and rockets.

Everyone was surprised at Shane's collection.

"I love watching firecrackers," Melba said. "Let's go outside and celebrate!"

Enthusiastically, everyone followed Shane as he carried the hefty box outside and placed it on the picnic table. Like schoolgirls at a party, Melba and Hazel started rummaging through the firecrackers, looking for which ones they wanted Shane to light first, while Solomon, Ethel, Raymond, and Alma sat around the picnic table, anticipating one of Shane's great firework shows.

"I hope you brought your Dubble Bubble chewing gum so we can stick a few of these babies together for the ultimate fireworks display," Isaac said and smiled.

"Surely, you didn't think I would forget that." Shane grinned, then pulled a box of matches and his Dubble Bubble chewing gum from his front pocket and laid them squarely on the picnic table. Then he unwrapped two pieces of the gum and popped them into his mouth.

The excitement grew as Hazel and Melba handed Shane two rockets. He planted them firmly in the ground far from the picnic table, stuck them together with his wad of chewing gum, and lit their fuses. Everyone held their breath, listening to the fuses burning, and then, with a great burst of energy, the rockets shot up, showering the evening sky with brilliant sparkles! Everyone oohed and aahed, eagerly awaiting the next dazzling display of fireworks. Melba, Hazel, and Isaac continued handing Shane firecrackers as Solomon, Ethel, Raymond, and Alma sat watching, their hearts filled with joy—a perfect celebration.

33

GOOD JOB, MOM
May 4, 2020

"SOMETHING CRAZY happened to me today," Chris said, anxiety ringing in his voice.

"What do you mean? What happened?" Charlie asked, sitting down next to him at the kitchen table after coming home late from work.

"After you left for work this morning, I went for a bike ride to Fisher Point like I usually do. When I got home, I took a shower and then went across the street to get the mail," Chris said, his voice shaking. "This is where it gets crazy . . . but I swear I'm not making this up—it really happened!"

"What happened?"

"A red-tailed hawk dive-bombed me!" Chris blurted out. "I was walking back from getting the mail, and a red-tailed hawk buzzed my head so close I had to duck to get out of the way. Then the hawk flew straight into the tree trunk and fell to the ground. It was like he was out of control or something. He just sat there for a minute like he was stunned, then flew away. It really freaked me out. Red-tailed hawks are skilled hunters—they don't dive-bomb people or run into trees!"

Charlie looked surprised. "Yeah, I've never heard of that before."

"It must have been Isaac messing with the hawk." Chris took a sip of his mojito. "Didn't Allison say people who've crossed over can use animals to send a message or get someone's attention?"

"Yes, that's what Allison and Tarra both said," Charlie answered. "In fact, I remember Tarra saying Isaac would present himself as a hawk. Remember, I told you that after my reading with her. She said we were to keep our eyes out for a hawk!"

"Oh yeah, I remember that, now that you mention it," Chris said. "Isaac must have influenced the hawk to get my attention, since I haven't been able to get a message from him any other way. But that really freaked me out! I swear that's what happened."

"Hey, you don't have to convince me," Charlie said. "I've been having weird stuff happen to me ever since Isaac passed."

"I know, I thought you were . . . I thought you were losing it when you said he talked to you in your dreams, but now I believe you," Chris said, taking another sip of his mojito.

"I'm glad you finally know what I'm talking about," Charlie said. "I understand how you might have thought I was going a little crazy, but you just don't really understand these things until they happen to you. I'm so glad this happened!"

"Me too." Chris finished his mojito, then got up to make another.

"How was your bike ride?"

"Great. I finished the trail without coming out of my clips." Chris did a little jig where he stood at the kitchen counter. "I'm so thankful Dr. Wang put me on these meds; I feel so much better. I've enjoyed skiing for the last couple of months, and now I'm enjoying riding my mountain bike. I love my new Pivot; it's a killer ride."

"I can't believe how much stronger you are!" Charlie got up and hugged Chris, then put a slice of bread in the toaster.

"You know, tomorrow is May fifth," Chris said. That was Charlie's birthday. "And I have to say, you're really difficult to shop for. A few years ago, I got you a nice down vest and coat, which I know you wear because you are always cold. But you never wear the nice blouses I got you last year."

"It was very kind of you to get them, but I'm more comfortable in a T-shirt and a pair of 501s," Charlie said. "Blouses just don't work for me."

"Yeah, but *I* might like to see you in a dress or something pretty."

Chris groaned as he sat back down at the kitchen table with his mojito.

Charlie spread some strawberry-rhubarb jam on her toast and joined him at the table. "I'm sorry, I just don't like to wear dresses, which is exactly why I don't own a single one ... but you already know that about me."

"I'm just saying you're very difficult to shop for, and you say there's nothing you want or need, so I had no idea what to get you for your birthday." Chris let out a breath of frustration. "But I decided to get you something anyway because it's not right to have a birthday without a present."

"That was really sweet of you, but you didn't need to get me anything."

Chris rolled his eyes. "Is there anything you'd like to do tomorrow for your birthday, since you have the day off?"

"I just want to do something with you. Spending the day together is far better than anything you could buy me. Maybe we can take the dogs out for a walk."

"That sounds nice, and maybe we can go to dinner afterward."

After lunch the next day, Chris left to do errands and returned with a bouquet of white daisies and a chocolate cake he had ordered from the bakery. He put the flowers in a glass vase and arranged them on the kitchen table. Then he placed the cake on a plate, went to his closet, and brought out a square present. The wrapping paper had different-colored letters, spelling *HAPPY BIRTHDAY* against a blue background. It was the same wrapping paper they'd used the last time they celebrated Isaac's birthday. The top of the package had a white ribbon Charlie recognized from the Christmas bows they'd boxed up and no longer used. After the day that forever changed their lives, they no longer trimmed the house with brightly colored lights or decorated the Christmas tree—merrymaking had become a thing of the past.

Looking at the wrapping paper and white ribbon took Charlie back to ground zero—Isaac's eyes stared blankly ahead as the ventilator forced air into his lungs, his heart racing, but he wasn't alive.

"Make a wish," Chris said, lighting the cheery candles on her birthday cake.

I wish Isaac weren't dead, but I'm so thankful he's still with us, Charlie thought, then blew out the candles.

"I didn't know what to get you, but I hope you like it."

Charlie unwrapped the present to find a square box with a picture of an illuminated moon on the side. It read: *DIAMETER 10 INCH MOON LAMP*. She opened the lid, looked at the white moon safely nestled inside the box, and then ran her fingertips over the rough surface of the moon's craters, making a hollow, scratchy sound like sandpaper stretched over a drum.

"I'm giving you *the moon* for your birthday," Chris said, grinning. "It's a small rendition of the actual moon, which you can use as an evening light. It reminded me of the giant moon we saw at the Museum of Natural Science in Houston. I thought you might like it."

"That was very sweet of you," Charlie said, taking the moon from the box.

She walked to the living room, placed the moon on the console table, and plugged it in. Chris turned the moon on with the remote and tried various color settings.

"I think white's best, don't you?" he asked.

"Yes. It looks great. This'll make a nice evening lamp."

"Then you like it?"

"Yes, thanks for giving me *the moon* for my birthday!" Charlie smiled, kissing and hugging Chris. "It was very thoughtful of you."

"I'm glad you like it. Would you like to take the dogs for a walk and then go out for dinner? I thought we could go to Hiro's for sushi."

"Sure, that sounds nice. We haven't been there since Thanksgiving."

After taking Dexter and Cobalt out for a walk along the Arizona Trail, Charlie and Chris went to Hiro's and asked to be seated at their favorite table in the back of the restaurant. They ordered green tea, then looked at the menu.

"This was one of Shane's favorite places to eat," Charlie reminisced. "He recommended this place to Isaac and me because he used to come here with his aikido buddies."

"I'm glad he did." Chris turned the sushi menu toward her. "I thought we could get some California rolls, eel, miso soup, snow crab, yellowtail, and an order of smelt roe."

"Okay. You can have the fish eggs, and I'll stick to the California rolls and miso soup."

The waiter walked over and placed two small dishes of wasabi on their table. "Have you decided what you'd like to order?"

"Yes." Chris gave the waiter their order.

Charlie and Chris enjoyed the rest of the evening talking over dinner, then drove home and went to bed early because Charlie was tired and had to work the following morning.

—

Over the next few weeks, Chris rode his bike almost daily and occasionally went golfing. In his spare time, he watched sports on TV and puttered around the house. On Charlie's days off, they took the dogs out for walks, watched movies in bed with popcorn, and Charlie worked on her painting of Isaac. They felt a tremendous sense of relief with Chris's significantly improved health and not having to spend time in Houston.

One morning, while making breakfast, Charlie had an idea.

"Hey, handsome, would you like to go see my aunt Mable for a couple of days? Ever since Isaac passed, I've been meaning to go see her. It might be fun to take a little road trip."

"That sounds nice," Chris said. "Can you get the time off?"

"I sure hope so. I've been working my butt off to make up for the time I took off, so I think my boss will let me go."

"When would you want to leave?"

"Do you want to leave tomorrow if I can get the time off?"

"I'm game if you are."

The next morning, Chris and Charlie put their suitcases into the car and headed toward Elko, Nevada. En route, they listened to one of Charlie's favorite books, *Slaughterhouse-Five*, by Kurt Vonnegut. Since it was a five-hour audiobook and the drive was over nine hours, they had plenty of time to listen to it before reaching their destination. Charlie had been unable to quite remember why she'd liked the book so much, but since Chris had never read it, she was happy to listen to it again. While Chris drove, they listened to the main character, an American soldier named Billy Pilgrim, confront the fundamental question about the meaning of life and death after being captured in Dresden by the Germans during World War II.

"That's it!" Charlie said, pausing the audiobook. "I knew there was something in this book I needed to remember. Billy Pilgrim is saying that the most important thing he learned is that it only appears that we're dead at the time of our death and that all moments—past, present, and future—have always existed. He says that it's only an illusion 'that one moment follows another one, like beads on a string.' What he's saying is that even though the moments in our lives pass, they still exist and always will."

Charlie continued, "It reminds me of what Robert Lanza said in *Biocentrism*—that death is an illusion, and there are an infinite number of 'now' moments in a person's life that are *not* arranged in a linear fashion. What if those 'now' moments are like the still frames of a stop-motion picture—they only appear to be moving because they're played rapidly in sequence, but the individual frames are inanimate? Then, the individual frames—the 'now' moments in someone's life—are like the individual beads on a string, separated only by the smallest unit of length, the Planck length. If you removed the string, the individual beads—all the 'now' moments in a person's life—would float around the person like bubbles in the air but remain connected to that person through quantum entanglement."

Chris listened intently.

"If that were the case," Charlie said, "then one of our bubbles—one of our 'now' moments—would be us driving in this car right now, and another bubble would be when you, Isaac, and I were hiking to the teahouse in Canada, and still another bubble would be the moment Isaac died. If you remember, Robert Lanza said that our bodies die at the moment we call death, but our consciousness only moves from one 'now' moment to another. What Kurt Vonnegut is saying is similar . . . that a person is in bad shape at the time of death, but he's perfectly fine in so many other moments. They're both saying death is not the end—that there are an infinite number of 'now' moments in a person's life."

"I remember you telling me that Allison said time was different on the other side," Chris added. "I wonder if our bubbles that surround us, our 'now' moments—the past, present, and future—which all exist simultaneously and forever, would explain why mediums can see into the past and future. Those 'now' moments would be no further away from us than the present."

"Good point!" Charlie said. "I didn't think of that. Apparently, Robert Lanza, Allison, and Kurt Vonnegut are saying similar things, but from very different angles."

Chris flashed his wide cat grin. "So it goes."

"Nice!" Charlie smiled and hit play on the audiobook.

A couple of hours after listening to the end of *Slaughterhouse-Five*, they arrived in Elko, Nevada, and Charlie's aunt Mable and uncle Russell welcomed them into their home with open arms. Since it was late, they visited briefly, and then Aunt Mable showed Charlie and Chris to the spare bedroom, where they slept comfortably.

Early the next morning, Charlie heard someone puttering around in the kitchen and got up to find her aunt Mable making a pot of coffee.

"Good morning, sweetheart. Would you like some coffee?"

"I'd love some."

Aunt Mable poured two cups and added creamer to hers.

"Would you like some?"

"No thanks; I drink it black."

Aunt Mable set the creamer on the countertop next to the coffeepot. "Let's sit at the dining room table. We can catch up while we drink our coffee."

"That sounds nice."

While they were visiting, Chris walked into the kitchen, made himself a cup of coffee, and joined them.

"When Russ gets up, I'll show you the rest of the house," Aunt Mable said. "But he usually stays in bed until later. He needs his sleep. I think he's getting Alzheimer's."

Charlie placed her hand on Aunt Mable's. "I'm so sorry to hear that."

"It's bound to be one thing or the other," Aunt Mable said. "We're not the spring chickens we used to be. Russ is close to ninety years old."

"How long have you guys been married?" Charlie asked.

"Practically our whole lives," Aunt Mable chuckled. "We've been together for sixty-two years, and I'll tell you a little secret about staying together. It's really very simple. First, you must be faithful, and second, you must make good gravy. My Russell loves gravy, and it will cure just about anything."

Chris smiled. "Words from the wise."

Charlie pointed to a photograph of her aunt Melba on a small table next to Russell and Mable's bedroom. "I love that photo of her; she was so beautiful."

"Yes, she was." Aunt Mable turned to Chris. "Have you ever seen the photograph of my dear sister?"

"No, but I'd like to."

Quietly, so as not to wake Uncle Russell, Aunt Mable walked to the small table near her bedroom, and Charlie and Chris followed. Aunt Mable picked up the studio portrait of her twin sister, Melba, and showed it to Chris. Melba had her short dark-brown hair loosely curled to frame her face, had a radiant smile, and was wearing long, sparkly rhinestone earrings.

Aunt Mable angrily explained to Chris how her sister had died.

"Charlie told me what happened," Chris said, shaking his head. "What a nightmare!"

"There isn't a day that goes by that I don't think about my dear sister and that awful day." Aunt Mable set the photograph down, then they returned to the dining room table. "And I knew something terrible was happening the night she was murdered. I woke up frantic in the middle of the night and tried to get ahold of her, but she wasn't home."

"My mom knew something terrible was going on too," Charlie added. "I think my mom begged Aunt Melba not to go out that night because she felt something terrible would happen, but Aunt Melba thought my mom was just worried for no reason."

"You're right," Aunt Mable said. "Your mom had a premonition beforehand, but I knew something terrible was happening at the time of her death."

"I think you're both sensitive to paranormal activity. Doesn't it run in our family?" Charlie asked.

"Yes, my grandmother Ethel was visited by my mother, Alma, shortly after she passed," Aunt Mable said. "Grandmother Ethel said she saw and heard my mother on two different occasions. She was worried about her kids, but Grandmother Ethel assured her she'd take care of them. After that, she never heard from my mother again."

"That seems crazy, but not really. . . . I've told you about everything that happened to me," Charlie said. "Still, it makes you wonder."

"It certainly does," Aunt Mable said just as Uncle Russell, dressed in slippers and blue-and-white striped pajamas, walked in and sat down at the table.

Charlie offered to get him coffee.

"Much appreciated," Uncle Russell said. "I take it black."

Charlie got up, brought Uncle Russell a cup of coffee, and then made eggs and toast for everyone. Later, after lunch, Aunt Mable, Uncle Russell, and their grandson Travis took Charlie and Chris up to Lamoille Canyon in the rugged Ruby Mountains for a bit of sightseeing.

The following morning, Charlie got up early because she couldn't sleep. She quietly made a pot of coffee, opened her computer on the raised countertop, and started working on *Charlie and the Rainbow Trout*.

Aunt Mable got up, poured herself a cup of coffee, and then stood beside Charlie.

"Sweetheart, I saw you were up by the light under the door. What are you working on?"

"I'm writing a children's book," Charlie explained. "It's based on a true story about me when I was just a kid. It helps me to keep busy, and of course, I plan to dedicate it to Isaac."

"Oh, bless your heart, honey. What's the story about?"

"Do you remember the small creek that ran in front of our house when we lived in Hailey?"

"Yes, you were still pretty young then."

"In the spring, the creek would fill up, and the trout would swim into the creek, but as fall approached, the creek would dry up, and the fish would get trapped in the lowest part of the creek underneath the bridge. I used to catch them, put them in a bucket, and then return them to the Big Wood River." Charlie showed Aunt Mable the book's cover illustration.

"Oh, that's a darling picture of you sitting in the mud," Aunt Mable chuckled. "Your mom never could keep you clean, but she tried!"

Charlie laughed. "It wasn't her fault. . . . She did her best. I just didn't like wearing dresses or getting my hair combed. In fact, that's how the book starts. See, here's the illustration of my mom trying to comb my hair." Charlie showed Aunt Mable the fifth illustration of the book.

"Oh, she'd love that picture if she could see it," Aunt Mable said. "I love the grasshopper in your hand and how the other two grasshoppers have escaped from the bug barn and are jumping around on the bathroom floor."

"I'm trying to make Isaac proud," Charlie said, continuing to explain the story. She was showing Aunt Mable more illustrations for the book when suddenly, Aunt Mable looked toward the ceiling as if she were listening to someone. She stood there frozen for a moment, then looked back at Charlie.

"I just got a message, and the message is 'Good job, Mom,'" Aunt Mable said, filled with awe. "That had to be Isaac!"

34

TWO OR THREE DAYS
June 30, 2020

EATING AT PREGO, in the heart of Houston's Rice Village, had become a tradition for Chris and Charlie. One that they always followed before Chris checked into MD Anderson for treatment and after he was released from the hospital. There was a sense of ambivalence and dread when dining prior to Chris being admitted to the hospital for treatment, but after his discharge, they were relieved and grateful because he had survived yet another round of chemotherapy, transfusions, and other treatments.

"I have to say, I like this fettuccine primavera better than the Mediterranean sea bass I had the last time," Chris said, then motioned to the formally dressed waiter. "But I'm still going to have them box up the rest so I'll have room for dessert."

The waiter came over, took their dessert order, and left.

"Tomorrow's my first day of radiation," Chris sighed. "I hope it will help the meds be more effective, like they were a couple of months ago."

"Me too, handsome," Charlie said. "You were doing so great from the beginning of March to the middle of June, but then you started feeling bad again. Hopefully, the radiation will help, and you can get back to riding your bike."

"I'm not looking forward to the radiation treatment, but I've had it before, when I had thyroid cancer. I guess this will be similar," Chris said. "I'm glad we visited your aunt Mable and uncle Russell. It was incredible how Isaac got that message to you through her. It's really good to know Isaac's still out there watching over us."

"Watching Aunt Mable get the message directly from Isaac felt like a miracle. I'll never forget that as long as I live," Charlie said. "I hate that they won't let me into the hospital with you because of COVID. But if you're feeling afraid and worried while you're getting radiation, just talk to Isaac and ask him for guidance—he can hear you."

The waiter came to the table, handed Charlie a cup of coffee and a piece of the double chocolate cake, and then gave Chris a second glass of chardonnay and a serving of vanilla bean panna cotta with fresh berries.

"I'm so glad you're here with me," Chris said after the waiter was gone. "I couldn't get through this without you."

"I'm happy to be here for you. It's the least I can do."

"I was just thinking about when you took me to the emergency room," Chris said, then took a bite of his dessert. "Do you remember that? It was before New Year's Day . . . just after the second or third round of chemo. I was losing so much blood—I'd have been a *dead man* if it weren't for you."

"That was a dangerous situation," Charlie agreed. "The problem was the doctor in the ER was only looking at your hemoglobin level when you were admitted, which was 7.1, and since someone has to be at 7.0 or below for a transfusion, they were going to release you. I understand that's their protocol, but I needed the doctor to look at the trend of your blood loss over the last few days rather than just that day's level because it didn't adequately reflect our situation. I finally got the doctor's attention by showing her the copy of your lab values that I had in my bag. Those numbers *clearly* showed that you'd been losing about a pint of blood every day since your last transfusion."

"I remember the doctor was irritated with you," Chris said. "Then she left, saying she'd review my chart."

"And when she came back, she said they were admitting you per Dr. Wang's orders, so she must have called him. I was afraid you'd lose so much blood that you'd pass out in the hotel, and I wouldn't be able to wake you up," Charlie said, frustrated. "There was no way I was going to let them release you—you can't afford to lose a pint of blood every day!"

"No kidding," Chris agreed. "That's why I'm so glad you're here with me. Thanks for everything—I love you with all my heart!"

"I love you too, handsome." Charlie squeezed Chris's hand, then looked at the clock hanging on the wall. "We'd better get going soon. You need to check into the hospital. Your room should be ready by now."

"It really sucks that you can't go into the hospital with me."

"This whole COVID thing really sucks, if you ask me."

After Chris and Charlie finished their desserts, Charlie drove Chris to MD Anderson Cancer Center and got in line with the other cars whose drivers were picking up or dropping off their loved ones. Chris reached over and squeezed Charlie's hand as they slowly approached the entrance.

"I'll call you after I get checked into my room."

"Okay, I'll be at the hotel." Charlie put the car in park at the front entrance. Then she got out, opened the hatch, and handed Chris his suitcase. They kissed goodbye, and just before Chris entered the building, he turned around and waved forlornly. Charlie blew him a kiss, and then Chris disappeared into the massive medical fortress.

Charlie sighed, then drove to the hotel. She was in her room talking to a secretary at the hospital regarding MD Anderson's COVID-19 guidelines when her phone rang. She excused herself from the first call and then answered Chris's call.

"Hey, handsome, how are you?"

"I'm okay," Chris said. "I got unpacked, but I'm sick of this hospital and this room. I wish you could be here with me."

"I wish I could be there too. I hate being stuck in this hotel and not being able to come and see you," Charlie said. "At least before, I could get you something to eat, talk to the nurses and doctors, and just be there for you. It's going to be difficult for me to know how you're tolerating the treatments now. That doesn't sit well with me."

"I talked to my nurse. Tomorrow's going to be a tough day," Chris said. "They're sending me to get a CT, and then I'll get my first radiation treatment."

"Is there anything I can do for you?" Charlie asked. "I could get you something to eat while you're there. I called the hospital, and they said I could drop food off at the front entrance, and they'd deliver it to your room."

"I'll think about it and let you know tomorrow." Chris sighed. "Right now, I'm just going to watch something on my tablet and go to sleep. I'm sick and tired of this place!"

"Okay, I hope you sleep well," Charlie said. "Will you call me in the morning? I don't want to call you in case you're sleeping."

"Sure. I'll call you when I get up."

"Love you."

"I love you too," Chris said, then hung up.

Charlie worked on her painting of Isaac for the rest of the evening to pass the time. His eyes called her name, slowly emerging from the paper as she delicately added minuscule amounts of black paint to the thick white paper.

When she didn't hear from Chris the following morning, Charlie grew concerned. She waited until 11:30 a.m., then called him and left a message. Next, she called the nursing station and learned Chris had been scheduled for radiation early that morning. She decided to surprise him by delivering him a care package, hoping it would be waiting for him when he returned to his room. She quickly drove to the store and bought a bag full of Chris's favorite snacks, including a six-pack of root beer, and delivered it to the front entrance of MD Anderson. A staff member there assured her that the care package would be taken directly to Chris's room. Charlie was walking down the hall to their hotel room when her phone rang.

"Hey, beautiful, I just got back to my room."

"Are you okay? How was your radiation treatment?"

"I'm okay. Sorry I didn't call you earlier. It's been a hell of a day. First, they took me to get a CT and I forgot to take Isaac's ashes off again, so we got CT'd together a second time." Chris laughed. "Then they took me to get the radiation treatment, which was no walk in the park, and I couldn't call because they wouldn't let me take my phone into the radiology department. When I got back, the kidney guys came and said they were concerned about my creatinine levels. It's just been one thing after the other."

"That sounds rough. I wish I could be there to help you," Charlie said. "Did you get the bag of treats I sent you?"

"I saw it on the table but haven't had time to open it yet."

"If you're hungry, there are a lot of different snacks I thought you might like."

"That was sweet of you," Chris said. "I ordered lunch, but as you know, I'm not crazy about this hospital food. It's sometimes cold by the time it gets to my room, so it'll be nice to have a little backup."

"What other treatments are you scheduled for today and tomorrow?"

"The nurse said my hemoglobin is low again, so I'll probably be getting a transfusion later today. But they want to wait a day before they give me the second round of radiation."

"I wish I could be with you and hold your hand."

"I wish you could too."

"Is there anything I can do for you?"

"Not that I can think of, but it's nice to know you're here and I can call and talk to you on the phone," Chris said, his voice wavering.

Hearing Chris cry over the phone, isolated in his hospital room, broke Charlie's heart. "Oh, handsome, I feel so bad for you. I wish there were something I could do."

"I'm going to get off the phone," Chris said, his voice trembling. "I'll call you in the morning."

"Okay, I love you."

"I love you, too."

As anticipated, Chris received a transfusion that evening, and then two days later, he was given his second radiation treatment. Chris called Charlie after he returned from radiology, but he wasn't feeling well and kept the conversation short. After hanging up, Charlie quickly drove to Prego and placed a to-go order for Chris's favorite entrée and dessert: fettuccine primavera with grilled carrots, asparagus, and mushrooms, and vanilla bean panna cotta. When it was ready, she delivered it to the hospital and then sent Chris a text: *I'm sending you a little something special, and it's on its way to your room.*

Chris called Charlie after he finished his meal.

"Hey, beautiful. Thanks for the surprise. That was delicious!"

"I thought you'd like something good to eat."

"I loved it. Thanks, I ate every bite!"

"I'm so glad you enjoyed it. How are you doing?"

"Earlier today, the kidney guys came back and said they need to place a central line so I can get dialysis tomorrow. I thought I would get out of here after radiation, but now I have to get dialysis first."

"Dialysis through a central line? That sounds awful!" Charlie cringed. "When are they going to do that?"

"They're trying to schedule it now, but knowing them, they'll probably come and get me in the middle of the night just to make sure I don't get any sleep."

"Isn't that the truth? It's impossible to get a good night's sleep when you're in the hospital."

"I guess I should try to get some rest now. . . . I'm beat," Chris said. "Thanks for dinner. It was delicious and very sweet of you."

"Okay, I hope you get some sleep. Love you, handsome."

"Love you too, beautiful. I'll call you in the morning."

After surgery the next day, Chris sent Charlie a photo of himself reclining in his hospital bed, wearing a faded blue gown with a central venous catheter placed on the left side of his neck. He looked stressed, worn out, and exhausted. The text read: *Can't talk now. They're taking me to dialysis. I'll call later.*

While Charlie waited to hear from Chris, she surfed the internet to take her mind off the situation. She came across Andy Grammer's song "Don't Give Up on Me." She watched the video of him performing the song with children seated in an auditorium and paid particular attention to the lyrics about how lovers don't give up on each other when faced with their darkest hours. Instead, they stand up and fight for one another. Before she knew it, a wall broke inside her, and a flood of sorrow poured out. With tears streaming down her face, Charlie copied the link to the song and sent it to Chris. Later that evening, Chris called.

"I watched the video," Chris said, his voice wavering.

"I'm glad you got it," Charlie said, tearing up at the sound of Chris's shaky voice.

"My throat's been hurting. I haven't been able to eat since you brought me dinner from Prego."

"That's the last time you ate?" Charlie felt alarmed as tears rolled down her face.

"Yes. I'm sorry to go, but it hurts to talk. I need to get off the phone."

"Okay, I understand," Charlie said. "I'm going to call the nursing station and see if I can get into the hospital. It's not right for you to be alone in your condition."

After Chris hung up, Charlie called the hospital. She spent the rest of the day wrangling with the nurses and doctors. Finally, the following morning, the hospital notified her that she had received permission to stay with Chris, with the understanding that once she entered his room, she wouldn't be permitted to leave again. As Charlie packed her suitcase, she called Chris and told him she was on her way and would be staying to take care of him.

When Charlie entered Chris's room, he was sitting on the side of his bed in his faded blue hospital gown, connected to an IV pole. He looked beaten down and worn out, and his stomach was visibly swollen.

Charlie kissed Chris on the cheek. "You look like you're in pain."

"It hurts to talk," Chris whispered, pointing to his neck, then motioned that he needed to go to the bathroom.

"I understand." Charlie helped Chris to his feet and walked him to the bathroom. He closed the door, and Charlie stood outside waiting. When he was finished, she walked him to the side of his bed, and he sat down. As Charlie asked Chris a few questions, he either nodded or shook his head because it hurt too much for him to talk. She called the nurse to Chris's room to get an update.

"Ever since Chris's throat started hurting, he won't take his meds for me." The nurse retrieved a small Dixie cup containing Chris's pills from the cabinet over his sink. "Would you like to try?"

"Sure," Charlie said, taking the Dixie cup. "Would you like me to help you take your meds?" she asked Chris.

He nodded, defeat in his eyes.

Charlie took a small blue oval pill from the Dixie cup and gave it to Chris. He put it in the back of his throat, took a sip of the water Charlie was holding for him, and then leaned back as far as he could while holding on to the bed rail to help the pill slide down his throat. They tried the same procedure with the second pill, but this time, it caused Chris to choke, and he spat the pill back up.

"We're going to have to skip the meds for now," the nurse said, taking the Dixie cup from Charlie's hand. "I don't want Chris to choke. I'll call his doctor and see what he wants me to do, and I'll get back to you."

Once the nurse was gone, Charlie helped Chris lie down and get comfortable, and then he dozed off and on while watching sports on his tablet for the rest of the day. Sitting next to him, Charlie noticed that Chris had changed . . . that his eyes no longer closed all the way when he slept. As his eyes rolled back, his eyelids covered his irises but not the whites below. It made Charlie feel eerie. She stood up and paced the floor, nervously biting her fingernails as she watched over Chris while he slept.

In the morning, a staff member came and took Chris to dialysis in a wheelchair. While he was gone, the doctor who was on rounds came in to talk to Charlie.

"I'm sorry to tell you this, but your husband has only two to three days to live," she said.

"WHAT!" Charlie screamed.

"You'll need to make arrangements," the doctor said sympathetically. "We can take care of him here until he passes if that would be the easiest for both of you, or we can discharge him home to you, but you'll need to decide soon—we don't have much time. When your husband returns from dialysis, you'll need to discuss this with him and then let your case manager know what you've decided."

Charlie stood there paralyzed by fear—speechless—shocked into silence.

"Do you understand?"

Charlie nodded but did not respond.

The doctor placed her hand on Charlie's shoulder and then walked out the door.

35

TRUST
The Other Side

WHEN ISAAC HEARD the oven timer beep, he grabbed a pair of rooster-patterned oven mitts from the kitchen counter and handed them to Hazel. She put the crowing roosters on and pulled the second tray of golden-brown angel biscuits from the oven. Hot air poured from the stove, filling the room with both warmth and the comforting smell of freshly baked pastries. Hazel placed the biscuits on the cutting board in the middle of the kitchen table, removed the oven mitts, and then sat down with the Williams family for breakfast.

Solomon took a hot biscuit from the tray and looked at Shane, who was sitting beside him. "When are you, Hazel, and Isaac going over to Edith's?"

"After breakfast," Shane said, opening a new jar of huckleberry jam for Ethel. "The last time Isaac and I visited Chris at the hospital, we noticed his soul had started separating from his body. Edith was there too, and she asked us to gather at her place to prepare for Chris's journey home."

"It was a great honor for her to ask Isaac to help Chris cross over," Hazel said. "Ensuring the safe passage of a loved one is one of the most important things we can do."

Isaac smiled.

"Since angel biscuits are Chris and Isaac's favorite, I made an extra batch so you can take them to Edith along with some huckleberry jam," Ethel said. "Please let Edith know we're thinking of her and Chris and that we wish him a gentle crossing. And please let her know we'll all be there for his celebration."

"Will do," Hazel said.

"Oh, that reminds me. I wanted to write down the recipe for Edith." Isaac went to the kitchen counter and got a piece of paper and a pencil, then sat back down.

"I'm so proud of Chris for achieving his goals!" Shane said. "He's completed the two life lessons he set out to learn before he was born."

"Me too," Isaac agreed as he wrote down the recipe. "I was a bit worried there for a while, but I'm so happy he prevailed. It's been a painful and difficult journey for Chris and my mom, and losing Chris will be very difficult for Mom, but now that she knows I'm still with her, she'll be strong enough to walk this journey on her own. And when she finds moments of happiness, she'll know it's the universe letting her know she's on the right path. As for Chris, I'm thrilled he's achieved his goals, and I can't wait to see him!"

Feeling anxious to leave, Isaac finished his breakfast and placed the huckleberry jam and angel biscuits in a wicker basket, which Ethel had lined with a beautifully embroidered dish towel. Then he folded the piece of paper on which he had written the recipe and tucked it inside the basket.

Isaac smiled. "I'm ready when you guys are."

"You're right, little man; we should get going." Shane finished his biscuit, then stood up to leave. "We don't want to keep Edith waiting."

"We'll see you all later," Hazel said, finishing her coffee.

As Isaac, Hazel, and Shane said goodbye, the Williams family wished them well.

—

Traveling instantly by thought, they arrived at Edith's and knocked on her door. She welcomed them into her 1960s-style ranch home—her version of heaven. Edith's short brown hair was neatly curled, and she was wearing pearl earrings, a maroon blouse patterned with small green leaves, gray slacks, and loafers.

Isaac handed Edith the wicker basket and showed her the recipe. "We brought you some huckleberry jam and angel biscuits. My mom always made these for Chris and me, and I'm sure he'd love it if you make them for him after he gets settled in."

"We also brought you these flowers," Hazel said, handing Edith a bouquet of sunflowers. "Isaac told me how much Chris loved yellow flowers, so we stopped near the Big Wood River and picked these for him."

Angel Biscuits

2 1/4 t dry Yeast
1/4 C warm water
1 t Sugar
1 1/4 C Buttermilk
1 egg

4 C White Flour
3/4 C Butter
2 t Baking Powder
1 t Baking Soda
1 t Salt

Stir Sugar into the warm water, then add yeast and set aside. Next, combine dry ingredients, then cut in the butter until crumbly. Mix egg and buttermilk, then fold in the yeast. Lightly mix the dry and wet ingredients just until they come together. Place dough on a floured counter and roll to 1/2 inch thick. Cut biscuits with floured glass and place on a greased and floured cookie sheet. Let Rise for 15 minutes, then Bake at 375°F for 25 minutes. ♥♡

Edith took the bouquet and walked into her living room, where two couples sat at a table playing bridge, eating hors d'oeuvres, and drinking Coke and Crown Royal.

Edith introduced them. "Shane, Isaac, and Hazel, this is my brother Bill; his wife, Mildred; and my brother Chick and his wife, Faye."

Edith's brothers and their wives stood up and greeted Isaac, Shane, and Hazel, and they all made small talk for a few minutes. Then Edith asked the visitors to follow her to the kitchen to put the flowers in a vase. As they left, her brothers and their wives sat back down and continued playing their bridge game.

As they entered the kitchen, they saw two horses sticking their heads through the top half of a white Dutch door with a brown frame. Seeing Isaac's surprise, Edith set the flowers and basket down on the counter and picked up a bowl of apples.

"Would you like to feed the horses?" she asked.

"Sure, that sounds fun." Isaac grinned. "What are their names?"

"This is Chris's horse, Sunny." Edith stroked the brown Appaloosa's nose. "He's a good-natured boy, but he's been a little restless as of late—he's looking forward to seeing his trusted riding buddy. And this big boy is my horse, Geronimo," Edith said, rubbing the palomino's nose, which stood well above Sunny. "Although I have to use a step stool to get into his saddle, he's a gentle giant and wouldn't hurt a fly."

"Chris told me about Sunny," Isaac said. "I remember him telling me how you and your family would ride your horses to the sand dunes, cook hot dogs and marshmallows, and then ride back home. He also told me about when he used to go on weeklong camping trips with Sunny. The way he told it, Sunny got spooked once and ran off in the middle of the night, but luckily, Chris found him the next day. He really loved his horse, so it's great to finally meet him."

"Those are fond memories," Edith said.

Eyeing the apples in Edith's hands, Geronimo and Sunny neighed and shook their manes. "Let me show you how to feed them." Edith took a green apple from the bowl, placed it flat in her hand, and fed it to Geronimo.

Isaac was a little nervous. "I've never fed a horse before."

"Just keep your hand flat and you'll do just fine," Edith said. "They're very gentle and won't hurt you."

Isaac placed an apple flat in his hand and held it under Sunny's nose. Sunny took the green apple and crushed it in his mouth as the juice drizzled down his lips. Then Sunny and Geronimo nudged Isaac with their noses, begging him for more.

"Looks like you've made yourself a couple of new friends." Edith smiled. "You can go ahead and feed them the whole bowl of apples. There's plenty more where those came from."

Isaac grinned and then continued feeding Sunny and Geronimo while Hazel and Shane sat down on barstools at the kitchen counter.

Edith took a pitcher of iced Lipton black tea from the refrigerator, poured four glasses, and returned the pitcher to the fridge. While Shane and Hazel sipped their iced tea, Edith took a vase from underneath the kitchen sink, filled it with water, and arranged the sunflowers. Then she placed them on the far end of the kitchen countertop next to a bouquet of irises and white lilies and a bright bouquet of mixed wildflowers her brothers and their wives had brought.

Hearing the commotion, Edith's two shepherd dogs, Big Guy and Cowboy, and her dachshund, Wendy, ran into the kitchen through the dog door and begged for treats. She opened the cupboard, gave them each a dog biscuit, and then they ran back outside, wagging their tails. Chris's black Lab, Quill, was comfortably curled up on a brown rug patterned with orange and yellow flowers in the middle of the kitchen, eagerly awaiting the arrival of his master. Edith offered him a treat, but he refused it. Instead, he just laid his head down between his paws.

Edith sat down on a barstool adjacent to Hazel. "I'm so glad you're here to help prepare for Chris's celebration. I'm proud of him, and I'm so excited to see him!"

"Me too," Isaac said. "We all have different life lessons, but often the most difficult lessons can offer the greatest rewards."

Isaac fed the last apple to Sunny, then took a seat between Hazel and Shane.

"Isaac's lesson, humility, is a perfect example," Shane said. "Having a brain injury at birth made Isaac understand how painful it is to live with physical and mental disabilities, which caused him to see all people as equals, including those less fortunate. As a result, he looked out for the downtrodden—those who struggled as he did. He couldn't prevent what happened to him, but he could help others."

"And lessons can be tricky at times," Hazel said. "I was disgruntled in my last life because I had to help take care of my nine younger siblings, including three sets of twins, and then raise all my kids by myself. But when I learned that one of my life lessons was to serve others because I had previously been very selfish, it all made sense—two sides of the same coin."

Shane raised one eyebrow. "I sort of messed up.... I loved adventure, but I often got myself in sticky situations by not being cautious."

"You can say that again," Isaac joked.

"We don't always get it right the first time," Shane laughed, nudging Isaac. "I might not have got the end of my life right, but I still learned many valuable lessons. It's a good thing there's always a next time if we choose for there to be."

"Well, I'll certainly need a next time," Hazel said. "I haven't mastered forgiveness, but I've made progress, thanks to Shane. Still, forgiveness is a tricky lesson."

"Isn't that the truth!" Edith agreed. "I'm still working on that one myself. I've had a difficult time forgiving Chris's dad, Cliff, for how he treated our kids."

"You can't make others do the right thing.... That burden's for them to carry. It's part of their lesson," Shane said. "All you can do is what you know to be right. You adopted Chris and Clair and gave up your career to care for your children. You can be proud because, at the end of the day, you did right by your children."

"Many years ago, I delivered a message to Chris in a dream, telling him to get in touch with Charlie, his old girlfriend from high school, because I knew they could help each other achieve their life lessons if they got married. Later that day, Chris sent Charlie an email, and by the end of the week, they were talking on the phone, and the rest is history." Edith took a sip of her iced tea. "And it's because Isaac contacted Charlie that Chris was able to learn one of his two lessons—death is not an end. The hope of seeing Isaac again gave them the strength to carry on, and now Chris won't be afraid of crossing over.... What a tremendous gift to give to another person. Thanks, Isaac. You've not only saved your mom, but you've also saved my son!"

"You're welcome, but I had a lot of help from my grandma Hazel, Uncle Shane, and the rest of the Williams family back home."

"Many thanks to all of you!" Edith said, raising her glass.

They raised their glasses and cheered.

"Chris's second lesson was to experience unconditional love. Cliff and I adopted both him and his sister, Clair, when they were newborns, but we never told them they were adopted, because I didn't want them to question their self-worth. One day, when Chris was young, he came up to me and told me he thought he got his curly hair from me. After that, I never let the kids know I didn't have naturally curly hair. I just got a babysitter to watch them when I went to get my hair permed at the salon." Tears welled up in Edith's eyes. "Those are the days I miss the most."

She paused, then her expression became more serious. "However, they eventually found out they were adopted, and that was a very ugly and difficult situation. Now, I wish I had told them because, after I passed, Cliff remarried and cut Chris and Clair out of the inheritance that I had left for them, and the kids were forced to sue their father to get it back. During the lawsuit, Cliff stated that he felt the property and trust belonged to him because Chris and Clair were adopted! That's how they found out, and it hit Clair and Chris like a ton of bricks. It caused Clair to have an identity crisis because she felt that everything she had been told was a lie. She felt betrayed and questioned her relationships with her relatives, which made her sad because she and Chris loved their aunts and uncles and had fond memories of visiting them during summer vacations. Chris, on the other hand, felt like he finally understood why his father never loved him. Cliff plans to apologize to Chris after he crosses over, but I know it won't be easy.... Chris felt very betrayed by his father."

"That's terrible," Hazel said. "I certainly hope he'll try to make amends."

Isaac and Shane agreed.

"After that, Chris struggled with his sense of belonging and his concept of love. It's impossible to understand unconditional love when you don't have a reference," Edith said. "It's easy for a parent to love a child unconditionally when they're young because the child can't take care of themselves, and they depend on their parents for their every need. However, as the child grows up, conditions start to get put into place. Parents ask their kids to clean their rooms, eat dinner, do their homework, and pick up after themselves. Over time, this often changes their unconditional love into a love that has conditions, but not always. Since Chris never had children, he's never experienced that kind of unconditional love. As a result, he based his ideas of love on feelings he had for his parents and his romantic relationships."

Edith sipped her iced tea, then continued. "Love can also change slowly into something else. That happened with Chris's first marriage. It started with love, but Chris became unhappy as their relationship became weighted over the years. That's when I stepped in and delivered a message to Chris in his dream . . . the one about reaching out to Charlie."

"I remember Chris telling me about that dream," Isaac said. "But I didn't know that you had intervened."

"When Chris first married your mom, he thought maybe he had finally found unconditional love, but he was wrong," Edith said.

Shane, Hazel, and Isaac all looked alarmed.

Edith smiled, then explained. "Like most couples, their love had many conditions—it was calculated . . . based on the benefits and hindrances of their relationship." Edith took another sip of her iced tea. "Chris didn't come to know unconditional love willingly—it was forced upon him by circumstance. As he's battled cancer, little by little, he's been forced to relinquish his independence . . . his control of the situation. When Chris finally surrendered and trusted Charlie to care for his every need, that's when he finally found unconditional love. At last, Chris understood that unconditional love carries no shield—that it's based on trust."

They raised their glasses and cheered, "Here's to Chris."

36

HOMEWARD BOUND

July 6, 2020

PANICKED, CHARLIE PACED the room, trembling as she wept. She could hardly catch her breath through the stream of tears as her mind raced. Knowing Chris would be back from dialysis at 10:00 a.m., she checked the clock hanging on the wall: 9:47 a.m.

There's no way I can do what I have to do. . . . I can't tell Chris he has only two to three days to live! And how am I supposed to ask him if he wants me to take him home to die or stay here at the hospital? I just can't say those words, but I have no other choice.

Sobbing, Charlie grabbed another tissue, then looked at the clock as she paced the floor: 9:55 a.m. Her stomach sank. She didn't want Chris to be wheeled back into his room, she didn't want to have to say those words, and she didn't want to be in the horrific situation they were in. She didn't want to be an army of one. She wanted Chris to be well. She wanted to go home and have everything go back to normal. But before she knew it, the door opened, and the transporter wheeled Chris back into his room, transferred him to his bed, then left.

Feeling a sense of urgency, Charlie walked to the side of Chris's bed, adjusted his pillows to make him more comfortable, then sat down next to him and took his hand. She looked at his pale, exhausted face and saw that he was listless. He looked into her bloodshot eyes. She was desperate. Frantic.

Charlie wiped her tears with her hands. "I don't know how to say this, but the doctor said you only have two to three days to live!"

"Two to three days?" Chris questioned, his voice frail, almost a whisper.

"Yes, and you told me you didn't want to die in the hospital," Charlie said. "Do you want me to take you home?"

Chris nodded, then reached out and placed his hand on Charlie's leg. She tried to hold back her pain, but a flood of tears broke through and poured down her face. Charlie bent over and buried her face in her hands. Chris didn't say a word or cry; he just quietly watched Charlie lose control of herself.

Charlie was inconsolable for the next couple of hours while Chris remained calm. At noon, Charlie finally stopped pacing the floor and did the math in her head. *I have two to three days to get Chris home. It will take me most of the day to get out of here, and I have a twenty-hour drive in front of me. That's not going to leave me much time to spare! I need to stop crying and get things done. I'll have to cry later.*

Charlie dried her tears, called the case manager, and told her they needed to get things in place so she could drive Chris home. She explained the urgency of the situation, and within the hour, the case manager brought in the first form she needed to sign in order to discharge Chris from the center into Charlie's care. Charlie read the top of the form: *OUT-OF-HOSPITAL DO-NOT-RESUSCITATE (OOH-DNR) ORDER, Texas Department of State Health Services*. On the left side of the form was a black silhouette of Texas with the word *STOP* written in white letters across it. Charlie noticed Chris's name had been written on the first line of the form. It had been dated July 6, 2020, and signed by the doctor on rounds and two nurses.

The case manager stood next to Chris's bed and explained the DNR form to him. "Is this what you want?"

Chris nodded, pointing to his neck.

"It hurts Chris to talk," Charlie explained.

"Can you sign the form?" the case manager asked.

Chris shook his head.

"Would you like me to sign the form for you?" Charlie asked.

Chris nodded listlessly.

Charlie signed and dated the DNR and then gave it back to the case manager. "What do I need to do next?"

"You need to find a hospice care provider in your area to care for Chris when he gets home. They'll have to deliver oxygen and other equipment to your house, so you'll need someone there to let them in. Now that I have this form signed, I can get you the official DNR printed on orange paper, which you'll need to keep with you at all times. Keep it readily accessible in case of an emergency. Any officer will recognize the orange DNR in case something happens while you're driving," the case manager said.

"I understand," Charlie said, her heart sinking.

"I'm going back to my office to order the oxygen tanks to be delivered to your room so you'll have them for the drive home," the case manager said. "Call me as soon as you've decided which hospice care provider to use so I can send them the paperwork."

"I'll look into it right now and call you as soon as possible."

After the case manager left, Charlie searched the internet on her phone, found a reputable hospice care provider, and made arrangements. When she was done, she called Teresa and arranged for her to stay at the house to receive the equipment. She gave Teresa the hospice care provider's phone number and the security code to her garage door.

When she was done, Charlie called the case manager and updated her about the arrangements. Next, Charlie called Chris's nurse, informed her of the situation, and asked her to get a stat order from the doctor to remove Chris's central line. All of this took a considerable amount of time.

Charlie looked at the clock: 2:51 p.m.

The case manager returned to Chris's room and, handing Charlie the DNR, reminded her one more time to keep it with her at all times in case of an emergency.

"I understand," Charlie said, taking the orange piece of heavyweight paper.

After the case manager left, Charlie glanced at the clock: 3:02 p.m. She sat down next to Chris, took his hand, and informed him that she was working on getting him discharged from the hospital so they could go home. Chris nodded, motioning for Charlie to get him a sip of water. She held the cup near his dry, parched lips and placed the straw in his mouth. Chris took a sip, but it was difficult for him to swallow. He leaned his head back, barely managed to get the water down, then squeezed Charlie's hand.

Charlie set the cup of water on the bedside table. "While we're waiting, I'll get our things packed."

Chris nodded, his eyes half empty, moving toward vacant.

Charlie was packing Chris's suitcase when a man dressed in black MD Anderson scrubs entered with a wheelchair.

"I'm here to take Chris down to have his central line removed," the man said, helping Chris into the wheelchair.

Charlie got up, kissed Chris on the cheek, and squeezed his hand. "I'll be right here waiting for you to get back."

Chris smiled, and then the man wheeled him out of the room.

As Charlie continued packing, she heard her phone ring.

Charlie answered, then Teresa gave her an update. "We made it to your house. I've called the hospice care provider, and they're on their way to bring the equipment. They want you to let them know when you're about thirty minutes away from your house so they can send the hospice nurse here to meet you."

"Okay, thanks for helping me."

"Of course," Teresa said. "I went to the store and bought some flowers and food. I'll start cleaning the house and strip the bed so it will be nice and clean for Chris when he gets home."

Charlie looked at the clock: 4:45 p.m. "Thanks. I need to go before the case manager leaves for the day."

"Okay, please drive safe," Teresa said, hanging up the phone.

Worried that the oxygen tanks weren't there yet, Charlie called the case manager. She called the oxygen-tank supplier and then called Charlie back.

"I located the truck carrying your oxygen tanks. It's on the east side of town, and they still have several orders to deliver before they stop at the hospital," the case manager explained. "They said they hope to deliver your order by eleven tonight."

"Eleven!" Charlie exclaimed, her heart rate increasing as anxiety struck. *I don't have that much time to spare!*

"I'm sorry; I wish there were more I could do."

Trying to calm down, Charlie paced the floor for a while, then began packing up the rest of their belongings again. Finally, the door opened, and the man dressed in black scrubs wheeled Chris back into the room. The man transferred Chris into bed, got him comfortable, then left. Charlie walked to Chris's bed and looked at the large dressing on the side of his neck, where they had removed the central line. Chris reached for Charlie's hand and squeezed it.

"The only thing we're waiting for is the oxygen tanks," Charlie said. "Once they're here, we can go."

Chris nodded, surrender in his eyes.

"I hate having to say this, but if something happens while I'm driving and I'm not able to pull over, you need to go toward Isaac! He'll be on the other side waiting to help you cross over."

Chris squeezed her hand.

Charlie looked at the clock: 7:40 p.m.

"I only slept a couple of hours last night because I was too upset, and I'm worried about being too tired to drive twenty hours straight to get home. I should lie down and see if I can rest."

Chris nodded and let go of Charlie's hand.

Charlie lay down on the couch and covered herself with a hospital blanket. She was exhausted, but her mind continued to race. She forced herself to stay still until she eventually fell asleep, but after a while, she woke suddenly in a panic. *What time is it?* She got up quickly to look at the clock: 9:44 p.m. She looked out the window at the sea of city lights for a few minutes, then walked to where Chris lay awake in his hospital bed. Her heart sank, noticing how frail he looked.

"Should I go to the hotel and check us out there while we wait?" Charlie asked.

Chris shook his head. "No, don't leave me," he whispered.

"Okay, we'll do it together," Charlie said, understanding his fear of being left alone. "It will only take a few minutes anyway."

Chris smiled, squeezing Charlie's hand.

The door opened and a flood of light spilled into the room. "I have your order for three oxygen tanks with a conserving device and a concentrator," a broad-shouldered man said. "I'm sorry I'm late."

Charlie thanked him and told him he could leave them in the hall. After she'd signed the paperwork, he left.

She looked at the clock: 11:20 p.m.

She rummaged through her suitcase, found the lighter and a large white candle, and placed them on the windowsill. Then she took the photograph of Isaac from her bag, put it on the windowsill, and lit the candle.

"Isaac, I need your help," Charlie whispered. She looked into Isaac's eyes, the window to his soul. "I'm right here, where the candle is burning in the windowsill of this skyscraper in Houston." She looked out over the sea of city lights flickering against the night sky. "I'm right here, and I need your help! We need to leave as soon as possible, but I'm worried about driving twenty hours while I'm already exhausted, and I'm also afraid of running out of time. I don't know what the right thing to do is, Isaac. I need to know if it's safe for me to drive home." She grew quiet and listened to her heart for Isaac's answer—*yes*.

Charlie walked over to Chris. "We need to get out of here and get on the road."

"Okay," Chris whispered. "Can you get me a shirt and a pair of pants? I want to change before we go."

Feeling a sense of urgency, Charlie wanted to ask Chris if he could wear the clothes he already had on, but she didn't want to upset him or go against his wishes. Concealing her impatience, she opened his suitcase and found Chris a clean T-shirt, a pair of loose-fitting pants, clean socks, tennis shoes, and his favorite orange baseball hat.

While Charlie helped Chris change out of his pajamas into his clothes, she asked the nursing assistant to find a cart to transport their suitcases, concentrator, and oxygen tanks to their car. Once he was dressed, the nurse pushed Chris in his wheelchair toward the elevator while Charlie and the assistant followed with the cart. When they reached the exit, Charlie hurried to the parking garage, then drove Chris's Touareg to the patient pickup area. While the nurse helped Chris into the passenger seat, Charlie and the assistant loaded their belongings into the back of the car. After Charlie had thanked the nurse and her assistant for their help, she checked Chris's seat belt. Then she kissed Chris, got into the driver's seat, and then squeezed his hand as they drove away from MD Anderson Cancer Center for the last time.

Charlie parked outside their hotel. "Should I just go in, get our stuff, and check out?"

Chris shook his head, unfastened his seat belt, and removed his nasal cannula.

"You need to keep your oxygen on," Charlie said, alarmed.

Chris shook his head and got out of the car defiantly.

Charlie hurried to the other side of the car and gave Chris her arm to help stabilize him as he walked toward the hotel's entrance. Chris clung to the handrail leading up the stairs but then, losing his strength, stumbled. Charlie caught his fall, and then Chris hung on to Charlie's arm as they walked into the hotel, took the elevator to the fifth floor, and walked down the long hall to their hotel room. Charlie gathered their belongings while Chris slowly walked around. Charlie wondered what he was thinking but didn't ask. She put her computer over her shoulder and tucked her black-and-white painting of Isaac, which she had placed between two pieces of heavy cardboard before going to the hospital, under her arm. Then Charlie wheeled her suitcase with one hand while Chris held on to the other as they walked to the lobby, checked out, and got back into the car. Charlie helped Chris put his nasal cannula back on and gave him a pillow, hoping he would sleep while she drove to San Antonio.

Before they drove away from the hotel, Charlie looked at the clock on the dashboard: 1:02. She took a deep breath, exhaled, then texted Teresa: *Leaving Houston.*

Chris settled into his seat and slept while Charlie drove through the night. As they reached San Antonio's city limits, the sun's rays colored the horizon, fading the sky from a midnight blue to a mixture of crimson reds and cadmium oranges.

When Charlie pulled into a gas station, Chris woke up.

"We're in San Antonio," Charlie said. "I'm just stopping to fill the car with diesel. Is there anything I can get you?"

Chris shook his head.

Charlie went inside to use the restroom while Chris stayed in the car. He had no need to use the restroom, as he had stopped producing urine due to kidney failure. When Charlie got back to the car, she took a drink from her Nalgene water bottle. Spying a small bag of stone-ground wheat crackers in the back seat, she grabbed them and put them next to the Nalgene bottle. When she got back into the driver's seat, she checked the clock: 5:37 a.m. She texted Teresa, not taking time to say anything other than their location: *San Antonio.*

Charlie pulled out of the gas station, took the on-ramp to Interstate 10, and headed west toward El Paso, which was eight hours away. As Charlie drove, Chris settled into his seat, rested his head on his pillow, and closed his eyes. While Chris slept, Charlie became lost in her thoughts.

When Isaac first died, there was nothing but pure misery . . . darkness. But I began to feel a little hope that Isaac wasn't gone forever when I started getting signs: the dreams, the hawk, the lights flickering in the living room, Schmiggs, and the laundry light. And then there was the message Isaac sent directly to me through Aunt Mable, which was nothing less than extraordinary. Isaac has certainly made his presence known, which means we can't truly be separated—we're two sides of the same coin. Nothing can divide us, not even death!

At the sound of the rumble strip at the side of the road, Charlie returned her attention to the task at hand. She moved into the middle of her lane and glanced at Chris, glad he was peacefully resting. Knowing she wouldn't waste time buying coffee or food, Charlie ate two of the six crackers, saving the rest for later. She took a drink of water, looked out the window, and remembered all the times they had passed through that area over the last eleven months. While Charlie continued reviewing past events, she drove down the endless roads of Texas, staring blankly ahead as the mind-numbing broken white line on the pavement repeatedly flashed before her eyes. *All this has been so crazy. I can see how these sorts of things, especially the paranormal activity and near-death experiences, could be the stuff of religious texts. In the beginning, it was easy to dismiss a single sign, but now, when I add all these events together, it's changed my perspective on dying—it's a transition, not an end. Now Isaac is free of all the horrible suffering he had to endure while he was alive! May he be forever free!*

Wanting to make good time, Charlie increased her speed to eighty miles an hour, the speed limit through some stretches of Interstate 10 between San Antonio and El Paso. *Tarra said Chris's kidneys were weak, and he was just getting dialysis through a central line due to kidney failure! Maybe it's like she said; we're here to learn specific lessons and once we've completed them, we move on. If that's the case, death isn't an end but a graduation, which means Chris must have completed his lessons, whatever they were. I'm glad he knows there's something after death and glad we've shared the time we had together. Maybe EVERYTHING IS AS IT SHOULD BE. Life is like the two sides of a coin: sometimes brutal, other times full of wonder and joy. I accept both, and I'm not afraid of either. I can lean into both and learn the lessons each has to offer. Doing this would help me get out of my victim mode and do something good with this terrible situation. I'm so thankful to see the world from this new perspective—what an incredible gift Isaac has given me from the other side.* Charlie started to get choked up, but she forced herself to hold back her tears. *I better think about something else. I can't afford to start crying—I need to get Chris home!*

Chris shifted his weight in his seat.

"Would you like me to turn on some music?"

Chris gave her a thumbs-up.

Charlie selected classic rock radio from her Pandora collection, and the first song, "Street Fighting Man" by the Rolling Stones, made Chris smile. He did a little jig to the music in his seat, and Charlie joined him by singing along and tapping her feet to the beat of the drum. They looked at each other, grinned, and then continued listening to music as they drove down the highway. They guessed each new song's name as they started to pass the time, just as they'd done on their countless journeys to and from Houston, but this time, only Charlie guessed the song, and Chris either gave her a thumbs-up or a thumbs-down because using his voice hurt.

Since she was planning to drive straight through El Paso, Charlie stopped in Fort Stockton to fill the car with diesel. While they were there, Charlie drew up a dose of Dilaudid into a syringe, put it into Chris's mouth, and squeezed it into the side of his cheek. After he swallowed it, she removed his fentanyl patch from his right shoulder and placed a new one on his left shoulder. Before getting back on Interstate 10, Charlie texted Teresa: *Fort Stockton.*

The pain medication caused Chris to feel drowsy, and he fell asleep with his head resting on his pillow. Hoping he would sleep soundly, Charlie turned the music off and concentrated on the road.

As they arrived at the edge of El Paso, the sun was directly overhead. Charlie looked at the clock on the dash: 1:28 p.m. Then she subtracted an hour in her mind, as they'd gained an hour when they entered Mountain Daylight Time. They had made good time, only stopping to get fuel, but El Paso was still far from home, and despite the sprawling city's aggressive and hectic bumper-to-bumper traffic, Charlie could barely stay awake. The repetitious sound of the wheels speeding along the highway and the repetitive, mind-numbing, flashing broken white lines lulled her toward sleep as she watched the road mindlessly. She felt the lack of coffee—the caffeine drip that kept her brain operating—and her mind began to wander, slowing her thinking and reflexes. Charlie knew she was in trouble. She rubbed her eyes, trying to keep them open, and ate two more crackers, then washed them down with some water. She hoped that would help, but it didn't—her mind was drifting from exhaustion, with eight hours still to go.

Charlie thought about turning the music back on but didn't want to wake Chris, as he seemed to be resting peacefully. She opened the center console compartment of the car, looking for anything to help her stay awake. She found a small pair of her nursing scissors—with thin, sharp needle-nose points—and picked them up. Charlie was too tired to try to figure out how they got there. She never drove Chris's car to work and always kept her nursing equipment in her work backpack. Still, there they were, in her hands.

She closed the center console compartment, then, in a last-ditch effort, pushed the sharp ends of the scissors through the fabric of her Levi's into her thigh, hard enough to get her attention but not hard enough to break the skin. For the next forty-five miles, every time she felt her mind start to wander, she pushed the scissors in, and the sharp pain refocused her attention. By the time they were thirty miles north of El Paso, she had gotten a second wind and was able to put the scissors back into the center console.

As Charlie drove toward Socorro, New Mexico, she remembered how Allison had described Isaac. *He's a bright light . . . like what we would call an angel, and he's capable of helping you with whatever you need.* Next, she remembered how Tarra had described him. *Isaac's an old soul in a young body.* Charlie smiled. *Those are perfect descriptions of my little guy.*

She thought about eating the last two crackers, which reminded her that Chris had eaten his last meal days ago, when she had ordered takeout from Prego and delivered it to the hospital. Reluctantly, she ate the crackers, washing them down with water. As she took the exit into Socorro, Chris woke up. While Charlie filled up the car's fuel tank, she texted Teresa: *Socorro.*

As they traveled from New Mexico to Arizona, the blue sky gradually grew dark while the brilliant sun slowly disappeared below the horizon.

Charlie pulled over in Winslow and called the hospice care provider to let her know she would be home soon. When she checked the clock on her phone, she noticed they'd gained an hour because the majority of Arizona doesn't observe daylight saving time. Charlie merged back into traffic, and forty-five minutes later, she finally took the first exit into Flagstaff.

Pulling into her garage at last, she checked the time on her phone: 7:27 p.m. Teresa held the door open and Chris held on to Charlie's arm as they walked from the garage to their bedroom, Chris stumbling and barely making it because he was so weak.

He sat down on the edge of the bed, where the hospice nurse connected Chris to the oxygen concentrator and then took his vital signs. His oxygen saturation was at 50 percent, even though the oxygen was at its maximum flow rate. The nurse tried to replace Chris's nasal cannula with a face mask to increase the oxygen, but Chris refused to wear it, so she put his nasal cannula back on. While Charlie and the hospice nurse got Chris comfortable in bed, it was clear that his life forces were leaving him.

As Teresa walked the hospice nurse to the front door, the nurse gave Teresa her business card and asked her to call if they needed help or if Chris passed during the night. Once she was gone, Teresa returned to Chris and Charlie's bedroom and sat on a chair beside the bed.

Charlie held Chris's hand while she sat beside him on the bed. "You're safe at home. Cobalt and Dexter are on the bed with you, and I'm not going anywhere. I love you, and I'll stay right here by your side."

"I . . . I . . ."

"It's okay; save your energy, handsome. I know you love me too," Charlie said, finishing his sentence for him.

Chris nodded, closing his gray-blue eyes for the last time.

Charlie held his hand as he began his journey to the other side.

"I'm so glad you made it home safe, but you look beat." Teresa stood up to leave. "Why don't you lie down next to Chris and get some sleep?"

Charlie curled up next to Chris with her hand over his heart. Teresa covered Charlie with a blanket and then, closing the door behind her, left to go sleep in Isaac's room.

At 1:27 a.m., Charlie woke suddenly. As she watched, Chris took his last two breaths.

Charlie grabbed Chris by the shoulders. "Go toward Isaac. I know he's there waiting for you. Go to him, and after you get to the other side, you better find a way to let me know you're all right!" Charlie ran down the hall, woke Teresa up, and they ran back to be with Chris. Teresa sat on a chair while Charlie sat next to Chris, holding his hand. Charlie wept as they sat with him in the wee hours of the morning as he made his journey home.

When the sun came up, Charlie called the hospice nurse, who came to record his death and take possession of his narcotics and then left. Afterward, Charlie and Teresa went to the kitchen and made coffee, then reminisced about their fondest memories of Chris, at times crying and then at other times laughing. Looking at Teresa's beautiful flowers on the kitchen table, Charlie took them from the vase and walked to the bedroom, where Chris's body lay in bed. She placed the flowers on his chest, put her hand around his cold face, and kissed his forehead.

When Charlie returned to the kitchen, she saw Teresa in the living room.

"Isn't this the moon lamp Chris gave you for your birthday?" Teresa asked.

"Yes."

Teresa turned the moon on. "Let's keep it on for Chris."

"That's a great idea," Charlie said, smiling.

Three days later, Chris was cremated with the small pendant containing some of Isaac's ashes around his neck. Charlie imagined Isaac's and Chris's ashes mixing together in the fire, which made her smile and cry at the same time. *At least they're together,* she thought.

That night, Teresa and Charlie got ready for bed, and then Charlie talked to Isaac for a few minutes. When she was done, she blew out his candle, turned off Chris's moon lamp, and went to bed. In the middle of the night, Charlie woke up, seeing a light in the hall. She thought Isaac must have triggered the laundry light but then realized the light was fading from bright to dim and back again, which the laundry light never did.

Getting out of bed, Charlie glanced at the time on her phone: 1:27 a.m. *That's the same time Chris died.* She walked down the hall to the living room and found Chris's moon glowing in the dark! Charlie's heart jumped as she stood there staring at the moon shining bright, fading, then shining bright again. *I know I turned the moon off before I went to bed,* Charlie thought. She looked toward the kitchen and noticed that the lights on the appliances were off. Then she looked out the window and saw that the streets were dark. That's when Charlie realized the power was out. Still, Chris's moon glowed brilliantly, even though the neighborhood was pitch-black!

Charlie stood frozen, staring at the moon—elated.

37

THE CELEBRATION
The Other Side

CHRIS HAD FELT NO PULL from the earth—no gravity—as he had separated from his body three days earlier. He had felt only weightlessness. At last, he was free . . . free from the pain that had tortured his body, free from anxiety, fear, worry, and sorrow. Euphoria settled over him, knowing he was truly released. Looking down at his lifeless body, he watched Charlie grab his shoulders and listened to what she had to say. Then Chris said goodbye to his broken body, his loved ones, and his life as he knew it and turned to face a brilliant light that beckoned him in the great darkness. *Go to Isaac; he's there waiting for you.* Chris heard Charlie's words echo in his mind. *He must be near the white light,* Chris thought. He stepped forward into what seemed like an enormous tunnel. He felt confused, and then it dawned on him—the only thing he could hear was absolute silence.

Just go to the light—Isaac will be there, Chris kept reminding himself as he walked toward the beacon shining bright in the distance. Occasionally, he looked around, but he didn't waver from his path. With every step, the light grew more radiant, warm, and inviting until Chris approached the end of the tunnel and stepped into the light. Realizing the brilliant light *was* Edith and Isaac, who had come to take him home, Chris was overcome with elation. Pure joy.

"Welcome home," Edith said, putting her arms around her son, covering him with her radiant light. "I've missed you so much. It's so good to see you!"

"Mom, is that really you?" Chris wept, his heart bursting with joy. "I've missed you every day since you passed. . . . It seems like a lifetime ago."

"It *was* a lifetime ago," Edith said, pulling him closer. "But you're here with us now."

Not able to hold back any longer, Isaac threw his arms around Chris, showering him with white light.

"We've been waiting for you!" Isaac said. "I'm so glad you made it through the dark tunnel. For some people, that's the hardest part, and that's why we're here—we've come to bring you home."

"I looked for you like Charlie told me." Chris smiled, realizing he could hear again and wondering why Isaac was so young.

"Just before you crossed, I woke my mom, knowing you'd need to listen to what she had to say as you made your journey home." Isaac threw his arms around Chris again. "It's so good to see you! We have so much to show you."

"I've missed you. You're a sight for sore eyes, my friend," Chris said. "By the time I was ready to cross, I knew death wasn't an end, and I wasn't afraid to die. What a tremendous gift you've given me. Thank you!"

"What are friends for?" Isaac smiled. "Soon, you'll understand everything. It's time we go to the garden."

"Yes, come with us," Edith said. She motioned for Chris to follow her to a nearby garden surrounded by a white picket fence.

Chris and Isaac walked side by side behind Edith, but then Isaac ran ahead, opened the gate of the white picket fence, and held it open. After Chris and Edith entered the beautiful garden, Isaac closed the gate behind them. They walked along a winding path through wild sunflowers, blue flax, red and yellow columbine, royal-blue-and-white rocket larkspur, and bright-pink catchflies toward a garden courtyard. The courtyard was speckled with dancing sunlight shining through the overhanging branches of blooming dogwood trees, their crisp white flowers gently moving on the light breeze. At the center of the patio were three stone benches around a small pond with several sunfire water lilies, their white-and-yellow centers encircled by bright-pink petals. A blue dragonfly alighted on one of the water lilies, cleaned its enormous turquoise-colored eyes, then darted off, chasing a smaller yellow-and-black striped dragonfly, a potential mate.

Around the pond, various potted flowers were beautifully arranged with an array of colorful blooms. Across the patio were garden beds filled with black-eyed Susans, Rocky Mountain penstemons, and Shasta daisies. A grove of aspen and pine trees lay behind the flower beds, where a small wooden bridge arched over a quiet babbling stream, the fresh mountain air perfumed by the pitch of pine trees. Beyond the bridge was a ranch house surrounded by green pastures flanked by the Teton Range, home of Grand Targhee Resort, which was covered with new powder.

As Edith, Chris, and Isaac walked through the garden to the patio, Chris saw a closed book lying on top of one of the benches. Isaac picked it up, then sat on the bench facing the lily pond and placed the book on his lap.

"Come," Edith said, looking at Chris and kneeling at the pond's edge.

Chris knelt next to his mom and looked into the water. There, he saw a reflection of himself as a fully restored, strong, healthy twenty-two-year-old man with thick, curly blond hair and the same gray-blue eyes as his mom.

Chris looked at Edith, surprised. "I'm young again!"

"Yes, the age when you were the happiest." Edith smiled. "This courtyard is your version of a perfect garden and reflecting pool. Keep looking. . . . You have much to learn."

That explains why Isaac is so young, Chris thought. He settled his eyes back on the pond. As he gazed into the water's reflection, the water showed him all the events in his life, making it clear to him why he had made the choices he did. The majority of the events were positive, but he saw the mistakes he had made in various situations. He acknowledged both, owning his errors as well as his accomplishments. Next, Chris saw what effects his actions had on others. Again, most were positive, but Chris was not without faults; he had hurt some people with the choices he made. As Chris reviewed his life, he took mental notes on what he could improve and what he needed to learn if he chose to return at some other time. Then Chris saw Charlie's reflection and heard her words echo in his mind: *You better find a way to let me know you're all right!*

Chris looked at Edith and Isaac. "Charlie's worried about me. I need to let her know that I'm here . . . that I made it to the other side."

"Think of something that will get her attention," Isaac said. "You know, like how I got your attention with the hawk, but think of something that she'll know is you, then send her a message—a sign."

"I know just the perfect thing." Chris closed his eyes and lowered his head, concentrating and intuitively knowing what to do. After a moment, Chris raised his head and opened his eyes. "You should have seen Charlie's expression! She was OVER THE MOON . . . so to say." Chris grinned. *How ironic—now I'm the one sending messages!*

"You're going to get the hang of this in no time," Edith said. She sat down on the garden bench next to Isaac, and then Chris sat down beside her. She bent down and picked up a blue-and-white toy boat concealed in the grass beside the bench, where she had placed it earlier. "You set out to learn two important lessons and achieved both. I'm so proud of you—a job well done," Edith said, handing Chris the toy boat. "May this be a reminder that you can sail across any water you set your mind to cross."

"I remember this boat," Chris said. "You gave it to me when I was just a child. You were the best mom! Thanks for giving me the greatest childhood a kid could ever ask for," Chris said, wiping tears of joy from his eyes.

Edith held Chris's hand. "You're the finest boy a mother could ever wish for. I love you with all my heart!"

Isaac handed Chris the brown journal he had been waiting to give him. "This is a book of your memories and adventures to review. As our journey continues . . . as we make more memories here, they'll be added to your book. And when my mom thinks of us as she continues her journey, those memories will also be added to your book of memories."

"Then our journey with Charlie continues?" Chris asked.

"Yes, absolutely! We remain connected to our loved ones. They're part of our heaven."

"I think I'm going to like this place," Chris said, flashing his Cheshire cat grin.

"Would you like to walk to the bridge?" Edith asked. "It's a lovely place."

"Sure." Chris placed the blue-and-white toy boat on the pond to sail among the water lilies and dragonflies.

Edith, Chris, and Isaac walked along the trail through the black-eyed Susans, Rocky Mountain penstemons, and Shasta daisies to the aspen and pine tree grove, where the arching bridge crossed a small stream. Songbirds sang and flittered about them as they walked to the middle of the bridge, faced the creek, and then rested their arms on the railing of the wooden bridge.

"Some people are sent back by a family member or a loved one they've never met at this point, because it's not their time to cross. Others, like yourself, arrive here after asking for their crossing to be delayed until they can say goodbye to a loved one or take care of something important. In your case, that meant getting back home, where you were comfortable. We waited until you were in your own bed with Charlie at your side so you could have a good death—a death of your choosing." Edith put her arm around her son. "Once you cross this bridge and step onto the ground on the other side, you cannot return. Say your last goodbyes, then when you're ready, Isaac and I will walk you over to the other side."

"So you guys made sure Charlie would get me home?" Chris asked, tucking his journal under his arm.

"Yes, my mom asked me if it was safe for her to drive you home, and I assured her it was," Isaac said. "She's working on self-reliance—trusting her intuition. She's making progress, but she still has a way to go."

"Thanks, Isaac. You're a true friend." Chris smiled, took a deep breath, and consciously let go. "I'm ready when you guys are!"

Edith and Isaac took Chris's hands, walked to the end of the bridge, stepped onto the country road to the other side, and didn't look back. As they walked toward the ranch house, Chris's black Lab, Quill, came running down the road, eager to meet his master. Chris handed his mother his book of memories, wanting to greet his faithful friend with open arms.

Chris knelt on one knee. "Come on, boy. Come on!" he called, patting his legs.

Quill quickened his pace and almost knocked Chris over as they met, his tail wagging as he buried his head in Chris's chest.

Chris hugged Quill as tears streamed down his cheeks. "Good boy! It's so good to see you."

Quill barked ecstatically, then ran circles around his master.

Chris stood up to see Sunny, his brown Appaloosa, neighing and trotting toward him.

"Come here, Sunny!" Chris said, patting his legs again.

Sunny threw his head back, neighed, and then broke into a gallop, running so fast he passed Chris and had to double back around to greet him. Chris reached out his arms, placed them around Sunny's neck, and gave him a long hug. Sunny neighed and nudged Chris with his muzzle as Quill pushed against his legs.

Chris bent down, petted Quill one more time, then took hold of Sunny's mane and jumped onto his back. Filled with excitement, Sunny reared up onto his hind legs, landed, and then started trotting around Edith and Isaac. Quill ran around them, barking enthusiastically.

As they approached Edith's ranch house, Edith's dogs—Big Guy, Cowboy, and Wendy—joined Quill, creating quite a commotion. Next came Edith's horse, Geronimo, who was also eager to see Chris after so long. Geronimo trotted up next to Sunny and nudged Chris with his head.

"Good to see you, boy," Chris said, putting his arms around Geronimo's neck, then rubbing the bridge of his nose.

Geronimo neighed, then turned and trotted down the road, leading the way to the front yard, where Chris's family and friends had prepared his homecoming celebration. They had set the picnic table with a bright-yellow tablecloth, placed flowers in the center, and prepared Chris's favorite foods. Next to the table was a large box of fireworks.

As Edith, Isaac, and Chris arrived, the crowd of family and friends circled around Chris, cheering him on and showering him with love and flower petals as he sat on Sunny's back, his heart filled with immense joy. Chris caught Isaac's eye and motioned him over. Isaac made his way through the cheering crowd and stood next to Sunny. Chris reached down and took hold of Isaac's hand, and with a little help from friends, Chris lifted Isaac onto Sunny's back just in front of him.

"Thanks for watching over Charlie and me in our time of need!"

Chris said, flower petals sprinkling down on him and Isaac as they sat on Sunny's back. "Things were very difficult for a long time, but we both came to know you were still with us . . . that you had just gone ahead. Thanks; you saved both of us!"

Isaac smiled. "Through the darkness, love prevailed."

EPILOGUE

January 12, 2023

TWO AND A HALF YEARS LATER, Charlie worked with Mrs. Davies, the director of living exhibits at the American Museum of Natural History (AMNH) in New York City, to install Queen Izzy into her new custom-made formicarium. The exhibit was part of AMNH's new Richard Gilder Center for Science, Education, and Innovation.

In 2020, when the Audubon Butterfly Garden and Insectarium in New Orleans announced that they planned to move from the US Custom House to the Audubon Aquarium campus, Zack called Charlie, and they arranged for her to pick up Queen Izzy and care for her until they opened their new facility. However, Queen Izzy's colony grew so large over the next two years that Zack and Charlie agreed to have her placed at AMNH, and Zack would receive Queen Ladybird Jack, whom Chris and Charlie had collected from the same area of the Painted Desert as Queen Izzy, but two years later, in July 2019. Queen Ladybird Jack got her name because she had a birthmark—a dark spot on her right shoulder—and because Charlie had worked with a Navajo woman named Ladybird Jack and had always thought she had a great name. Zack and Charlie debated whether Queen Ladybird Jack looked more like Cindy Crawford or Marilyn Monroe. Charlie went with Marilyn. Zack remained on the fence.

"I'm so thrilled that Queen Izzy will be part of the American Museum of Natural History," Charlie said as she carefully transferred one of the large repletes from its traveling container into its forever home. "I'll always be in your debt for making this happen."

"We're pleased to have her!" Mrs. Davies said, placing a small replete into the formicarium. She spoke with a heavy British accent even though she'd lived in New York for over two decades. "Thanks so much for bringing her all the way from Arizona."

"Sure, of course . . . happy to do it. But that was a long drive!" Charlie smiled. "There's nothing quite like driving cross-country with ants in the winter."

"Indeed," Mrs. Davies agreed.

After they moved the rest of the repletes, larvae, and pupae into their new formicarium, Charlie carefully transferred Queen Izzy, placing her next to the larvae and pupae, where she would stay to protect them. With Queen Izzy securely placed, Mrs. Davies and Charlie carefully put the glass on the front of the formicarium. Next, they attached the formicarium to the foraging area and transferred the workers into it. When they were finished, they watched as the first workers entered the formicarium, surrounded Queen Izzy, and started cleaning her. The rest of the workers began setting up their new home, cleaning repletes, and attending to the larvae and pupae.

"Oh, that's sweet how the workers are taking care of Queen Izzy," Mrs. Davies said.

Charlie agreed. "I'm just glad we got her transferred safely—that always stresses me out."

"What are you doing tomorrow?"

"I don't really know. . . . I'm a bit spent from the long drive."

"Would you like to meet tomorrow, get a cup of coffee, and walk through Central Park before checking in on the girls?"

"Sure, that sounds nice."

"On our way, we could stop at the farmers' market just outside the museum," Mrs. Davies suggested. "I usually stop there on Sundays to pick up what I need for the week."

"Sounds like a good place to get some local jam and honey."

"Indeed."

The next day, after a lazy morning and a stroll through Central Park, Mrs. Davies and Charlie checked on the colony and adjusted their environmental controls.

"Wow, that looks fantastic," Mrs. Davies said. "Everyone I showed them to last night is fascinated by them. This is awesome!"

"It certainly is." Charlie smiled, knowing Isaac and Chris were smiling with her.

"I'm going to go get my assistant, John—he will want to see this. I'll be right back."

"Okay, I'll clean the glass to make it pretty."

While Mrs. Davies went to get John, Charlie tidied up, imagining Isaac and Chris on the other side. Isaac was sitting on a white sandy beach, listening to the ebb and flow of the waves while contemplating the bigger questions in life. His heart was content, knowing his mom knew he was still with her—she had found the answer to the question she held closest to her heart. Chris was skiing endless slopes of fresh powder. Afterward, he would enjoy scrumptious meals and cocktails with his mom, his aunts and uncles, Isaac, and the Williams family they had invited over for dinner. Knowing how happy they were now and thinking about how much Isaac and Chris had suffered when they were alive, she felt glad they were free and restored to perfect health— Charlie wouldn't have brought them back even if she could. She looked forward to sitting on the beach with Isaac and eating dinner with Chris and the gang one day. And in the meantime, she'd work hard to make them proud. Charlie wanted to make sure that the next time she saw them, she'd have earned their smiles.

BIBLIOGRAPHY

Access to Insight, Barre Center for Buddhist Studies. 1998. "Aghatavinaya Sutta: Subduing Hatred (1)." Translated by Thanissaro Bhikkhu. https://www.accesstoinsight.org/tipitaka/an/an05/an05.161.than.html.

Allen, Kimberly A., and Debra H. Brandon. 2011. "Hypoxic Ischemic Encephalopathy: Pathophysiology and Experimental Treatments." National Library of Medicine. PMC PubMed Central. https://www.ncbi.nlm.nih.gov/pmc/articles/PMC3171747/.

Amazon Prime Video. n.d. "Mushi-Shi (English Dubbed)." Accessed July 22, 2022. https://www.imdb.com/title/tt0807832.

American Cancer Society. 2015. "Treatment of Thyroid Cancer, by Type and Stage." https://www.cancer.org/cancer/thyroid-cancer/treating/by-stage.html#:~:text=If%20cancer%20is%20confirmed%2C%20a,removed%20and%20tested%20for%20cancer.

American Museum of Natural History. 2014. "Analyzing Extinct Ants in Amber." https://www.amnh.org/explore/news-blogs/research-posts/analyzing-extinct-ants-in-amber.

American Thyroid Association. n.d. "Low Iodine Diet." Accessed July 21, 2022. https://www.thyroid.org/low-iodine-diet/.

Ancestry. n.d. "Bynar Tree, Chaloner Ogle [cousin] 1745–1747 National Maritime Museum, Greenwich, London." Accessed July 21, 2022. https://www.ancestry.com/mediaui-viewer/tree/58561509/person/48038332205/media/5af77d0c-1912-414c-bc72-497dbac49e0f?_phsrc=Qkn649&_phstart=successSource.

Ancestry. n.d. "Bynar Tree, Solomon Walker Williams [great-grandfather] 1879–1958." Accessed August 18, 2022. https://www.ancestry.com/family-tree/person/tree/181486182/person/402357735511/facts.

Archaeology. 2016. "The World's Oldest Writing." https://www.archaeology.org/issues/213-1605/features/4326-cuneiform-the-world-s-oldest-writing.

Armstrong, Lawrence, and Benjamin J. Stenson. 2007. "Use of Umbilical Cord Blood Gas Analysis in the Assessment of the Newborn." National Library of Medicine. PMC PubMed Central. https://www.ncbi.nlm.nih.gov/pmc/articles/PMC2675384/.

Associated Press. 2010. "'Heretical' Copernicus Reburied as a Hero." https://www.cbsnews.com/news/heretical-copernicus-reburied-as-a-hero/.

Attenborough, David. 2013. *Africa*. Episode 5, "Sahara." BBC. https://www.bitchute.com/video/JDrJtGJ2ZMTu/.

Bible Study Tools. 2021. "Bible Verses About Dreams." https://www.biblestudytools.com/topical-verses/bible-verses-about-dreams/.

Bible Study Tools. n.d. "Ecclesiastes 1:4–5. King James Version." Accessed July 21, 2022. https://www.biblestudytools.com/nkjv/ecclesiastes/1.html.

Bible Study Tools. n.d. "Micah 7:18. King James Version." Accessed July 21, 2022. https://www.biblestudytools.com/nkjv/micah/7.html.

Bibleinfo. n.d. "Who Wrote the Bible." Accessed August 22, 2022. https://www.bibleinfo.com/en/questions/who-wrote-the-bible.

Bobrow, Catherine S., and Peter W. Soothill. 1999. "Causes and Consequences of Fetal Acidosis." *Archives of Disease in Childhood - Fetal & Neonatal Edition* 80, no 3: 246–9. https://fn.bmj.com/content/80/3/F246.

Britannica. n.d. "Genesis." Accessed August 17, 2022. https://www.britannica.com/topic/Genesis-Old-Testament.

Britannica. n.d. "Mina: Unit of Weight." Accessed July 21, 2022. https://www.britannica.com/science/mina-unit-of-weight.

Britannica. n.d. "Space-Time: Physics." Accessed August 8, 2024. https://www.britannica.com/science/space-time.

Britannica. n.d. "Thermodynamics: Entropy." Accessed July 21, 2022. https://www.britannica.com/science/thermodynamics/Entropy.

Britannica. n.d. "The Sun Was Eaten: 6 Ways Cultures Have Explained Eclipses." Accessed August 21, 2022. https://www.britannica.com/list/the-sun-was-eaten-6-ways-cultures-have-explained-eclipses.

British Museum. n.d. "Cuneiform tablet with the Atrahasis Epic." Accessed July 21, 2022. https://www.bmimages.com/preview.asp?image=00032581001.

British Museum. n.d. "The Gilgamesh Tablet." Accessed July 22, 2022. https://www.britishmuseum.org/collection/object/W_K-3375.

British Museum. n.d. "Object: The Rosetta Stone." Accessed July 22, 2022. https://www.britishmuseum.org/collection/object/Y_EA24.

British Museum (blog). 2017. "Everything You Ever Wanted to Know About the Rosetta Stone," posted July 14. https://blog.britishmuseum.org/everything-you-ever-wanted-to-know-about-the-rosetta-stone/.

British Museum (blog). 2017. "The Lion Man: An Ice Age Masterpiece," posted October 10. https://blog.britishmuseum.org/the-lion-man-an-ice-age-masterpiece/.

Brown, Brené. 2012. *Daring Greatly*. New York: Penguin Random House.

Brown, Brené, host. 2020. *Unlocking Us* podcast. "I'm Sorry: How to Apologize and Why It Matters, Part 2 of 2," interview with Dr. Harriet Lerner, May 8. https://brenebrown.com/podcast/im-sorry-how-to-apologize-why-it-matters-part-2-of-2/.

Bub, Jeffrey. 2001. "Quantum Entanglement and Information." Stanford Encyclopedia of Philosophy. Last modified February 22, 2019. https://plato.stanford.edu/entries/qt-entangle/.

Buck, Pearl S. 1931. *The Good Earth*. New York: John Day.

Buehler, Jake. 2019. "World's Fastest Ants Found Racing Across the Sahara." *National Geographic*. https://www.nationalgeographic.com/animals/article/silver-saharan-ants-fastest-desert.

Burj Khalifa. n.d. "Facts & Figures." Accessed July 21, 2022. https://www.burjkhalifa.ae/en/the-tower/facts-figures/.

Bynar, Charlotte. 2021. *Charlie and the Rainbow Trout*. Indianapolis: Archway Publishing.

Bynar, Charlotte. 1989. *David Bowie Is*. https://www.bynar.com/david-bowie.

Bynar, Charlotte. 2013. *Isaac*. 2022. https://www.bynar.com/isaac.

Cartwright, Mark. 2016. "Inca Religion." World History Encyclopedia. https://www.worldhistory.org/Inca_Religion/.

Castro, Danny, Sachin M. Patil, and Michael Keenaghan. 2021.

"Arterial Blood Gas." *StatPearls*. https://www.ncbi.nlm.nih.gov/books/NBK536919/#:~:text=PaCO2%20%3E%2040%20with%20a%20pH,compensation%20for%20a%20metabolic%20acidosis).

Central Connecticut State University. 1992. "Allocution of the Holy Father John Paul II." https://bertie.ccsu.edu/naturesci/cosmology/galileopope.html#NoteB.

Cetintas, Ramazan. 1998. "Chapter 34: Longest Adult Life." Book of Insect Records. University of Florida. https://entnemdept.ufl.edu/walker/ufbir/chapters/chapter_34.shtml#:~:text=A%20queen%20ant%20Lasius%20niger,from%20adult%20emergence%20to%20death).

Christensen, Christian. 2022. "Who Are Sköll and Hati in Norse Mythology? Get the Facts." Scandinavia Facts. https://scandinaviafacts.com/who-are-skoll-and-hati-in-norse-mythology/.

Churchill, Penny. 2020. "A Sprawling Castle Once Owned by the Naval Commander Who Ended the Piratical Career of the Real-Life Jack Sparrow." *Country Life Magazine*, January 25. https://www.countrylife.co.uk/property/sprawling-castle-owned-naval-commander-ended-piratical-career-real-life-jack-sparrow-210636.

Cline, Platt. 1935. "Some Place Names of Mesa Verde." *Mesa Verde Notes* 6, no 1. http://npshistory.com/nature_notes/meve/vol6-1d.htm.

Clottes, Jean. 2002. "Chauvet Cave (ca. 30,000 B.C.)." The Metropolitan Museum of Art. https://www.metmuseum.org/toah/hd/chav/hd_chav.htm.

Cook Museum of Natural Science. n.d. "About the Cook Museum." Accessed July 21, 2022. https://www.cookmuseum.org/.

Crawley, William. 2010. "Galileo: What Really Happened?" *Will and Testament* (blog). BBC. https://www.bbc.co.uk/blogs/ni/2010/06/galileo_what_really_happened.html.

Crumm, David. January 27, 2009. "The Importance of Dreams in American Indian Tradition." ReadtheSpirit.com. https://readthespirit.com/explore/the-importance-of-dreams-in-american-indian-tradition.

Dalley, Stephanie. 2000. *Myths from Mesopotamia: Creation, the*

Flood, Gilgamesh, and Others. Revised edition. New York: Oxford University Press.

Danchevskaya, Oksana. 2011. "Concept of Soul Among North American Indians." Moscow State Pedagogical University. https://www.se.edu/international-student/wp-content/uploads/sites/85/2019/09/NAS-2011-Proceedings-Danchevskaya.pdf.

Davlin, Melissa. 2013. "Idaho Woman Works to Keep Mom's Killer in Prison." *Idaho Press*, May 11. https://www.idahopress.com/news/state/idaho-woman-works-to-keep-moms-killer-in-prison/article_0b5448a4-1002-5679-9963-2b01978cb9d1.html.

De Benavides, Fray Alonso. 1630. *The Memorial of Fray Alonso de Benavides, 1630.* Arizona Memory Project. https://azmemory.azlibrary.gov/nodes/view/309218.

Drane, John. 2011. "The Bible as Library." BBC. https://www.bbc.co.uk/religion/religions/christianity/texts/bible.shtml.

DuBois, Allison. n.d. "Reading and Events." Accessed August 22, 2022. https://www.allisondubois.com/readings-events/.

Durant, Charlie, Max John, and Rob Hammond. 2019. "Six Amazing Facts You Need to Know About Ants." The Conversation, June 20. https://theconversation.com/six-amazing-facts-you-need-to-know-about-ants-100478.

Einstein, Albert, and Besso, Michele. 1972. *Correspondence 1903–1955.* Paris: Hermann.

EN Thanatos TV. 2020. "What Really Happens When You Die / Peter Fenwick's Studies of End-of-Life-Phenomena." YouTube, March 11. 1:00:27. https://www.youtube.com/watch?v=aiEYQyUjAQA.

Exploratorium. 2000. "The Big Bang." https://www.exploratorium.edu/origins/cern/ideas/bang.html.

Fenwick, Peter. 2008. *The Art of Dying.* London: Continuum.

Fenwick, Peter. 2017. "Perceptions of Beyond the Near Death Experience and at the End of Life." Royal College of Psychiatrists. https://www.rcpsych.ac.uk/docs/default-source/members/sigs/spirituality-spsig/spsig-archive-fenwick-perceptions-of-beyond-in-the-near-death-experience-and-at-the-end-of-life.pdf?sfvrsn=7b6e14f3_2.

Fine, Arthur. 2017. "The Einstein-Podolsky-Rosen Argument in Quantum Theory." Stanford Encyclopedia of Philosophy. Last modified October 31, 2017. https://plato.stanford.edu/entries/qt-epr/.

G. E. Healthcare Inc. 2012. "OPTISON (Perflutren Protein-Type A Microspheres Injectable Suspension, USP)." https://www.accessdata.fda.gov/drugsatfda_docs/label/2012/020899s015lbl.pdf.

Girard J., J. Reneau, S. Devata, et al. 2019. "Evaluating Acalabrutinib in the Treatment of Mantle Cell Lymphoma: Design, Development, and Place in Therapy." *OncoTargets and Therapy*, September 30. https://www.ncbi.nlm.nih.gov/pmc/articles/PMC6777435/.

Golden, Frederic. 1984. "Science: Rehabilitating Galileo's Image." *Time*, March 12. https://time.com/archive/6855482/science-rehabilitating-galileos-image/.

Gonzales, Fernando F., and Steven. P. Miller. 2006. "Does Perinatal Asphyxia Impair Cognitive Function Without Cerebral Palsy?" *Archives of Disease in Childhood - Fetal Neonatal Edition* 91, no 6: 454–9. https://www.ncbi.nlm.nih.gov/pmc/articles/PMC2672766/.

Grant, Edward. 2007. *A History of Natural Philosophy: From the Ancient World to the Nineteenth Century*. New York: Cambridge University Press.

Gutenberg. 2005. "Three Translations of the Koran (Al-Qur'an) Side by Side," Verse (7:199). Translated by Abdullah Yusuf Ali, Marmaduke William Pickthall, and M. H. Shakir. https://www.gutenberg.org/cache/epub/16955/pg16955-images.html.

Handwerk, Brian. 2017. "How Ants Became the World's Best Fungus Farmers." *Smithsonian Magazine*, April 12. https://www.smithsonianmag.com/science-nature/how-ants-became-worlds-best-fungus-farmers-180962871/.

Harvard Forest. n.d. "Life Cycle." Accessed July 21, 2022. https://harvardforest.fas.harvard.edu/ants/life-cycle.

History. 2015. "9 Things You May Not Know About the Ancient Sumerians." https://www.history.com/news/9-things-you-may-not-know-about-the-ancient-sumerians.

History. 2015. "9 Things You May Not Know About Isaac Newton."

https://www.history.com/news/9-things-you-may-not-know-about-isaac-newton.
History. 2017. "Fertile Crescent." https://www.history.com/topics/pre-history/fertile-crescent.
History. 2017. "Mesopotamia." https://www.history.com/topics/ancient-middle-east/mesopotamia.
History. 2017. "Sumer." https://www.history.com/topics/ancient-middle-east/sumer.
Holian, Brian. 2014. "International Practices of Patient Release Following Iodine-131 Therapy." Office of Federal and State Materials and Environmental Management Programs. https://www.nrc.gov/docs/ML1421/ML14217A350.pdf.
Houston Museum of Natural Science. n.d. "Cullen Hall of Gems and Minerals." Accessed July 21, 2022. https://www.hmns.org/exhibits/cullen-hall-of-gems-and-minerals.
Houston Museum of Natural Science. n.d. "Everyday Fabergé." Accessed July 21, 2022. https://www.hmns.org/exhibits/permanent-exhibitions/faberge/.
Houston Museum of Natural Science. n.d. "Fabergé: From a Snowflake to an Iceberg." Accessed July 21, 2022. https://www.hmns.org/exhibits/faberge.
Houston Museum of Natural Science. n.d. "Herzstein Foucault Pendulum." Accessed July 21, 2022. https://www.hmns.org/exhibits/permanent-exhibitions/pendulum/#:~:text=First%20exhibited%20in%201851%20at,pendulum's%20swing%20appears%20to%20change.
Houston Museum of Natural Science. n.d. "Lester & Sue Smith Gem Vault." Accessed July 22, 2022. https://www.hmns.org/exhibits/permanent-exhibitions/gem-vault/.
Houston Museum of Natural Science. n.d. "Moon by Luke Jerram." Accessed July 22, 2022. https://informal.jpl.nasa.gov/museum/content/first-steps-next-steps-celebrating-apollo-11-and-future-lunar-exploration.
HuffPost (blog). 2011. "Why You Will Always Exist: Time Is 'On Demand.'" Updated January 14, 2012. https://www.huffpost.com/entry/biocentrism-why-you-will-always-exist_b_820183.

Invertebrates in Education & Conservation Conference. n.d. Terrestrial Invertebrate Taxon Advisory Group. Accessed July 21, 2022. https://entsoc.org/event-calendar/2024-invertebrates-education-and-conservation-conference.

Iowa State University, Department of Entomology. n.d. "Insect Zoo." Accessed July 22, 2022. https://www.ent.iastate.edu/insectzoo/.

Isaac's Ant Foundation. n.d. Accessed July 21, 2022. https://www.isaacsantfoundation.com/.

Isaac's Ant Foundation. n.d. Scholarships. Accessed July 21, 2022. https://www.isaacsantfoundation.com/scholarships.

Johns Hopkins Medicine. 2017. "Blueprint to Reduce Wasteful Blood Transfusions." https://www.hopkinsmedicine.org/news/media/releases/blueprint_to_reduce_wasteful_blood_transfusions.

Johns Hopkins Medicine. 2016. "Study Suggests Medical Errors Are Third-Leading Cause of Death in the U.S." https://hub.jhu.edu/2016/05/03/medical-errors-third-leading-cause-of-death/.

Jones, Alexander R. n.d. "Ptolemy." *Britannica*. Accessed July 22, 2022. https://www.britannica.com/biography/Ptolemy.

Kansas Public Radio. 2013. "Regional Headlines for Thursday, April 25, 2013." https://kansaspublicradio.org/kpr-news/regional-headlines-thursday-april-25-2013.

Kerr, Ally. 2004. "The Sore Feet Song." Recorded at Quince Records, Tokyo, Japan. YouTube. 3:09. https://www.youtube.com/watch?v=VBBFDb0hC4Y.

Kumar, Giriraj, and Ram Krishna. n.d. "The Cupule Replication Project." Rock Art of India. https://rockartindia.org/understanding-the-technology-of-the-daraki-chattan-cupules-the-cupule-replication-project.

Lanza, Robert. n.d. "Archive of Books." Accessed July 22, 2022. https://www.robertlanza.com/category/books/.

Lanza, Robert, and Bob Berman. 2009. *Biocentrism: How Life and Consciousness Are the Keys to Understanding the True Nature of the Universe*. Dallas: Benbella Books.

Lanza, Robert. n.d. "Has History Occurred Yet? Evidence Suggests the Past Isn't Set in Stone." Accessed July 22, 2022. https://www.robertlanzabiocentrism.com/has-history-occurred-yet/.

Lanza, Robert. 2020. "The Impossibility of Being Dead: The Key to Immortality Lies in How Quantum Physics Applies to the Everyday World." *Psychology Today*, November 11. https://www.psychologytoday.com/us/blog/biocentrism/202011/the-impossibility-being-dead.

Lanza, Robert. 2011. "The True Nature of Death and Eternity." *Psychology Today*, December 11. https://www.psychologytoday.com/us/blog/biocentrism/201112/the-true-nature-death-and-eternity.

Lazarus, Clifford N. 2019. "Can Consciousness Exist Outside of the Brain? Is Consciousness Actually a Property of the Universe like Gravity or Light?" *Psychology Today*, June 26. https://www.psychologytoday.com/us/blog/think-well/201906/does-consciousness-exist-outside-the-brain#:~:text=In%20fact%2C%20Fenwick%20believes%20that,%3B%20rather%2C%20it%20filters%20it.

Leagle. n.d. State v. Williams, 234 Kan. 233 (1983). *Supreme Court of Kansas*, opinion filed October 21, 1983. Accessed July 22, 2022. https://www.leagle.com/decision/1983467234kan2331448.

Library of Congress Online. n.d. "Image 11 of the Einstein Theory: Relativity and Gravitation with Some of the Most Significant Implications for the General Reader." Accessed July 22, 2022. https://www.loc.gov/resource/gdcmassbookdig.einsteintheoryre00grub/?sp=11&st=pdf&r=-0.317%2C-0.252%2C1.739%2C1.739%2C0&pdfPage=48.

Library of Congress Online. n.d. "Physical Astronomy for the Mechanistic Universe." Accessed July 22, 2022. https://www.loc.gov/collections/finding-our-place-in-the-cosmos-with-carl-sagan/articles-and-essays/modeling-the-cosmos/physical-astronomy-for-the-mechanistic-universe.

Mahoney, Michael. 2008. "The Mathematical Realm of Nature." In *The Cambridge History of Seventeenth-Century Philosophy*, edited by Daniel Garber and Michael Ayers. Cambridge University Press. Accessed September 9, 2023. https://www.cambridge.org/core/books/abs/cambridge-history-of-seventeenthcentury-philosophy/mathematical-realm-of-nature/3E00EDDD0D598FAD4F1ECF6D6B963C61.

Mangold, Sarah A., and Joe M. Das. n.d. "Neuroanatomy, Reticular Formation." *StatPearls*, updated July 26, 2021. https://www.ncbi.nlm.nih.gov/books/NBK556102/.

Mark, Joshua J. 2011. "The Atrahasis Epic: The Great Flood & the Meaning of Suffering." World History Encyclopedia. https://www.worldhistory.org/article/227/the-atrahasis-epic-the-great-flood-the-meaning-of/.

Mark, Joshua J. 2009. "Bible." World History Encyclopedia. https://www.worldhistory.org/bible/.

Mark, Joshua J. 2021. "Code of Ur-Nammu." World History Encyclopedia. https://www.worldhistory.org/Code_of_Ur-Nammu/.

Mark, Joshua J. 2017. "Enki." World History Encyclopedia. https://www.worldhistory.org/Enki/.

Mark, Joshua J. 2017. "Enlil." World History Encyclopedia. https://www.worldhistory.org/Enlil.

Mark, Joshua J. 2020. "Eridu Genesis." World History Encyclopedia. https://www.worldhistory.org/Eridu_Genesis/.

Mark, Joshua J. 2016. "Ghosts in Ancient Egypt." World History Encyclopedia. https://www.worldhistory.org/Ghosts_in_Ancient_Egypt/.

Maxwell, Nicholas. 2019. "Natural Philosophy Redux." *Aeon*. https://aeon.co/essays/bring-back-science-and-philosophy-as-natural-philosophy.

Mayo Clinic Online. n.d. "Drugs and Supplements: Rituximab (Intravenous Route)." Accessed July 21, 2022. https://www.mayoclinic.org/drugs-supplements/rituximab-intravenous-route/side-effects/drg-20068057?p=1.

McCoy, Daniel. n.d. "Skoll and Hati." Norse Mythology for Smart People. Accessed July 25, 2022. https://norse-mythology.org/skoll-hati/.

Melville, Herman. 1851. *Moby Dick*. New York: Harper & Brothers.

Mesopotamian Gods & Kings. 2014. "The Ur-Nammu Law Code." https://www.mesopotamiangods.com/the-ur-nammu-law-code/.

Montalbano, William D. 1992. "Vatican Finds Galileo 'Not Guilty.'" *The Washington Post*. https://www.washingtonpost.com/archive/

politics/1992/11/01/vatican-finds-galileo-not-guilty/1092b119
-440e-4fb6-b990-cc7f8a662f0d/.
Monterey Bay Aquarium. n.d. "Kelp Forest." Accessed July 22, 2022.
https://www.montereybayaquarium.org/visit/exhibits/kelp-forest.
Mulder, Megan. 2014. "Dialogus de Systema Cosmicum, by Galileo
Galilei (1635)." ZSR Library. https://zsr.wfu.edu/2014/systema
-cosmicum-by-galileo-galilei-1635/.
NASA. 2017. "Eclipse History." August 21, 2017. https://eclipse2017.
nasa.gov/eclipse-history#:~:text=The%20ancient%20Chinese%20
believed%20that,also%20means%20%22to%20eat%22.
NASA. 2017. "Eclipse: Who? What? Where? When? and How? Total
Solar Eclipse." https://eclipse2017.nasa.gov/eclipse-who-what
-where-when-and-how.
NASA. 2017. "What Is an Eclipse?" https://www.nasa.gov/audience
/forstudents/5-8/features/nasa-knows/what-is-an-eclipse-58.
National Center for Atmospheric Research. n.d. "Galileo Galilei
(1564–1642)." Accessed September 19, 2024. https://www2.hao
.ucar.edu/education/scientists/galileo-galilei-1564-1642.
National Center for Atmospheric Research. n.d. "Nicolaus
Copernicus (1473–1543)." Accessed September 19, 2024.
https://www2.hao.ucar.edu/education/scientists/nicolaus
-copernicus-1473-1543.
National Horseshoe Pitchers Foundation. 2006. "The Official Rules/
Regulations, Guidelines, Specifications for the Sport of Horseshoe
Pitching." https://www.horseshoepitching.com/wp-content
/uploads/2024/02/RGS2024revjan2024.pdf.
National Park Service. n.d. "Bats." Accessed July 21, 2022. https://
www.nps.gov/cave/learn/nature/bats.htm.
National Radio Astronomy Observatory. n.d. "Welcome to the Very
Large Array!" Accessed July 22, 2022. http://www.vla.nrao.edu/.
Navajo Dictionary Online. n.d. Accessed July 24, 2022. https://www
.navajodictionary.com/.
Navajo People. n.d. "Navajo Code Talker. Navajo Code Talkers
History." Accessed July 22, 2022. https://navajopeople.org/navajo
-code-talker.htm.
Navajo People. n.d. "Navajo Language. Diné Bizaad: The Navajo

Language." Accessed July 22, 2022. https://navajopeople.org/navajo-language.htm.

Navajo Word of the Day Online Dictionary. n.d. Accessed July 24, 2022. https://navajowotd.com/.

Nield, Christopher T. 2017. "The Amazing Secrets Behind 'Flying Ant Day.'" The Conversation. https://theconversation.com/the-amazing-secrets-behind-flying-ant-day-79686.

NPR. 2008. "The Secret Society of Superorganisms." *All Things Considered.* https://www.npr.org/2008/11/29/97547749/the-secret-society-of-superorganisms.

Omo-Aghoja, L. 2014. "Maternal and Fetal Acid-Base Chemistry: A Major Determinant of Perinatal Outcome." *Annals of Medical & Health Sciences Research* 4:8–17. https://www.amhsr.org/articles/maternal-and-fetal-acidbase-chemistry-a-major-determinant-of-perinatal-outcome.html.

O'Raifeartaigh, Cormac. 2017. "Einstein's Greatest Blunder?" *Scientific American.* https://blogs.scientificamerican.com/guest-blog/einsteins-greatest-blunder/.

Overduin, James. 2007. "Einstein's Spacetime:." Gravity Probe B Testing Einstein's Universe. https://einstein.stanford.edu/SPACETIME/spacetime2.html#curved_spacetime.

Patel S., and S. Sharma. n.d. "Respiratory Acidosis." *StatPearls,* updated June 12, 2023. https://www.ncbi.nlm.nih.gov/books/NBK482430/.

Peesay, Morarji. 2017. "Nuchal Cord and Its Implications." *Maternal Health, Neonatology and Perinatology* 3, no 28. https://www.ncbi.nlm.nih.gov/pmc/articles/PMC5719938/.

Penn Museum. n.d. "The Babylonian Story of the Creation and the Earliest History of the World." Accessed July 22, 2022. https://www.penn.museum/sites/journal/199/.

Penn Museum. n.d. "Law and Love, a Hymn, a Prayer, and a Word to the Wise." Accessed July 22, 2022. https://www.penn.museum/documents/publications/bulletin/17-2/law_love_hymn_prayer_word.pdf.

Pew Research Center. 2009. "Many Americans Mix Multiple Faiths." https://www.pewresearch.org/religion/2009/12/09/many-americans-mix-multiple-faiths/.

Phys. 2019. "Laborer, Doorkeeper, Future Queen: Neurobiology in Turtle Ants Reflects Division of Labor." https://phys.org/news/2019-03-laborer-doorkeeper-future-queen-neurobiology.html.

Phys. 2019. "Scientists Unveil the First-Ever Image of Quantum Entanglement." https://phys.org/news/2019-07-scientists-unveil-first-ever-image-quantum.html.

Plain of Six Glaciers Tea House. n.d. Banff & Lake Louise Tourism. Accessed July 22, 2022. https://www.banfflakelouise.com/business/plain-six-glaciers-tea-house.

Rafferty, John R. n.d. "The Great Molasses Flood and 6 Other Strange Disasters." *Britannica*. Accessed July 22, 2022. https://www.britannica.com/list/7-strange-disasters.

Rayor, Linda S. 2016. "Hidden Housemates: Australia's Huge and Hairy Huntsman Spiders." The Conversation. https://theconversation.com/hidden-housemates-australias-huge-and-hairy-huntsman-spiders-55017.

Reuters. 2010. "Astronomer Copernicus Reburied in Polish Cathedral." https://www.reuters.com/article/us-poland-copernicus/astronomer-copernicus-reburied-in-polish-cathedral-idUSTRE64M24920100523.

Rickshaw. n.d. "Menus." Accessed July 22, 2022. https://www.eat-at-rickshaw.com/menu/.

Ruth, Vineta J., and Kari O. Raivio. 1988. "Perinatal Brain Damage: Predictive Value of Metabolic Acidosis and the Apgar Score." *BMJ* 297, no. 6640: 24–7. https://pubmed.ncbi.nlm.nih.gov/2457406/.

Saneh, Hala, Maga D. Mendez, and Vijay N. Srinivasan. 2022. "Cord Blood Gas." *StatPearls*. https://www.ncbi.nlm.nih.gov/books/NBK545290/.

Santa Croce in Florence. 2014. "Galileo's 450th Birthday." https://santacroceinflorence.wordpress.com/2014/02/13/galileos-450th-birthday/.

Saunders, David. 2015. "Dreams and ESP." Psi Encyclopedia. The Society for Psychical Research. https://psi-encyclopedia.spr.ac.uk/articles/dreams-and-esp.

Sheehy, Sara. 2017. "Sun Valley Solar Eclipse August 21, 2017. Everything You Need to Know for the 2017 Solar Eclipse in Sun Valley, Idaho." *Visit Sun Valley*, Summer 2017. https://www

.visitsunvalley.com/bucket-list/everything-you-need-to-know-for-the-2017-solar-eclipse-in-sun-valley-idaho/.

Siegel, Ethan. 2019. "This Is Why Einstein's Greatest Blunder Really Was a Tremendous Mistake." *Forbes*. https://www.forbes.com/sites/startswithabang/2019/10/29/this-is-why-einsteins-greatest-blunder-really-was-a-tremendous-mistake/?sh=4adc9c5350f4.

Simon, Leslie V., Muhammad F. Hashmi, and Bradley N. Bragg. 2022. "APGAR Score." *StatPearls*. https://www.ncbi.nlm.nih.gov/books/NBK470569/.

Skyscraper Page. n.d. "Petronius Compliant Tower." Skyscraper Source Media. Accessed July 22, 2022. https://skyscraperpage.com/cities/?buildingID=23522.

Smith, Stephen. 2022. "Dreams and Visions." OpenBible.info. https://www.openbible.info/topics/dreams_and_visions.

Smoky Mountain Ancestry. n.d. "Solomon Walker Williams." Accessed July 22, 2022. https://www.smokykin.com/tng/getperson.php?personID=15456&tree=Smokykin.

Spar, Ira. 2009. "Flood Stories." The Metropolitan Museum of Art. https://www.metmuseum.org/toah/hd/flod/hd_flod.htm.

"Sri Lanka Tripitaka Project: Pali Tipitaka Source Texts." Access to Insight. Accessed August 23, 2024. https://www.accesstoinsight.org/tipitaka/sltp/.

State Symbols USA. n.d. "Nine-Spotted Ladybug: New York State Insect." Accessed July 22, 2022. https://statesymbolsusa.org/symbol-official-item/new-york/state-insect/nine-spotted-ladybug.

Steinbeck, John. 1937. *Of Mice and Men*. New York: Covici Friede.

Stony Brook University. n.d. "Radiation Oncology." Accessed July 22, 2022. https://cancer.stonybrookmedicine.edu/diagnosis-treatment/radiation-oncology/info/radioactive-iodine.

TEDx Talks, TEDxBrussels. 2011. "Peter Fenwick: The Art of Dying Well." YouTube, November 23. 9:24. https://www.youtube.com/watch?v=U-CXpReUpiM.

TEDx Talks, TEDxVitosha. 2020. "Master Shi Heng Yi: 5 Hindrances to Self-Mastery." YouTube, February 13. 18:36. https://www.youtube.com/watch?v=4-079YIasck.

Tokyo Sky Tree. n.d. "Highest Point: 634m." Accessed July 22, 2022. https://www.tokyo-skytree.jp/en/about/spec/.

Torres, Isabel. 2013. "ScienceShot: How Ants Avoid Eviction." https://www.science.org/content/article/scienceshot-how-ants-avoid-eviction.

Truong, Alain R. 2015. "Jeweled Masterpieces Float Before Your Eyes at the Lester and Sue Smith Gem Vault." https://alaintruong2014.wordpress.com/2015/01/21/jeweled-masterpieces-float-before-your-eyes-at-the-lester-and-sue-smith-gem-vault/.

Ueshiba, Morihei. 2007. *The Art of Peace*. Translated and edited by John Stevens. Boston: Shambhala Publications.

UW Medicine. n.d. "I131 Radioactive Iodine to Treat Thyroid Cancer: What to Expect and How to Prepare." Accessed July 22, 2022. https://www.uwmedicine.org/sites/default/files/2018-10/181019_Radiology_Preps_I131-Radioactive-Iodine-Therapy-Treat-Thyroid-Cancer.pdf.

Van der Spek, Robartus. J. n.d. "Commodity Prices in Babylon 385–61 B.C." International Institute of Social History. Accessed July 22, 2022. https://iisg.nl/hpw/babylon.php.

Van Dongen, Josanne D. M. 2020. "The Empathic Brain of Psychopaths: From Social Science to Neuroscience in Empathy." *Frontiers in Psychology* 11, 695: 1–12. https://www.ncbi.nlm.nih.gov/pmc/articles/PMC7241099/.

Van Gogh, Vincent. 1887. *Self-Portrait*. Art Institute of Chicago. https://www.artic.edu/artworks/80607/self-portrait.

Voltaire. 1759. *Candide*. Geneva: Cramer Brothers.

Vonnegut, Kurt. 1969. *Slaughterhouse-Five, or The Children's Crusade*. New York: Random House. Audible.

Weintraub, Pam. 2016. "There Is No Death, Only a Series of Eternal 'Nows.'" *Aeon*. https://aeon.co/ideas/there-is-no-death-only-a-series-of-eternal-nows.

Wu, Sheng-Ka, Po-Chun Chu, Wen-Yen Chai, et al. 2017. "Characterization of Different Microbubbles in Assisting Focused Ultrasound-Induced Blood-Brain Barrier Opening." *Scientific Reports* 7, 46689: 1–11. https://www.ncbi.nlm.nih.gov/pmc/articles/PMC5397978/.

Yale Law School. n.d. "The Code of Hammurabi." Translated by L. W. King. Accessed July 22, 2022. https://avalon.law.yale.edu/ancient/hamframe.asp.

Young, Robert and William Morgan. 1987. *The Navajo Language: A Grammar and Colloquial Dictionary*. Albuquerque: University of New Mexico Press.

Zimmerman, Lee. 2017. "David Bowie's Berlin Trilogy: *Low*, *Heroes*, and *Lodger* Reconsidered." Best Classic Bands. https://bestclassicbands.com/bowie-berlin-trilogy-review-low-heroes-lodger-12-17-21/.

ABOUT THE AUTHOR

© John Running, printed with permission form the Cline Library

Charlie Bynar is an author and international artist whose David Bowie portrait was featured in the Victoria and Albert Museum's five-year traveling exhibition, *David Bowie Is*. Additionally, after her son died, Charlie founded Isaac's Ant Foundation and installed ant exhibits across the country in his memory including at the American Museum of Natural History in New York City. She published her first children's book, *Charlie and the Rainbow Trout*, in 2021. *Through the Darkness* is her first work of narrative nonfiction.

Made in the USA
Las Vegas, NV
28 October 2025